In the Wake of the Jomon

In the WAKE
of the

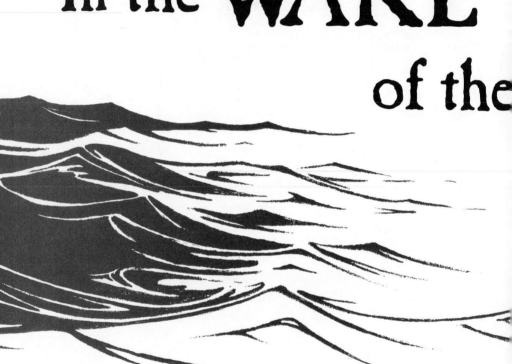

Jon Turk

JOMON

Stone Age Mariners and a
Voyage Across the Pacific

International Marine / McGraw-Hill

Camden, Maine · New York · Chicago · San Francisco · Lisbon · London · Madrid
Mexico City · Milan · New Delhi · San Juan · Seoul · Singapore · Sydney · Toronto

The **McGraw·Hill** Companies

1 2 3 4 5 6 7 8 9 10 DOC DOC 0 9 8 7 6 5

Library of Congress Cataloging-in-Publication Data
Turk, Jonathan.
  In the wake of the Jomon : stone age mariners and a voyage across the Pacific / Jon Turk.— 1st U.S. ed.
    p. cm.
  Includes bibliographical references.
  ISBN 0-07-144902-7
  1. Prehistoric peoples—Travel—North Pacific Ocean. 2. Jåomon culture. 3. Turk, Jonathan—Travel—North Pacific Ocean. 4. Ocean travel—North Pacific Ocean. 5. Kayaking. I. Title.
  G88.T87 2005
  970.01′1—dc22   2005003142

Unless noted otherwise, photographs by Jon Turk
Maps by International Mapping Associates
Design and illustrations by Dennis Anderson

To my expedition partners Franz Helfenstein, Chris Seashore, and Misha Petrov, and to all the wonderful people along the Siberian coast who helped us on our way. This journey would not have been possible without you.

Contents

The floor of the
North Pacific Ocean
(World Ocean Floor: Bruce E.
Heezen and Marie Tharp, 1977)

RUSSIA

Kamchatka
Peninsula

Sea of
Okhotsk

Kuril Islands

JAPAN

NORTH

PACIFIC

OCEAN

——— Modern shoreline

·········· Ice age shoreline

Maximum extent of glaciation,
18,000 years ago

- - - 1st leg (June 14–August 21, 1999)

——— 2nd leg (May 19–September 9, 2000)

0   250   500 mi

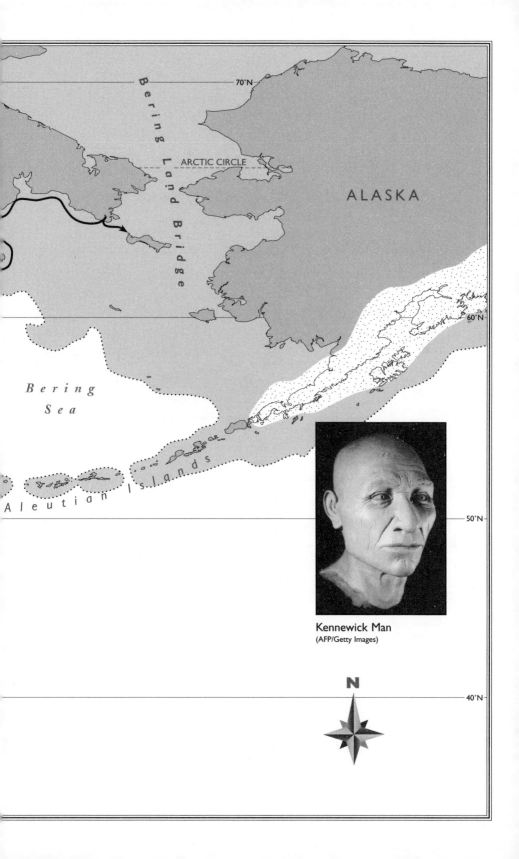

70°N

Bering Land Bridge

ARCTIC CIRCLE

ALASKA

60°N

*Bering
Sea*

Aleutian Islands

Kennewick Man
(AFP/Getty Images)

50°N

N

40°N

N

S e a   o f   O k h o t s k

Sakhalin Island (RUSSIA)

Sunset colors lighten the sky on our first sail with Jenya.

Franz brewing up hot soup in the ruins of Yuzno Kurilsk.

Chirpoyev Island

Shear waves and whirlpool, July 14-15

Arrive lighthouse, July 13

Urup Island

Kurilsk
Jenya leaves the expedition, June 25

Iturup Island

K u r i l

Kunashir Island

Yuzno Kurilsk
Meet Jenya, June 17

JAPAN

Nemuro
Launch, June 14, 1999

Battling the surf with heavy,
cumbersome WindRiders.

Kamchatka Peninsula

Petropavlovsk Kamchatsky
**Stop for the winter,
August 21, 1999**

KAMCHATKA
(RUSSIA)

Rescued by army tank, August 18

Severo Kurilsk
Phone call to my father, August 10

Paramushir Island

50°N

Oneketon Island

—— *Ekarma Island,* **July 26-27**
Shiashkotan Island

**Big storm,
July 23**

Rescued from the surf by soldiers in a
World War II Russian army tank.

Simushir Island

N O R T H   P A C I F I C

O C E A N

I s l a n d s

Sailing with "decks awash"
and "a bone in her teeth."

45°N

Our gear deteriorated
rapidly and we were con-
stantly making repairs.

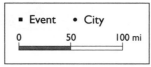

■ Event   • City

0   50   100 mi

R U S S I A

Portaging to narrow inland creek to navigate around heavy sea ice.

Caught between angry surf and a rocky coast, Misha fights his way into deep water.

Cape Rubicon

Vvenka

Il'pyrskiy

Apuka

Ossora
Chris left, July 4

Cape Govena
Rounded point, July 14

**River passage and portage,
June 25–30**

Ozernaya River Delta

Ust' Kamchatsk

Kamchatka
Peninsula

Zhupanova
Caught in ice, May 27

Cape Kronotsky

Jon muscles the boats to safety over jammed ice floes. (Chris Seashore)

Petropavlovsk Kamchatsky
Launch, May 19, 2000

Zhupanovsky Volcano rises above the coastal plain.

ARCTIC CIRCLE

Chuckchi Peninsula

ALASKA

Uel'Kal

Bering Strait

65°N

Anadyr

Enmelen
Nunligran

Providenya

Point Geka
Walrus skull site, August 13

Gambell, Alaska
Arrive September 9, 2000

Gulf of Anadyr

Beringofski

St. Lawrence Island

Meynypil'gyno

ALASKA

Cape Navarin

60°N

Misha rounds the last rocky
point before turning into
Providenya Bay.

House and fish drying rack in Meynypil'gyno.

B e r i n g   S e a

55°N

Hardy Russians offered food
and shelter along the way.

50°N

A l e u t i a n   I s l a n d s

N

■ Event   ● City

0   50   100 mi

Author's Note

WHEN I sit down to a meal with people, or squat around a campfire, I refuse to create a barrier between us by pulling out a tape recorder. Instead I enjoy the easygoing camaraderie of the moment, then transcribe the conversations in my notebook as soon as I am alone. Naturally, I don't remember everything verbatim, and the dialogues in this book are all written from memory, usually a few hours after the event. Yet I believe that this approach produces a more accurate view than if I held a microphone in people's faces or sat aside, observing, with notebook in hand.

One joy of the expedition was meeting the hardy Russians, Koryak, Chukchi, and Inuit who live along the northeast coast of Siberia and who sheltered, harbored, and fed us along the way. We talked in a confusing mixture of Russian, Koryak, and English. I speak a little pidgin Russian and understand a few simple words and snippets of conversation. Misha's English is quite good, and I would have missed many nuances without his patient translations. In the book, conversations spoken in Russian (and English translations of Russian) are printed in italics. I tried to mimic Misha's English syntax whenever possible.

Anthropologists debate the exact dates of many events in the distant past. Although an accurate chronology is exquisitely important to develop our understanding of Stone Age history, the details can be dry and technical. Rather than participate in arguments I'm not qualified to judge, I present many dates as ranges. Thus, I say that Kennewick Man or his ancestors arrived in North America between 20,000 and 9,500 years ago and defer to the experts for more precise numbers.

In researching this book, I used a scattergun approach, following leads that struck my fancy. I conscientiously read three basic research journals: *Science* and *Nature* cover a broad range of scientific pursuits from nuclear physics to anthropology, while *Arctic Anthropology* focuses on people of the North. Sometimes I skimmed magazines for weeks without finding anything pertinent, then some amazing gem appeared that I never would have dreamed of investigating had I been feeding keywords into Google. Finally, I subscribe to several popular science magazines: *Scientific American, Science News, Discover, Archaeology, Archaeology Odyssey,* and *Discovering Archaeology.* I list my major reference books in the annotated bibliography.

For the gearheads among my readers! Franz, Misha, Chris, and I measured distances in nautical miles, recorded by a GPS. I use the terms "miles" and "miles per hour" rather than "nautical miles" and "knots," just to make life easier for my non-nautical friends and readers. A nautical mile is about 15 percent greater than a statute mile, a critical difference in navigation but an insignificant correction in a narrative set against the vast Pacific.

Franz and I completed the passage from Nemuro to Petropavlovsk Kamchatsky in WindRiders. They were great boats, amazingly stable in steep seas. We would have died in a lesser craft.

Misha, Chris, and I paddled north from Petropavlovsk Kamchatsky in plastic Prijon Kodiak sea kayaks. I chose Prijon because their kayaks have the toughest plastic and because the Kodiak is an elegant boat. I prefer plastic over fiberglass or Kevlar because I'm willing to sacrifice weight and speed for the assurance that a boat won't break in the surf.

We wore Lotus Designs paddling jackets and PFDs (lifejackets) on the kayak passage. Lotus makes top-notch paddling gear, and its parent company, Patagonia, has a refreshing environmental ethic.

We wore wet suit Farmer-John bottoms during the second year because I have an old man's irrational, atavistic opinion that neoprene is the best material for the conditions we faced.

I have four great financial needs in my life: gear, gas, grub, and airfare. I thank the folks at Polartec and Gore-Tex for the cash grants for airplane tickets and their help with the gear. Our Gore-Tex suits kept us dry in the Kurils, and Polartec base layers over our core kept us as warm as possible in one of the wettest, coldest environments on Earth.

One final thought: If anyone is planning a vacation or expedition in Kamchatka, I recommend contacting Martha Madsen at explorekam@elizovo.ru.

I encourage you, my readers, to visit my website and to drop me a line expressing your feelings or criticisms about my work.

Jon Turk
www.jonturk.net
jon@jonturk.net

Prologue

MY KAYAK slid gently off a wave and settled into an eerie calm, sheltered by mesmerizing gray-green walls of water. A part of me relaxed, even though I knew that this moment of peace was ephemeral. To windward, the next wave reared higher and steeper than its neighbors. The wave loomed, then overreached itself and hung above my head. An instant later, cascading droplets leaped over the precipice and exploded into a growing line of white.

A kayak is so long and skinny that it should roll down the face of a breaking wave like a window shade gone amok. But just before the wave crashed onto my deck, I grabbed the turbulent water with my paddle and cocked my hips to set the edge of my kayak. The motion was automatic and relaxed by now; I felt as though I was resting on the shoulder of a friend rather than combating an enemy. The wave broke against my left cheek, washing away the encrusted salt from the previous wave and leaving a new coating to crystallize in my beard, eyelashes, and even the small hairs inside my ear.

I had launched this journey from Japan fifteen months previously to follow a small group of Stone Age mariners who—all evidence suggests—migrated to North America between 20,000 and 9,500 years ago. Most likely these long-forgotten sailors made their journey in open log canoes, paddling these same waters and marveling at the same menacing waves and the same magic that bears a small, frail boat over their crests. I had come here to share the thoughts, dreams, fears, and exaltations of these ancient seafarers—and in some indefinable way to understand why they had set out across this roiling and tempestuous sea.

At the moment, however, wonder was overshadowed by an acute pain in my elbow that jerked me rudely back into the present. I reached into a small waterproof bottle in my life vest, shook out a white oblong pill, and swallowed it. Soon its anti-inflammatory drugs entered my bloodstream. These molecules were designed to attach themselves to sites of tissue inflammation, but my body was a forest of sore, injured, and inflamed tissues. How were the molecules to know where I wanted them to go? I shouted down into my bloodstream, "Skip all the minor things—the countless little aches and pains, the sore muscles. You can even forget the bruised

I

vertebrae. Go for the elbow tendon! The left one!" Another wave hit, and when I leaned against my paddle my inflamed tendon throbbed. "Go for the elbow tendon," I whispered hopefully.

The long Arctic summer was sliding into autumn, and the sun was finally dipping into the sea. A quarter moon glowed orange as it hung incongruously above the sun, like two companions on the same watch rather than alternating guardians of day and night. The first stars appeared in the eastern sky, then suddenly more twinkles appeared to the south. It took a few seconds to realize that this wasn't some strange celestial event but the streetlights of Gambell, Alaska. After a passage of 3,000 miles, I had finally crossed the North Pacific.

The Stone Age mariners saw no streetlights, yet somewhere near here they must also have rejoiced to a feeling of accomplishment and relief. When they sailed, the sea level was lower than it is now; more land was exposed, and a map of the North Pacific—had one existed then—would have looked different. At about this latitude, the ancient coastline of North America veered toward the southeast. As the weary sailors turned southward, they must have realized that they were at last heading toward warmer, more temperate lands.

Misha pulled ahead in his fire-engine-red kayak. For months I had been joking with him, "You get the red kayak because you're the Communist Russian." He always smiled patiently at my weak humor, revealing his prominent gold tooth and disarmingly blue eyes. I would smile back, wondering how he managed to maintain such a tidy appearance in this remote land of ice and storm. His Viking-blond beard was always neatly trimmed, and there was never a smudge of campfire soot on his cheek or a stray fish scale lodged in his moustache.

Misha's kayak dropped into a trough between two waves until it disappeared, leaving only his brown hat, which seemed to float like an apparition in a medieval legend. I had watched that brown hat bob on the waves for so many miles; it had stared at me when Misha bent over the campfire and greeted me when we awoke on cold, foggy mornings. Misha and I had been strangers four months ago, and now we'd be fast friends for the rest of our lives.

Enough idle thoughts. I forced ten quick strokes, then tried to hold the faster cadence.

I searched for danger one last time, running through the mental checklist that had kept me alive through all the crossings and sudden storms of this journey: barometer, steady; sea, steep but not rising; clouds, fluffy cumulus with no indication of a nascent storm. Good. I punched the "where am I" button on the GPS and the screen blinked our position:

I scrolled through the menu:

Six miles—two hours to go.

Throughout the voyage, I had been deluding myself that we were in no great danger. But all the while I knew that this was a transparent, self-protective lie. We had been paddling across a vast, turbulent, unpredictable ocean. The ghostly truth had hidden itself in the folds of my brain, whispering its demoralizing logic and slipping into the shadows when I tried to exorcize it. Now the floodgates opened, and fear welled up inside me. For a brief moment, my body shook with adrenaline; but now that the fear was free to speak, the danger was over. Six more miles and we would be safe. The anxiety had no direction or purpose, so it spilled out of my body and dissipated into the great sea and sky. I felt drained, empty, exhausted, cleansed.

My elbow still throbbed, but it didn't matter anymore. We were going to make it. I switched off the GPS and concentrated on an efficient paddle stroke, using my torso as much as possible to relieve pressure on the elbow. The dark, menacing sea was flecked with white foam and offset by streaks of red-orange twilight that shimmered from the wave tops. "Concentrate on this sea, these colors, this feeling," I reminded myself. "You'll never be here again." But I couldn't achieve a Zen-like focus for more than a moment.

Instead I saw my journey from beginning to end. I remembered the tidy harbor in Japan where we had embarked, and all the rough-hewn outpost camps in Siberia. I saw mirror-smooth calms and hurricane-force katabatic winds screaming down from glaciated peaks. I also saw mysterious, quixotic dreams—just wisps of thought—that propelled the Stone Age mariners, and me, across this inimical and capricious ocean.

For the past several years, I had been obsessed with two questions: How had Stone Age mariners crossed this northern ocean, and why? The quest had consumed me, but the answers had proved elusive—as I had always known they would—flickering over the next wave top and whispering behind the next headland but always receding, just beyond reach. At night, asleep in ancient campsites, I chased phantoms through dreams, struggling to interpret signs and images. The answers I sought were out there, hidden in the shadows beyond ocean swell or firelight, if only I could see them.

Kennewick Man

"Unusual travel suggestions are dancing lessons from God."

Kurt Vonnegut, *Cat's Cradle*

IN JULY 1996, two college students were walking barefoot along the muddy banks of the Columbia River, near Kennewick, Washington. One of the men stubbed his toe against a hard object, bent down, and dug up a human skull. The students hid the skull and raced back to town to call the sheriff.

The sheriff suspected a murder, but had no corroborating evidence and no leads. So he passed the skull to James Chatters, a forensic anthropologist. In Chatters's words, "When I looked at the skull, right off the bat I saw it had a very large number of Caucasoid features, in particular a long, narrow braincase, a narrow face, and a slightly projecting upper jaw." The skull was discolored, indicating that it was quite old. Chatters reasoned that the college students had unearthed the remains of a nineteenth-century European settler or fur trapper.

Examining the site where the skull had been found, Chatters dug carefully in the mud and unearthed a remarkably complete skeleton. It belonged to a man about five feet nine inches tall. A dark gray object was embedded in the man's pelvis. Bone had grown around the object, just as a tree trunk will—after decades—encase a nail head. Suspecting that the object was metal, Chatters X-rayed the pelvis. The X-ray detected no metal, but a CAT scan revealed a leaf-shaped stone spear point. To Chatters's surprise, the point resembled a Cascade point used by Amerindians between 4,500 and 9,500 years ago. Clearly this was no modern murder but a much deeper mystery.

Next, Chatters shaved a sample from the skeleton, which he called Kennewick Man, and submitted it for radiocarbon dating. The laboratory reported that Kennewick Man died between 9,300 and 9,600 years ago. Columbus sailed to the Western Hemisphere in 1492, and Leif Eriksson landed on Labrador in 1000. No one could reasonably explain why a Caucasoid skeleton had died in central Washington more than 8,000 years before the Vikings reached North America.

When I came across the initial account of Kennewick Man, I wanted to reach behind the news to read the human story of those mud-encrusted bones. Who was he, where did he come from, and how did he, or his ancestors, travel across harsh lands to reach the placid shores of the Columbia River? I cut out the article, taped it above my computer monitor, and reread it whenever my concentration wandered from the screen. Though I knew virtually nothing about this Stone Age traveler, I tried to invent plausible scenarios. Did he sail the Atlantic or walk across Siberia? In my quiet moments, I fantasized that I could build a time machine and chat with him around a campfire. Was he talkative or taciturn? Jolly or somber? Kind or brutal? I imagined that if I could pose one question, I would ask him why he had abandoned his homeland to cross the unimaginable wilderness between worlds.

After staring at the clipping for a few weeks, I began to feel that Kennewick Man's adventurous life might have mirrored my own. Sometimes I pretend that my life is not really dangerous; but just so I don't fool myself too much, I have reserved a space on my wall for photos of close friends who have died in mountains or on stormy seas. I know the details of each accident—an avalanche, a rogue wave, a fall into a crevasse. When I see their smiling faces, I think of all the close calls I have experienced. Then I pause and contemplate slowing down, growing an herb garden, and spending more time with my grandchildren. But just when I begin to lean toward domesticity, some seemingly random image takes hold. Right now that image was staring at me from the clipping above my computer monitor. A group of travelers had embarked on a huge adventure, and one of them— or one of their descendants—had died on the muddy banks of the Columbia between 9,300 and 9,600 years ago. I felt linked to this man and wanted to follow in his footsteps.

After a few weeks, Chatters and other scientists determined that their initial assumption was wrong. Kennewick Man was not a European. Enigmatically, his cranium closely matched the skulls of Polynesians from the South Pacific and the Ainu from Japan. Extrapolating back in time, Chatters hypothesized that Kennewick Man might have been a Jomon or one of the Jomon cousins or ancestors from Southeast or south-central Asia.

The details are shrouded in the mist of a time, about 40,000 years ago, when Cro-Magnon artists and toolmakers were settling the forests of Europe and their contemporaries, the Neanderthals, were sliding toward extinction. At the same time, half a world away, Southeast and south-central Asia were populated by a group of *Homo sapiens* who would become the most prolific explorers in human history. One faction of this core group sailed southward across open-water straits to colonize Australia. Others migrated eastward into the Pacific, and their Polynesian descendants eventually spread over a third of the watery planet. A third contingent moved northward to become the Jomon, who settled in Japan and later—as Kennewick Man's skull suggests—continued onward. Much farther onward.

The conclusion that Kennewick Man was a Jomon or a related Southeast Asian was startling, because it contravened one of the oldest and most deeply entrenched paradigms of Western Hemisphere anthropology. In 1923, archaeologists discovered two stone projectile points among the bones of extinct bison near Colorado City, Texas. Over the following few decades, many similar, finely crafted tools and weapons were found in the south-central United States. The people who made these points thrived between about 13,500 and 8,500 years ago and were called the Clovis and Folsom cultures. The Clovis/Folsom people were descendants of Siberian big game hunters from northeast Asia. In turn, they are ancestors of modern Amerindians. For many years, most archaeologists argued that these people were the first Americans and that they walked from Siberia to Alaska. According to this paradigm, the sea level was lower during the last ice age than it is today, and the Bering Land Bridge connected Siberia to Alaska. These Siberian people followed game herds across this land bridge to the ice-free plains of Alaska.

More recently, however, archaeologists have uncovered new sites and found new bones to assure us that this is not the whole story. In his book *Bones, Boats, and Bison*, archaeologist James Dixon lists thirty-nine sites from Alaska to Chile that predate the Clovis and Folsom remains. Unfortunately most of these sites contain no human bones. As a result, according to another expert, Thomas Dillehay, "We are extraordinarily ignorant about certain aspects of the first immigrations to the Americas: their anatomical features, their religious beliefs, where and how they buried their dead, and the kinds of languages they spoke. We are left instead with a wispy trail, eroded by time and blurred by missing information." Yet, of the eleven oldest skeletons found in the Americas, ten are more similar to the Kennewick Man and the Jomon than to northeast Siberian Asians, the Clovis/Folsom people, and modern Amerindians. For example, the Spirit Cave Man, found in a dry desert crypt in Nevada, is about 9,400 years old and has cranial features similar to those of Kennewick Man. Thus it is likely that he, too, was related to the ancient Jomon. Two Minnesota skulls, one 7,000 and the other 8,700 years old, are also similar. An 11,500-year-old woman from Brazil has been linked to Southeast Asians and Australians.

One afternoon while compiling this information about Stone Age migration, I put down my papers, took off my reading glasses, and stared out my office window into a dense Montana forest of aspen, Douglas fir, and Ponderosa pine. My mind wandered back thirty-five years to when I was a young Ph.D. student in chemistry at the University of Colorado, and I remembered a time well past midnight when I was working alone in the instrument lab, waiting for the computer to spit out data from my latest experiment. Finally the printer disgorged a piece of paper; when I looked at the numbers, my mind raced. I had just proved that one of the established paradigms in a minuscule corner of human knowledge was wrong. A door had been opened, and looking through it I could see exciting ramifications of my discovery. This is what makes science so compelling—the opening of doors and the sudden appearance of new conceptual vistas.

Despite the thrill of discovery, I had abandoned my scientific career to become a writer and an adventurer. But now, catalyzed by the discovery of Kennewick Man, I was returning to an intellectual quest. I shuffled the papers on my desk and reread the seminal lines of text highlighted in yellow marker.

The old paradigm was an oversimplification. The Clovis people weren't the only migrants to the Americas, and they probably weren't the earliest. Stone Age migration to the Western Hemisphere was more complicated, fascinating, and varied than scientists had previously dreamed.

In archaeology, unlike chemistry, you can't design an experiment to answer the next question. Looking into our Stone Age past is more like solving a mystery. Gathering the scant clues, you must try to tie them together with a string of deduction and innuendo. I imagined fur-clad figures warming themselves around a campfire, bonded by the shared travails of a long journey. In my reveries it was winter, and the people were camped along the northeast coast of Siberia, bathed in the electric magic of the aurora borealis. They were people like us—with bodies that knew hunger, minds that knew fear and yearning, fingers and toes that could be broken or frostbitten or called upon to do extraordinary things. Yet their upbringing and environment were so radically different from my own. Could I understand their thoughts and motives? What were they doing up there in the bitter cold, unimaginably detached from the rest of humanity, just a half step behind the receding ice age glaciers?

I HAD never heard of the Jomon before, and my desktop encyclopedia had no mention of them anywhere. Western culture—and certainly my encyclopedia—focuses primarily on people who built cities and developed agriculture. But when I dug into the literature, I learned that these people thrived in northern Japan for 10,000 years, thousands of years longer than any of the familiar cultures that dominate our history books.

The Stone Age Jomon were hunter-gatherers, potters, and mariners. All humanity started as hunter-gatherers, from our earliest hominid forebears until agriculture gradually dominated, starting about 10,000 to 12,000 years ago. The early Jomon fished in rivers and bays, pursued sea mammals, and hunted deer in the mountains. They collected shellfish in the intertidal zones and nuts and berries in the forest. The Jomon left no written histories, so we have no direct record of their religion or philosophy. Yet, from a combination of clues, we can deduce the salient features of these people's lives and culture. In the intriguing book *The Other Side of Eden: Hunters, Farmers, and the Shaping of the World*, anthropologist Hugh Brody notes that all hunter-gatherers, from pygmies in the equatorial rain forest to hunters of the polar ice, share a common cultural structure. People lived in small units of about thirty-five individuals. These units were loosely tied into larger tribes that met at gatherings, where young people could find mates, but the larger concentrations always disbanded after the festivities were over, because too many people in one place would deplete local game, leading to starvation.

Everyone in a small clan knew one another, and many were close relatives. Each person had an essential function in the tribe and was both a contributor and dependent on other people's contributions. If one hunter killed a deer, the meat was shared communally, because the next day someone else might be successful whereas the first person might come home empty handed. Women's contributions were considered equal to men's. Societies were egalitarian. There were chiefs and shamans but no laws and rulers like those in urban agricultural societies.

We know that Jomon adventurers left their homes in what is now Japan and made the long and arduous journey to a new continent. We don't know why, but from studies of hunter-gatherer cultures we can be certain that no king or clergy ordered the migrants to undertake the passage. They left of their own volition and proceeded into the unknown because that is where they wanted—or needed—to go.

The Jomon were among the first Stone Age potters on the planet. Japanese archaeologist Tatsuo Kobayashi offers a useful analysis to help us appreciate this development. He divides all human artifacts into two general categories. Class A objects are made of natural materials such as stone, bone, and wood. The manufacturing process involves chipping away at the original material to make something smaller and more useful. Thus a toolmaker flakes an irregular hunk of obsidian to make a symmetrical, delicate spear-head. By contrast, class B objects are manufactured by combining materials to make something larger and with a significantly different form and function than the raw materials. Humans made simple class A objects early in our evolutionary history, but it took an additional *two and a half million years* before some visionary genius designed the first class B objects. This massive technological leap was made about 35,000 years ago with the invention of rope and woven cloth. Pottery was the second class B object.

Looking up from my reading, I glanced around the office at the twenty-first-century electronic devices I usually take for granted, and I reminded myself that they are mere extensions of the first simple artifacts manufactured by twisting shredded bark into a rope or molding a lump of clay into a cooking pot.

Perhaps one day a Jomon—most likely a woman, given the division of labor—was squatting by a riverbank or in a campsite, molding clay into a pot, when she thought, "This would be prettier if I gave it design." Perhaps she then pressed a seashell into the soft clay to make a small, decorative imprint. Soon, Jomon potters everywhere decorated their work by pressing shells and rope into the clay. Over the centuries, artists refined and highlighted these simple designs and offset them with elegant borders of sculpted clay. Later potters shaped narrow-based vases and storage vessels with gracefully curved lines.

When I was a child, my teachers made me believe that Stone Age humanity was defined by its functional tools, weapons, clothing, and pottery. But when I studied Jomon pots, I was struck by the integration of art with function. The Jomon were pragmatists who molded and fired clay into vessels that could hold water, berries, or soup, but they were also artists who took the time and effort to add design and beauty to their work.

The Jomon, and their ancestors on the Asian mainland, were also proficient mariners. Stone Age sailors reached Australia 46,000 years ago; New Ireland, off the coast of New Guinea, 33,000 years ago; the Solomon Islands 29,000 years ago; and Okinawa, off the coast of Taiwan, 32,000 years ago. The longest of these passages involved hundred-mile open-water crossings to new homelands far beyond the visible horizon. Thus 35,000 years before Kennewick Man's time, Stone Age east Asians were sailing significant distances across open water. Even in their daily lives, the Jomon hunted and traded on the sea. Harpoon points in tool caches and sea mammal bones in ancient garbage heaps prove that the Jomon hunted seals and whales. Tools and weapons found in a Jomon village site on the Japanese island of Honshu were made of obsidian that had been collected from an uninhabited island twenty miles offshore.

So we know that the Jomon were innovators, skilled artisans, and accomplished sailors. We also know that the Jomon, or other east-central Asians, migrated to the Americas and left their bones in a muddy riverbank in Washington, a dry desert cave in Nevada, and other locations. But we know essentially nothing about that journey itself.

Most anthropologists hypothesize that these people sailed or paddled across the Pacific Rim to North America, a supposition that is supported by the discovery of ancient nets, fishhooks, and other tools along the coast from British Columbia to Peru. In addition, one of the oldest human bones found in the Western Hemisphere was discovered on Santa Rosa Island, off the southern coast of California. The bone, apparently female, is 13,000 years old. Even during the period of lowest sea level, Santa Rosa was five miles from the mainland. John Johnson, an archaeologist who studied these bones, stated, "You have to conclude that she did not swim. These people had boats."

Kennewick Man is a single skeleton devoid of context. We would love to find his home campsite and unearth pottery shards with design patterns that match those of the Jomon in Japan, but we haven't yet and maybe never will. The early Stone Age Americans lived in small bands; they didn't build much, and they didn't leave much behind. In some sites we have artifacts but no skeletons; in others we have skeletons but no artifacts. Scientists try to fill in the spaces, but the trail is faded and fogged by time.

We don't know when Jomon seafarers reached North America. Perhaps Kennewick Man was one of the initial migrants, or perhaps he was born on this continent many generations after his ancestors had left Japan. Scientists debate when the first humans arrived in the Americas. According to a recent article in *Scientific American*, current opinion ranges from 15,000 to 50,000 years ago. Without entering into a long argument, I'll accept a general consensus date of about 20,000 years ago. (As a time reference, the most recent ice age glaciers reached their maximum extent about 18,000 years ago.) Kennewick Man is about 9,500 years old. Therefore, we can assume that he or his ancestors arrived here between 20,000 and 9,500 years ago.

Whatever the exact date, the migration was an incredible maritime accomplishment given the technology of the time. As a comparison, the great Polynesian navigators began colonizing the South Pacific about 5,000 years ago and reached Fiji 3,000 years ago. Polynesians may have covered much greater open-water distances, but the Jomon crossed the frigid Arctic 6,500 to 17,000 years before the Polynesians crossed the balmy South Pacific.

Columbus, Magellan, and other European sea captains of the "Age of Discovery" were Johnnies-come-lately who sailed thousands of years after the earliest oceanic pioneers.

Although we have no record of the Jomon boats, it seems probable that these people made their daring passages in primitive dugout canoes. A dugout is a class A object made by hollowing out a log—easier to conceptualize than a boat framed with ribs and covered by hide or bark. Cultures all around the North Pacific Rim used dugouts well into the modern era. By the fourteenth century, the Ainu of Japan and the coastal tribes of Alaska and British Columbia were making long, routine passages in seaworthy, ornate, cedar-log canoes. It is frustrating but hardly surprising that, so far, we have found no direct archaeological evidence of prehistoric Jomon dugouts. Wood rots rapidly in the moist North Pacific environment, and late Paleolithic coastal villages have been flooded by rising sea level during the past 15,000 years.

Using what I knew so far, I began to conjure an image of the Jomon's journey. I envisioned a small group of sailors loading a cedar-log canoe with provisions and dragging it to the water's edge. Most probably they were dressed in deer hide garments covered with waterproof parkas made of translucent dried salmon skin or the stomach of a great whale. Friends and relatives stood on the beach while the travelers hung together, already bound by the shared trepidation and excitement of their uncertain future. After tearful good-byes, eager hands slid the canoe into the waves. Paddles flashed in the morning sun. Then I lost sight of them.

WE LACK archaeological data to fill in the details, but we can use the scant clues we have to deepen our understanding of this migration. Interpretation of Kennewick Man's bones tells us that he was a member of a tribe and not a hapless loner. He had suffered two near fatal accidents: one was a spear wound; a second traumatic event, perhaps caused by a fall or a kick from a large animal, had caved in his chest and broken six ribs. Both injuries were debilitating, and no one would have recovered quickly from either. Not many modern readers have been stabbed with a spear, but many of us know that a broken rib is so horribly painful you can barely breathe, eat, sleep, or lie down. Certainly with six broken ribs, you couldn't hunt, walk long distances to gather berries or tubers, or set a net and haul in a heavy load of squirming, struggling salmon. In short, no matter how tough he was, a lone hunter-gatherer couldn't have fed himself until he healed from these injuries. Someone—friends, family members—must have nursed him slowly back to health.

Similarly, the 9,400-year-old Spirit Cave Man did not live alone. He was buried in a secluded cave in the western Nevada desert dressed in a rabbit-fur robe and wearing a pair of moccasins that were lined with bulrushes and patched with antelope hide. He was wrapped in a woven blanket. This ceremonial burial indicates that he was supported by a family and a tradition that believed strongly in the afterlife. Clearly the Jomon had migrated in sufficient numbers to establish homesites in diverse locations and create a viable culture in their new homelands. This analysis argues against some accidental journey such as might have occurred if a lone boatload of hunters had been blown off course and followed prevailing currents to the New World. No, these brave and skillful sailors must have crossed the North Pacific intentionally as a tribe, with men, women, elders, and children.

All evidence indicates that these people were a dominant culture in North America 9,500 years ago. Now they are gone. What happened? In a recent article in the British journal *Nature*, archaeologists argue that members of the Pericu tribe, which lived in Baja until about 600 years ago, were direct descendants of the Jomon or other Southeast Asians. If this is correct, then Kennewick Man's descendants survived until about the time Columbus sailed to the New World.

In Asia, the Jomon made major contributions to art and technology. They crossed the Arctic, colonized one of the last remaining frontiers of the Earth, and may have survived for roughly 10,000 years in their new homeland. They hunted, fished, and collected berries and roots. Youngsters fell in love and married. Warriors attacked and defended. Families huddled against the winter cold as the ice age glaciers retreated. These people almost survived the ravages of time. But then, somehow and for some reason, they were overrun by the more powerful or more numerous northeast Asian migrants who eventually became the Amerindians.

TO A SAILOR, a sea story is empty without a tactile and immediate description of the ocean. If I wanted to flesh out my image of the Jomon migration, I had to follow their passage in a small boat, from continent to continent, over one of the most turbulent oceans in the world. Only in that manner could I feel the sea in all its moods, hear ice grinding against rock, and bask in the joy of those glorious days when one's survival appears improbable but feels assured. In short, I needed to sail or paddle a small boat across the North Pacific from Japan to Alaska.

A reenactment of the Jomon voyage would provide insight into the Stone Age migration and at the same time might help me explore another question that began to plague me: *why* did those adventurers abandon their home in the lush bamboo forests of Japan, with salmon in the rivers, deer in the forests, and seals in the bays, to paddle across the frigid Arctic? Anthropology texts argue that Stone Age people migrated when pushed out of their homeland by warfare or starvation or when pulled into new lands by a promise of rich hunting grounds. Yet I can't intuitively imagine that people would leave a productive, temperate environment and move into northeast Siberia to seek an easier existence. I've traveled by dogsled through the Arctic in the dead of winter and spent many years at sea—in sailboats, kayaks, and commercial fishing boats—and I wasn't convinced that the dictates of war or the stomach could explain such a voyage. Perhaps it's my own romantic proclivities, but I believe that pragmatists resolve their problems on land; they don't paddle across the Arctic in a hollowed log. I felt sure that some other motive or complex amalgam of motives must have driven the Jomon mariners across the North Pacific Rim.

I knew from my days as a chemist that scientific ideas usually begin with unsupported intuition. Starting with a wispy, poorly formulated blue-print, you move forward, secretly wishing to prove your hypothesis but always ready to accept data that dispel it. I had a hunch that the Jomon migration was motivated by something other than pure pragmatism, but how could I be sure I was on the right track when they lived many thousands of years ago, produced no written record, and left scant fossil remains?

I directed my attention instead toward the Polynesian colonization of the Pacific. Because the Jomon and the Polynesians had evolved from common ancestors, perhaps the great Polynesian voyages held clues to the Jomon migrations. Almost immediately I found a respected anthropologist who shared my opinion that maritime migrations weren't always launched to alleviate suffering and seek an easier or safer life. Writing in *Timewalkers*, published by Harvard University Press, Professor Clive Gamble asked:

> Were they [the Polynesian explorers] impelled out into the ocean by over-crowding or starvation . . . or was it a heroic tradition inspired by a worldview of discovery in which prestige went to those who founded colonies and made return voyages?

Professor Gamble argued that the first wave of Polynesian colonization occurred *before* their Southeast Asian homelands became overcrowded. Furthermore, the continued migration raced much faster across the Pacific than could be explained by an exploding population alone. He concluded that although famine, warfare, and overcrowding explain some Polynesian migrations, these factors don't by themselves account for the Polynesian wanderlust. In many cases, he reasoned, sailors set out on deliberate passages of discovery, not desperate dashes for escape and survival.

Could I ascribe the same logic to the Jomon migration to North America? I logged on to the Internet to find population data that would support or refute my hypothesis, and in an incredible 0.78 second, Google led me to pay dirt. In the period extending from 15,000 to 10,000 years ago, the population of the entire Japanese archipelago was less than 22,000 people, well below the potential carrying capacity of the land. Over the next 5,000 years, that population increased over fivefold, to more than 100,000 people. Thus the migrants left their homeland thousands of years *before* the population explosion. When the first sailors headed into the unknown, there was land and food enough to support a much larger Jomon population than had then existed. Overcrowding, it seemed, was not a catalyst for migration.

So what was the impetus? We can't reach into prehistory and interview Stone Age explorers, but we can listen to modern Polynesian navigators. In his book *The Last Navigator*, Steve Thomas listed three motivations for long passages across the Pacific. Navigators set off into the unknown "to prove themselves at sea, to escape overcrowded islands, and to exercise their will to rule." In Thomas's view, escaping overcrowding was only one of an amalgam of motives. Piailug, the Polynesian navigator prominent in Thomas's book, eloquently summarized his own ageless propensity for exploration: "I am a *navigator*, I don't want to stay long on land. Sometimes when I am caught in strong winds and big waves, I am afraid—oh yes, I am afraid. But when the wind dies and the waves are lower, I make myself strong again to search for the island, and to keep going."

The literature of migration reveals a complex list of motives for moving into unknown and hostile lands. Of course, famine, poverty, warfare, and religious persecution have been significant driving forces in many cases. Some adventurers, like Erik the Red, were murderers fleeing justice and reprisal. But we can also compile a long list of nonpragmatic, romantic, and religious motivations such as fame, shamanistic visions, Gamble's "worldview of discovery," and a deep, unadulterated genetic urge for adventure.

TEN pages after his analysis of the Polynesian migration, Professor Gamble seemed to be writing me a personal note:

> The past is closed to travelers. We visit it in our imaginations. We reconstruct its processes from the evidence that survives. We interpret the results according to our principles and purposes. But we can never experience the past, not even vicariously if we were to live in a cave, make fire by rubbing two sticks together, and hunt animals with flint-tipped spears.

But I was planning to relive the past by following the ancient Jomon mariners across the North Pacific in a small boat. From the beginning, I recognized the limitations of this endeavor. No, I couldn't go back in time, but I could get a little closer than I would if I stayed in my comfortable office, reading books and searching the Internet. And, ultimately, all these explanations and rationalizations didn't matter. Kennewick Man had set an inexplicable hook in my soul. I had followed my inner urges for thirty years and I wasn't about to change.

I EARNED my Ph.D. in chemistry in 1971, then stuffed my diploma in the glove box of a 1964 Ford Fairlane, lashed a canoe to the top of the car, and headed into the Arctic. While paddling down great rivers in the Northwest Territories and the Yukon, I forfeited a secure career as a research chemist with a house in a cul-de-sac subdivision and a country club membership. I returned south to live in shacks, tepees, and abandoned chicken coops. I raised three wonderful children—but endured two difficult divorces. I climbed snowy peaks—and was pummeled down a mountainside in an avalanche that could have killed me. I kayaked desolate oceans—and swam to shore, alone, injured, and shipwrecked on a remote beach near Cape Horn. The only real constant in my errant life was that—time and time again—when faced with the option of following a dream or doing something pragmatic, I followed the dream.

Now I was in my mid-fifties and, despite my wandering, had a safe career as a science writer, money in the bank, a small house in the Montana mountains, three grandchildren, and a loving wife. But I was still dreaming, and I was determined to paddle across the North Pacific.

I bought maps and started soliciting sponsors. If Jomon migrants embarked from Hokkaido, their most direct route north would have traversed the Kurils, a long, narrow chain of volcanic islands. The northernmost island in the Kurils is only ten miles from Kamchatka, a peninsula protruding from northeast Siberia. A mariner could follow the Kamchatka coast to mainland Siberia, then continue onward to Alaska.

In my atlas, the North Pacific Ocean and the Bering Sea are colored light blue—the same shade as a swaddling blanket for a newborn boy. I'd sailed these waters on yachts and commercial fishing boats. I'd once run a forty-six-foot sloop bare poled before hurricane-force winds off the coast of Washington, and I'd pulled nets in horizontally blowing snow while green water rolled over the wheelhouse of a fishing boat in southwest Alaska. The baby-blue color in the atlas didn't fool me. Sudden, intense storms and abrupt current shears rule the North Pacific.

Yet, though I had profound respect for this ocean, I knew that aboriginal people from many parts of the globe had navigated some of the most dangerous seas in the world in small boats. The Yaghan of southern Chile lived within sight of Cape Horn, built bark canoes, and sailed on the edge of the Antarctic Ocean. The Koryak, Chukchi, Aleut, and Inuit of the North Pacific Rim hunted ice-choked Arctic seas from sealskin kayaks and larger, walrus-hide boats called umiaks, and many Pacific Rim peoples routinely made daring crossings in dugout canoes.

From my own experience, I'd learned that even the tiniest boats are amazingly seaworthy. I remembered the day that I paddled around Cape Horn in a kayak that was sixteen feet long and twenty-two inches wide and weighed sixty-two pounds. The waves off the Cape were as high as a three-story building and weighed millions of tons. I bobbed and wove, slid off the wave faces, dodged the offshore breaks, then eased into the calm of a natural harbor. Navigating in the grip of such overwhelming force, like a wily judo master pitted against a heavyweight opponent, I drew strength from my own weakness. The elegance of my craft and the subtle movements of my arms and hips kept me alive. I was outthinking—not overpowering—the ocean, and as I rose to the crest of a giant wave and surfed down its eastern face, wind in my hair, I felt as though I were manipulating gravity and time, zooming around the galaxy with impunity.

When I looked at the atlas, I saw structure in that baby-blue ocean. I saw swell and offshore break—surf beating against weathered sea stacks. All these images terrified and excited me until I became obsessed with a vision of myself as a splash of color on a steel-gray sea.

But I also realized that my proposed passage promised to be more than an ocean adventure. Because I planned to travel in a small boat, I intended to return to shore and camp nearly every evening. Today, the Kuril Islands and the Siberian coast form one of the most isolated and remote wildernesses on the planet, punctuated only by a string of small, forlorn villages along the coastline, inhabited by a mix of aboriginal people and Russians. I wondered if the Russians were refugees from Soviet gulags, or down-and-outers with nowhere else to go? Or had these modern settlers intentionally forfeited the relative comforts of western Russia to the allure of a frontier?

I wondered: what common bonds—if any—united the Siberians, the Jomon voyagers, and me?

THE main character in any sea story is not the captain or the narrator, but the boat. Once under way, sailors spend every moment of every day feeling the motion of their craft. Even now, I can vividly recall the awkward wallow of a fishing boat in a steep sea or the smooth roll of a performance yacht on a broad reach. A kayak is the world's smallest oceangoing vessel, and I love its simplicity and elegance. All the same, I didn't think I could complete the passage in a kayak. On other kayak expeditions I had averaged seventeen miles a day, but to cross the North Pacific Rim I proposed to travel three thousand miles in a hundred days of favorable summer weather. There was no way I could average thirty miles per day, nearly twice as fast as I had paddled on previous expeditions. Furthermore, for the first eight hundred miles, the route followed the Kuril Island chain. The longest crossing between islands is forty miles, and many of the crossings are twenty-five miles. I imagined the urgency and terror of paddling across deep water in a kayak. Alone and vulnerable in a seemingly infinite space, buoyed by swells that can turn angry in a hurry, I would be living on borrowed time. I didn't like the sound of that; I needed a different boat.

A WindRider is a modern sailing trimaran molded out of impact-resistant plastic. It is sixteen feet long, about the same length as a sea kayak. The sailor sits in the central hull; two outriggers, one on each side, stabilize the craft. A WindRider is also similar to a kayak in that you sit in a cockpit that is sealed by a waterproof sprayskirt. Waves can wash over the deck and soak the sailor, but they won't sink the boat. However, whereas a sea kayak has a round bottom and draws only a few inches of water, the WindRider has a substantial keel. This keel and the boat's two outriggers provide enough stability to support five times as much sail as I have ever dared raise on a sea kayak. In a fair breeze, a WindRider can clip along at eight knots. At that speed, a forty-mile crossing would be almost trivial, and even a three-thousand-mile passage seemed reasonable.

Unfortunately, the keel, the pontoons, the mast, and the rigging are heavy, and as a result a WindRider weighs 250 pounds, four times as much as a sea kayak. The weight may seem insignificant—after all, boats are buoyed by the ocean—but serious problems arise at landing sites. When you are fighting your way in or out through turbulent surf, your boat must be light enough to lift, drag, and paddle even when loaded with a hundred pounds of gear and food. I can muscle 165 pounds of kayak and gear, but 350 pounds is a different matter. It may seem counterintuitive, but a minuscule boat is safer than its slightly larger cousin. I carefully weighed the advantages and disadvantages of the WindRider and finally decided that, even though it was dangerously heavy, its speed was essential to the success of the expedition.

Once I had outlined the route and chosen the craft, I needed a competent partner.

DURING THE summer of 1997, I went river kayaking with friends. We were preparing to launch when several paddlers from Colorado and Oregon drove up and asked to join us. One of the Oregon boaters was Franz Helfenstein, a balding, barrel-chested man with a slight potbelly and a salt-and-pepper beard. When he told me he was a mathematics professor at Central Oregon Community College, I thought he clearly looked the part. Nevertheless, Franz was one of the best boaters I had ever seen, and he was a veteran of several extreme first kayak descents in the jungles and deserts of South America.

But competence alone isn't sufficient. On a long expedition, partners must share a common passion for the journey. As my friendship with Franz deepened, I realized that he was a quiet man, not prone to discussing his emotional underpinnings. At the same time he was a chronic dreamer and an unrepentant follower of dreams. This attitude was a perfect comple-ment to his skills and a necessary qualification for crossing the North Pacific in a small boat. When I asked Franz if he would join me, he contemplated my question briefly, smiled, and answered simply, "Why not?"

I made e-mail contact with Martha and Yelena from Yelizovo Tour Service in Kamchatka. These women normally arrange logistics for tourists who are visiting Kamchatka to gawk at volcanoes, fly-fish in pristine streams, or view the abundant wildlife. When I asked if they could arrange the visas and permissions for our novel expedition, they agreed.

Soon Martha wrote back that we couldn't get permission unless we traveled with a Russian guide. In this context, the word "guide" was bureaucratic doublespeak. No one in modern times had ever sailed across the North Pacific Rim in a small boat, and Franz and I were unlikely to find someone who matched our expertise. Therefore, our guide would be someone who was unfamiliar with the route and less skilled than we were. Nevertheless, rules were rules. Several people applied for the job but then backed out when they learned the details. In March I received an e-mail:

> Dear Jon and Franz,
>   Well, today, a man named Evgenie Filimonov asked to travel with you. Jenya is 35 years old, a former volcanologist with many years experience climbing the volcanoes on Kamchatka. He has limited experience at sea but seems quietly confident that he can master the boat with your help. Also he has much experience working with foreigners (volcanologists) on various expeditions so he is looking forward to working with you. I explained your plan and asked him if he was definite and he assured me, yes.
>
>   Martha

Franz had never been to sea before, but he was an expert kayaker. Jenya, though, was a geologist with no experience in small boats. People would call me a dangerous crackpot for traveling with these two, but I trusted Franz completely. I worried about Jenya's lack of experience, but I couldn't think of any other options. In addition, I felt that communication was important. We expected to meet fishermen and soldiers along the way who would have valuable information about currents and safe landings. I rationalized that our need for an interpreter was greater than the risk of traveling with an inexperienced stranger. Perhaps, even more fundamentally, I'm an unabashed optimist and gambler. I wrote back that if he had a strong spirit, we would gladly share our adventure with him.

Polartec and Gore-Tex supplied cash grants, and Wilderness Systems (manufacturers of the WindRider) shipped three boats. My brother Dan, who works in Tokyo and speaks fluent Japanese, generously offered to take time off from work to help us prepare for our launch from northern Japan.

Expedition logistics require careful attention to detail—from a comfortable office chair in a warm room with a telephone, a keyboard, and a computer monitor. Then one day it's time to leave the safety of home and start the journey. On my way out the door, I looked up at a photo of my old friend Mugs Stump. I remembered meeting Mugs many years ago in the Anchorage airport. He was holding a small paper bag in one hand. He took me aside and told me to look inside it. It was crammed with hundred-dollar bills.

"What's up, Mugs? Did you just rob a bank or something?"

"No, amigo. Just came back from fishing in Cordova." Then he paused.

"I got fifteen grand in this bag," he said, and shook it a few times like a kid with Halloween candy. Mugs was a big, heavily muscled man who had played professional football. He fixed me with an intense, almost aggressive stare.

"So what are you going to do now?" I asked.

He smiled. "I'm going to get me a stronger bag so the money doesn't fall out. Then I'm going to go climbing until it's all gone."

Mugs came back from the Himalayas with numerous technical first ascents—and a dislocated shoulder. He emptied what was left of his money bag in a surgeon's office, then went fishing again. He died guiding clients on Mount Denali.

In my photo, Mugs is dressed in winter clothing and his hair is wildly messy. He's smiling devilishly, silently urging all viewers to follow their passions wherever they lead. I was carrying a few thousand dollars in cash, a one-way plane ticket to Japan, and my passport. I hefted my seabag and set off.

IN EARLY June 1999, I was sitting in the passenger seat of a rental car, looking at the ocean while Dan drove. We were in Hokkaido, on the northeast edge of Japan. I thought about my wife, Chris, back home in Montana. I pictured our house, nestled into the forest at the end of a dirt road, with the snowy peaks of the Bitterroot Range in the background. Chris and I had shared a dozen arduous expeditions to the Arctic and to the mountains of central Asia, but when I'd asked her to join this expedition, she declined. There were too many uncertainties and too much risk, and she didn't think she was strong enough to complete the journey. I missed her already. Then I recalled my three grown children: Nathan, a computer programmer; Reeva, a veterinarian; and Noey, an organic farmer and rock climber. Their children, my grandchildren, would receive postcards but no summer visit from Grandpa. I was in Japan, headed across the North Pacific Rim.

The evening sun danced highlights on gentle ripples that lapped against the shore. Fishermen in open skiffs were dressed in short-sleeved shirts and baseball caps as they worked their nets. Thirteen miles to the north, a snow-capped volcanic peak rose prominently over the undulating gold-blue sea. The peak rose above Kunashir, the southernmost of the Kuril Islands—Russian territory. I had studied the meteorological and oceanographic data, but I was relieved to see with my own eyes that our passage to Kunashir shouldn't pose any technical difficulties. Beyond that island we would find another island, and beyond that yet another. Beyond the islands, the northeast coast of Asia stretched toward the Arctic Circle and Alaska. The sea was calm, but the ocean remains the largest, most primeval wilderness on Earth. I had come to feel vulnerable and inconsequential; now, with the ocean and the vast sweep of our journey in front of me, I felt—well—vulnerable and inconsequential.

I thought back to a time, years before, when my three children and I were motoring a sixteen-foot open skiff across Kachemak Bay, near Homer, Alaska. The fuel pump cut out and the motor died just as a sudden afternoon gale whipped the placid bay into a confused frenzy. As I put the oars in the locks and started rowing for shelter, the children continued playing cheerfully in the stern. I wondered, "Don't they realize that we're in subarctic waters, in a storm, in a small open boat?" But in their minds, none of that mattered; they were perfectly safe in Daddy's care. Now as I gazed at the gently curving horizon, I needed to combine adult competence and awareness with the blind faith of a child.

Franz was still in Oregon finishing his school year. Jenya had been unable to obtain a visa for Japan and would wait for us in Yuzno Kurilsk, the first Russian village, where we were to make camp. Dan and I spent that night in the port city of Nemuro and located our WindRiders, which had been shipped ahead. The following morning we drove to a small fishing harbor, but when Dan asked permission to rig our boats and launch, the men shook their heads. I couldn't understand the words, but the message came across clearly: "No. No! *No!* No geek-tourist-American-foreigner-adventurer sailors in the way of Japanese commerce."

Dan pleaded and persisted until one of the men directed us to the Nemuro Yacht Club. I expected a secure harbor with tall-masted yachts, floating wharves, and a spacious lounge and chandlery. Instead we drove into the parking lot of a karaoke bar and walked across a log-and-plank bridge that sagged over a muddy creek reeking of cannery waste. A hundred years ago live salmon had schooled up the creeks; now ground fish guts oozed downstream through the lifeless eutrophic water. The club owned a narrow stretch of land between this creek on one side and a commercial shipyard on the other. I saw no harbor and no yachts, just a concrete ramp leading to the tide zone through a low wall. There were two buildings on the property: a boat shed and a clubhouse perched on fifteen-foot wooden pilings. The members had raised their clubhouse to give it a commanding view of the sea, like a "widow's walk" rising above a Victorian house in a New England whaling town. But unlike tidy Victorian houses with their intricate trim and precise angles, this structure was helter-skelter and resembled nothing more than a tree house built by unsupervised eighth graders.

The man gave us the key to the building and drove off. We climbed rickety steps to a small room with an old hatch cover as a table and plastic crates as chairs. The refrigerator was full of beer but held no food. We found a small grocery store, bought rice and vegetables, and cooked our dinner over a rusty propane stove.

The next day as we unpacked the WindRiders, fishing boats motored past, their hulls slapping rhythmically against small wavelets. Fog slid over the volcanic peak on Kunashir so subtly that it seemed as though the island had drifted northward, beyond the horizon. In the adjacent boatyard, one man was grinding old paint from a fifty-foot trawler, another was laying fiberglass across a taffrail, and a third was welding a rudder. The sound of the grinder, the smell of fiberglass resin, and the welder's staccato flashes were familiar from the days when I'd worked in Alaska, prepping a fishing boat for sea. I spread out my tools.

In the rush of attending to last-minute details, I had almost forgotten about Kennewick Man and his Jomon ancestors. Now, with our boats and the ocean in front of me, I wondered again why the Jomon had set out on this epic journey so long ago.

Much of human history is a chronicle of warfare and territorial disputes. Maybe the conventional explanations were correct, and the Jomon had left Japan to flee a victorious army and brutal repression. But if the exodus was forced, why didn't they go south, toward warmth? Maybe their enemies had come from the south, denying them that route. But if that were the case, given the slow and dangerous travel of the Stone Age, people could escape by moving just a few hundred miles. Instead these migrants kept traveling. If we assume that the Jomon followed the arcing passage across the North Pacific Rim, Kennewick Man's bones lie an incredible 8,000 miles from his ancestral homeland in Hokkaido. Of course the Viking passage from Norway to North America occurred over the course of three generations, and the Jomon's journey may also have proceeded incrementally. Still, I held firm to my belief that pragmatism alone couldn't have driven these wanderers into the Arctic.

I slipped the WindRider's pontoon into its stanchion. The volcanic peak on Kunashir reappeared cloudlike as the fog thinned, then disappeared again, and finally stood out sharply against a patch of blue sky. I tightened a bolt securely, thinking that if a pontoon broke loose at sea, we would capsize and die.

It would not be possible to solve all the mysteries, but I could start by addressing one simple question: how difficult is it to cross the North Pacific in a small open boat?

If I could share the seas, the storms, and the surf with these Stone Age mariners, I could better understand the consequences of their choice, the magnitude of their voyage, and the demands the voyage must have made on their primitive technologies and their maritime and survival skills.

No, I couldn't go back in time, but I could tether myself to these brothers and sisters of the sea. The Jomon mariners built no cathedrals with lofty buttresses and sweeping arches. Their legacy was their journey—wispy, ephemeral, blurred in the fog of time. I wanted to share the vibrations of that journey, to better understand my ancestors—and, yes, myself.

BACK in Oregon, Franz gave his last exam, stayed up all night grading papers, then boarded an early morning flight to Japan. After crossing seven time zones and enduring another sleepless night on the train from Tokyo to Nemuro, he arrived at the yacht club. He took a nap while

Dan and I drove to the market to buy food. I tried to calculate how much food we needed for our thousand-mile passage to Petropavlovsk. It was simple enough to divide a thousand miles by our expected daily average of thirty miles and calculate that we needed food for thirty-three days. But my calculations were based on two uncertain assumptions. I didn't know if we could maintain that speed, and I didn't know how much food we could procure along the way. There are no large cities between Nemuro and Petropavlovsk Kamchatsky on the Kamchatka Peninsula, but my maps showed a dozen villages. I had e-mailed Martha asking whether we could buy groceries at these outposts, and she replied that, with hard economic times and poor communication in Russia, it was impossible to tell where people lived or what was going on. Maybe the villages were abandoned; maybe they had grocery stores. She didn't know.

I stood in the middle of an immaculately clean Japanese supermarket. Unblemished vegetables were arrayed artistically in colorful displays. Meat and fish overflowed open refrigerator units. My mind drifted to previous expeditions when my starving body had begun to digest its own flesh. I recoiled at the image but embraced it all the same, because I had come here not only to sail across the Pacific but to seek the asceticism that the journey would demand.

Lacking any way to logically calculate how much food we'd need, I simply decided to fill the boats with as much food as we could conveniently carry. With our clothes and camping gear lashed onto the trapezes that stretched between the pontoons, I estimated that each boat could carry about the same volume as one shopping cart. Therefore, I needed to fill three shopping carts with food—one for each boat. I put a ten-kilo bag of rice in each cart, added cooking oil for needed fat, threw in a pile of noodles as Franz had requested, then tossed in a random selection of spaghetti, dried tofu, dried fish, and packaged condiments. Dan translated the labels on the packages, but I didn't even try to remember all the instructions.

Then we went to the immigrations office to clear customs. The smiling officer in the starched uniform politely explained that he wouldn't give us permission to embark. As I stared, open mouthed, he said that Japan and Russia were still technically at war. At the end of World War II, Russian marines had captured the southernmost Kuril Islands *after* the Japanese had surrendered—an action that Japan still believed to be illegal. In the intervening fifty years, an odd catch-22 had evolved. Even though the Russians now control the Kurils, the Japanese still claim them. As a result, the officer explained, "You don't need an exit visa because we believe that you're not leaving our country."

Then he smiled and continued, "But, in fact, the Kurils are part of Russia, so the Japanese coast guard will arrest you if you sail without an exit visa."

I froze in disbelief. After two years of planning, promises to sponsors, and steadfast commitment, at the last moment we were to be denied permission to sail! I couldn't imagine simply just turning back and flying home. I wanted to argue, but I kept my mouth shut and showed no emotion. Dan averted his face from the immigrations officer momentarily and rolled his eyes. Then he picked up the phone and called the Japanese State Department. Faxes spat back and forth between Nemuro and Tokyo. By evening, we obtained our permission.

The shortest distance between Hokkaido and Kunashir is thirteen miles. The Japanese demanded that we depart from the immigrations office in Nemuro, however, and we weren't allowed to land on Russian soil until we reached their immigration port in Yuzno Kurilsk. As a result, our thirteen-mile passage telescoped to fifty-five miles—an insignificant distance in a yacht, but twice as long as any previous passage I had made in a small boat like the WindRiders.

Sunday morning, June 13, was glorious and sunny. The shipyard was quiet, and several couples appeared at the yacht club. Women set up hibachis, started charcoal fires, and sat in the sunshine while their husbands and boyfriends donned wet suits and dragged Windsurfers and Jet Skis to the waterline. Our WindRiders fit the festive mood and seemed ideal for a short sail in the bay followed by a picnic with girlfriends. But we were headed across the Pacific Ocean.

Dan agreed to sail Jenya's boat to Nemuro harbor so we could clear customs. After that, I planned to tow Jenya's boat to Yuzno Kurilsk. As we departed, the wind picked up and we rode a rising sea for the three-mile passage. Dan and Franz were both grinning with excitement as we sailed through Nemuro's busy commercial harbor and tied up near the coast guard station.

The immigrations officer filled out two international manifests. Mine read:

> Captain: Jon Turk
> First mate: nil
> Crew: nil
> Passengers: nil

Engine: nil
Cargo: nil

Franz and I bivouacked under a storage shed near the boats, and Dan checked into a local hotel. Our papers listed our debarkation time as 4:00 A.M. the following morning.

Passage to Petropavlovsk

"The sea and the hills offer challenges to those who venture upon them. . . . And in meeting them as best he can, lies the sailors' or the mountaineers' reward. An essential difference is, perhaps, that the mountaineer usually accepts the challenge on his own terms, whereas once at sea the sailor has no say in the matter and in consequence may suffer more often the salutary and humbling emotion of fear."

W. H. Tilman, *Mischief in Patagonia*

I WOKE in the predawn darkness, clicked on my headlamp, and looked at my watch: a few minutes before 3:00 A.M. Franz was already sitting up in his sleeping bag. He looked at me, smiled, and nodded, "Let's do it."

I nodded back and grinned. "OK. Let's do it."

I climbed out of my sleeping bag, dressed, walked onto the dock, and hefted my boat. Although the WindRider is heavier than a sea kayak, I could still lift the bow off the ground with one hand. Suddenly concept collided with reality, and with the boat and the sea before me I realized—as if I hadn't known it before—that I planned to cross the Pacific Ocean in this diminutive craft. I reminded myself that adaptability and wariness—not power—would be my salvation.

A thin line of gray announced the coming dawn and dulled the running lights of fishing boats in the straits. Gentle wavelets lapped the shore, but I had been a sailor long enough to understand that this serene ocean could quickly morph into a maelstrom. In order to survive, I would have to avoid both reckless elation and enervating terror. I resolved to navigate between these extremes, neither lulled to complacency by the undulations of a placid sea nor paralyzed by internal or external chaos.

I took a deep breath. Everything out there was unknown save for one certainty: the ocean, the land, the sky, and the journey itself would change us. Travelers are always changed. The person who arrives is always a little different from the one who departed.

Franz was standing beside me. I had known him for only a short time: we had kayaked a few rivers together, and I had visited his home, watched him work on a beautiful wooden dory in a small, cluttered garage, and been to his office at the college. We hadn't spilled our souls over a long night and a bottle of tequila, but we didn't need those unspoken words. He was standing here, and that was his statement.

I repeated softly, "OK. Let's do it," and we stowed our gear and lashed the waterproof duffels to the trapezes.

Dan arrived with six lunches from a convenience store, each consisting of rice, fish, and condiments arrayed neatly on Styrofoam and garnished with a sprig of plastic parsley. The trays looked silly, but we would be hungry enough to eat three lunches each later in the day.

The Jomon voyagers who launched from these same shores more than 10,000 years ago were, we must assume, experienced sailors, familiar with the lulling softness and unpredictable ferocity of the sea. Maybe that initial expedition covered only a short distance, and the migration proceeded incrementally—perhaps haphazardly—over several years or even generations. I looked north toward Siberia and Alaska. If the Jomon could sail this ocean with their primitive tools and boats, it seemed logical that Franz and I should be able to repeat the journey with twentieth-century technology. But, I wondered, did the Jomon possess some innate survival skill or tenacity that we had lost over the centuries? There was only one way to find out.

When we finished packing, Franz suggested that I tow Jenya's boat because I was the more experienced sailor. I nodded and uncoiled a rope. After securing the towline, I looked back out to sea. A twelve-knot wind blew directly through the mouth of the harbor breakwater, and there wasn't enough space to tack against it. I picked up my paddle and climbed into the cockpit.

Dan pushed me off; I took a few deep strokes and moved resolutely into the wind—for about thirty feet. Then the towline tightened and pulled the nose of Jenya's boat into the wind. WindRiders are not designed for paddling—the hull is too deep and your stroke is impeded by the pontoon stanchions. I bent my arms and back into the effort and bashed my thumb against the heavy aluminum stanchion, but with the added weight and resistance of Jenya's boat I gained only a few feet toward the breakwater before a gust blew me backward and Jenya's boat smacked against the boat ramp. Paddling hard, I jerked the towline taut again and lurched forward once more. The pleasant ripple of wave against hull replaced the fingernails-on-blackboard sound of plastic grating against concrete. But after half an hour of vigorous paddling, I was only a few feet from shore.

Dan watched stoically as I struggled with the boat, the wind, and ultimately with my emotions. I had traveled only a few feet of 3,000 miles—a half hour of a hundred days—and I couldn't allow frustration to overwhelm me. I rested for a second, looked around, and took a few deep breaths. The gray predawn light brightened, and fishermen collected near the dock to load their nets and gear. A polished coast guard cutter glided powerfully into the harbor.

Franz tied a long line to my bow and the two of us clambered onto the dock and muscled the boats outward to the edge of the breakwater. Then, while Dan held the rope, I jumped back into my cockpit and, paddling frantically, gained a few yards of sea room before attempting to raise sail. But a strong gust blew both boats against the breakwater into a tangle of floating polyethylene line, discarded motor oil containers, old watermelon rinds, and other harbor flotsam. I pushed free with my paddle, but another gust pushed me sideways again, and this time I collided with the coast guard cutter, its diesel quietly idling. The watch on deck looked away, as if not wanting to witness my dishonor.

Franz sailed clear and was waiting for me in deep water while Dan stood on the dock looking concerned—whether about this blow to my ego or about my fate for the next few months, I wasn't sure. Finally, bathed in sweat from exertion and frustration, I paddled clear of the cutter and raised sail. Dan waved and shouted something like "good luck" or "bon voyage"; his words were blown back by the wind. I waved hurriedly and trimmed the sail. Then the boats lurched forward and I set a course northeast, toward Alaska.

The mainsheet hummed, the bow parted waves into gentle foam, and the hull rocked pleasurably. Relieved and exhausted, I settled into the cockpit and pulled the sprayskirt over the cowling to form a watertight seal. This would be my epicenter, so I wiggled around to feel the tiny, enclosed space. The seat was raised a few inches off the floor; when I stretched out my legs, my feet reached sliding foot pedals that controlled the rudder. The hull of the WindRider is deeper than that of a normal sea kayak, so I had room to bend my knees and stretch my legs. I had only two controls at my hands: a tiller that duplicated the rudder pedals, and the mainsheet. The Wind-Rider is a simple rig.

Jenya's boat snapped the towrope taut, then surfed on a swell. It caught up with my boat and ran alongside, almost passing me, like a dog so eager for a walk that it carries its leash in its teeth. Jenya's boat was moving so well that it seemed to be under sail, or perhaps it was just apologizing for its stubbornness in the harbor. Franz passed me with both hands held high, giving me thumbs-up, and I raised two thumbs up in return. I needed to forget the recent commotion—not only the last hour, but all the preparations of the past month: the airplanes, sponsors, long lists of gear, and immigrations officers. For the remainder of the summer, my job would be to sit in this cockpit, observe the slow changes around me, and dodge storms and headwinds. As land receded into the distance, Nemuro Harbor grad-

ually lost its sharpness, until only the bluish outline of distant hills remained.

Franz took out his GPS, and I could see him keystroking input data and
staring at the tiny screen. Finally he looked up and called across to me,
"We've gone seven miles in the first hour of sailing. It's now 8:00 A.M. and
it's 48 miles to Yuzno Kurilsk. At this rate, we'll be there at 3:00 in the afternoon." Then he paused, gave me thumbs-up again, and shouted, "Yeehaw!
Alaska here we come!" I shouted back and we pantomimed high-fiving each
other across the wind and waves.

An hour later the wind died, and we drifted aimlessly on a long swell. I
cut into the plastic wrap of one of the lunches. Franz paddled close, but
we didn't talk. I was thinking about Chris and our beautiful home in the
forest. I saw the small brown house with blue trim on a knoll, surrounded
by Douglas fir and Ponderosa pine. Beneath their boughs, trillium were
spreading white blossoms over the dun, needle-covered earth. In Chris's
garden, guarded by a high fence to deter deer and elk, the first shoots of
sugar snap peas, garlic, and chives would be poking out of the ground. But
those were visions to drift off to sleep with at a campsite—not for voyaging.
At sea, I promised myself, I'd keep my focus within the surrounding horizon. I hadn't come halfway around the world to long for home.

After a few hours a stiff headwind pushed the sea into six-foot waves,
which steepened as the afternoon progressed. White foam rolled over the
deck, slammed me in the chest, and passed astern. Jenya's boat lost its play-
fulness and once again became my nemesis. As I tried to tack, my boat
stalled against an oncoming wave while Jenya's boat raced down the back of
the receding wave to ram my stern. Then the situation reversed; I accelerated down the back of a wave as Jenya's boat collided with a wave front,
and the towline snapped taut and jerked me to a stop. When I lengthened
the towline, Jenya's boat careened wildly and turned its beam to the sea. I
shortened the rope again, trying to find a happy medium.

Frustration is such an unpleasant but tenacious emotion. With my brain
half out of control and my nerves firing scattershot jolts of useless energy,
I felt as though I had drunk forty cups of truck-stop coffee. I wanted to
cut Jenya's boat loose, then sail past Yuzno Kurilsk, Jenya, and the Russian
immigrations officials and head directly to Alaska without a stamped passport or a guide.

Just as these foul thoughts reached a crescendo, my boat stalled on top
of a wave as Jenya's boat leaped forward. The towline went slack and formed
a loop, which, by some evil happenstance, wrapped around my rudder and

pulled tight. I lost steering, my boat drifted into the wind, and the sail flapped wildly. A wave rolled over my head and Jenya's boat rammed my stern.

This mini emergency snapped me out of my sniveling. I released my sprayskirt, then climbed out of the cockpit and wiggled across the back deck on my stomach, like a lizard on a limb. My body weight depressed the stern—and me—half underwater. Nevertheless, hooking my toes against the cowling for balance, I inched closer to the rudder. A wave hit hard and threatened to wash me off the deck, but I held on by clasping my arms around the bottom of the hull. Though I was wearing a waterproof dry suit, the wrist gaskets leaked and cold water seeped into my clothing. The next wave turned my boat to starboard so that the sail caught the wind and the craft lurched forward. If I went overboard now, I'd be left treading water in the middle of Nemuro Straits while the boat raced ahead. It occurred to me that we should have rigged safety harnesses, but this was no time think about what we should have done. I wiggled toward the stern until my fingers grasped the tangled towline. But just at that instant, my boat rose and the line pulled taut, grinding my fingers into the rudderpost. A second later the boat slid off the wave and dipped its stern and my head underwater. Just as oxygen starvation set in, the line slackened and I unraveled the tangle. Back in the cockpit, I trimmed the tiller, pulled my sprayskirt tight, and resumed course—wet, cold, but now fully alert.

B Y DINNERTIME the wind abated, the swell subsided, and the saturated colors of midday had slid into the soft pastels of evening. We were only two or three miles from Kunashir Island—close enough to discern individual trees in what had been a homogenous smear of green. Throaty trucks rumbled along a road that paralleled the beach. Franz paddled in close, threw me a line, and tied his boat to mine so we wouldn't drift apart and lose sight of one another in the oncoming inky blackness. According to the GPS, we had sailed twenty miles from Nemuro and were still thirty-five miles from our destination at Yuzno Kurilsk.

It was illegal to land on Kunashir Island before clearing customs, and we couldn't paddle or sail to Yuzno Kurilsk before dark. If we were to land and get caught, the Russians would expel us and the expedition would end immediately. Instead we dropped sail, drifted slowly with the tidal current, and resigned ourselves to spending the night at sea. I opened my second luncheon tray, picked out the thin plastic parsley, and offered it to Franz with mock ceremony, as if I were a page offering a feast to a king. But the joke wasn't that funny, so we ate in silence. The meager meal was insufficient after a hard day, but most of our food was stashed securely in watertight hatches or bags, and we decided to save our last two lunches for the morning.

With its outrigger pontoons, my boat was stable enough that I could stand up and stretch my legs. I turned in tight circles like a dog looking for a bed, then sat back down in the cockpit. Still restless and cramped, I pressed my feet against the rudder pedals, then bent my knees to flex the joints. I was still wet from my ordeal with the rudder, and the first chill of night sent shivers through my torso. I opened the zipper on my dry suit so my body heat would drive the moisture from my clothing before the deeper cold set in after midnight. Lying down was impossible. I dozed for half an hour, then woke. Phosphorescent algae danced a blue-green glow as gentle ripples caressed the hull. A crescent moon backlit gray clouds, and Franz's boat appeared ghostlike in shadow. Blue and red lights of fishing boats dotted the straits, and the bright light of a moored ship provided a navigational marker. We had no lights or radar reflectors so we just sat back and hoped we wouldn't be run over in the darkness. I thought about calculating our speed of drift, but it didn't matter anyway. As the evening wore on, I began shivering more vigorously, so I zipped my dry suit closed and waved my arms to speed up blood flow.

Franz woke and we discussed our situation. We were cold, hungry, exposed, and uncomfortable, but our WindRiders felt seaworthy, the sea was calm, and we were in no immediate danger. An expedition begins like a love affair: in the beginning, everything is wonderful, even hazard and discomfort. I dripped water on the deck and watched the luminescent algae slide across the plastic, and drop into the black sea. Then I dozed fitfully, waking periodically to shift position, wave my arms, shiver, sip water, or munch on a candy bar.

I remembered the advertising brochure for WindRiders that featured a photo of blue sky, a fair breeze, and a square-jawed male at the tiller. A bikini-clad woman was riding on the trapeze with one leg stretched out straight, the other bent provocatively, and her torso twisted to offer a full view of her chest and smiling face. Our experience bore little resemblance to the brochure.

MORNING ILLUMINATED a gray, billowy sky. We ate the last of our lunches, turned into the light southerly wind and tacked to clear a sand spit, but with Jenya's boat in tow, we covered a measly three miles in five hours. As soon as we rounded the spit, the south wind veered to the north, directly on our nose again. By dinnertime, we had eked out only five miles in twenty-four hours. We were exhausted, hungry, and thirsty; after thirty-six hours in the boat, we were still thirty miles from town.

It seemed silly to spend a second miserable night in the boats when Ku-nashir Island was only a hundred yards away. We could see no roads or buildings, and discovery seemed unlikely, so we paddled through the surf and landed on a sandy beach. The coast was dotted with concrete bunkers—whether built by the Japanese to defend against a Russian attack or by the Russians to defend against the Japanese, I wasn't sure. We cooked hot noodles flavored with curry, then set up our tents. I fell into a deep sleep.

The following day we battled more intermittent calms and headwinds, and by dark we were still within sight of the previous night's camp. We were worried that Jenya would assume we had abandoned the expedition. If he gave up and went home, we would be in real trouble, so we stayed in the boats and hoped for wind.

With the sea calm at twilight, we tied the boats together and tried to get comfortable. I dozed for a few minutes, then opened my eyes to watch the moon and stars appear and disappear behind slow-moving clouds. The night reminded me of emergency bivouacs in the mountains, and I re-membered sitting on a narrow ledge, tied into the rock, watching moon shadows of rock spires drift slowly across glaciated peaks. Now, the gentle rocking of the boat and the cosmic infinity of the heavens felt deeply re-laxing, but my stomach, undeterred, called for a hot dinner, and I started to shiver. I reminded myself that I was cold and hungry because I had cho-sen to be here.

I had grown up reading sea stories, memorizing passages from the clas-sics that often calmed and reassured me when I felt stressed. As the algae sparkled in unreal colors, I remembered a verse from *The Rime of the Ancient Mariner:*

> About, about in reel and rout,
> The death-fires danced at night.
> The water, like a witch's oils
> Burnt green, and blue, and white.

I couldn't quite remember the shipwreck scene from *Lord Jim*, but I did better with the opening of *Heart of Darkness*. Finally I settled on my favorite lines, from the first paragraph of *Moby-Dick:*

> Whenever it is a damp, drizzly November in my soul . . . whenever my hypos get such an upper hand of me, that it requires a strong moral principle to prevent me from deliberately stepping into the street, and methodically knocking people's hats off—then I account it high time to get to sea as soon as I can.

Ishmael would have thought it perfectly agreeable to be hungry and shivering out here in a small boat. Melville almost makes you believe that everyone has a secret urge to go to sea in order to shed the pent-up frustration of a safe, predictable life on land. Did the Jomon adventurers respond to such an urge on an unrecorded day 10,000 or more years ago?

A DEEPWATER strait separates Borneo and Sumatra in Southeast Asia from an archipelago called Wallacea, off the coast of Australia. Even when the sea level was low during the ice ages, Wallacea was separated from the mainland by twelve miles of open water. This strait formed an ecological boundary called Wallace's Line. While Asian animals inhabited the peninsula north of the strait, the southern archipelago was populated only by animals capable of swimming or flying across open water.

In 1968 a Dutch missionary found stone tools on Flores, an island south of Wallace's Line. The tools were located near the bones of a species of elephant that lived only north of the straits. The missionary hypothesized that Stone Age mariners must have paddled across, carrying a handy chunk of elephant meat for their larder. Because this species of elephant became extinct 750,000 years ago, the missionary reasoned that hominids had paddled across the straits before that time. Most scientists discounted this find and its conclusions, arguing that ancient hominids were not sophisticated enough to build boats. In the late 1990s, however, Australian scientists revisited the missionary's site on Flores and found fourteen stone tools adjacent to bones of animals that had lived only north of Wallace's Line. Accurate dating established that the tools and bones were between 900,000 and 800,000 years old. Mike Moorwood, leader of the research group, concluded that early hominids had indeed built boats and paddled across the straits. In an interview he stated, "People couldn't have crossed the strait in any significant number by accident, hanging onto logs or crude rafts. . . . I think you need directed water craft. You'd have to have some means of steering, and some means of propulsion. If you try to put a few logs together and jump on it, you're probably going to die."

If we accept Moorwood's conclusion, then the raft or the log canoe predates any other means of travel—other than walking—by a huge margin. Consider five dates:

Efficient walking: 2.5 million years ago
Watercraft: 850,000 years ago
Horseback riding: 6,000 years ago
Steam locomotive: 250 years ago
Rocket ships: 40 years ago

Imagine plotting these dates on a linear scale the width of this page. If we place walking on the left-hand margin and rocket ships on the right margin, the log raft or dugout canoe lies near the center of the page. Horseback riding is about 0.01 inch from the right, crammed tightly against other modern technologies such as steam locomotives and rocket ships.

In October 2004, researchers found a nearly complete skeleton of an extinct hominid on the island of Flores. The skeleton was remarkable because it was a new species, probably an evolutionary descendant of *Homo erectus*. The adult female stood only three feet tall and had died a mere 18,000 years ago. Thus, after that original migration some 800,000 years ago, a small population of *Homo erectus* on Flores apparently became genetically isolated from the rest of humanity long enough to evolve into a new species. This evidence suggests that these people didn't sail back and forth across the straits and find marriage partners on the mainland. The original migration must have been an extraordinary occurrence. Was it initiated by a charismatic adventurer, a shaman with visions, or a terrified band of fugitives fleeing war, starvation, disease, or a natural disaster? Why did they remain isolated for so long? We may never be able to answer these questions.

By almost every standard, hominids were quite primitive 800,000 years ago. Modern humans, *Homo sapiens*, hadn't even evolved yet, and the Southeast Asian mariners were probably *Homo erectus*. Most Asian *erectus* sites contain only simple hand axes and cobblestone choppers. Not only were his tools primitive, *Homo erectus* didn't utilize sophisticated language. No one could propose tying some logs together and paddling across the straits. Perhaps one individual (our anonymous visionary) started making a crude raft while others watched—first in silent amazement, then with dawning recognition.

This early Stone Age boat journey is so extraordinary that many archaeologists favor some other explanation for Moorwood's finds. Even if we reject his conclusions, however, positive evidence dates boatbuilding and ocean travel to 45,000 to 50,000 years ago.

In 1974, anthropologists uncovered the skeleton of a lightly built man in the dry desert dunes of Australia. He had been ceremoniously buried with ocher-colored soils sprinkled over his body. His hands were clasped together with his fingers intertwined around his penis. The skeleton is about 40,000 years old, but other evidence indicates that humans were present in the area 50,000 to 46,000 years ago. This man or his ancestors had sailed to Australia. If we assume they followed a relatively short route across narrow straits rather than an extended passage across the Indian Ocean, then these original settlers must have come from Southeast Asia. To put this time frame in perspective, art, ritual burials, and other signs of advanced cognition appeared about 50,000 years ago in Africa and 40,000 years ago in Europe. Thus, at the same time Cro-Magnon artists were painting images on the walls of caves in southern France, Southeast Asians were not only burying their dead but building boats and voyaging across the sea.

I would love to know what type of boat people built 850,000 years or even 50,000 years ago, but ancient boats were made of wood, reed, or hide and can't withstand the ravages of time. The oldest direct image of a boat is not the craft itself but its fossil imprint. About 7,000 years ago, sailors stored a reed boat in a stone building in the Kuwaiti desert. The floor of the shed was coated with an asphalt-like substance called bitumen, which had oozed out of the oil-rich ground. When the boat was set on the bitumen, it left an impression like the fossil footprint of a dinosaur. The boat rotted away, but the imprint remained. Close examination showed that the boat was made of reeds bundled together with rope and coated with tar. Imprints of barnacles on the bottom of the boat reveal that the craft had been used in the ocean. Other evidence indicates that by the third millennium BC, Arabian traders were sailing to India, and ocean trade from the Middle East to China was common a few thousand years before European square-riggers made the journey.

Thus there is abundant evidence that diverse Stone Age people built boats and, in the words of Ezra Pound, "set keel to breakers, forth on the godly sea." The crossings to Flores, Australia, Okinawa, and other islands off Southeast Asia all occurred prior to the Jomon migration 20,000 to 9,500 years ago.

A GENTLE wind puffed against my cheek. The sail flapped, the boom swung, and the sheet tightened. Waves crashed in the darkness, but the surf was at least a quarter mile away. I turned on my headlamp to check the compass, then adjusted my course to parallel the coast.

Many anthropologists argue that Stone Age *Homo* were pragmatic survivalists, that travel was dangerous and insecure and thus motivated solely by compelling need or opportunity. Unless people were "pushed" from their homes by famine or warfare or "pulled" by some great and immediate promise, they stayed put. Surely this paradigm holds true in most cases, but I still couldn't help believing that occasionally people may have set out for other reasons, such as a spiritual quest or the joy of adventure. I tried to mentally re-create the feel of every boat I'd sailed in, from the tactile immediacy of a kayak to the sleek heel of a racing yacht and the raw diesel-driven power of a ninety-foot crab-fishing boat in the North Bering Sea. If Stone Age humans were at all like us, wouldn't they have exalted in the pure, glorious, improbable cleverness of survival at sea, when waves loom above you and then almost magically slide beneath your boat? And once ancient boatbuilders and navigators became addicted to this feeling, it seems perfectly logical to me that they would have yearned to sail beyond the horizon. All it takes is one Columbus or Magellan, charismatic in the thrall of their dream, to convince others that the need or the opportunity is great enough—no matter how improbable—to justify the hardship.

Of course it's a personal bias, but I kept thinking that the pragmatists had come later. Perhaps the first boatbuilders and sailors had been romantics.

The wind slacked off, the mainsheet drooped, and I started shivering again.

A TAILWIND rose a few hours before dawn, and we sailed smartly into Yuzno Kurilsk just after noon. Our optimistic one-day sail had turned into a four-day slog. At the harbor mouth, we sailed past several half-sunken ships that merged with the mud. No boats plied the waters, and the shore cranes looked immobilized with rust. We couldn't see a dock or a habitable building, so we headed for a small opening between four listing and rusted ships, with their paint long gone, deck winches scavenged, and windows shattered.

A tall, well-built man in casual clothes stood silently above the tide line, watching us. Franz and I stepped out of our boats and waded through rainbow-colored refractions of sunlight on floating oil. We pulled the boats ashore, taking care not to cut the hulls on torn and jagged iron, then tied them off to an ancient flywheel buried in the sand and filth. The man on the beach watched, his arms folded on his chest.

Franz walked up to him. "Hi, are you Jenya?"

"*Da, zdrastvoote.*" *

Franz, who spoke no Russian, looked at me quizzically.

I translated, "He said, 'yes, hello.'"

I extended my hand and returned the greeting in Russian, "*Hello, Jenya, pleased to meet you. I'm Jon. This is Franz.*"

We all shook hands. Franz turned away and walked down to the boats, and I followed him. He shook his head. "This is ridiculous; our interpreter doesn't speak any English."

Jenya remained motionless, watching us stoically.

A military vehicle arrived, and two officers stepped out looking immaculate in pressed green uniforms, sparkling insignia, and broad, flat-topped hats that resembled dinner plates. One addressed me curtly: "*Passports, documents.*"

I handed him the papers, and he climbed back into the car and told Jenya to get in the back seat. Then they all drove away, leaving Franz and me alone on the beach. We looked at each other, then I shook my head slowly. "Franz, I don't care if he speaks English or not. Did you look at his face? That guy hasn't been outside all winter. He looks soft and sad, and he didn't help tie the boats off when we pulled to shore. We've got problems."

Another vehicle pulled up. The driver jumped out and opened the back door for an officer. The man was tall and strong, about fifty years old, with white hair. His uniform and shoes were spotless, and the four gold stars on his shoulder complemented his prominent gold front tooth. He greeted us in heavily accented English, plunked down two forms on the hood of the car, and passed us each a pen.

The form was written in Russian, so he pointed to the first line. "*My name.*" We wrote our names.

He pointed to the second line and ordered us to write "*USA.*"

---

* Throughout the book, Russian conversations are italicized.

We wrote as instructed, then filled in "Japan" on the third line.

Then he pointed to the fourth line: "*USSR.*"

I looked up, questioning. The Soviet Empire had imploded eleven years previously. Had this officer made a mistake, or was he reflecting nostalgically on the past?

He smiled mysteriously.

I looked around at the ruined infrastructure of economic disaster. Millions of Russians had lost their jobs after Gorbachev raised the capitalist dream in 1988. Yet, in most parts of the country, conditions had gradually improved until the economic collapse of August 1998. At that time, the Russian stock market plummeted by 94 percent, the currency devalued from eight rubles to a U.S. dollar to twenty-five rubles to a dollar, and Moscow defaulted on $40 billion in domestic bonds. Was this officer reminiscing about the Communist dream that created an empire and sent the first man into space? Or was he thinking fondly of the Soviet dictators who controlled the economy, eliminated personal freedom, and murdered 70 million of their own people in the gulags?

"*USSR?*" I queried.

He shrugged sadly. "*Nyet, Russia.*"

When we were done, the officer pulled a round official stamp from his pocket and imprinted our papers, and told us to hand them to the immigrations officers when we left the country. Then he climbed into his car and drove away. A young soldier with an automatic assault rifle walked casually down the road toward us, sat on an old tire, and lit a cigarette. Curious children collected, and an attractive young woman in a short skirt passed by pushing a baby carriage. The soldier shooed the children away, but they didn't retreat far.

Franz and I had eaten only a few candy bars in the past twenty-four hours, so we unpacked a stove, crouched in the lee of a ruined building devoid of roof or windows, and rummaged through the food bags for noodles. I asked the soldier for water, and he pointed down the road. But when I started walking in that direction, he stopped me.

"*Potom* [later]," he said, and waved me back to the beach with the muzzle of his Kalashnikov.

We cooked the noodles with water we had carried with us, then Jenya returned with our documents. He announced in English, "We go."

Franz and I were exhausted. It was late in the afternoon. I wanted to show Jenya how to sail. We wanted to sleep.

"We go tomorrow."

Jenya raised his hands to pantomime, "I don't understand."

I couldn't speak proper Russian, just a few words and phrases with a verb or two thrown in every now and then, but I searched my brain to see if I could remember the word for "tomorrow." "*Zavtra*," I said emphatically.

"*Nyet, we go.*"

I tried to explain that we had a few things to do—change money, buy food, fill our water bottles, and mail letters to our families back home.

"*Nyet, nyet, nyet. No bank, no store, no water, no post office, no international fax, no phone. We go today! We go now!*"

I didn't want to leave before we at least obtained some information. My map was sprinkled with numerous small, round dots, and I needed to know which dots were populated towns and which were abandoned ghost villages. Where could we expect to find people and food? I pointed to a circle and asked, "*People?*" Jenya responded, "*Maybe.*" I pointed to another circle. "*Maybe.*" And another, and another. "*Maybe, maybe, maybe.*"

Then Jenya formed his first English sentences, speaking slowly and searching for every word: "Maybe people, maybe no. My country is destroyed. We go now."

I looked into Jenya's face, thinking, "This is your country. You mean you don't know where the towns are? We have eight hundred miles of island wilderness to sail across before we reach mainland Asia. Doesn't anybody know what's out there?" But he stared back, bored and inscrutable.

"OK," I muttered to myself. "OK. But wait a moment. We absolutely need water."

Jenya remained silent. I held up my empty canteen and said, "*Voda.*"

The soldier shook his head. "*Nyet.*"

I wanted to shout, "I'm the captain of an international vessel in international waters and you are bound by the international law of the sea! Have you ever heard of the Safe Harbors Act? You can't send a boat out to sea without proper support, without drinking water. I'll take you and your rag-tag general with the shiny shoes to The Hague and see what the international tribunal has to say about that!"

But it would do no good. The soldier was a kid with a gun, and by now the officer was in his office where he didn't have to look us in the eye and personally banish us.

I shrugged. "We go now."

We set sail at five o'clock that afternoon with one liter of water for the three of us and a guide/interpreter who spoke almost no English and had never been in a small boat before. Franz lashed his WindRider to Jenya's so he could stand on Jenya's boat and show our new companion how to sail. Thus encumbered, we sailed away from the oil-soaked beach. At the harbor mouth, I swung north to follow the coast, but Franz and Jenya were so engrossed in their sailing lesson that they continued a mile out to sea. The mistake would have been inconsequential if the wind had held, but it didn't.

I took a photo of Franz and Jenya's colorful boats reflected in mirror-calm water and backlit by the setting sun. Then I started paddling toward shore, motivated by a desire to avoid another cold, hungry, sleepless night in the cockpit. But Franz and Jenya, their boats still lashed together, were lagging. Although Franz was driving his paddle into the water with long, powerful strokes, Jenya was dipping his paddle fecklessly, with the air of a nonchalant dilettante.

I called out "Jenya!"—perhaps a bit harshly. Then I placed my palms together and held them against my cheek to pantomime sleep. To complete the message, I pointed to shore and stroked vigorously with my paddle. Jenya smiled wanly and continued with his short, pathetic paddle strokes.

We inched toward shore. About midnight a dark silhouette of land loomed above us. Faint reflections of starlight shimmered on small ripples in the sea. Closer to shore, deep-throated surf reverberated against the night. Franz suggested that I go in first, then guide him and Jenya to a safe landing.

I paddled toward shore until my boat rose on the rising swell that directly preceded the break. I was afraid to paddle farther for fear that the surf would dash me against the rocks. My headlamp was too dim to reach across the darkness and only blinded my night vision, so I turned it off. The map had showed a small river nearby. River deltas often make good landings because they are sandy, not rocky, so I paddled along the coast, alert for some sign that we were near the river.

This was the fourth night of our expedition. Franz and I had spent two nights at sea and one on shore, flouting international law. Now I was preparing to land through turbulent surf in pitch-blackness. I didn't know Jenya, but I'd had an unfavorable first impression: he hadn't helped us pull our boats to shore when we first landed at Yuzno Kurilsk; he had no information about our route and wouldn't ask for any; and he had paddled pathetically. Maybe this wasn't a fair appraisal—maybe we had overwhelmed him with our delayed arrival and abrupt departure. What was he thinking out there in the darkness?

Forget about Jenya. My job was to find a route to shore. I couldn't see into the night, and my only information came from the motion of the boat and the steepness of the swell. But wait: was I using all my senses?

I listened to the surf, straining to discern slight changes in pitch. Could I distinguish the sound of surf crashing onto sand from the boom of surf on rock? A hundred yards away, a wave swished into foam, which hit land with a thud. But was it rock or sand? I needed more signals. Could I recognize the distinctive smell of seaweed clinging to rock? I sniffed into the darkness, but to no avail.

Hunter-gatherer people knew every rock, undulation of the coast, safe harbor, and dangerous reef that lay close to their native villages. Those who ventured beyond those confines entered the unknown, just as we were doing. This, I thought, must be the challenge and the joy that have motivated all adventurers for all time, from the first hominids who walked out of Africa two million years ago to the Jomon who paddled this coast in prehistoric mists—the glory of seeking an intimate connection to the unknown. I stopped paddling and bobbed on the waves. Then I felt a slight brush of warm air against my face—warm, soft air that smelled sweetly of flowers. It was the signal I needed—a warm breeze carried by a river flowing across the land. The soft sand of the river delta would be our salvation.

"I'm going in," I shouted, without explaining my reasoning.

Franz shouted back with complete trust, "OK!"

I turned the boat toward shore and took a few strokes. A wave lifted my boat, then passed and broke a few feet in front of me. The following wave curled and broke under the hull. The boat hung for an instant, then accelerated toward the beach. I surfed the foam, riding high on the speed, the sound, and the glow of the luminescent sparkles that danced across the bow. The keel crunched smoothly onto soft sand, and I jumped onto the beach.

Franz came in next, and Jenya managed the surf landing competently. It was much easier to pull the boats up the beach with three men than with two. I rested my left hand on Jenya's shoulder and extended my other in greeting.

"*Zdrastvoote*." I smiled. What I wanted to say was, "Hello, welcome to the expedition. We're going to have a grand adventure." But for now, he would have to surmise the full greeting from the simple "hello."

We drank cool fresh water from the river and cooked a hearty meal over a cheery campfire. That night, before drifting off to sleep, I thought again about the Jomon sailors who had preceded us. The archaeological record in the Kurils is scanty. In a recent issue of *Arctic Anthropology*, Ben Fitzhugh, one of the foremost experts on Kuril anthropology, wrote, "A

Paleolithic occupation of the Kurils, while not currently in evidence, is possible." In other words, the Jomon may have been here, but we haven't found their campsites. The oldest evidence uncovered so far consists of 2,000-year-old Jomon relics in the southern Kurils. At any time someone might discover a new site that will open a window on these details, but it is also possible that we will never know. Perhaps the original mariners moved so quickly through the Kurils that they didn't stop to build villages. Perhaps they did stop, but their structures have rotted beyond recognition in the damp, foggy, island air. Then, too, the sea level was lower when the Jomon voyaged than it is today. Parts of the Sea of Okhotsk, west of us, are so shallow that today's seafloor was dry land when the Jomon passed through here. If they built villages on this low-lying plain, the rising sea would have obliterated the remains.

THE next day dawned calm and sunny, and we launched into a friendly sea. Jenya seemed to enjoy the nuances of light-air running, reaching, and tacking. Maybe my initial impression had been wrong, and the three of us would evolve into a team. That evening we made a relaxed camp, and his reserve seemed to be softening.

The following morning we tacked into a light headwind, sweating under the hot sun. In the early afternoon, we rounded a rocky point and headed across the mouth of a large bay. Inland, a volcanic peak was covered with abundant snow. Suddenly, at the head of the bay, the line between sea and sky became fuzzy, and the ocean turned from blue to white. After years of sailing along mountainous coastlines, I was familiar with intense afternoon winds, called williwaws. They form when warm air cools as it flows over snow-clad mountains. The cold, dense air sinks and spills rapidly onto the sea.

I released my sprayskirt, climbed out of the cockpit, and stepped forward to reduce the amount of sail I was carrying. But the williwaw struck so suddenly that the Dacron slipped free of my grasp and flapped wildly. The front deck of a WindRider is not much wider than a gymnast's balance beam, and with the hull frolicking in the gale I could easily have gone overboard. I took a quick look around at Franz and Jenya a few hundred yards away, each fighting with his sail. We were together out here, yet each of us bore primary responsibility for his own survival. If I slipped into the sea, my boat would lurch out of reach. Maybe Franz and Jenya would see me, or maybe they wouldn't; even if they did, there was no guarantee that either would be able to get to me. I dropped down on one knee and stretched the other leg out to the pontoon for a wide, stable stance.

This wasn't The Tempest, The Typhoon, or The Perfect Storm; it was just a garden-variety Kuril Islands afternoon squall. Nevertheless, a steep sea roared across the bay, and the wind blew foam off the tops of the white-caps. I completed the reef, secured the sail, and tightened the mainsheet. The boat accelerated, with the upwind pontoon dancing across the wave tops, the downwind pontoon knifing through the water, and the mast bending like a pole ready to vault. One moment the upwind pontoon would rise into the air; then a breaking wave would wash white foam across the deck, hitting me in the chest. I headed toward a tall bluff a few miles away that would provide shelter from the wind.

Suddenly I realized that I had been so engrossed in my immediate world of hull, rope, wave, and sail that I hadn't seen my companions for several minutes. I looked to my left and saw Franz's boat skipping alongside, but Jenya was nowhere in sight.

I yelled "Jenya?" and pantomimed "Where?" We both looked back to a small dot behind us. Franz and I shrugged, came about, and retraced our course. When we reached Jenya, he was hunkered down in his cockpit, with no sail up, bobbing helplessly in the sea.

Didn't he realize that an offshore wind would blow him out to sea, not to safety? How do you explain to a man paralyzed by fear or confusion, with wind howling, foam blowing, and cleats banging—when you speak only a few words of his language and he speaks only a few words of yours—that there are two kinds of death: active and passive? He could die fighting the gale, pushing his boat toward safety, or he could sit in the cockpit and drift toward a helpless demise in the broad Pacific. We hadn't come here for that. We were here to embrace the sea and overcome our fears; if we capsized trying to survive, so be it.

I wanted to shout, "Unfurl a third of your sail and point for the bluff. When a big wave rolls in, turn into the wind momentarily to take the impact on the nose, then back off and pick up your course. In less than an hour we'll reach the lee." But I lacked the vocabulary for that.

I sailed as close to him as I could. Jenya didn't look scared, just sad and dreary, as if contemplating how unfair it was that he should die out here with these two insane Americans. I pointed to my sail, then to the distant shore. But before I could say anything, a wave turned my boat, the wind grabbed my sail, and I rocketed off into the squall.

When I looked back, Jenya was sailing alongside Franz. Their brightly colored sails looked jaunty against the tan rhyolite cliff in the distance. Masts gyrated as their boats rolled with the beam sea, and I realized that I must also look bright and jostled out here in the big ocean. I was soaked, cold, and scared, but I was also a sailor, back at sea. The water rolling over the deck and the spray in the air weren't harbingers of disaster but a friendly hello, as if saying, "I'm the ocean and you've come here to play, so here's water in the face, old chum. Welcome back."

The sea was calm as soon as we crossed into the wind shadow of the cliff. Thirty seals floating in the lee barked a greeting as we paddled toward a tiny protected beach and pulled our boats to shore. Franz was ebullient; he high-fived me and pranced around the beach shouting, "What a storm! This is what we're here for, amigo! What a ride!"

Jenya was pale, somber, and obviously shaken. Why was he here? I knew he was an unemployed vulcanologist who had recently been divorced, but beyond that he remained enigmatic. He must have understood that this was just the beginning. Maybe he was only now starting to comprehend the scale of our adventure.

Jenya turned away and walked quietly down the beach, alone. I left him for a few minutes, then followed. He watched me approach, and when I was close he bent down and picked up a baseball that had washed up on the sand. It was battered, and part of the covering flapped loosely. I picked up a piece of driftwood and assumed a batter's stance. He pretended to throw the ball but held it in his hand. I motioned for him to actually throw it, but he smiled and carefully set it back down on the rocks.

OK. He was playful enough to think about throwing it. Maybe that was all I could ask for. Maybe that would be enough.

OUR landing had put us at the northeast tip of Kunashir Island, poised for the twenty-mile crossing to the next island, Iturup. The next day there was no wind and the sea was flat. If we had been in kayaks, we could have paddled to Iturup, but with the WindRiders we had to wait. It had been a week since Franz and I had left Nemuro. We had sailed fifty-five miles from Nemuro to Yuzno Kurilsk in four days and had worked through calms and storms for twenty miles in two days with Jenya. Now we were sitting on the beach going nowhere at all. At this rate, it would take us ninety-three days—all summer—just to reach Petropavlovsk, which was only one-third of the way to Alaska. I wrote in my journal, "We are working as hard as we can, but we aren't even coming close to traveling as fast as we had planned. Because of the calms and headwinds, the Wind-Rider's potential speed is meaningless."

We were camped in a small cove, about a quarter mile across, bounded on both sides by high cliffs. I walked along the beach and tried to ignore my frustration over schedules and commitments. I had told myself and my sponsors that we would sail to Alaska, but winds and currents now controlled our fate. Perhaps we had encountered a week of anomalous weather. Maybe our luck would change.

The sun was warm, so I stripped down to a T-shirt, sat on a smooth, wave-sculpted rock, and watched the placid sea. Despite the peaceful day, I was surrounded by abundant evidence of roiling nature. Nearby basalt cliffs had formed when molten lava was blasted into the air by an explosive volcanic eruption. After the rock had cooled, winter storms eroded smooth surfaces to form delicate features such as the seat I was resting on. These winter storms had also tossed driftwood and trash high up the beach, a hundred yards beyond the summer high tide line.

I walked to the storm line, stooped down, and picked up a piece of rope bigger around than my wrist. The rope had been spliced into a loop that was then rent apart by a violent force. Nothing breaks a rope this thick during normal working conditions. This rope was broken during a gale as desperate crews fought crashing waves to rescue a heavy trawl or pull a crippled ship off a lee shore. I could picture it; I've seen it: A ship rises and the rope slackens, then the ship falls off the wave, dropping its entire weight onto the rope. The ship shudders, the line pops with a loud crack, and men drop onto the deck as the rope snaps back like a deadly rubber band, snaking through the air with enough force to break, shatter, and decapitate.

Above the high tide line, a few woody bushes grew low to the ground, and higher up, battered, gnarled trees clung to the hillsides. We were close to 45° north, about the same latitude as Salem, Oregon, on the other side of the Pacific. Along the Pacific coast of North America, Salem is temperate, supporting huge fir and cedar forests and lush farmlands. The climate along the northeastern Pacific is so mild that coastal forests grow as far north as Alaska. But the weather here on Kunashir is ruled by harsh winds blowing southward from the Siberian tundra. Kunashir has enough moisture and sunlight to support a forest, and volcanic soils are generally rich in nutrients, but the vegetation is sparse and stunted. The weather here is harsher even than in the windswept valleys beneath the glaciated peaks of the Alaskan coast and the Saint Elias Range. The detritus, the rope, and the trees all told a sobering story. We must be careful; this placid sea could turn against us in a heartbeat.

Walking back toward camp, I picked up a small, curved piece of yellow-brown pottery, polished on the inside and decorated with carefully etched parallel lines on the outside. I showed it to Franz and Jenya. Jenya nodded and said, "*Ainu.*"

The smooth ceramic with its simple design took me back into the past. Over time, the ancient Jomon intermarried with their trading partners on the Asian mainland, and this interracial mixture evolved into a new culture, the Ainu. The people had moved north, hunting, trapping, and fishing for their subsistence. They called this place home and they loved it. They viewed their world in animistic terms, ascribing souls to all objects and natural phenomena. Like many other hunter-gatherers, they saw little separation between themselves and their environment.

Kayano Shigeru, a Japanese Ainu who was born in 1926 near the south coast of Hokkaido, wrote in his book *Our Land Was a Forest:*

> [My father] taught me that when walking in the mountains, we were not to startle the gods of the mountains by raising our voices or otherwise creating disturbances. "When you're walking by the river or the edge of a marsh, don't move a rock without reason," he said. "If you lift a rock to get fish bait, you're expected to put it back where it was." Now that I think back, I see that my father was imbued with the spirit of a hunting people.

Shigeru's grandmother told him that "a god dwells in each element of the great earth . . . in the mountains off in the distance, the running waters, the trees, the grasses and flowers. One must not arbitrarily cut down trees, one must not pollute running water, even birds and beasts will remember kindnesses and return favors."

The Ainu believed that gods, called *kamuy*, could be animals, plants, minerals, any geographical place, or any natural phenomenon. A person could cut a tree or kill a salmon, but only if he or she performed the proper ceremonies. Thus the Ainu culture was based on a solidarity between people, their environment, and *kamuy*. A hunter found food by passing unob-trusively through the landscape. If the hunter destroyed his environment, the deer would vanish. Therefore, *kamuy nomi*, the belief that the environ-ment was god and must be treated reverently, was religion and survival guide in one neat package. Even after the Jomon and Ainu had lived on the land for 13,000 years, the hillsides remained forested and the rivers still teemed with fish.

Turning in my hand a ceramic shard of those people, I thought about the Ainu who lived on this beach amid ubiquitous reminders of nature's power. It was hardly surprising that the Ainu saw *kamuy* in the rocks, wind, and waves. It seemed, at that moment, perfectly natural that a person should pray to nature.

After lunch I made another effort to bond with Jenya. Because conver-sation was limited by our lack of shared language, I sat down to show him photos of my home and family. He reached out and grasped a photo of Chris, who was standing on skis and smiling, with snow-covered fir in the background. He explained slowly, in Pidgin English and Russian, that his wife had found a new boyfriend and had left him. Then he looked up.

"*Me, no wife. No home. No little boy.*"

He stood and walked lugubriously to his belongings, unwrapped a video camera, inserted a tape, and handed me the device. The tape showed a scene from a past Christmas with his wife and son. She was smiling and happy, and the little boy was running around a decorated tree. When I looked up, he repeated, "*Me, no wife. No home. No little boy.*"

I said, "Many women," and waved my hand across the cosmos, but he shook his head. Then I tried "Friends" and pointed to Franz and me, but he was inconsolable. I left him alone and walked back down the beach. At first I thought, "I don't understand this guy; he's not having any fun out here." But then it hit me—maybe Jenya wasn't strange. He was afraid of the storm, and he missed his estranged wife. Franz and I had left our partners and our homes and were prancing around the beach with thumbs up, high fives, and yahoos; maybe we were the weird ones.

WHAT WERE the Jomon sailors whose route we were following like? Were they outcasts? Were they visionaries? Did others look at the migrants and wonder why they were eschewing their villages, their relatives, and the safety of their tribe? I was positive, at least, that the Jomon migrants were eccentrics, and that made them kindred spirits.

W E LAUNCHED the next day in a ten-knot wind and sailed into the strait. The boats danced in the wind, holding good speed, without tension. Within a few hours Kunashir lost its sharpness, and the volcanic peaks on Iturup loomed larger. We heard surf pounding against rocks. Gulls wheeled around us, then returned to their nests on the black volcanic rock, which was splotched white from their droppings. We sailed into a circular bay about four miles wide. Franz beckoned us toward the shelter of a cliff where we could slow down, chat, and regroup.

We were hoping to find a river flowing into the bay, and another beach with a good landing, but there was no valley here, no river, and no beach. Instead, the bay was ringed entirely by steep cliffs. In some places vertical rock was fractured into columns; other cliffs were composed of undulating curlicue rock, formed when viscous, fluid lava freezes. I looked at my nautical chart and saw that even close to shore the water was 1,500 feet deep, enough to drown the Empire State Building. It took me a few moments to understand the landscape. Then I shouted to Franz, "We've sailed into a caldera!" The entire Kuril Island chain is a volcanic arc above the boundary between two colliding tectonic plates. From the east, the Pacific Ocean floor—a chunk of rock about fifty miles thick and covering almost one-third of the planet—crashes inexorably into Asia, the Earth's largest continent. Under these unimaginable forces, the ocean floor buckles and dives into the Earth's mantle, sinking about as fast as a person's fingernails grow. This diving plate has formed a trench 34,600 feet deep on the ocean floor. By comparison, Mount Everest is 29,000 feet above sea level. Thus if you could cut off Mount Everest at sea level, turn it upside down, and drop it into the Kuril Trench with a big splash, it would leave more than 5,000 feet of water from the mountain's base to the surface, deeper than the ocean off the eastern seaboard of the United States. When the sinking oceanic plate reaches the Earth's mantle, it stirs up hot magma, which rises to form volcanoes. Over time, the volcanic peaks have risen above sea level to form the Kuril Islands.

About four million years ago, a series of volcanic eruptions deposited successive layers of lava on the seafloor. Then about 3.2 million years ago, before hominids had walked out of Africa, this undersea mountain rose to form the island of Iturup. Later, deep within the bowels of the volcanic mountain, hot lava rose and pressure built until a violent eruption ripped the mountain apart. The rock exploded into a huge mushroom cloud of fine dust that blew away with the wind, leaving behind a deep hole—the caldera we had just sailed into. I raised a clenched fist of excitement and victory. We had sailed into a volcanic crater, a vortex of nature's power, where solid earth had exploded into dust and had collided with the ocean. So far, the *kamuy* of earth, sky, and sea had granted us safe passage, and I hoped they would continue to if we paid them proper respect. Don't challenge the *kamuy;* live with them. Don't try to overpower them, because they can blow a mountain into the sky. But with the right blend of cleverness and reverence, we could dance with the gods—and sail to Alaska.

Franz grinned and shouted "Ba-boom!" He covered his head with his hands to ward off an imaginary shower of fiery ash and hissing volcanic bombs.

Then I remembered that Jenya was a professional vulcanologist, so I tried to include him in the excitement. "*Caldera, da?*"

He didn't understand the word "caldera," and I didn't know the Russian translation, so I said, "*Vulcan, da?*"

He nodded with a bored expression. Then, as if teaching an obvious lesson to a child, he waved his hand laconically across the entire landscape. "*Vsya, vulcan* [it's all volcanic]."

I wanted to shout: "It's the power, Jenya! Don't you get it? We're here to stand on the edge and look in. We step close to the power and then step back. If you don't get excited when you're sailing into the maw of a place where nature's powers have met in a cataclysmic embrace, then maybe you just shouldn't be here."

W̅E SAILED forty-eight miles the following day, but we managed only nine the next, in light winds and calms. That afternoon, while we were making camp, two Russian men with ragged clothes, patched boots, and unkempt beards approached us on the beach. They were shouldering hunting rifles. We all said hello, but when they realized how bad my Russian was, they sat down and talked with Jenya. Jenya took out his maps, and the strangers were clearly offering information about locations to the north. When they left, I asked Jenya to explain what he had learned, but he shook his head, walked away, and sat by himself on the outskirts of camp. Franz and I gathered firewood, fetched water, and cooked dinner while Jenya looked on, offering no help.

The next evening Jenya sat down next to me with a phrase book, a dictionary, and a piece of paper. The phrase book was written for mariners, not tourists. Instead of translating "How do you buy tickets to the ballet?" it was filled with sentences such as, "My engine room is flooded and we have lost the pumps."

Jenya turned to the medical section and ran his thumb down a long list of ailments: heavy bleeding, broken leg, and so forth, until he came to "severe heart attack." Then he made a complete English sentence, "I have severe heart attack."

I asked incredulously in Russian, "*Schto* [what]?"

He consulted his dictionary and wrote slowly in English on his crumpled, water-stained paper, "I have pain in heart."

Was he talking about a real heart attack, or the emotional pain caused when his wife left him?

He wrote another line, "I am leave."

"*To where?*" I asked in Russian.

"*Petropavlovsk.*"

But we were in the wilderness, on an island. We had seen no towns and only two people in the five days since we left Yuzno Kurilsk. I asked him how he was going to leave. He explained that the men with rifles had told him that the village of Kurilsk, twenty-five miles north, had an airport.

I was angry. My map showed a small, round circle at Kurilsk, and I had asked Jenya several times whether it was a functioning town. Could we buy food? Send mail? He had always said, "I don't know," or "Maybe."

Now he told me that the town was large enough to have an airport. Surely someone in Yuzno Kurilsk had known of its existence. And even if by some incredulous happenstance no one had, the men with rifles had told him about the town yesterday.

Franz took the news with equanimity. Jenya's strength was welcome during launching and landing, but otherwise he had been only marginally helpful when we were in camp and a liability at sea. If he left we would probably have to abandon his boat, which was a monetary loss, but our checkbooks were far away and financial balance sheets seemed abstract.

On the following morning, June 24, we launched into a calm, dense fog.

The Kuril Islands not only form the boundary between two tectonic plates, they lie at the confluence of two opposing weather systems. The Japanese current carries moist, tropical air northward, while cold arctic air descends from the polar ice cap and the Siberian tundra. When these two masses collide, moisture condenses into an incessant fog. Although it was disconcerting to be floating only a few hundred yards from shore and at the same time be out of sight of land, it was peaceful to drift within a great expanse of enshrouding uniformity. However, when the sun burned through the fog in midmorning, we realized that we were only a hundred yards from camp. I unpacked hand lines and we caught seven fish. By early afternoon we were still in the same place. We could see several old, abandoned military tanks half buried in the hillside above us, their rusted cannon peering threateningly across the bay. The war toys seemed silly out here in the vastness. Why would someone defend this uninhabited bluff, on this island, near this volcano? Why would someone attack?

A gentle breeze from the southwest crinkled the sea into wavelets, so we raised sail. When the wind picked up to twenty knots, we reefed down and the boats heeled over until the upwind pontoon skimmed through the air. Jenya sailed like a master, with spray in his face, not like the frightened novice he had been the week before. I even thought I saw a slim smile break through the sadness. And why not? This was the sensation every sailor craves: decks awash, with "a bone in her teeth." I imagine that the first caveman who hacked at a hardwood log with a chip of obsidian dreamed of this moment, when the wind blows, the salt water fills your sinuses, and the boat flies over the waves. Why was Jenya quitting now, when he was learning his boat and even grinning at the sea?

I wasn't sure whether he was afraid of the danger, oppressed by the calms and boredom, or overwhelmed by the time commitment. Maybe he thought he could woo his wife back if he hurried home to Petropavlovsk. The reasons were irrelevant. Jenya wasn't happy here; he was leaving.

People have gone to sea for millennia, but most people, throughout time, have embraced the safety of villages. Even though the Ainu hunted, fished, and traded on the open sea, their main deity was Fuchi, fire goddess of the hearth. The two essential spiritual components of every Ainu house were a hearth and a sacred window that faced upstream, toward the spawning grounds of the holy salmon. Fuchi mediated with all other gods, so all *kamuy* rituals started at the hearth. If you wanted to cut down a tree, embark on a voyage, hunt deer, or pick roots and berries, you started at the hearth and implored Fuchi to negotiate permission from the appropriate gods or goddesses. Thus the hearth was not only the place where families joined at the end of the day, it was the focus of their spirituality.

In a similar manner, the Tlingit Indians, who lived along the northwest coast of British Columbia and Alaska, revered the home. Even though the Tlingit navigated along the coast, fished, and hunted sea mammals, their legends encouraged people to embrace the safety of land. Many Tlingit stories started with someone leaving home and being swirled into a whirlpool, battered by storms, eaten by devilfish, or kidnapped by capricious frog people. But perhaps the most terrifying fate suffered by people in the Tlingit legends was loneliness. Their stories were full of people who, through ineptitude, laziness, adultery, jealousy, or contentiousness, were exiled from their villages, families, and hearths into the forest or onto the broad wilderness of the sea.

Most villagers can't imagine why fellow humans embrace discomfort and possible death just to travel to some strange and distant place. When Russian explorers first penetrated the central highlands of Kamchatka, a Koryak chief summed up the quintessential domestic view of the world. The chief could "imagine that no people in the world are so happy as themselves, regarding all the accounts that strangers give of the advantages of other countries as so many lies and fables, for they say, 'If you could enjoy these advantages at home, what made you take so much trouble to find us?'"

Once again my anger at Jenya was tempered by an awareness that he was acting perfectly normally by abandoning the expedition and leaving us to our fates.

DESPITE calms, fog, and headwinds, we paddled into Kurilsk the following evening. A military officer was waiting for us on the beach. He was good looking, about forty years old, with a medium build, a carefully trimmed moustache, and crow's-feet forming around his eyes. A few tufts of carefully groomed blond hair offset his incipient baldness, and I could see three gold teeth between his thin lips.

Armed soldiers appeared on the bluff above us, dark and impersonal against a gray sky. Was this going to be a repeat of our experience in Yuzno

Kurilsk? I tried to make eye contact with the officer. Maybe if I could hold his attention for a moment, he would look into our salt-encrusted faces and imagine our exposed journey over the open sea. Maybe he would see that we were friendly and had stories to tell. Maybe then he would take us home and feed us around a warm fire in a cozy kitchen.

He asked for our passports, and when I smiled he looked up to the bluff and barked a command. Soldiers slid down the hill, waving their AK-47s to herd us into a tight circle around the boats. Then the commanding officer motioned to Jenya, and they walked off together. I offered cigarettes to our guards and they accepted gratefully. They paced slowly back and forth, Kalashnikovs at their hips, puffing away contentedly.

The fog was so thick that water beaded on our raincoats. A ramshackle wooden fence guarded the top of the bluff, and beyond that lay a low building with peeling paint and a radar antenna. A fishing boat moved slowly in the harbor, and I heard clanging that sounded like a fish cannery, but I wasn't sure. The soldiers let me walk ten yards to either side of our boats before ordering me to halt. I walked inland about fifteen yards and saw clear signs that surf washed over the entire beach during a storm.

I wasn't quite sure why we were under guard; our papers were in order and we had committed no crime. Perhaps this was a sensitive military zone, but I couldn't imagine what military secrets were hidden behind the rotten, listing fence. Jenya returned and explained that the officer, a major, was holding our passports and would return them when we departed.

Then Jenya clutched his heart, grimaced, and repeated, "I have pain in heart. I go to Petropavlovsk tomorrow." It seemed too dramatic. I wanted him to tell the truth and simply say that he wasn't addicted to playing judo master against a powerful ocean. Maybe Franz and I thought it was fun to leave our jobs, homes, and wives to brush against forces that could crush us in an instant—but the journey made no sense to him. In the abstract it had sounded like a paying gig; in the concrete it was obvious madness. I said nothing.

The following morning, an eight-year-old girl in a clean, frilly dress walked into our camp, after half carrying and half dragging a heavy sack across the beach. She said she was the major's daughter, and her parents had sent her down with a gift of bread and potatoes. I thanked her and squatted in the sand to show her photos of my home in Montana, my grown children, and my young grandchildren. She nestled up to me and squirmed her way into my lap to get a closer look at the pictures.

The soldiers inched closer to look over my shoulder. I've been in places, like the Middle East, where enemies genuinely hate each other, but no one here was angry. The major was a well-mannered gentleman whose mother had evidently taught him to offer hospitality to strangers. For some reason he couldn't invite us for dinner, but he trusted us enough to send his daughter as an emissary. Likewise the soldiers saw us as people, not as feared enemies. I gave the little girl a postcard of two black bear cubs climbing a tree. She pointed at the bear and offered me a short Russian lesson:

"*Medved.*"

I answered, "*Da, Medved. Engleeski:* bear."

"Bear," she repeated tentatively but with surprisingly clear pronunciation. Then she jumped up, clutched the photograph with two hands, and ran home to show it to her parents.

The major came down an hour later and told us that Jenya could go to town to buy groceries. I gave Jenya fifty dollars; he walked off, and returned in an hour with bread, sausage, spaghetti, tins of meat and milk, and change in Russian rubles. After lunch, we dismantled Jenya's boat and carried the pieces to a shed near the beach. The major promised to ship the boat to Sakhalin, then have it forwarded to Petropavlovsk, where we could pick it up. I didn't know it then, but I would never see it again.

After we locked the shed door, Jenya shook our hands and left. The major started to walk away, but I motioned that I had a few questions. I squatted in the oil-soaked dirt and drew a crude map of Iturup and the surrounding islands. Maps are a universal language among travelers, hunters, and soldiers. The major poked his finger at our present location and said "*Kurilsk,*" to indicate that he was oriented to my drawing. I drew a line along the northwest shore of the island and said in Russian, "*We go here.*"

He nodded.

Then I drew two short arrows, one leading to the west side of the next island, Urup, and the other to the east. He smudged out the arrow leading west and extended the arrow along the east coast.

"*You go here.*" Then for emphasis he pointed to the west coast and said, "*Nyet. Danger.*"

I nodded and extended the map all the way to Kamchatka, six hundred miles away. "*Where people?*" I asked.

He poked a dot at the northern edge of the chain and said, "*Here. Severo Kurilsk.*" Then he waved his hand over the central five hundred miles and said, "*Here, no people. No food.*"

From what little I could see, I estimated that about a thousand people lived in Yuzno Kurilsk and another thousand lived in Kurilsk. But for the next five hundred miles, the islands were uninhabited. Surely this was one of the most isolated regions in the world. We carried an emergency locator transmitter (ELT) that could send a distress signal to a satellite in a dire emergency. But unless our lives were in immediate danger, we had no means of communicating with anyone.

I stood, and we shook hands warmly. Then, gently, as if apologizing, he pointed me back to the beach. As I started to walk away, he tapped me on the shoulder and said, "*Tomorrow, good weather.*"

I replied, "*Good. We go tomorrow. Early.*"

He handed me our passports and papers. I thanked him; he shook my hand again and wished me good luck.

When I returned to the beach the guards were gone, but there were two deep lines drawn in the sand, about twenty yards apart, to indicate the perimeter of our camp. I'm an honorable man, and my mother taught me manners. I stepped into our prison and didn't leave until we set sail the following morning.

W E EKED out fifty-four miles over the next four days, tacking into diabolical headwinds, running blind through incessant fog, and landing and launching through treacherous surf. One night I dreamt that I was at sea; my boat wouldn't respond to the tiller, and the sail was flapping wildly. I woke up and realized that a gale had loosened the rain fly on my tent. I crawled outside, secured the fly, and slid back into my sleeping bag. By this time the wind was strong enough to bend the tent poles and press the cold nylon against my face. Instead of feeling desperate, I felt secure and peaceful because we were on land, and I fell into a deep sleep.

I woke around noon and stepped outside. The wind was driving foam off the tops of the waves, and small waterspouts gyrated across the sea. Franz and I built a driftwood fire in the shelter of a large boulder and cooked a pot of rice. High cliffs protected the cove from the full force of the gale, and the boulder provided further shelter. Six waterfalls waved in the breeze, their mist dancing iridescent rainbows over the black basalt. The wildflowers hadn't bloomed yet, but the undergrowth was intensely green. We had left Japan less than three weeks before, but our boats were already deteriorating.

The battens had torn loose from the sails, so we sewed spares in place with our strongest thread. The impact of surf landings had loosened the rudder mounts. We stiffened them with an extra bolt; we didn't have the tools or material for a complete repair. When we were finished with our chores, I bundled up in warm clothes and sat on an exposed rock with a cup of tea. Then I took out my journal, holding the pages carefully so they wouldn't catch the wind, and wrote:

> We're not going to succeed on this expedition. Whatever we do, I'm going to return and tell my sponsors that we didn't make it to Alaska. So why don't I go home now? Because, ultimately, neither the sponsors nor the destination is that important. I'm out here because it's fun. . . . Well, fun is a non-word and I don't know its meaning anymore. I'm out here because after all these years, that's who I am.

Waves crashed against the cobbled beach and threw spray into the air, so I moved into my tent. Ensconced, I recalled an Ainu exhibit at the Smithsonian Museum in Washington, D.C. The museum curators had set a ten-foot model of an Ainu trading canoe against a large painting of five frightened, fur-clad sailors rowing beneath a breaking wave. Ainu canoes were built out of a cedar log. First the boatbuilders hollowed the log, then they filled the hull with water, which was then heated with hot stones. The hot water softened the wood so they could spread the sides of the canoe apart, providing more beam amidships. Finally the Ainu lashed wooden planks to the sides to give the craft a higher profile for a heavy sea. On the museum model, the planks were tied with rawhide, but early Russian explorers reported that Ainu made string from whale baleen. Japanese and Russian accounts both report that Ainu trading canoes were up to fifty feet long and were routinely used for extended ocean passages. A finished boat weighed five hundred to a thousand pounds and was large enough to carry crew and trade goods.

Over time the Ainu became prolific traders, whereas the Japanese developed agriculture and metallurgy. Ainu seafarers loaded their boats with salmon and furs, sailed to southern Japan, and returned home carrying rice, steel tools, tobacco, cloth, and sake. Ainu navigators also sailed north to the Amur River to trade with the Chinese for silk, metal, and glass. Early Russian explorers reported that the Ainu introduced swords and steel pots to the Stone Age hunters on Kamchatka.

Eventually the Japanese decided to conquer the Ainu rather than trade with them. The story is sickeningly similar to the histories of so many other places in the world: after a few setbacks, large, well-coordinated armies of the agro-industrialists overpowered the hunter-gatherers, stole their land, killed off most of the inhabitants, and destroyed the culture, leaving a few skeletal remnants of the past.

As a small-boat sailor, I understood how the Ainu and the Jomon before them could navigate these waters in a hollow log. The major trick is patience—don't go out when it's nasty; paddle like hell, and bail like a madman if you get caught in a storm. But I find it even more amazing that people survived in a harsh environment such as the Kurils. Although Franz and I were slowly moving north, we would freeze and starve to death before we could sew our own clothes and hunt, fish, and gather food along the way.

One of the earliest direct accounts of aboriginal existence in the Kurils comes from Stephen Krasheninnikov, who traveled to the Russian Far East with Vitus Bering in 1736. Krasheninnikov was twenty-four years old when he arrived in Kamchatka with orders from Her Imperial Majesty, Anna Ivanovna, Empress of all the Russians, not to come home until he had completed a thorough description of Kamchatka and the Kurils, including the animals, plants, geography, geology, and people. Bering sailed to Alaska and the Aleutian Islands while Krasheninnikov stayed on the east coast to complete his assignment.

To the south, on Hokkaido, and to the north, on Kamchatka, large rivers supported abundant salmon populations, and in turn the salmon supported relatively large human populations. But there were never many salmon in the Kurils, and as a result the area has never been well populated. Snippets from Krasheninnikov's book *The History of Kamtschatka* provide a keen insight into life in the Kurils:

> [The Ainu in the Kurils] feed for the most part on sea mammals, and sometimes upon fish.
>
> They anoint the points of their darts and arrows with the poison juice which is squeezed from the root of a special plant . . . The very largest whales, when they have received a slight wound from such a poisoned weapon, cannot bear the sea for any considerable time; but throwing themselves upon the shore, expire most miserable, with terrible groans and bellowing.
>
> They harvest nettles in the months of August or September, and lay them to dry in the shade . . . They first split them with their teeth, then peel off the skin, and beat them. After this they comb them and spin them between their hands . . . The thread of the first spinning they use for sewing but to make their nets they double and twist it; but the nets, after all, never last

above one summer. The nets they use for fishing, which is absolutely necessary for the support of life.

They have a net made of the hair of whales' beards, composed of several
rings; this is spread on the ground, and to a ring in the middle they bind a
magpie; round the net is drawn a cord, the ends of which are held by a person concealed in a pit near at hand, who, when a fox springs upon the bird,
draws the cord and gathers the net, which surrounds the fox.

They make great use of the birch bark, which they strip from the trees
while yet green; and cutting it in small pieces, like vermicelli, eat it with dried
caviar . . . They also ferment this bark with the sap of the birch, which makes
an agreeable drink . . . They eat everything they can get down, even the dri-
est plants and the nastiest rotten mushrooms . . . However, the natives have
obtained such a knowledge of plants, and their use both in food and medicine
. . . that one shall not find so much knowledge of this sort among any barbarous nation, or even perhaps among the most civilized . . . Hence the people . . . can find food and medicine everywhere.

[Their clothes] are made of sea fowls, foxes, sea beavers [sea otters], and
other sea mammals and are generally composed of skins of very different
creatures, so that it is rare to see a whole suit made of the same sort of skins.

There grows upon the seashore a whitish high plant, resembling wheat.
They mow it with a scythe, made out of the shoulder blade of a whale; which
they whet so well by grinding it upon a stone, that they bring it to a very good
edge. Of this plant, they make cloaks . . . smooth within . . . and rough without, which makes the rain run more easily off them.

Imagine the tasks required to go fishing, Ainu style. First you must
scrape a log for a few years to carve a boat. Then you paddle over a stormy
and treacherous ocean to a small island to locate obsidian for a harpoon
point. You quarry and shape the obsidian by bashing it with another rock,
then you lash your point to a long stick. You walk through the forest, dig
up special roots, and grind them into poison. When all this is done, you go
charging back into the ocean, kill a whale, drag it to shore, extract its shoulder blade, and rub the bone against a rock until the bone is sharp enough
to harvest nettles. Now you're getting close—all you have to do is split the
nettles with your teeth, spin the fiber into string, and macramé a net. Finally
you set the net and catch fish. And don't forget that the net lasts only a year,
and you have to harvest more nettles the following spring.

Of course, no one went fishing in this linear manner. I imagine a group
of Ainu adolescents dressed in feathers, fox skin, and dried grass. They ea-
gerly ask the elders if they can take the boat by themselves, but a boat is
too valuable to entrust to youngsters, so one of the older men accompanies

them. A whale spouts in the distance, and they paddle hard, with the blind audaciousness of youth. A whale would feed the entire village for the winter, and people would talk about their bravery and skill throughout the dark, cold times. But the whale is wary, and it sounds before the boys can throw their poison-tipped harpoons. Tired, they land on a distant beach to dig clams and collect seagull eggs. They set a net along the beach, walk inland to harvest nettles, then return to pull in a few fish.

KRASHENINNIKOV VISITED the Russian Far East roughly 275 years ago, yet his observations of the Ainu provide insight into the lives of their Jomon ancestors who lived 9,500 to 20,000 years earlier. In most hunter-gatherer societies, people depend mainly on foods that are easy to harvest. Thus Stone Age maritime cultures relied heavily on shellfish. During the early Jomon period, sea temperatures in the southern Kurils were warmer than they are now, and shellfish were abundant. Clams and oysters are rich in protein. Fish were also important in the Jomon diet. The oldest Jomon net fragments in Japan are 8,000 years old; however, because nets rot quickly and are not preserved well in the fossil record, the Jomon could have been making nets much earlier, though we don't know for sure. We also don't know when the Ainu ancestors might have begun using poison-tipped weapons. Most of the sea mammal bones in early Jomon sites came from juvenile fur seals, which are much smaller and less formidable than adult seals or whales. On the other hand, people almost certainly scavenged dead whales that washed up on the beach—if they dragged meat and blubber home, but not the skeleton, there would be no fossil record of these scavenged whales. In addition, analysis of Stone Age garbage heaps near Jomon villages indicates that they hunted bear, deer, fox, and hare. A variety of plants were also essential to their diet.

Though we know little about Jomon settlements in the Kurils, it seems probable from scant evidence that isolated populations either lived on or visited these lonely islands for a least a few thousand years, maybe more.

Tools, bones, and bits of pollen or leaves tell us what people ate and how they hunted. In addition, by analyzing human skeletons, scientists can deduce how old people were when they died, what they ate, what injuries they may have sustained, and how often they struggled through periods of starvation. Good skeletal data are not yet available from the Kurils, but Kennewick Man's remains tell a fascinating story.

Anthropologists estimate that Kennewick Man was forty to fifty years old when he died. He had all his teeth and no cavities, but the tops of his teeth were worn flat almost to the gums, causing chronic toothaches for a decade before he died. His teeth had probably been worn down from eating coarse, unwashed plant roots. A chemical analysis of his bones indicated that, in addition to roots, his diet consisted of nuts and berries and abundant salmon. This diet closely parallels that of other aboriginal people in the Pacific Northwest.

In addition to his two major injuries—the broken ribs and spear wound—Kennewick Man had suffered several minor ones. He had fractured his left elbow, and his left arm had withered; he had been hit on the head; his right shoulder socket had been chipped; and he had arthritis in numerous joints.

From the structure of any bone, an anthropologist can determine whether the muscles attached to that bone were strong or weak. Kennewick Man was heavily muscled. Anthropologist James Chatters also noticed that certain muscles in the Kennewick Man's face and jaw were surprisingly strong. These well-developed muscles aren't those needed for practical functions such as chewing but rather are associated with facial expression. Chatters thinks that the muscles were strengthened as a result of maintaining a strained but stoic expression through years of intense pain.

This picture of a hard life in the Stone Age is supported by additional data. James Dixon, curator of archaeology at the Denver Museum of Natural History, analyzed thirty-eight North American skeletons between 8,000 and 11,000 years old. According to Dixon, about one-fourth of the population died when they were children. Most of the others died in their twenties or thirties, only 10 percent lived to age forty, and only one, Kennewick Man, possibly lived to see fifty.

At least 10 percent (and probably more) endured one or more periods of starvation.

Most of the older skeletons showed signs of severe injury, and about 25 percent of the people appear to have died from an accident.

Several individuals suffered severe infections and tooth abscesses. The Spirit Cave Man may have died from a raging toothache.

Surprisingly, women generally died younger than men. Even though men risked injury and death during hunting and warfare, childbirth and breast feeding took a harsh toll on women during the hungry times. Whereas a few men lived into their forties, most women died in their twenties or early thirties.

Dixon wrote, "These very limited and sketchy data suggest that these rugged men and women led harsh lives, periodically suffering from hunger, infections, broken bones, and violence . . ."

Yet a Stone Age life was not one of unadulterated misery. Dixon concluded, "Just as there were times of hardship and hunger, there must have been times of comfort and abundance. Burials suggest an intellectual and metaphysical life encompassing the natural environment, the spiritual world, and belief in an afterlife."

WATERSPOUTS WHIRLED across a chaotic sea. The ocean would calm down eventually and we would continue north along this ancient sea route. The journey was consuming all our strength, time, and energy, but we were supported by boatbuilders and clothing factories in the United States and by rice farms in Japan. Unlike us, the Jomon had to collect food while they traveled. Forget, for a moment, hard-to-define concepts such as danger, risk, or human spirit, and look instead at simple arithmetic—calories in versus calories out. Travel not only consumes calories, it takes time away from food gathering. So migration is a double whammy that imposes a tremendous burden just to survive.

This caloric analysis provides an argument against my thesis that people may have migrated out of a romantic urge to explore. The costs seem too great. But the same argument could be used against pragmatic migration. A pragmatist maximizes his or her chances of survival, and it would take monstrous famine or war to chase a logical person away from Japan and into these islands with nothing but a stone-tipped harpoon and a parka made of dried grass.

But early *Homo sapiens* walked out of Africa and spread across the world. They colonized tropical paradises, deserts, and the high Arctic. Whatever their reasons, Jomon sailors left behind their goddess of the hearth and sailed along these rocky, storm-tossed islands.

I N ORDINARY times, when I am living in Montana with Chris, I give free reign to my changing moods. But these weren't ordinary times. Franz and I were on a lonely island chain, in two absurdly small boats, in the middle of a vast ocean. At the beginning of the journey I had promised myself to avoid emotional highs and lows, even internally. Thus when I was untangling the towrope on our first day, I reminded myself to "hold on tight—don't embellish—don't think about the consequences—just hold on tight." Survival was paramount, and we had to remain functional at all costs. Nothing else mattered. As a result, I tried to hold my feelings within and remain blandly unemotional, inside and out.

My mind remained acutely alert to external details, but it frequently went blank internally. Maybe this is the mental state that Zen masters talk about. Live in the moment and ignore the past, the future, or any analysis of the moment. I don't know. But I do know that although this semi-suspended mental void was joyously simple, it was unsettling to my Western consciousness. As I write this, three years after the voyage, I can vividly picture a rogue wave that threatened to capsize my boat, a shearing crosswind, a flower that incongruously grew out of a rocky beach, and the look on Franz's face as he squinted into the wind. But I can't recall my thoughts during many of those long days at sea, and I don't remember much of what Franz and I talked about around our campfires.

As the days and miles passed, Franz and I became a competent team. The Jomon had traveled as a tribe, but Franz and I began this journey as two near-strangers. We hadn't played together when we were toddlers, and we didn't have elders to guide us, or children and wives to temper our macho maleness. Yet we managed to work through the niggling hassles that arise between two people who were cooperating on life-and-death decisions. We lived out our dreams, we kept each other alive, and—against formidable odds—we would complete our passage to Petropavlovsk.

ON SUNDAY, July 4, Independence Day back home, a light breeze blew and we launched early, headed for the twenty-six-mile crossing to the next island, Urup. Within the dream state of watching but not thinking much, I formulated and repeated a hopeful mantra: twenty-six miles—in fifteen hours of daylight—less than two miles per hour—fat city—piece of cake. Low-angled sunlight reflected off the backs of the waves, shadowing their western faces. We tacked north into deeper water, and the sea flattened dramatically. I pointed to the northeast and shouted jubilantly, "Twenty-six miles in fifteen hours!" and Franz replied with a raised fist.

Water bubbled up behind my stern, creating a cheery singsong gurgle in harmony with the rhythm of the broad, easy swell. A thin line of fog hugged the sea, and another fog bank formed higher in the sky, leaving a thin window that drew my soul toward the horizon. Perhaps if I were a Jomon shaman, perhaps even the leader of the travelers I was following, I could leave my body and zoom around that expansive circle of blue, speeding up and flying faster and faster like a whirling dervish until I collapsed in ecstasy back into my cockpit. But after half an hour, the two separate fog layers coalesced into a dense, encapsulating fog that held my spirit captive.

When I am sitting in a WindRider in the middle of the ocean on a clear day, my eyes are four feet above the water and the horizon is 2.3 miles away. I visualize myself in the center of a small expanse within the much larger ocean vastness. But when the fog closes in, the visual world shrinks to a hundred feet or less. A hundred feet isn't that much smaller than two miles when compared with the size of the Pacific Ocean, but the diminished horizon feels so confining that I imagine apocalyptic disasters germinating in the haze.

The wind fell off around noon and the sails went limp. The waves had flattened to an almost imperceptible swell seeming to emanate from every compass point at once. My boat rotated clockwise while Franz's, only a few feet away, rotated counterclockwise, as if we were two meshed gears. We slowly spiraled away from each other until the fog softened the bright red and yellow of Franz's hull and parka. Large boils bubbled out of the sea as if ferns were rotting beneath us in a Cretaceous swamp. But the water was more than half a mile deep, and the upwellings were generated by restless currents funneling through undersea canyons to collide against submerged cliffs taller than the granite monoliths of Yosemite. The eerie peacefulness made us apprehensive; we bobbed helplessly while the hours passed.

Just when I started to worry that we wouldn't make landfall before dark, the wind picked up from the west. At 3:00 P.M. our GPS showed land at 8.5 miles, bearing 87°, and we were traveling at four miles an hour.

Long ago, in an old, high-ceilinged school building with windowpanes that rattled because all the glazing had dried up and fallen out, I'd learned in Miss Edgett's seventh-grade class that multiplying speed by time of travel gives distance covered. I considered it among the most useful things I'd been taught in school. I ran a quick calculation through my head and shouted to Franz, "We should reach land in 2.1 hours, about 5:00."

Franz is a math professor, so he had to agree.

Then the sea—not the wind but the sea—started to assume a different character. The broad swells bunched up, and small wavelets began to jump about. The bubbles emanating from my stern changed to *gurgle, slap, gurgle, slap*, adding a sinister syncopation to the melody. Driven inexorably by the moon above and the rock beneath, the currents were changing. At 4:00 P.M. we took another GPS reading. Land was now 8.1 miles, bearing 55°, and our speed remained steady. Yes, we were sailing at four miles an hour, but the current was sweeping us southeast, into the Pacific. In an hour we had progressed only 0.4 mile toward our goal. At this rate, we would spend the night at sea. Well, we had done that before. But then we had been closer to land and to civilization. Out here in the ocean wilderness, the prospect of spending a night at sea in a sixteen-foot boat was intensely frightening.

I reminded myself once again that fear could be my friend or my enemy. Right now, fear told me that danger lurked, but I knew that already. I pushed my fear aside, calmed myself, and stared toward the island I couldn't see, as if the power of thought would draw me there. We altered course to buck the current, and our speed dropped until we weren't moving anywhere at all.

In the next hour the current weakened, then reversed. The ebb tide had been drawing water out of the Sea of Okhotsk; now the current was moving back in with the flood, and we resumed our progress toward land. The wind picked up and we were hopeful, again, that we would reach safety before dark.

There was no golden sun sinking into the western ocean, instead the fog darkened gradually as night approached. Wind was driving against the current and we were now sailing in shallow water; the waves steepened to a nasty chop. The cold wetness was irrelevant; we were approaching land, camp, warmth, and safety. We heard the surf when the GPS gave our position as two miles from Urup, but we couldn't see a thing. At 0.25 mile the surf sounded loud and urgent, then the GPS read 0.2 mile, then 0.1 mile, and we both stared into the haze. Franz looked down at his GPS and shouted, "0.05 mile from Urup, 250 feet!" I felt the waves change shape as they touched bottom, and suddenly I saw breakers pounding against rocky cliffs.

"Land! Rocks! Turn right, now!"

Our map showed a protected cove less than a mile away. The bow wake created the illusion that we were plying through the water at five to six miles an hour, but the GPS assured us that we were again sailing to a standstill against a fast-moving current. After a few frustrating minutes of staring at his tiny GPS screen, Franz looked up and said in a soft, measured voice, "The current must be backing off. We're moving forward again. We're close, real close."

Our boats rose on one wave, slid sideways off another, then twisted on a reflection from the opposite direction. The GPS told us that we were at the mouth of the cove, but the wave pattern indicated that uncharted shoals and sea stacks guarded our landfall. A GPS is useless if hazards aren't on the map, so I turned it off and stared into the haze, reluctant to enter the danger zone without vision.

Then, incredibly—deus ex machina, heroes on white horses in cheap novels—the fog lifted. A green cliff appeared, white foam curled around a half-buried shoal, and breakers crashed against a looming sea stack. We caught wind in our sails, skirted the shoals, and ducked into the lee of a high cliff just as twilight surrendered to darkness. Two-inch ripples caressed a kelp-covered beach, and we steered to a gentle landing on soft sand.

Franz and I didn't prance around the beach high-fiving each other as we had a few weeks previously after our first storm. This time we were physically and emotionally exhausted. We ate a candy bar, pitched our tents, said a weary good-night, and retired without cooking dinner. I stripped off my wet clothes, tossed them in a clammy heap at the foot of the tent, and slipped into dry long underwear. Out there, in the ink-black sea, surf was bashing against the cliffs and wind was whistling through the rocks.

Then an animal called from the cliffs above us. It was eerie, like the sound of a baby's cry, "*Whaaa.*" Then it called again, with the same pitch and rhythm as before.

The cry ululated in the wind, modulated by the surf; then it was closer and more distinct—inscrutable and lonely. It seemed to be the wilderness and the sea welcoming us to safety and at the same time reminding us that our travails weren't over. This was our celebration, quieter and more poignant than some backslapping huzzah. Franz and I unzipped our tent doors and shined our flashlights into the night. The beams reflected off the glassy eyes of a fox, moving its head quickly back and forth to observe both of us. Suddenly the eyes disappeared and our lights reached toward nothingness in the darkness. We said good-night again and I dozed into sleep, thinking, "We've done three crossings. Nine more to go."

THE storm intensified during the night. The next morning I wrote in my journal:

> There was a non-visual quality to the adventure yesterday. For most of the day the waves were small. We couldn't see anything in the fog. Even if we did everything that the *National Geographic* guys told us to do, we couldn't have photographed a current that was washing us out to sea or the nightfall that threatened to envelop us. The danger was real, but invisible and ephemeral.

Franz and I built a cheery driftwood fire, cooked a hot meal, forgot the past, and looked into the future. I'm generally guilty of excess optimism on an expedition: "Conditions are going to improve; things will get better; the wind will be at our backs." But this time I was feeling sobered and frightened. Ahead of us, the islands were smaller and the crossings were longer; we could expect the fog to be even thicker; and there was less shelter and more open ocean. The weather patterns and current systems were becoming increasingly complex.

About 30,000 years ago, more than 20,000 years before Kennewick Man's time, the Jomon ancestors lived in southeastern China, between Hong Kong and Korea. Some of these people migrated north and became the Jomon. Others moved south, eventually became the Polynesians, and colonized a fourth of the Earth's surface, often sailing long distances upwind to atolls that were mere specks in the vast South Pacific. At the dawn of the Industrial Revolution, when Europeans were conquering the world from their clumsy square-rigged ships, the Polynesian double-hulled canoes were the fastest, most seaworthy craft on the planet.

I once visited the American Museum of Natural History in New York and stopped in front of an impressive Haida dugout canoe. The Haida are Amerindian people who live along the west coast of British Columbia. The canoe in the museum is sixty-three feet long and was carved from a single red cedar log. By comparison, Christopher Columbus's flagship, the *Santa Maria*, was a hundred feet long, but his two accompanying caravels were shorter, about fifty feet each. In the display, a Haida chief stands alone on the stern. Several nobles stand five feet in front of him, and one of the nobles holds a carved stick. A museum guide explained that the chief's job was to navigate and to communicate with the powerful gods of wind and storm. It was *tapus* for any crew member to walk past the nobles toward the stern and the chief. The noble with the ornate "talking stick" mediated between the crew and the chief. The modern word "taboo" is derived from this Haida no-man's-land, or *tapus* zone, in their traveling canoes.

When the guide had gone on ahead, I lingered, remembering that the Polynesian navigators also isolated themselves on the back deck and also communicated through a "talking chief" with a "talking stick." The parallels could be coincidental—an example of convergent cultural evolution—but it seemed more likely that these rituals had a common root in common ancestors. This cultural commonality supported the hypothesis that early Jomon mariners carried their traditions into Polynesia and North America.

Browsing the museum bookstore, I had stumbled across the title *Across*

Before Columbus? Evidence for Transoceanic Contact with the Americas prior to 1492. The first chapter argued that Stone Age pottery found in Equador is remarkably similar to Jomon pottery. It is possible that these similarities, too, were unrelated, but four observations imply that Jomon potters sailed to the New World and brought their artistic styles with them: First, the pottery markings were complex. Second, the markings were artistic and not functional. Third, the Jomon artistic style evolved over 6,000 years of gradual elaboration, whereas the comparable South American pottery appeared suddenly. Finally, the dates of the pots are contemporary on both sides of the ocean.

Complex functional traits frequently appear in societies that are not in contact with one another, because invention evolves toward maximum efficiency. For example, if two disparate cultures invented the wheel, you could argue that clever people independently came up with the same idea. But there is no inherent engineering imperative for artistic styles. It is highly unlikely that South American potters suddenly and independently developed a pottery style identical to the Jomon style.

South American pottery dates from between 4,300 and 5,600 years ago—at least 3,700 years after Kennewick Man. Possibly these later Jomon sailed across the ocean in double-hulled catamaran canoes. Alternatively, they could have followed the coastal route south from what is now Oregon and Washington. The important point is that the Jomon crossed the Pacific at least once and possibly multiple times over thousands of years.

In the last thousand years, without exception, the most successful long-distance explorers came from wealthy, powerful, technologically advanced societies. Poor people who were trampled by their enemies or were starving from crop failures did not have the wherewithal to build ships and cross oceans.

Similarly, the Japanese Jomon were not down-and-outers. The oldest Jomon skeleton found to date is an 11,000-year-old male who died about the time that a band of migrants must have sailed toward North America. The twenty-year-old man was buried in a ritual fetal position, his torso facing upward and his knees angled to the right. One humerus was withered, indicating that the luckless individual was born with a deformity or had suffered a debilitating bone disease later in life. Yet he lived with this disability and was buried punctiliously, indicating that the Jomon cared for their disabled.

The prehistoric Jomon constructed the largest monument built by any hunter-gatherer culture in the world. At San'nai Maruyama, archaeologists have uncovered six foundation posts for a tower estimated to be sixty feet tall. This structure must have been a shrine, watchtower, sundial, or monument built by people who had the time and resources for community and spiritual pursuits.

The Jomon migrants might have been an oppressed group within a more opulent society. We'll never know. But we do know that any Stone Age migration across an ocean was carried out by competent mariners: men and women who loved the sea, built fine boats, and started out healthy and with enough food to survive the rigors of travel.

I had followed the Jomon migrants into the open sea, and now I felt that their restless ghosts shimmered in the fog and paddled alongside us, like the Navajo skin-walkers—phantom horsemen who rode across the desert and vanished in an eye-blink. Although Kennewick Man may not have been one of the original sailors, his visage stared back from the spirit canoe that we followed through calm and storm. He had a long, almost Roman nose, a thin face, and a slightly back-sloping forehead. Some reconstructions picture him with an enigmatic smile—self-assured and commanding. Others show a slight grimace of pain, probably from the wounds that he carried to the grave. But Kennewick Man wasn't alone in the canoe. Lest we forget, the Jomon migrated as a clan, with women at the paddling thwarts and children playing in the bilges amidships. Sometimes, in the dream state of a long paddling day, I saw my grandchildren in the canoe: Cleo practicing graceful dance steps; Jaimon already growing into a man and intently flexing his childhood bow; Julian, the actor, imitating the facial expressions of the adults; Dimitri, with his inimical smile, watching Jaimon play with his adult toys; and baby Aiden, silent, alert, and observant. All the people in the dream canoe were dressed in hides, covered with waterproof parkas of fish skin or whale stomachs. They smiled at me and I smiled back, and in our silence they urged Franz and me onward, into the unknown.

PEACEFUL days are usually a joy on a long expedition, but during the next week, tranquillity was our enemy. July 9 dawned foggy and utterly calm, so we sat on the beach. We had been sailing for twenty-six days and had averaged less than ten miles a day. Unless we increased our speed, we might run out of food and perish in these lonely islands. Even if we survived, it was frustrating to fail so utterly. I tried to raise my spirits by reasoning that we were making as much progress as possible and we might as well accept our fate and enjoy this wild land. But I wasn't Zen enough to live in the happiness of the moment. Franz and I discussed the situation and resolved to paddle.

It is a pleasure to paddle a craft that slices efficiently through the water, but the WindRider was an exercise in frustration. The seat was so low that I had to reach over the cockpit to take a stroke. This awkward reach reduced my power, so I tried sitting on the back deck, but the aluminum boom kept bashing me in the head. I lashed the boom to one side and paddled on the other until my arms were tired. When I switched sides, I scraped my knuckles against a sheet block. I lashed the boom farther out until a gentle wind backfilled the sail and pushed me south as fast as I was paddling north. Then I lowered the sail, but a slight tailwind rippled the sea, so I raised the sail, but the wind fell off almost immediately. In eight hours we progressed 6.7 miles; I can easily paddle 25 miles on a calm day in a sea kayak.

We landed, exhausted and frustrated, in a dense fog. The beach was composed of black volcanic sand, moistened enough by the fog to stick to everything. It crept over our shoes and lodged abrasively between our toes. Despite our utmost care, sand mixed with our food, sidled into the teeth of every zipper we owned, and marched steadfastly into our sleeping bags. But the sand was only the beginning. In the fog, we had inadvertently camped a hundred yards away from a dead whale stranded on the beach.

We sat in the cool dampness eating a starchy, gritty glop of overcooked rice mixed with Japanese noodles and a feeble pinch of packaged flavoring. The stench of the whale tickled the hairs in my nostrils, expanded past the sinus cavities, and settled on my tongue. I was trying hard to chew without clamping my jaws together and abrading my teeth on the sand. As I was half chewing and half swallowing the tasteless mush, Franz started a conversation.

"Fifty-five miles in five days."

I said something intelligent like, "Yeah."

We masticated our glop in silence, but I felt obligated to hold up my end of the conversation.

"That whale sure does stink."

"Yeah."

Then the conversation stalled, so we finished dinner and went to sleep early.

We woke to a dense fog and still no wind. Seagulls soared out of the mist, landing to peck out strips of putrid whale. We squatted on the sand, and Franz broke the silence.

"I guess I'd rather paddle than stay here."

I nodded. "OK."

So we paddled away from Dead Whale Beach, gained sea room, and headed north. I tried to ignore the petty frustrations and bend my back steadfastly into each stroke. So be it, I thought; we would struggle all day for another five to six miles. Then the morning fog set in, dense and damp, and my mind drifted.

Thirty years earlier I had been hiking near the Continental Divide west of Boulder, Colorado. Gray storm clouds spoke of a swirling blizzard over the high peaks. To the east, bright sunshine beat down on the Great Plains, and people were likely walking around town in short sleeves and Bermuda shorts. The sunshine seemed to be moving toward me from the east as the storm approached from the west. I climbed to the top of a knoll, put on a down jacket, and watched the battle between dark and light, storm and warmth. The two weather systems drew closer. Snow swirled over an adjacent ridge; sunshine danced yellow against the granite cliffs of Boulder Canyon. Then, with an unusual suddenness, I was enveloped in an impenetrable whiteness—fog. I felt that I had bought tickets to a show and the announcer came out and said that the actors were on strike but we could look at the closed curtain as long as we wanted.

Fog.

The Kingston Trio once sang, "Oh, out here they have a name for wind and rain and fire." These are elemental forces that stir deep emotion. But no word about fog.

Fog is the Joker with one eye white and one eye black and only the vaguest outline of chin and ears. The light meter of your camera reads f/11 at $^1/_{250}$ of a second—lots of light—but you can't see a thing.

On a clear night, you can navigate by stars or discern the dark silhouette of shore. But in the fog—even though there is so much light that you almost need your sunglasses—you see only wispy nothingness. Grayness to the right looks like land. Yes, I can see the outline of one mountain folding against another. But no, there is no land to the east; trust your map and compass and don't head toward the Joker's grin.

Night is orderly and predictable, calmly moving through its allotted cycle. But Joker drops in unannounced, pounces, retreats, and pounces again.

"I need a quarter-mile visibility. Joker, please, just an instant, so I can get a bearing. I want to see how far we've paddled."

"No! Ha ha! I thought you said that you could trust your instruments!"

Then, poof . . . green hills, dark rock, a cove. Haven't I seen that rock before? And what is that concentration of seagulls surrounding something large and inert? Joker, don't tell me!

We had been paddling for three hours, but despite our efforts a current had pushed us backward a few hundred yards. Franz didn't say a word but turned his boat toward shore. We both cranked hard on our paddles and slowly, painfully, gained the lost distance. The boats crunched quietly onto the black sand and we stepped out.

On the outside chance that I hadn't noticed, Franz remarked, "Dead Whale Beach."

I didn't have an intelligent or upbeat response, so we made camp in silence.

B Y THE afternoon of July 13, we were a mile from the northeast tip of Urup. We beached in a protected cove and scampered to a plateau covered by knee-high grasses and ground-hugging sedges. After a short walk, we were surprised to see several one-story duplexes and a few machinery sheds nestled beneath a large steel lighthouse. Most of the buildings had torn roofs and broken windows, but a few were in reasonable repair, and smoke rose from three chimneys. A dog barked, and I recalled that the major in Kurilsk had told me that there were no people in the central Kurils. No people, huh? The dog barked more urgently until a woman stepped outside.

Franz and I introduced ourselves, and she told me that her name was Svetia. Her husband, Volodia, came outside and we shook hands. I explained that we were Americans and had come from Japan by boat.

Volodia asked, "*By ship?*"

"*Nyet. Small boat.*"

"*Ah, a yacht!*"

"*Nyet, not a yacht, like a kayak.*"

They didn't understand the word "kayak," so I searched for and finally remembered the Russian word for a native skin boat, "*baidarka*."

"*Baidarka?*"

"*Da, baidarka.*"

We all stood awkwardly in the afternoon twilight, until Svetia suddenly became animated. "*Well, come in, have some tea. Did you say baidarka? From Japan?*"

Numerous travel writers have elaborated on the dreariness of Russian housing—the lack of paint, the flaking plaster, the paucity and poor quality of the furniture. But we had been cold and wet for weeks. When Svetia opened the door, I felt a blast of warm air mixed with the rich aroma of baking bread. A bare lightbulb hanging by a frayed wire cast a cheery glow over the room. Torn patches of wallpaper with faded roses reminded me of my mother's flower gardens when I was a boy. We took off our wet shoes and parkas and walked across the pine floor to stand by the coal fired *petchka* (stove).

Svetia, a heavyset woman, was wearing a plain print housedress; Volodia was tall, lean, and weather-beaten, his large hands stained with machine grease. I explained our journey in my limited Russian as Svetia boiled tea water. She had only three cups, so she served Volodia's tea in a drinking glass. Svetia told me that she and Volodia had been living there five years, and we were the first guests. When I nodded, she repeated her statement a few more times to be sure that I understood.

She pulled bread out of the oven. The loaf was nothing like the Russian rye you buy in an American supermarket and certainly nothing like health-food bread baked with sunflower seeds and walnuts. It was peasant bread from the steppes—hard on the outside, soft and full in the middle—wholesome without any frills. There was no jam or butter, and no sugar for the tea, but they weren't necessary.

Five people lived in this isolated island settlement—two couples and a single man. Volodia and his partner, Sasha, maintained the electric generator to run the lighthouse. Sasha stopped in to greet us, but his wife, Luda, was too timid to visit. Losha, the bachelor, was a trapper who had lived on the island for twelve years. Although the nearest village, Kurilsk, lay only 120 miles to the southwest, the lighthouse people never ventured that far in their battered open skiff. Once a year, a ship anchored offshore to unload food and fuel. And then it was back to isolation for another twelve months. Because there was no commerce in the area, the lighthouse wasn't a warning for commercial vessels, but still these people toiled to maintain the small orange glow, shining where no one saw it. Perhaps the light was an announcement to the world that this island was Russian soil, not an uninhabited wasteland.

We chatted while Svetia cooked four small meat patties and a pot of buckwheat garnished with cooking oil and local herbs. There were only two stools in the kitchen, so we moved the table into the living room. Franz and I sat on a tired old couch with lumps and exposed springs. I shifted my weight to find a reasonably comfortable depression, thinking that just about anything was more luxurious than another night in a WindRider. Svetia put two meat patties on my plate and two on Franz's. She heaped buckwheat on all four plates, heated a precious can of green peas, and spooned them over the buckwheat. I protested that there were four people and four patties, so we should each eat one, but Svetia refused. In many places that I've traveled, the poorest people, with barely enough to eat, are the most hospitable.

In one corner of the room, a shiny new Sony entertainment center stood out incongruously, like a technological altar, above the threadbare rug, peeling paint, inadequate furniture, and bare wires of this outpost home. The conversation lagged because my Russian was inadequate, so Volodia plugged a class B shoot-'em-up into the VCR. So often, blood and bare breasts form the first lobe of civilization reaching into the wilderness—a stupefying litany of sex and violence with such narcotic effects. I wished that I could speak better to draw my generous hosts away from the screen and into real conversation.

Losha walked in to watch the final scene, in which blond men and near-naked women prevailed over evil. Then I spread out our maps. The next island, Chirpoyev, was seventeen miles away. After our last crossing, Franz and I were worried about the tidal currents between islands.

I explained in Russian, "*Tomorrow, we go to Chirpoyev.*" I reminded Losha, in case he hadn't heard, "*Our boats are very small. Not ships, not yachts, but baidarkas.*"

"*Baidarkas?*"

"*Da, baidarkas. Very small. You understand?*"

"*Da.*"

Then I pointed to the channel that we intended to cross. "*Danger?*"

"*Nyet.*"

"*Big waves?*"

"*Nyet.*"

"*Strong currents?*"

"*Nyet.*"

"*Where are big waves, strong currents?*"

Losha pointed to a distant crossing in the northern Kurils.

Franz said, "We'll worry about that when we get there," and I rolled up the maps.

IN THE morning, Svetia cooked a huge plate of fried potatoes and dried our shoes by the stove. I didn't tell her that dry shoes were superfluous because we walked into the water every morning to push the boats clear of surf and rocks. When we had finished eating, she waved good-bye from the kitchen door and Volodia and Losha followed us to our boats. Snow-covered Chirpoyev, a nearly circular volcanic island about three miles in diameter, stood out sharply in the distance against a clear blue sky and a mellow sea. The wind blew from the southwest, promising a downwind run. Franz and I looked at each other and grinned. Even as a worst-case scenario, if the wind held for only two hours, we would sail far enough toward the island that we could paddle the rest of the way if necessary.

We prepared for sea and pushed our boats to the water's edge, but I hesitated. Dry shoes felt good; the ocean was cold and wet, and we were warm and dry. Then I braced myself, waved good-bye, thanked the men, and sloshed off into the ocean. With visibility and wind, we launched easily through the shoals and breakers and turned northeast. A series of tiny islands stretched eastward from the tip of Urup. Under normal conditions we would have scooted between the islands and headed directly for Chirpoyev. We were both river kayakers, used to paddling inches away from rocks. Any self-respecting kayaker should be able to run through a hundred-yard opening between islands.

But I swung wide, and Franz called out, "How come you're heading east?"

"There's something funny going on here."

"What?"

"I don't know. It's just weird."

The wind was blowing out of the southwest, but the swell was coming from the north. What was driving it? I spilled wind to let Franz catch up and explained that I felt uncomfortable sailing between rocks into a sea I didn't understand. I preferred to sail due east until we reached deep water. Franz listened and agreed.

The black basalt islands were capped by green grass and stained white with guano from the gulls that wheeled overhead. Waves broke against the north sides of the islands, and the fractured swell re-formed and expanded southward into the Pacific. A faint coolness wafted across my face. Almost instantly the blue sky became fuzzy, as if I were losing my eyesight. The fog wasn't blowing in from somewhere, like a cloud traveling across the sky. Instead, mist formed spontaneously as the air cooled around us. I looked up for a last visual bearing before the land disappeared from view.

Then we seemed to sail off the edge of the Earth into a sea like no other I had ever experienced. Without howling wind, rising storm, or warning, the placid ocean suddenly reared into fifteen-foot breaking waves. A wave steepened, curled, and trapped air as it collapsed. Then the trapped air escaped with a deep-throated *whoosh* as tons of water dropped out of the sky. The peaceful day had been torn apart. I felt as though I had been skiing across a sunny slope when suddenly I was engulfed by a massive avalanche. I was instantly terrified, and fear led directly to that familiar, detached hyperalertness. It was too eerie to be frightening and, once I registered what was happening, too frightening to be eerie.

To our right, a tidal current from the Pacific was flooding toward the Sea of Okhotsk. To our left, a tidal current from the Sea of Okhotsk was flooding toward the Pacific. A few miles to the southeast, the Pacific Ocean was six miles deep. A few miles to the northwest, the Sea of Okhotsk was only a few hundred feet deep. When these two unequal columns of water collided, they created a giant shear. The bulge from the Pacific stalled, but momentum piled up more behind it. The water had to go somewhere, so it rose straight up. I wondered why the waves weren't bigger. Why only fifteen feet? Why weren't they a mile high, two miles high? Fifteen feet, though, was quite enough.

A wave reared above me, and I let out the sheet and surfed down its face. I've surfed deepwater waves before, but this wave was steeper and faster than anything I had ever experienced. The foam formed behind me and cascaded closer. The boat accelerated, and I cranked the rudder hard to hit the trough obliquely. Despite my efforts, the bow dug in and stalled just as breaking foam slammed into my stern. The boat balanced on its nose, and

I lurched forward until I was standing on the rudder pedals. From this perspective, the gray ocean beneath looked dark and shiny; then it churned white. For a harrowing moment, I thought that the WindRider would cartwheel—but it flopped back down, right side up.

When the next wave reared, I knew it could kill me.

I sought refuge in a detached fatalism, the certain awareness that this moment was a consequence of my own free choices. The resignation felt deeply cathartic. The wave looked too steep to surf, so I pulled in the sheet to gain speed and turned sharply to meet the looming wall of water nose first. This time the boat reared until I felt as if I were sitting over the rudder. The boom jibed with a sharp snap as the wave crest curled into a white break that dropped down the smooth, oncoming face, hissing toward my boat. I had just enough momentum—or luck—to ride over the top, boom and sail flapping. Franz was fifty yards away, sliding off a wave face, looking brave and toylike in a colossal sea. When the next wave approached, I didn't know whether to surf away from it or charge into it. Instinctively I turned toward it, preferring to take what was coming head-on.

Franz appeared as the only splash of bright color against the damp mist, the gray-green sea, and curling white breakers. A wave reached above his mast, and his boat tilted on the dark face. The foam curled, fell, and seemed to engulf him. Franz was gone! I turned toward the place where I had last seen him, and sailed down a wave face and away from the break; then he appeared again, rising over a massive roller.

I'm not sure how long we were in the shear waves—probably about an hour. Eventually the current pushed us southward, off the continental shelf and into the deeper water of the Pacific. When we crossed this threshold, the huge waves suddenly disappeared and three-inch ripples slurped against the hull with a mellow cadence reminiscent of a Sunday outing on a backyard lake. The change was so dramatic that I feared it was a harbinger of some new danger. In my agitated state, anything new and inexplicable was innately terrifying. But after a few minutes, I realized we were safe. Franz sailed close and remarked grimly, "Don't ever trust a fur trapper for information about the sea."

I thought back to our conversation with Losha:

"*Danger?*"

"*Nyet.*"

"*Big waves? Strong currents?*"

"*Nyet. Nyet.*"

It didn't matter now.

LATER I read the following passage in Krasheninnikov:

> The channels are crossed in light boats, in less than half a day, but the passage
> is excessively difficult, because the tide runs very rapid in all of them; and
> when it happens to be a side wind, these small vessels are driven into the sea
> and lost . . . This passage requires not only fair weather, but likewise a slack
> tide. In the time of the flood, the waves are rapid and white, and so large
> that even in calm weather they rise two or three fathoms high. The Kuriles
> [Ainu] have a superstitious awe and veneration for these waves; and when
> they row over them, offer a sacrifice by throwing chips made on purpose,
> imploring a safe passage; the pilots also use conjurations the whole way.

That passage summarizes a whole library of sea stories. The Ainu sailors
had a "superstitious awe and veneration for these waves"—but they threw
a few wood chips in the water, chanted some "conjurations," and sailed
into the teeth of danger.

Were the Ainu nothing other than pragmatic traders, out making a living? Perhaps, but forging through those mountainous seas reinforced my
belief that some innate spirit of adventure had taken them far from Fuchi,
goddess of the hearth.

THE wind dropped off and we floated listlessly in dense
fog. Fear has many faces: acute terror, latent apprehension, even unreasonable
trepidation over a danger that doesn't exist. We faced no immediate danger at
the moment, just a vague, chimerical miasma. The boats rocked gently with
the sea's mellow cadence, but the lack of motion signified another danger.
Without wind, even a small current could carry us out to sea or, worse yet,
back into the shear waves. And if we bobbed out here long enough, eventually we would be engulfed in a storm. This vulnerability as a consequence of
tranquillity settled uneasily into my psyche. I tried to push my fear into distant corners of my brain, where it would become disoriented and lost, but it
peered out from within the maze, its elusive shadow intensely unsettling.

By the time the wind picked up in the early evening, we had drifted
southwest and were twenty-two miles from Chirpoyev, five miles farther
than when we had launched. I shrugged it off. We had wind now, the

barometer was steady, and there was no indication of bad weather. A night at sea would be uncomfortable but manageable, and we had done it before. In any case, I assumed we would reach landfall sometime the following day.

We lashed our boats together—pontoon to pontoon—so we wouldn't separate in the foggy night. The resultant craft—an awkward-looking penta-maran with two outside pontoons, two cockpit hulls, and one shared pontoon—was almost as wide as it was long. Though it didn't look elegant or maneuverable, one person could easily sail and steer the ensemble while the other slept.

I drew the first watch, and Franz dozed off. Dinner was a candy bar and a handful of peanuts, probably just short of 450 calories all told. It wasn't much, but it would see us through the night. After an hour I woke Franz, and he took the helm. Then, resting my chin against my life jacket, I tried to wiggle myself into a comfortable sitting position, and shivered until I warmed up enough to fall asleep.

We traded watches through the night, and with each shift I grew increasingly tired, hungry, cold, and scared. I reminisced about other ordeals to remind myself that pain is evanescent but the richness of an experience lasts forever. I remembered a time when I was climbing with my daughter Noey. When I tangled a rope on lead, we lost a precious hour and had to huddle together in the darkness on a tiny ledge through a long autumn night in the High Sierra. The discomfort of that night is long since gone, but the closeness of father cuddled against daughter remains.

By early morning, my dream images carried me from memories to semi-hallucinogenic imaginings. Kennewick Man was at the helm of my boat, and a chief with a "talking stick" stood between us. I nodded, and Kennewick Man returned the salutation with a slight grimace of pain, reminding me that I was in good hands as long as I accepted the minor discomforts of our passage. Jomon children were sleeping in the bilges, wrapped in fur blankets, looking like seals splayed out against the sturdy cedar hull. The Jomon voyagers drew strength from those tiny breathing forms at their feet, even as I could find refuge in thoughts of my family.

At dawn the fog was so thick that we couldn't see land, but my GPS showed that we were eight miles south of Chirpoyev, moving at three miles per hour. Franz woke and shook his arms vigorously to get the blood flowing. When he asked how we were doing, I told him that if speed multiplied by time really did equal distance in the Sea of Okhotsk, we would make landfall in time for a relaxing brunch. He muttered that speed times time *always* equals distance, and I didn't argue.

Just as I relinquished the tiller and started to doze, the placid sea bunched up into the now-familiar ripples formed by fast-moving currents. Franz took out his GPS and waited silently for the instrument to find three satellites on which to triangulate its calculations. Then he shouted, "Oh shit! Here we go again. Heading: 270°. Speed: 2.5 miles per hour."

We were sailing north, but a fast-moving current was carrying us west. After we had drifted for a few hours, the current veered toward the southwest. We were caught in a massive whirlpool formed by opposing tidal forces, and the swirling currents were carrying us back to the deadly shear waves.

I've kayaked in small river whirlpools where the water descends in a toilet-bowl-like turbulence complete with a swishing, sucking sound; but this swirl was ten to twenty miles wide, its very magnitude obscuring its danger. We were sailing north and heading west, then we were sailing north and heading southwest. That was all. Waves weren't breaking over the cockpit, and I couldn't reach out and touch the danger; I was left instead with a dull, helpless feeling in my gut that is paradoxically more muted and at the same time more intense than jittery, adrenaline-pumping terror.

Whatever the peril, we stayed calm. I reminded myself, "Live for the moment, Jon, because that's all you have. Watch the sea and record these images; they're what you're here for."

Real trouble was hours away, and we had time to make a plan. When the wind switched to the north, Franz suggested that we sail southeast on a broad reach in order to slide out of the whirlpool at an oblique angle. This course would take us farther into the Pacific Ocean, away from land, but it would also free us from the deadly shear waves. Once we reached deep water, we would spend a second night at sea, skip Chirpoyev altogether, and make landfall on the next island, Simushir. It was a good plan, and I agreed. We turned the tillers, trimmed the sails, and headed toward open water.

Franz took the helm and told me to catch some sleep in the relative warmth of midmorning. I ate another candy bar, then reached for my water bottle. The previous morning I had packed three quarts of fresh water, which had seemed more than adequate for a seventeen-mile crossing. But now I had only two quarts left and we were heading into the Pacific Ocean. How many days were we really going to remain at sea? I stashed the empty bottle, opened one of the full ones, and took a measured sip. I closed my eyes but couldn't sleep. There was no room for sloppy thinking. Were we making the right decision? Were there any clues in the sea or the sky that we were missing?

A long time ago, I read *The Voyaging Stars: Secrets of the Pacific Island Navigators*, by David Lewis. Lewis had sailed with traditional Polynesian navigators and documented how they navigated without compass or sextant. (Electronic navigational tools, such as GPS, didn't exist when Lewis wrote his book in 1978.) Polynesian nursery rhymes outlined star maps, and every youngster memorized sequences of guide stars from an early age. Celestial navigation was irrelevant in the Kurils, because it was generally too foggy to see the sun or stars, but the Polynesians also navigated by interpreting wave patterns. According to Lewis, a Polynesian navigator would place his scrotum on the sternpost to feel every complex vibration of the waves. A deep, underlying, low-frequency wave might be a residual swell from a distant trade wind, whereas overlying local winds formed higher-frequency surface waves. Navigators could detect islands that lay over the horizon by interpreting interference patterns in the waves.

My compass and GPS worked fine, and I didn't need to strip off my warm clothes and sail with my scrotum on the cockpit rim to determine my position or locate unseen islands. But my instruments and maps didn't locate currents or shear waves. I wanted to interpret every minute vicissitude of the sea and the sky, but I couldn't read a thing. Low-frequency waves seemed to rise vertically, and surface ripples emanated from all directions, driven by chaotic currents. Then the north wind dropped off entirely and we bobbed back into a purgatory of inactivity. With no power and therefore no speed, we were at the mercy of the slowly rotating whirlpool. We tried to guess where it would take us, but we could be no more precise than that. After sailing in the fog for thirty hours, I had lost all sense of direction, and without instruments I would have had absolutely no idea where we were or where we were heading.

I could imagine how, after a lifetime of training, a Polynesian navigator could sail 2,000 miles from Tahiti to Hawaii following memorized star charts and the feel of the sea. I had once kayaked off Cape Horn along the sea routes of the Yaghan, who had sailed that region until they were exterminated by white settlers in the nineteenth century. Before I had set out, it seemed unbelievable to me that the Yaghan had paddled bark canoes through the storm-tossed waters of Tierra del Fuego, but after several months I learned to read the water and the storm systems. After half a dozen expeditions in the high Arctic, it seemed reasonable to me that the Inuit could hunt from skin kayaks in ice-choked waters. I had started this journey to the Kurils with the attitude, "Heck, if families sailed the Pacific Rim with elders and infants ten thousand years ago in dugout canoes, then the passage shouldn't be all that difficult." But now I simply couldn't comprehend how anyone—ever—could sail seventeen miles from Urup to Chirpoyev without a compass and a GPS.

To appreciate the navigational challenge, imagine sitting in a shopping cart in the middle of a huge Wal-Mart parking lot—blindfolded. Someone twirls you around and drags you back and forth for a day or two, then asks you to stand up, still blindfolded, and walk directly to the store entrance. Good luck. Yet the Ainu traders routinely navigated from island to island and through the Pacific Ocean in the fog.

EVENTUALLY I began to understand how the seventeenth-century Ainu might have done it. When they were lost in the fog and caught in the swirling currents, they stopped paddling, lowered their sails, and waited. The currents would have drawn their boats into the Sea of Okhotsk or into the Pacific. But the swell patterns in the broad Pacific are notably different from those in the shallow inland sea. You don't need a genius navigator to discern the difference; even I can feel that. So the Ainu would have at least known which ocean they were in. When the fog lifted and they got a sun or star fix, they would have sailed in the general direction of land until they saw the comforting image of a snow-capped mountain rising out of the sea. Yes, I can see how they did it, but as Steve Thomas says in his book about the Polynesian navigators, this kind of blind sailing in a big ocean takes "fierceness, strength, and wisdom."

As we go further back in time, we have no written or oral records, so it's impossible to learn the secrets of Jomon navigation. Because they crossed an ocean, however, we can guess that they had some rudimentary knowledge of celestial navigation. They must have known they were headed northeast when the summer sun rose obliquely off their starboard bow, and I believe that they recognized the Pole Star. We can also reasonably assume that they read wave patterns to determine ocean depth and current direction.

The Jomon may have had an easier passage in this region because sea level was lower during the ice ages, and the Kurils weren't an island chain but a long, narrow finger of land enclosing an inland sea. Thus Stone Age mariners wouldn't have had to make open-water crossings or cope with shear waves and whirlpools. On the other hand, ice age weather was cold and turbulent, forming sea ice and formidable surf. Jomon dugouts were heavy and awkward relative to our plastic trimarans, and their passages into and out of the surf must have been arduous and dangerous. I wondered whether the Jomon navigators made long, multiday passages, landing only when they found sheltered bays. Or did they make landfall almost every night? Or did they sail through the inland sea, then portage back into the ocean? How many boats sank? How many crew died?

All during the long, windless afternoon we drifted slowly southwest, back toward Urup. We didn't talk much—there was nothing to say. If we had a little wind, at least we could discuss a strategy, but the only alternative now was to drift helplessly, plot our course nervously, and hope that we would miraculously avoid danger.

Then, for some inexplicable reason, the whirlpool swept us east of the shear waves. Once we were free, a small current spun us in the opposite direction and dropped us off—like two driftwood logs—at the same place we had been the day before. In thirty-six hours we had made one broad counterclockwise loop followed by a small clockwise ellipse back to our starting point. Now we were in calm water only six miles from our original camp. A gentle east wind picked up, aiming straight for Svetia's kitchen. Franz suggested that we return to land and regroup. I didn't want to retreat, but he was right.

The fog lifted as night fell, and the lighthouse blinked brightly in the dark. This was our second night at sea, and the cold, fatigue, apprehension, thirst, and hunger were beginning to deepen. We had eaten most of our available snack food, so dinner consisted of a shared Clif bar, 125 calories each.

A GPS is more accurate than your eyes. You may look at land and estimate that it is a quarter mile away, whereas the GPS will put your position precisely at 0.37 mile off. Nevertheless, vision is more comforting than digital numbers on an electronic display. The lighthouse announced in the darkness, "This is the end of the island . . . right here . . . at this spot . . . which you can clearly see. The light is operating because Volodia and Sasha revved up the generator and flipped the big switch. And to the left, Svetia is baking bread. Can you smell it?"

We swung wide of the lighthouse and approached our old camp a mile southwest from the tip of the island. Just as we were discussing how to work through the breakers in the dark, a current swept us eastward, back toward the tip of Urup and the shear waves. By this time, we were too exhausted to do anything but fight for our lives. As we paddled desperately and adjusted sail to catch every breath of wind, the blinking light got brighter. Then, sometime after midnight, we found a gentle breeze and made headway back west. By 3:00 A.M. we had broken free of the current and were a quarter mile from our camp. Reluctant to land through the surf and rocks in darkness, we dropped the sails and bobbed until first light. Then we recognized familiar landmarks and made our landing. After forty-eight hours at sea, we were safely back at our previous camp.

LACKING the energy to hike to the lighthouse or even to cook dinner, we pitched our tents and crawled into our sleeping bags. We woke at four that afternoon and gathered driftwood to cook a starchy mixture of rice, spaghetti, and Japanese noodles garnished with curry seasoning from Nemuro and a can of dogfood-like tinned meat from Kurilsk.

Over dinner, we reviewed our strategy. We could skirt around the shear waves next time, but the big problem was the combination of fickle winds and strong currents. Whenever the wind dropped, we were at the mercy of the currents, which could carry us in the wrong direction or, worse yet, push us helplessly into the roiling waves. To make a safe passage to Chirpoyev, we needed a steady wind. Looking back in our journals, we saw that we had enjoyed steady winds only two days out of the last fifteen, so the odds of a safe crossing were not good. But Chirpoyev wasn't safety; it was only a small island in the middle of the Kuril chain. We had eight more crossings after that, for a total of nine crossings before we reached mainland Asia. Franz calculated that the probability of making nine consecutive crossings in calm seas and favorable wind was roughly two in a billion. In other words, our odds of crossing uneventfully to Kamchatka were about the same as buying twenty lottery tickets and winning twenty consecutive lotteries. It wasn't going to happen. If we continued on, we were going to get hammered.

We sat for a long while, thinking. Then I remarked, "You know, Franz, hammered isn't the same as dead. We can stand up to bad conditions. The boats proved themselves in the shear waves. So, we'll go out and get beat up a little. Then we can regroup and keep on going."

Franz shook his head. "No. It doesn't always work like that, Jon, and you know it. I don't have to remind you about all your good friends who didn't return home from an expedition. But you've been lucky; you've never seen death up close."

Franz paused to collect himself, then told me the story of John Foss's death.

In 1998, Franz, John, and a third friend, Kurt, were making a descent by kayak of a river in the upper Amazon basin that had never been run before. They had navigated numerous dangerous rapids, and the next one waiting for them wasn't particularly easier or more difficult than the others. Kurt ran first and had a clean line. Franz ran second and also came through upright and smiling. John followed the route that the other two had taken. Then he slammed into a wave and disappeared. His body turned up downstream a week later.

John had done nothing wrong. Until the moment of his disappearance, his boating had been technically perfect. He hit the same wave that Kurt and Franz had run through. Most likely an errant current had pushed his bow down and trapped him beneath a submerged rock. The unsettling lesson is that when you are close to the edge, the smallest twitch of bad luck can kill you.

If we continued on toward Kamchatka, we could expect nine crossings and nine close encounters. We had been terrified in the shear waves, but nothing bad had happened. How close had we been to the edge? We asked the question, tried to answer it analytically, and couldn't reach a conclusion. You never know where the edge is until you step over it. And then it's too late to step back.

What if a storm had arisen just as we slid into the shear waves? What if we had bumbled into a rogue wave? What if we had run into shear waves while tied together in the middle of the night? What if . . . What if . . . What if?

If you insist on reducing your risk to zero, you'll never leave home. But if you don't leave slack for random chaos or bad luck, sooner or later you'll die.

I thought for a long time, then stood up. "Let's sleep on it and talk in the morning."

THE next morning we decided to quit.

There was only one problem. We were on an island in the middle of the Kuril chain and couldn't just buy an airplane ticket for home. The closest approximation of civilization was Svetia's kitchen, so we climbed up the bank and walked across the tundra to say hello.

Svetia and Volodia were surprised to see us. We explained what had happened and told them we were scared and wanted to retreat. Then we asked if they could make radio contact with the mainland. We had two requests: First, we had told our friends and relatives that we would reach Petropavlovsk by July 11. It was now July 17 and we were still six hundred miles from the city. Chris would understand that Franz and I might be stalled by bad weather, but to my eighty-two-year-old father, the sea was alien and foreign, and a schedule was a schedule. Even though I was fifty-four years old, I was still his little boy who had run off on some dangerous foolishness. He wanted to shelter me, and in turn I wanted to reach out and explain that we were scared but safe. We needed to call Martha in Petropavlovsk and ask her to relay a message home. Second, we wanted help reaching a commercial airport. Could Volodia ask whether there was a ship in the area? Volodia said that they had a scheduled radio contact the next day at ten.

The whole "town" gathered for the radio contact. Even Luda overcame her shyness and made an appearance. We walked to a large concrete building between the residential area and the lighthouse. The building consisted of two cavernous rooms—one for the generator and the other for the radio. Normally the generator operated only at night, but Volodia and Sasha fired up the beast for this occasion. The floor was slick with old crankcase oil, the walls and ceiling were black with diesel soot, and the shadowed corners were filled with ghosts of old machinery and parts. The motor itself was about the size of an engine that powers an eighteen-wheel tractor-trailer truck. There was no starter switch, but when Volodia connected a cable to a battery terminal, the connection sparked and the engine coughed to life. The crankshaft or the flywheel was out of balance, and the motor lurched back and forth on its tired mountings. The mounting bolts transferred the vibration to the building, making the floor jiggle and the windowpanes rattle.

Satisfied that everything was running properly, Volodia motioned me into the radio room. The radio was about thirty feet long, seven feet high, and four feet deep. Vacuum tubes glowed, current and voltage dials wavered, cooling fans whirred, and two large speakers cackled. By comparison, the long-distance radios on Bristol Bay fishing boats are about the size of a laptop computer and are powered by a car battery. I felt as though I were inside a giant time machine. As the building shook, my internal organs vibrated, and I imagined that I might suddenly whir beyond relativistic speed to land in the twenty-first century.

Volodia picked up the microphone. I caught the words, "*Sakhalin, Sakhalin . . . myak . . . Urup.*" Sakhalin was the closest mainland city to the south, and "*myak* ... *Urup*" meant that we were calling from the lighthouse on the island of Urup.

After the opening protocol, Volodia announced, "*There are two American tourists here.*"

"*American tourists? Where are they?*"

"*They are sitting right here.*"

"*And are they Americans? Are you sure?*"

"*Yes, I am sure.*"

I was amazed that I could understand this Russian conversation. Volodia carefully spelled out our names in Cyrillic script.

"*OK, we understand. How did they get there?*"

"*Baidarka.*"

Long silence. "*We asked, how did they get there?*"

"*Baidarka.*"

"*You mean yacht.*"

"*Nyet, baidarka. We have seen their boats; they are very small. Baidarkas.*"

"*Where did they come from?*"

"*Japan.*"

Another long silence.

"*Tell them to report to the pogranichniki* [frontier guard] *base on the north side of the island at fourteen hundred hours tomorrow. Fourteen hundred hours sharp.*"

Volodia looked at me and asked, "*Da?*"

I was puzzled. Was there was a *pogranichniki* base nearby? This was the first time anyone had told us there was a military base in the area. I asked, "Where?" and Volodia unrolled a chart and pointed to a small bay about ten miles away. I wanted to explain to him that there is no such thing as "fourteen hundred hours sharp" in our world of wind, storm, current, and sail. I wanted to say, "We'll do our best," but I didn't know the syntax. Then I searched my brain for the word "try." I wanted to say "we try"; or if I could remember only the infinitive, I would say "we to try." But I couldn't remember even that much, and the generator was throbbing, the room was shaking, the windowpanes were rattling, the whole town was looking at me, and a military man was waiting on the other end of the radio.

Volodia repeated, "*You'll be there at fourteen hundred hours sharp for a meeting with the commander of the pogranichniki station. Da?*"

And I said, "*Da.*"

Then Volodia asked the radio operator to contact our friends in Petropavlovsk.

After another long silence, he replied, *"Nyet."*

"Why?"

"Because it is impossible."

"Excuse me?"

"It is impossible. These Americans will talk to the pogranichniki commander tomorrow."

OUR immediate problem was to find a safe route around Urup to the north coast. If we sailed wide, we would encounter shear waves and currents, so our only reasonable alternative was to hug the shore. Franz and I hiked to the tip of the island. There was a channel, about fifty yards wide, between Urup and the first small island. A tidal current raced through the channel, but there were no whirlpools or waves. We watched for several hours and noted that the current stopped during the change in the tide. We calculated when the tide change would be the following day, and retired.

That evening I started a letter to my sponsors announcing our failure.

> Franz and I had a bold idea for a grand and daring sea adventure. We worked well together, took chances, and pushed ourselves hard. We didn't even come close to achieving our stated objective; in fact we only completed a little over 200 miles of a proposed 3,000 mile passage.

Then I felt too depressed to continue.

The following morning we paddled uneventfully through the straits and sailed a gentle breeze southwest toward the military base—southwest, away from Alaska. Sea lions barked from an offshore rock, but I couldn't feel the excitement of sharing the ocean with them. I kept repeating, "We're both alive, and that's what counts," but a different voice was whispering in the background, "You really blew it this time, Jon."

When we arrived at the base at 14:15, a young blond officer was standing alone on the beach, waiting for us. We shook hands and introduced ourselves. The lieutenant, Alexei, invited us inland to a carefully camouflaged complex of buildings. Fifteen men were stationed there to guard the island, though it wasn't clear why: Would the United States attack the soft underbelly of the Kurils as a jumping off point for Siberia and then on to Moscow, nine time zones away? Was Japan—which had no army to speak of—about to launch a preemptive strike to avenge their loss and embarrassment during World War II? And if either nation did attack Urup, could fifteen guys with Kalashnikovs and pistols stop them?

Alexei ushered us inside, and an aide brought bread, butter, salmon caviar, and tea. Alexei explained that he had direct orders to hold us on the beach under armed guard. We were absolutely forbidden to enter the base.

I helped myself to another piece of bread, slathered it with creamy butter, and heaped it with rich, salty caviar.

Alexei continued, *"But I have ignored my orders. You are cultured gentlemen, so I must invite you to share a meal with me."*

AFTER A snack, Franz, Alexei, and I took a Russian sauna, called a *banyo*. After undressing in a warm outer room, we stepped into the hot sauna with its crackling wood-fired stove, soot-blackened walls, flickering candlelight, and pungent smell of birch branches. We quickly broke a sweat in the intense heat, then soaked the branches with steamy hot water and beat our skin to increase circulation. When our bodies were tingly and red, we washed vigorously with dishpans of hot, soapy water. It was indescribably luxurious to be that warm and clean. After bathing, we ate dinner while listening to Jimi Hendrix. Then Alexi disappeared to call his commander on the radio. When he returned, his face was grim.

"A ship is coming tomorrow. But you are not welcome on it. You are not allowed to return to Kurilsk. Your papers say that you intend to travel to Petropavlovsk. That is the best thing for you to do. The commander ordered you to leave immediately."

He paused, *"You are brave men. You are romantics. I cannot treat you so poorly. You may spend the night here, but you must leave by six in the morning—sharp!"*

Then he put a Grateful Dead tape into the boom box and showed us pictures of his family back home. His mother was German and had been deported to Siberia by Stalin. There was a story there, perhaps a whole book, but I wasn't interested. I repeated his words to myself: "Your papers say that you intend to travel to Petropavlovsk. That is the best thing for you to do." No, he hadn't meant that. They didn't want to kill us, did they? Did they understand what we were up against? Maybe my comprehension of Russian was so bad that I had misinterpreted what he had said. Well, he had been very definite that we couldn't go on the ship. I was sure of that.

But of course we could sail back to Kurilsk. The major wouldn't shoot us. Maybe he would deport us, which is what we wanted anyway.

When we finally retired to our rooms, Franz and I sat on the edge of our beds. If we sailed back, the return journey would be a long, slow, discouraging struggle against the prevailing winds. We would have to reverse the dangerous crossing between Urup and Iturup, and we had no idea what would happen to us once we reached Kurilsk. And every mile of this journey would be another mile closer to defeat. I tried to rationalize that defeat is merely a relative term weighed against the expectations I had placed on myself. But I felt lousy.

Then, more as a way to rail against the gods than to formulate a plan, I blurted out, "Franz, let's head to Petropavlovsk. We can pull it off."

Franz looked at me carefully, then slowly reached into his dry bag and pulled out his maps. I held my breath as he spoke. "Well, I've been thinking about that too. We can survive nights at sea—no problem. It's the currents and shear waves that could kill us. So if we can devise a strategy to avoid the chaotic water, I agree with you; we should go for it."

I moved onto the edge of Franz's bed so we could look at the maps together. Our past words hung in the air: "If we head out into the central Kurils, there are two chances in a billion that we will have clear sailing. We're going to get hammered." But as we had also said before, "Hammered isn't the same as dead." With sudden bravado, we formulated a new strategy that seemed safer than the old one.

Tidal currents are weak in the open sea but intensify when they funnel through narrow channels between islands. Therefore, we could avoid the main turbulence by sailing into deep water. We drew a line from Urup to Chirpoyev and another from Chirpoyev to the next island, Simushir. In our past misadventure, we had found calm water when we were five miles from that imaginary line. We decided to double that distance and sail ten miles out to sea. The next decision was easy: we would go north into the Sea of Okhotsk, because the swells would be smaller there than in the Pacific. But then came the hard part—how would we get back to land? We would die of hypothermia if we tried to sail for a few weeks, like a yacht, and go all the way to Kamchatka.

When a current flows past an obstacle, like a rock or an island, it creates a calm water eddy on the lee side. Small objects generate small eddies; large obstacles generate large ones. We had failed to break into the eddy around Chirpoyev, but an island as big as Simushir would generate an eddy that extended far from land, where the currents were weaker. Therefore we planned to remain in the Sea of Okhotsk until we reached the current shadow of Simushir. Then we would hope for a safe landing.

Thus, in this revised strategy, we planned to skip the small islands altogether and head from one large island to the next. We would spend many nights at sea. Our first crossing, to Simushir Island, was eighty miles. It would be cold and uncomfortable, but we would avoid currents and shear waves. The possible flaw was that our new strategy disregarded a vital safety asset of a small boat: you can pull it on the beach and drink hot tea from your tent during a storm. But we weren't going to follow the coast or make short crossings between closely spaced islands; we planned to go to sea like a yacht. How would we fare in a gale?

I brushed the image aside and thought back to previous expeditions. On any classic adventure, there is a moment when you look at the mountain, the river, or the ocean and think, "It's too steep, turbulent, or unpredictable; I can't do it." But then you see a series of connecting cracks in the cliff or a line of green water through the rapids. As you continue to stare, the route becomes a clear and elegant path through danger. The joy and essence of an expedition is in finding and following such paths.

Sitting on the edge of our beds in a tiny military base on Urup, we couldn't see a route. But we had a simple plan to sail around the most dangerous water. This strategy entailed its own unique danger, but expeditions involve risk. The decision to go on isn't necessarily rational, and success is never guaranteed. After weighing all the factors, we agreed to head out in the morning, northward toward Simushir, then on toward Petropavlovsk. I felt the excitement and fear of action: tingly and alert, happy and terrified. Before going to bed, I silently resolved that I would return the following year to complete the journey to Alaska.

WE ATE an early breakfast with Alexei and pulled out our maps. I explained that we needed to know the exact position of all the villages, military bases, and outpost camps where we might find food or emergency help. Alexei shook his head and told me that this information was classified. I replied that, for us, it was a matter of life and death. He looked at us hard and glanced furtively over his shoulder as if someone might be watching. Then he nodded slowly, took out a pen, and marked five Xs on the map, indicating four military bases, with fifteen soldiers in each, and one meteorological station with five scientists. Some of these settlements were located on small islands that we couldn't visit, but others might supply essential succor. Finally he explained that Severo Kurilsk, 350 miles away, was a large fishing village with a few thousand people, grocery stores, and telephones.

We walked to the beach and loaded the boats. As I lashed my gear to the trapezes, I thought about the few abandoned Russian homesteads we had passed on Iturup and Urup. If Alexei was right, all the civilians had retreated to the mainland, and everyone who remained in the central Kurils was a soldier or a government employee. On these islands, the soil is poor, storms are frequent, fog is incessant, winters are long and bitterly cold, and infrastructure and transportation networks are nonexistent. Yet Krasheninnikov had estimated that several hundred Ainu lived in the central Kurils in 1740 at first contact with the Russians. Thus this is one of the few places in the world where the modern civilian population is smaller than the aboriginal population. The Ainu who had settled here must have been one tough bunch, and the Jomon who had voyaged through must have been even tougher.

When Franz and I were ready for sea, a deep engine throb drifted out of the fog. A whistle blew, disrupting the misty peace of a Kuril Island morning with a mechanical urgency. Alexei paced nervously. *"Quickly, quickly, it is the ship! You must go before they see you!"*

I didn't want to feel rushed, and what could they do to us now anyway? It was more important to stow everything properly and lash the bags securely in preparation for a long crossing. We could hear the ship's anchor chain rattle through its windlass, but Alexei calmed down as we finished packing. I was reminded of the Secret Sharer in Conrad's novel. I was the outlaw and Alexei was the officer—bonded in a private conspiracy that we should base our actions on common humanity, not on governments and rules. We shook hands warmly, and he gave me a military decoration as a memento.

"Thank you for the food, the friendship, and the banyo."

"Good luck. Godspeed."

The fog softened and the ship loomed gray and ominous out of the mist as we raised sail. A sailor waved and we waved back; then the fog closed in and we headed out to sea.

We chugged along at two miles per hour in a light wind, accompanied by the rhythmic gurgle of water rolling under the stern. Once again, our tangible universe consisted of a fifty-yard circle of visibility that moved with us. Somewhere beyond it was land, cobbled beaches, green grass, and safety.

After the mental turmoil of the past few days, I finally relaxed enough to feel the rhythm of the boat, the breath of damp wind, and the easy roll of an inland sea. The day was blissfully uneventful. In the evening, we lashed the boats together and settled into the uncomfortable but now familiar overnight routine. When darkness fell, I marveled at the all-encompassing blackness. North, south, up, down, east, west—it all seemed the same. I could be flying to the moon or sailing to Hawaii, or a current could be driving me backward. I switched on my GPS and stared at the tiny numbers—our focal point in the cosmos. We were headed in the right direction with no current drift.

I fought off drowsiness by reviewing our situation. Franz and I were both logical men and trained scientists. We had calculated our chances coldly and mathematically; then we had pushed the calculations aside in favor of bravado, and something else—stupidity? I didn't like the sound of that. Alexei had called us romantics.

Romance:

A narrative depicting heroic or marvelous achievements or even supernatural experiences, chivalrous devotion. . . .

Romantic:

Fanciful, unpractical, unrealistic. . . . Ardent, passionate, fervent. . . . That which emphasizes imagination, emotion and introspection, and often celebrates nature and freedom of the spirit.

Perhaps.

I REMEMBERED a time years before when I had been kayaking alone north of Cape Horn. A fast-moving storm drove me into the surf and broke my boat apart on the edge of the Antarctic Ocean. I walked for four days across windswept tundra back to a Chilean military base I had visited earlier. Heraldo, the radio officer, invited me in and shook his head. "You're too loco; you're a loco man."

Five years later, a friend and I were running dog teams along the east coast of Baffin Island, in the Canadian Arctic. The cold was so intense that the moisture in my eyes froze to form tiny icicles between my upper and lower lashes. On top of a pass, wind had blown the snow off the ground, and our dogs cut their feet on the sharp rocks. Blood glistened in the tracks as we descended to the sea ice. In the evening, we stopped at a small shack with several snow machines parked in front. When we opened the door, a wall of warmth burned the frostbite on my face. Four men in skin clothing were crouched around the carcass of a dead seal, eating slices of warm, raw liver. One of the younger men beckoned us toward the feast and said, "*You white men carry knives?*" We nodded, sat on the floor, and cut slices of liver for ourselves.

The young man pointed his knife at us as he addressed his friends, saying, "*They're white men, but they travel like hunters.*"

Romantic, loco, hunter: three different epithets for consistent behavior, reflecting the observers' biases. Alexei had joined the *pogranichniki* because he felt a romantic urge to see the frontier wilderness of the Kurils. Therefore he assumed that Franz and I were also on a romantic quest. Heraldo had joined the navy because it was a good job, and he had chosen to be a radio operator as a low-risk option. To him, adventuring was plain loco. The Inuit, on the other hand, were pragmatists, hunting to survive and traveling across the land to hunt. There was nothing romantic or loco about dogsledding over a pass in the dead of winter. It was just the way of things.

Romantic, loco, and pragmatist form a triumvirate. Maybe each of us is a unique amalgamation of these character traits, just as Greek philosophers believed that every object was composed of fire, earth, air, and water in various measures. One person might be born with a heavy dose of pragmatism, and another be innately romantic.

I had started this expedition with a guess that the Jomon journey, like ours, was based at least in part on a romantic sense of adventure. Franz and I hadn't learned anything concrete, but we had experienced the sea in all its moods, and now I was convinced that a pragmatist would head directly for the mainland, build a village, and settle down. The Stone Age Jomon needed a heavy dose of romanticism, mixed with a dollop of loco, to continue onward.

In the dream-space of a long night watch, I drew a possible parallel between our recent misadventures and the Jomon voyage. Perhaps the Jomon had initially fled warfare or an intertribal squabble, and now, in a like manner, Franz and I had been forced to sail northward by a warring party— the Russian bureaucracy. But we weren't going to stop at the first safe opportunity—and neither did the Jomon. Whatever propelled the Jomon, Franz, and me out to sea in the first place, once the spirit of the journey took hold, we were compelled to travel far beyond the bounds of necessity, or reason.

I FLICKED ON my headlamp to get a compass bearing, then turned it off and steered by the feel of the wind against my cheek. Franz had folded his arms across his chest, tucked his chin against his life jacket, and fallen asleep. The barometer was steady, a few stars twinkled through the night fog, and the waves passed gently beneath the boat. Everything was peaceful, but I was separated from the ocean by only three-eights of an inch of plastic, and the top of the deck lay only a foot off the water. Franz and I both knew that eventually we were going to get hammered.

FAVORABLE weather and moderate breezes held through the night and into the following day. By midafternoon we were close to the southwest tip of Simushir, and the currents were minimal, as we'd predicted. As we approached the island the fog lifted, revealing black basalt cliffs that reverberated with an echoed squawking that seemed to flow along the air currents like wisps of fog. The basalt was smeared with splotches of white, which at first appeared to be guano. But then I realized I was looking at the bellies of thousands of murres standing on ledges like tin soldiers, covering every nook and cranny in the rock wall. The smell of kelp near shore mixed with a base note consisting of an almost sweet-smelling musk. Dark clouds of the northern seabirds wheeled overhead, and more were swimming in the water all around us, fishing for silvery sardines.

Murres are black and white like miniature penguins; comical little birds. As I sailed close to one, it looked at me nervously and decided to flee. It could easily have dived and surfaced far away, out of danger, but instead its brain seemed to register, "Yikes, I'm a bird; I'm programmed to fly." And why not? Danger, for a murre, is far more likely to come from below than above. The bird swam away frantically, with an equally frantic flapping of its wings. After considerable effort, it lifted out of the water and got itself airborne, but just barely. Over the course of evolution, murres had traded the better part of their flying ability for aquatic skills; as a result, they couldn't seem to rise more than a few inches above the water. With its wings beating furiously, this bird seemed to run across the water like a cartoon roadrunner cleared for takeoff; then it belly flopped off the surface of a swell and ricocheted back upward. At last it gained elevation and airspeed, soaring around the boat while using its orange feet as ailerons and rudders. Some of the other birds, however, apparently realizing that this whole charade was a ridiculous waste of time and energy, folded their wings, dropped out of the sky, and disappeared under the water.

The basalt on Simushir is fractured at right angles, forming vertical cracks offset by small horizontal ledges. There was at least one murre on each ledge, keeping watch or warming its eggs peacefully. When an airborne murre decided to land, it would wheel close to the cliff, fold its wings, and fall onto the ledge, landing upright on its feet. Often the landing bird collided with another one on the ledge, and they would both shuffle about, seeming to look at each other with embarrassment and annoyance.

Waves broke against the cliffs, and a killer whale swam close, its high dorsal fin scalloping gently on the smoothly rolling sea. The black and white markings of the whale mimicked those of the murres, reminding me that similar protective coloration often evolves in disparate species that live in the same environment. I thought of the bird and the whale, swimming side by side, like two strange companions in a fairy tale.

The wind picked up and my keel got tangled in the thickening kelp. The boom jibed with a thud, and the impact bent the aluminum collar at its foot. I scrambled forward to jury-rig the damaged collar, feeling the excitement of overcoming hard times and the anticipation of danger ahead as we continued onward, toward Petropavlovsk and, eventually, Alaska.

Early that afternoon we reached a small bay. A *pogranichniki* base was perched on a nearby hill, but there were no signs of life. Franz and I pulled the boats above the high tide line and changed into dry clothes. After half an hour, doors burst open and two columns of soldiers in full battle dress poured out of the buildings. Each column consisted of five men with automatic assault rifles led by an officer with a drawn pistol and accompanied by a police dog. One column raced around a low hill, then doubled back, while the other headed straight toward us. When the men were twenty yards away, they spread out, surrounded us, and tightened the circle. Franz and I faced the commanding officer, who was in his mid-twenties.

I thought, "What do these youngsters and pimply teenagers think they're doing? Didn't someone radio ahead and tell them we were coming? Isn't the *pogranichniki* aware of us by now?"

I peered directly into the muzzle of a pistol, thinking of the bullet staring back out at me. Then I lifted my gaze toward the officer. The young man averted his eyes and shuffled his feet as if embarrassed and confused rather than angry. I scanned the circle of men and animals that surrounded us. The dogs seemed to think that this was great fun, and they wagged their tails as they stood obediently "on guard." None of the soldiers seemed particularly hostile. On the other hand, it's never wise to ignore a dozen men with loaded guns. I faced the commanding officer and reached out my hand.

"*Zdrastvoote.*"

He couldn't simultaneously hold his pistol and shake my hand, so he hesitated a moment, holstered the firearm, and reached out to return the handshake.

"*Zdrastvoote.*"

So far, so good. I walked around the circle to shake everyone's hand. Each man, in turn, took his finger off the trigger to greet me. After that, the soldiers seemed even more uncertain how to proceed. I stretched my arm toward the ocean and said, "*We have come from Japan. We are headed to Alaska.*"

The officer walked over to examine the boats.

"*They are so small! You have come far! Have you had many storms?*"

Then he remembered his official function and asked for our passports and permissions. After reviewing the papers, he told us that we were bad tourists for stopping at this military base.

I had no response. After an awkward moment, he asked, "*Are you hungry?*"

That evening, we all gathered around a large campfire, eating fresh bread covered with sugary condensed milk. Someone brought down a guitar and a bottle of vodka.

THE next day we sailed along the coast, camping that evening near the northeast extremity of Simushir. A chain of smaller islands stretched toward Kamchatka, and our chart showed squiggles and arrows indicating shear waves and currents. Funny, there hadn't been any squiggles on the fateful passage to Chirpoyev. Following our strategy, we plotted a long, arcing loop to the next large island, Shiashkotan, 175 miles away. The 80-mile crossing to Simushir had taken two days, so, on this passage, we expected to be at sea three nights and four days. Prior to this expedition, my longest crossing had been 25 miles; we were attempting a passage seven times as long as anything I had completed before. Neither Franz nor I knew how our bodies, our boats, or our luck would hold up. As I lay in my sleeping bag that night, tossing, I reminded myself that at times like this, when the mental commitment is firm and the danger obvious, it's important not to let the bogeyman of fear out of the closet.

Yet the wily devil reared his ugly head, mocking me: "You sure, hammered isn't the same as dead?"

In my half sleep, I responded, "Drop it."

But fear wasn't going to back down that easily. "Hammered can be awful close to dead."

I tried to turn the phrase into a song with a cheerful melody and a nursery rhyme beat so it would lose its dark foreboding. Something like:

> Jack and Jill went up the hill
> To fetch a pail of water
> Jack fell down and broke his crown . . .

But the bogeyman was tenacious.

Eventually, as I drifted off to sleep, optimism and certitude won out, but just barely. Even though I could still hear fear's muffled warnings, the sound of pounding surf filled me with a trusting fatalism that is the friend and enemy of all sailors.

The next morning we bundled ourselves in several layers of Polartec underwear, pants, and jackets, then slipped into our Gore-Tex dry suits. These clothes would be our sleeping bags and tents—a thin shell to keep water out and body heat in. Because we couldn't cook in the boats, we boiled some rice, added cooking oil for needed fat, and stored it in plastic bags. In addition we rationed a small stash of energy bars and some of our precious nuts. I estimated that we were packing about 1,500 calories for each day of the passage, a sustenance diet for a couch potato existence in front of the TV. In retrospect, I'm not sure why we didn't take more cooked rice. Perhaps the cold glop was so tasteless that hunger was an acceptable alternative.

We launched in a reddish sky and sailed all day on a perfect southwest wind. But late in the afternoon my altimeter jumped to 400 feet above sea level, signifying that a deep low-pressure system was moving in. Half an hour later the altimeter dove back down to 50 feet above sea level before reversing again and rocketing back up to 500 feet. My altimeter had never behaved so erratically. I hypothesized that a drop of water could have evaporated over the sensor, leaving behind a crystal of salt to induce spurious readings. But when the wind shifted to the northeast, where all storms in this part of the world seemed to originate, I began to believe the altimeter. I relayed my concerns to Franz, but he didn't say much. Instead he turned on the GPS and announced that we were making good progress and had already traveled twenty-eight miles.

We tied the boats together in preparation for the night, and I remarked, "Well, if speed times time equals distance in the Sea of Osh Kosh, by Gosh we'll be there soon enough!"

Franz was feeling edgy, and it was a lousy joke anyway. He reminded me again that speed times time *always* equals distance, and we were in the Sea of Okhotsk, not the Sea of Osh Kosh.

At dinnertime, we ate our cold, tasteless rice in silence.

The storm was building, and we reefed our sails. We had tacked into a steep sea before, and I told myself to ignore the fact that we were far from land. Being thirty miles from an island is no more dangerous than one mile; both are too far to swim. But the wind intensified until the waves broke against the side of my hood with a thud, and I was nervous.

As twilight edged into darkness, our old friends the algae cast their greenish sparkles across the sea. On a calm night, their colored glow outlines the edges of a bow wake like a friendly smile, but as the sea became chaotic, the luminescence only highlighted the breakers that charged out of the darkness. When the edges of a break hissed into the air, the algae sparkled not like a smile but an attacking horde. The breakers were hitting us from the starboard side, but at the same time our bows were plunging into the sea with enough force to throw additional water directly into our faces. I was half blind because I didn't have time to clear my eyes of the salt from one wave before the next one doused me again. When I tried to clear my eyes and senses, all I saw was aerated foam leaping out of an inscrutable blackness. Without vision or a horizon, we rocked vertiginously in the night, unsure of our balance or position.

We took in another reef, leaving a minimum amount of sail to maintain headway. Suddenly I felt a vibration from behind my seat, and the entire hull resonated. I thought, "Oh, shit, the main shaft bearing cracked." But that was, in a word, ridiculous—I wasn't on a commercial fishing boat in Bristol Bay, and the WindRider had no motor, propeller, or shaft bearing. Maybe the mast step had jarred loose, but no, the vibration was distinctly coming from behind my seat. It had to be the Achilles' heel of all trimarans, a pontoon attachment.

The trimaran had two pontoons, each attached by two crossbars, one forward and one aft. The four crossbars slid into the hull and were locked into place by stout stainless steel pins. I popped my sprayskirt, flicked on my headlamp, turned around, and checked the pins on the two aft bars. Both were fine. But when I grasped the port crossbar, I felt it vibrating madly. The port side was lashed to Franz's boat; the starboard was exposed to the storm. A wave broke into the cockpit, and I sat back down to secure the sprayskirt, pump the bilge, and think. The vibration changed tempo until it was syncopated by a distinct clicking.

I called over to Franz, "Hey! We've got a problem here. My pontoon attachment is loose. Maybe we're imposing too much strain by tying the boats together side by side. Maybe we should disconnect and tie bow to stern."

Franz wasn't excited about a complex and potentially dangerous maneuver, balancing on the slippery pontoons, to untie and retie the lashings in the middle of a stormy night.

"Don't worry about it. The boats are designed for this."

The wind was whistling in the rigging, and the waves were bashing into my body with disconcerting regularity.

"No, Franz, the boats are not designed for this. Not at all. We've tied them together, pontoon to pontoon, and we're in the middle of a gale. When one boat drops off a wave, its entire weight pulls on the pontoons."

Franz, one of my best friends in the world and my choice for an expedition partner, didn't answer, and I became agitated and urgent. "No one imagined that we would tie the boats together and sail into the middle of a stormy ocean. THE BOATS ARE NOT DESIGNED FOR THIS!"

"Look at the pontoons, Jon. They're held on with three-eighths-inch stainless steel pins. Those pins are strong enough to lift a truck. Check the lashings on your gear bags. Maybe they've wiggled loose."

I didn't answer but thought to myself. "It's OK, huh? Because he says so?" Then I felt it in my back, near the kidneys, where my diaphragm separates my lungs from my abdominal cavity. A sharp click, then a vibration. Yes, a vibration that wasn't in this boat before.

"FRANZ, LISTEN TO ME! I've lived in this boat for forty days! Something is wrong, big-time! I am sure of it! We've got to untie right now!"

Then a sharp crack rose above the storm, and my boat careened. The aft pontoon crossbar on the port side had disconnected from the hull. It was dragging, kicking up a plume of illuminated water, and transferring tremendous pressure to the forward crossbar. My fragile trimaran was breaking apart.

I envisioned that the added pressure would break the forward crossbar and my boat would capsize, spilling me into the ocean. Franz would sail away into the darkness, struggling with a crippled raft of one boat and one errant pontoon. There is no way he could turn in time to find me, and I would be left swimming helplessly in the Sea of Osh Kosh.

I jumped out of my boat and leaped across the two pontoons, grabbing Franz the way a rodeo rider grabs the horseman to pull himself free of the 1,500-pound bull that is threatening to throw, trample, and gore him. I held on tight, feeling his strength and thinking, "Franz, my friend, my buddy, I didn't mean to shout at you."

But I didn't need to say it.

Safety is relative, and as soon as my mind cleared I realized that all kinds of terrible calamities could occur in the next few seconds: a large breaking wave could fill my boat with water, my forward crossbar could break, or one of Franz's crossbars could detach. And then we would capsize and die. I crawled back onto the exposed trapezes and untied my duffel, thus salvaging my sleeping bag and tent and at the same time taking weight off the crippled boat.

I pulled out my knife, yelling, "Let's cut her loose! We can both limp back in one boat."

"No!"

"No?"

"I can fix it!"

Then, without explanation, Franz jumped over to my boat and dropped down on the back deck, lying on his stomach with his legs splayed out for balance. Steering from Franz's boat, I eased us off the wind to give the boats a more relaxed point of sail.

Franz shouted above the wind, "It's detached but not broken!" A huge wave rolled over both of us and washed Franz's headlamp off his head. The orange electric glow floated in the blackness, then disappeared. I thought, "If one crossbar detached, what's holding the others? We're going to expire like that light." But I'd experienced enough close calls in my life to know that you must ignore death when it grins at you. I screamed silently to myself, "You didn't mean that! Remember your mantra. Don't think about consequences. Just act!"

I shined my flashlight onto the other boat. Franz was struggling to slip the detached crossbar back into the hull while we careened and crashed over steep, breaking waves. One wave almost washed him off the deck. He momentarily lined up the crossbar with the slot in the hull, but the boat jerked and he lost the angle. He tried over and over, but the task seemed impossible. I wanted to do something, anything, but my job was to hold the flashlight and steer a steady course. If I hit a wave awkwardly, Franz would be washed into the sea.

Franz was acting heroically, but heroism is effective only if one's actions obey the laws of physics. Unless the boats lined up perfectly, Franz simply wasn't strong enough to lift 250 pounds of boat, plus gear, plus our body weight, plus all the excess water in the bilges to muscle the crossbar into the hull. Would the boats hit a lucky combination of swell and wind to line up on their own? Or would the boats hit an unlucky combination and break apart?

Waves reared out of the night, spume flew into the air, and the wind-driven foam hit hard. I felt that we were on the water, in the water, and under the water all at the same time. Irrationally, I told myself that Franz would succeed and our situation was not as precarious as it appeared. The boats careened as though we were about to capsize. And then the crossbar slipped perfectly into the hull. In an instant the motion of our strange penta-maran seemed normal, almost relaxed. It felt as though the storm had suddenly abated. But the wind kept howling and we weren't done yet.

Franz was holding the boats together with muscle and willpower. He shouted, "Get some rope and tie off one end!"

I unleashed the emergency throw line, secured one end, and passed the other to Franz. Then, steering awkwardly with my feet on the tiller, I reached across the trapeze to help lash our ungainly two-trimaran raft back together. When the lashing was secure, I crawled back to my boat and pumped the water out of the bilge. Then there was nothing more to do, so I sat back down in my cockpit. My mind was spent. I rested my chin against my life jacket, only vaguely conscious of the breaking waves, and dozed off blissfully for a fifteen-minute nap.

WHEN I opened my eyes, the blackness was less absolute. I flicked on my headlamp and looked at my watch: 3:45. I ate a small handful of nuts, took a sip of water, and adjusted our course. Fog obscured the sunrise, but the night slid into grayness, becoming brighter. The wind no longer lifted the spume into the air, the waves were breaking with less violence, and the lashings were holding. We had survived the night.

Franz and I untied the boats to ease pressure on the damaged crossbar, and we sailed separately. The wind diminished even further, so we raised more sail. As the waves gradually waned over the next few hours, occasional breakers washed over our heads, but they were infrequent rogues—the memory of the storm, not the storm itself. We made good progress, until the wind fell off completely and we drifted aimlessly in a dead calm.

With evening, the wind remained calm and we were exhausted, so we lashed the boats side by side again. For security, we backed up the normal lashings with longer ropes that stretched from hull to hull. The result looked more like a rat's nest than a final exam in a knot-tying course, but we wanted to avoid another midnight catastrophe. It was difficult to stay awake for one-hour watches, so we reduced the watches to half an hour. No matter how tired you are, you can stay awake for half an hour.

Even a good dry suit isn't completely waterproof in a raging gale, and we were wet and cold by the second night. I daydreamed about the relative comfort of a damp sleeping bag in a soggy, smelly tent. But the body adapts to hardship, and I wasn't acutely hypothermic. Relieved, I saw a few stars poking out of the fog.

On a yacht or a fishing boat, there are two environments: the cold, wet outside cockpit and the warm, dry living space down below. After three and a half hours on deck, the person on watch opens the hatchway and calls, "Your turn in half an hour." The next watch wakes up, yawns out of a comfortable sleeping bag, brews a hot cup of coffee, fixes a sandwich, dons foul-weather clothes, and climbs into the damp cold. But in our two-trimaran raft, we remained in the cockpits the entire time. I turned my head slightly and announced, "Thirty seconds." Franz blinked awake, moved his feet a few inches to the rudder pedals, and said, "OK, I got her. Still steering forty degrees?" And I replied, "Yup, she's yours," and took my feet off the rudder pedals. Then I wiggled about, waved my arms, nibbled on food, drank a sip of water, peed, and pumped the bilges. Once these chores were done, I dozed uncomfortably for fifteen minutes, woke, daydreamed, and waited for Franz's announcement, "Thirty seconds. Your turn coming up."

The third day slid uneventfully into a third night as we gurgled along briskly. My body seemed to have adapted to the cold, my stomach gave up churning over lack of food, and my joints stopped their useless complaining about being cramped. The fog lifted in the middle of the night, and the moon revealed a shadowy arc of islands that seemed close and inviting, yet distant and ephemeral. For weeks we had navigated by map, compass, and GPS, and now, paradoxically, visible landmarks seemed somehow untrustworthy. I compared my calculations with what I could see, and reassured myself that these were real islands, arranged like the pictures of islands on the chart. But I still envisioned my travel as a line across the chart rather than the passage of a real boat on a real ocean. My mind was getting fuzzy. I shut off my headlamp, forced myself to ignore the compass, and steered toward one of the ghostlike spots on the horizon. A whitish glow appeared in the east, then reddish rays wiggled and bounced off the wavelets, and finally the sun rose above the sea to bathe us in warmth.

I had never before watched the sea cycle through its moods from such an intimate vantage point. On previous small-boat expeditions, I had gone to shore and camped every night. In yachts and fishing boats there was always the cabin. The seascape changes when you sleep: night slides into day, storm settles to calm, calm is overpowered by storm. As a result, sleep interrupts your observations, as if you skipped a chapter in a good book. In an open cockpit, by contrast, your contact with the sea and sky is tactile and unrelenting. Blowing foam had filled my sinuses with salt spray so that the storm's mayhem invaded my body. At the same time, adrenaline raced through my bloodstream. Eventually the chaos had seemed to cyclone through my empty stomach and whistle through my hollow rib cage. As the storm subsided and the adrenaline slowly drained, the tension relaxed almost imperceptibly with the passing time. Finally, when the miasmic fog lifted and the sun rose above the protean sea, I welcomed each photon that delighted my exhausted body.

It would be logical to remember these four days at sea as a very real brush with death. Yet, looking back, what I remember instead is the primal beauty of phosphorescent storm seas, the admiration I felt for my expedition partner as he struggled to repair a broken pontoon at the height of the storm, and the gladness in my heart when the sun at last reappeared. These memories seem like ample compensation for fleeting hardships, which must be why adventurers keep heading out for more.

THE storm had blown us west of our planned course, so we decided to land on a small, uninhabited island, Ekarma, rather than Shiashkotan. When we reached the northwest corner of Ekarma in midafternoon, the basalt cliffs looked friendly and comforting. Once again our approach was through a forest of kelp that tangled around our keels. When a gust of wind drove my leeward pontoon beneath the clutching weed, my boat stalled out and rotated around the anchored pontoon. The boom jibed, and I scampered forward to unravel the tangle. Franz was swinging his paddle like a machete in a jungle, hacking his way through the dense kelp forest. Finally we reached a small cove ringed by a verdant valley. The kelp held the swell down, so we had an easy landing, without surf. As we heaved the boats up the cobbled beach, juvenile seagulls raced for cover in the rocks. I'd never seen young gulls running along the beach. On every other coastline I've visited, adults nested on high cliffs or lofty pinnacles, and chicks lived on these safe perches until they could fly. But here the gulls nested on the beach because there were no predators on the island. I had assumed that gulls were genetically programmed to build nests on inaccessible rocky perches, but here I learned that gulls were smart enough to evaluate the threat and nest accordingly.

We changed into dry clothes in the warm summer sunshine. We were safe—for the moment—although this sanctuary was temporary. No one had been on this island for a long time and no one was going to land here for a long time. In a month, the juvenile gulls would mature and fly; in two months, winter gales would drift snow onto the beach. We needed to rest, eat, fix my boat, and return to sea for another long crossing.

Despite hardly eating for four days, we were too tired to cook, so we munched a candy bar, pitched our tents, and went to sleep. That night another storm whipped across the sea. I was overjoyed to be in my tent.

After twenty hours in my sleeping bag, I dressed and walked out into the rain. Water flowed off my parka and dripped from my nose. The valley was covered with dense alder and shoulder-high, broad-leafed annuals. All of these plants grow only in very wet environments. When we had paddled into this cove, we had seen two creek beds and were absolutely certain we would find water. Strangely enough, however, both creeks were dry, and seagulls had nested in the creek beds. Franz woke up and we searched for a small seep or creek but could find neither. As soon as we set out our cooking pots to collect rainwater, the downpour subsided to a drizzle. Our map showed a large river half a mile over the next ridge. Because neither of us felt like getting soaked by tramping through the dripping wet vegetation, we decided to eat an energy bar for dinner and find water in the morning.

I returned to my tent and pulled my sleeping bag over me like a comforter. Then I spread maps, GPS, journal, and a well-worn copy of *Moby-Dick* across the top of my bag, feeling like an eight year old with chicken pox, all my toy soldiers taking up positions in the folds of my blankets. All I had to do was amuse myself quietly until the adversity passed and I could get on with life.

I keystroked new waypoints into my GPS memory, plotted our next passage, and wrote in my journal:

> Everything is going wrong today. Another storm blew in and we can't find water. But we're on land: Not out at sea, not on a hostile glacier in the Himalayas, or on a vertical granite wall, or in Antarctica, or at the North Pole. No! We are on mid-latitude, low-elevation land. It is a hostile island eschewed by all people and most mammals, but green things grow here and it won't sink into the ocean for another 100 million years or so. The wind doesn't churn the rocks into unstable towers that threaten to crush us and there is no winter cold from Siberia that will suck our body heat away and kill us. So everything going wrong here on Ekarma isn't so bad.

The storm continued into its second day, and I woke up to the sound of the tent flapping. We hadn't eaten a hot meal for five days, and today would be the sixth if we didn't find enough water to cook. I unzipped the tent, but it looked miserable out there, so I crawled back into my sleeping bag and dozed off. The wind calmed by midmorning, so we cooked a small breakfast with the last of our water. Then I loaded the empty bottles in my pack and set out across the ridge to locate the river that appeared on the map.

I climbed a muddy, slippery slope and fought through dense, wet overgrowth. After an hour I reached the rim of the river canyon and sat down to survey the landscape. A dozen horned puffins were standing in front of their burrows, watching me. This was odd. I'd seen puffins in the water and watched them fly to nests on rock cliffs, but I hadn't known that they also nest underground. Then again, puffins always look a little silly with their stumpy orange beaks and puffed-out, regal bearing and the way they fly with their orange feet flapping as rudders, so why be surprised to find that they live in burrows?

I scrambled to the valley bottom, but the riverbed was dry. Our situation was becoming serious. We needed to fill our water bottles and cook a hot meal before we set sail again; there could be no compromise on those points. I thought, "Ignore the abundant vegetation and the rain. Imagine that you're in a desert. Now, where would you look for water?" In the southwestern desert of the United States and in the Mongolian Gobi, you don't look for streams in the valley bottoms, because the water percolates into the soil and runs deep underground. Instead, you search for springs higher up, where the soil is thin and water collects on a layer of impermeable rock. Then I understood—Ekarma is covered with porous volcanic sand, so the streams dry up shortly after the snow melts. We had been looking in the wrong places.

I hiked up the streambed, careful not to crush seagull nests. Soon the nests and puffin burrows petered out, and black-capped chickadees hopped from branch to branch. The river valley became narrow, like a slot canyon in the Utah desert, except that here the canyon walls were composed of moss-covered basalt rather than dry sandstone. After half an hour, a fifty-foot cliff blocked further progress. In May, when snows were melting and the stream was running, a beautiful waterfall must have cascaded over the rock. If I wanted to be cautious, I would have walked back to the ocean, climbed out of the river valley, and ascended the mountain along the ridge, but I was tired, thirsty, hungry, and discouraged. I had been living on fifteen hundred calories a day for six days and didn't feel like retracing my steps to the ocean, then hiking back up only to gain fifty feet. No, the cliff wasn't that steep, the edges were sharp, and I was an experienced rock climber. I slipped my toe into a clean crack, grasped two positive handholds, and moved upward.

Thirty feet off the ground, I rested on a three-inch ledge. Above me, the handholds were rounded and wet for the next five feet, until the rock pitched back onto easy terrain. If I made a mistake and fell, I would be injured in this lonely and desolate place, with no possibility of medical attention. Then I would look back and say that I had been stupid. But if I succeeded, my gambit would look pretty smart. I wiped my hands against my jacket to dry my fingertips, then moved upward. My hands and feet held. I moved past the tenuous edges and slipped my fingers into a clean, positive crack. Soon I reached near-level terrain, where the streambed flattened out and the canyon walls receded.

I followed the streambed until I was a thousand feet above sea level, then decided to climb out of the canyon and look for a spring. Ten-foot alder protruded from the steep bank. I stepped up, but slid back down on the muddy soil. Then I grabbed an alder to pull myself up, but the branch yielded, spilling rainwater over my head. It seemed silly to get so wet on a desert-like quest for water, so I decided to collect raindrops from the leaves. I delicately pulled an alder to bring the leaves within reach, but most of the water spilled. After fifteen minutes I had harvested only a few precious drops. OK, I must attack this situation head-on. By simultaneously climbing, slipping, crawling, pulling, and squirming, I finally reached a knoll above the canyon rim. The sea and the sky were azure and the sun was warm, but there was no water. I pushed through the brush to the next knoll, and there, beyond the alder and high grasses, I saw a wide ring of waist-high white flowers. I hadn't seen that species before, and their circular growth pattern indicated that they were surrounding something ecologically important—maybe a vital nutrient, maybe water. The flowers exuded a sweet, succulent smell entirely different from the decomposition and decay that we had lived with for two months along ocean beaches. One last dense perimeter of alder guarded a small depression in the center of the flower patch. I dropped on my hands and knees and crawled through a damp world of greens and browns so far from wind, fog, ocean, and surf, and there it was— a tiny spring bubbling peacefully out of the ground. I lay down on my stomach, took a deep, long drink, rested for a moment, and drank again.

Thirst quenched, I unscrewed a bottle top and carefully collected a capful of water. Despite utmost care, I riled up the peat, leaf fragments, volcanic sand, crustacea, and insect larvae resting on the bottom of the pool. The clear spring turned brown, but every muddy capful trickled into my bottle like a blessing.

I HAD undertaken this long journey to follow an ancient migration path. Though a traveler can never visit the past, the storm at sea, the hunger, and the search for water had reduced my world to fundamentals. Out here in the Kurils, Franz and I were as close as anyone from the twentieth century can come to experiencing the essence of a Stone Age maritime migration.

Crouched in the green canopy, collecting precious water, albeit muddy, I set aside speculation about motives and appreciated, once again, the extraordinary difficulty of the Jomon passage. I imagined a small tribe of Jomon living in Japan. Survival involved fishing, hunting sea mammals and deer, making clothes, tools, and boats, and so on. Now I thought of the additional burden imposed by migration.

Surely some Jomon mariners died at sea. Even if there were no disasters, a Stone Age journey was incredibly difficult. Franz and I were strung out, hungry, weak, and exhausted. Yet if we survived the remaining crossings and reached Petropavlovsk, we would fly home to spend the winter in a warm house, with abundant food and doctors if we needed them. Then, strengthened, fortified, and resupplied, we could start out again in spring. If, on the other hand, Jomon migrants sailed through the Kurils, they would stop at the end of August and scramble to build winter shelters, collect food, sew clothing, and chip new tools. Travel consumes time and energy that could otherwise be spent on the most basic elements of survival. If you're sailing, you're not hunting or foraging. When you move to a new location, you have to build a new winter house. September must have been a frantic time for Stone Age migrants.

To add to their problems, migrants had to cope with unfamiliar territory. This search for water was a perfect example. When Franz and I sailed to Ekarma, we had every reason to believe that we would find water near the beach. Rain was abundant throughout the Kurils, and creeks had trickled into every cove at every landing since the beginning of our journey. What could be more obvious—rain falls on the mountain and flows to the ocean. But Ekarma's creeks were dry, and I had burned a few thousand calories and spent a half day searching for a spring. Franz and I weren't guilty of sloppy thinking; we just lacked local knowledge. Near my home in Montana, Chris and I didn't have to wander aimlessly around looking for water; we knew which creeks dry up in summer and which ones run all year. We also knew where to find huckleberry patches and where elk like to bed. For hunter-gatherers, intimate knowledge of the environment is critical. But the traveler moves beyond this circle of familiarity and must adjust to the unknown.

After filling the bottles, I stood to go—and banged my head against an alder. As soon as I started moving, the alders became gnarled, devious gnomes blocking my path, ripping at my clothes, spilling water down my neck, tripping me, and tossing me to the ground. But if I didn't move, I was safe in the lush canopy. I sat back down and watched insects crawl through the dirt and birds flit through the dense foliage.

But I couldn't stay here forever. Franz and I were alone on an uninhabited island. We had to repair the boats and push onward. This sense of aloneness suddenly seemed overpowering and frightening, and I longed to step off an airplane and see Chris's face in the crowd.

The image of Chris highlighted other challenges of a Stone Age migration. In a tribe's home turf, friends and relatives provided food, security, and safety, as well as love and companionship. If food was scarce in one region, hungry people could visit their families in areas of relative abundance. If one tribe was attacked, social contacts became military alliances. But once a band sailed away from its home territory, it became isolated in a way that we can only vaguely comprehend.

Alan Fix, an anthropologist at the University of California, has out-lined another cost of migration called the genetic migration load. People evolve to survive in their home environment: they develop genetic resis-tance to local diseases and gradually adapt body shape, skin color, and other physical characteristics to their homeland. But migrants step outside this circle of adaptation. A Jomon who moved from a temperate environment into the Arctic lacked the heat-conserving round face and squat nose of an Inuit. If an Inuit moved to Africa, he or she would be susceptible to a myriad of tropical diseases. So the Jomon migrants were not only sailing away from their allies, they were sailing away from their genetic makeup.

Hunger finally overpowered my lethargy and musings. I packed away the water bottles, hefted the load, and squirmed through the alders. I crossed the creek and traversed high ground to avoid the creek bed and the cliff. From the top of the drainage above our camp, I looked down at the sea spread out below, blue and placid. Waves looked like imperceptible rip-ples—inviting, welcoming, and mysterious.

No, of course I couldn't travel back in time, but I was peeking in the window. And when I thought about the Jomon migration, I had the same feeling I have when I watch Olympic athletes or listen to a fine piece of music. "Wow, look what human beings can do! And I'm a member of the same species. Lucky me." Yes, lucky me, I had inherited the genes that en-abled Stone Age migrants to survive incredible odds in unknown and often hostile ecosystems. And not just that—I had also inherited genes that made me choose to be here, not despite but because of the raw harshness of the place.

Franz and I had rhythm now. We had completed our longest crossing and had tested our brave motto, "Hammered isn't the same as dead." I ce-mented my resolve to return the following year and keep sailing or paddling until I reached Alaska.

WE COOKED a huge meal, then untied the lashings to examine my damaged boat. Although the crossbar was attached to the outside of the hull with a stout three-eighths-inch stainless steel pin, it was attached to the inside by an aluminum pop rivet. It was an engineering lapse, exacerbated by our folly of tying the boats together during a storm and thus exerting significantly more stress on the crossbar than it was designed for. We spent the afternoon drilling holes and reinforcing the attachments with heavy stainless self-tapping screws. The following morning, we put back to sea.

After a rough two-day sail to the next island, Oneketon, I wrote a single sentence in my journal: "It was a reasonable passage but a little blowy and I didn't sleep much because the sea was busy." Looking at the journal now, I realize that I was too tired and dazed to write. I no longer remember the details, but I do remember that we were cold and shivering when we landed at the *pogranichniki* base. By this time, the regional commander on the mainland had finally learned about our expedition. After reviewing the file, he dubbed us "The Two-American Suicide Expedition" and ordered the local commanders to assist us. We had ventured far enough into the unknown to escape antiquated cold war rivalries and bureaucratic labyrinths.

The base commander wasn't a talkative, backslapping, joke-telling guy; he was just quietly kind and generous. He fed us, loaned us warm clothes while our wet ones dried, fired up the *banyo*, and offered us a comfortable room with beds and clean sheets. A storm came through and we rested for two days.

We left the *pogranichniki* base on August 3 and sailed into the fishing port of Severo Kurilsk a week later. I walked along a dusty road to town, bathed in the security of small houses nestled into green hillsides. Franz and I had been at sea eight weeks, and the domesticity of town was both comforting and alien. At the harbor, I chatted with fishermen and reported to the *pogranichniki*. I went to the store and bought staples as well as ice cream, cookies, cucumbers, and oranges. Time is schizophrenic: on a sedate day on a flat sea, each hour seemed eternal, but now, looking back at the past eight weeks and eight hundred miles, our adventure had passed in an eye-blink.

Eternity or eye-blink, I had promised to phone home more than three weeks ago, so I walked to the post office and found a sullen woman sitting behind a dusty, empty desk under a barred window. I wrote my boyhood home phone number on a small piece of scrap paper, and she plugged black wire jacks into a big board. Then she directed me to an unlit wooden phone booth, and when I picked up the receiver, incredibly I heard my father's voice. The connection was crackly and slow, but I sensed a deep relief. I told him we were safe, and he reminded me to be careful.

Only later did I learn that he had seriously considered flying to Petropavlovsk and chartering a helicopter to rescue us. When I returned home, my sister wrote:

> You were supposed to call by mid-July and after you were three weeks late, Dad got quite worried and wanted to hire a helicopter to find you. So I said two things: (a) if he went, I was coming; (b) it was silly to go. We couldn't find you in the vast Pacific with one lone helicopter. After all, JFK, Jr. had just crashed in the water off Martha's Vineyard. The stretch of water was very narrow and he had the entire U.S. Navy looking for evidence of the plane. Nonetheless, it took days to find him. So, it was not likely that we would find you if you were ok. And it certainly was not likely (or useful) to find you if you had sunk. Moreover, we all understood intellectually that you were not on a precise timetable and we knew that the trip was going much more slowly than you had anticipated. Nonetheless, Dad wanted to find you.
>
> Fortunately, while all the negotiation was going on, you called. We were incredibly relieved.

Three days later, Franz and I made our last crossing—to Kamchatka. Tidal currents created standing waves reminiscent of the crossing from Urup. We surfed down some of them, met others head-on, and absorbed the slaps of green water in the face. When we finally slipped into the lee of the mainland, Franz's mast gyrated through smaller arcs until it stood upright, barely moving in a placid sea. We sailed north, found a sandy beach, and navigated through the surf, riding the swell, enjoying the acceleration and turbulence.

We had finally reached mainland Asia. I wiggled out of my dry suit and felt a warm, reassuring land breeze blow through my damp clothes. A tree was growing by a gurgling stream. It was the first real tree we had seen since leaving Kunashir, so we decided to camp in its shade. However, when I carried my duffel up the beach, I noticed abundant grizzly bear tracks in the wet mud. We searched for a flat camp that didn't infringe on the bears' territory, but their tracks, scat, and beds were everywhere.

In his book *The Shadow of Kilimanjaro*, Rick Ridgeway explains that although the Sierra Nevada in California is a designated wilderness area, all the grizzly bears have been exterminated. As a result, a backpacker loses that tingling awareness brought on by vulnerability. Rick walked across East Africa simply for the joy of sharing habitat with large and potentially man-eating lions and crocodiles.

Rick's party carried rifles, but we were unarmed. I was emotionally drained and wanted to feel safe. We were on the mainland now, and if the boats broke to pieces we could, in theory, walk across Siberia to Paris and stroll down the Champs-Elysées. I wanted to set my net, catch a juicy salmon, and grill it on an open fire without glancing over my shoulder in fear that a monster griz was shuffling into camp with nose down, beady eyes flitting back and forth, powerful muscles rustling shaggy fur.

I took a deep breath, exhaled slowly, and fought against my inner whiner. "OK, this place is full of bears. We exchanged the vulnerability of the Kurils for the vulnerability of a different wilderness. Stay aware, stay alert; that's the challenge and the joy."

Kamchatka is a long, narrow peninsula that protrudes from the eastern edge of Siberia. Local residents consider Kamchatka an autonomous entity, but most Western references list it as part of Siberia, which is a huge subcontinent stretching across nine time zones from the Ural Mountains to the Bering Strait. As one nineteenth-century explorer explained: "You could take the whole United States of America and set it down in the middle of Siberia without touching anywhere the boundaries of the latter territory. You could then take Alaska and all the states of Europe, with the single exception of Russia, and fit them in the remaining margin like pieces of a dissected map, and you would still have more than 300,000 square miles of Siberian territory to spare."

Siberia is a frigid land, with greater temperature extremes than Antarctica. Although summer temperatures can be quite hot, the meteorological station in Yukutiya has recorded winter temperatures of −90°F (−68°C) on several occasions.

In the sixteenth century, Siberia was such a terra incognita that Russians in Moscow imagined it was inhabited by fastastical monsters, reminiscent of the imaginary sea serpents that spread fear into the souls of Columbus's crew. Author Benson Bobrick cites one medieval text: "To the east of the sun, to the most-high mountain Karkaraur, where dwell the one-armed, one-footed folk." From this and other sources, Bobrick argues that: "Although by the end of the sixteenth century, because of explorations east and west, a large part of the world had been intelligibly mapped, Siberia had escaped the broad sphere of Renaissance discoveries." Bobrick is certainly correct that pre-sixteenth-century maps of eastern Asia were vague and inaccurate, but Siberia wasn't entirely unknown. In the thirteenth century, Genghis Khan and his successors swept out of the eastern steppes to conquer most of Russia, and they must have brought word about their neighbors near Lake Baikal and the forests to the north. After the Mongolian Empire collapsed, Russian soldiers and settlers moved east of the Urals. Between 1552 and roughly 1789, the Russians conquered the aboriginal people of Siberia in a series of brutal wars that paralleled the European conquest of North America. But there the similarities ended. Americans and Canadians assimilated the continent so that Los Angeles and Vancouver haven't become remote vassal states of Washington and Ottawa. The Russian Far East, on the other hand, has remained isolated from and politically subservient to Moscow.

Krasheninnikov records that in the eighteenth century, southern Kamchatka was settled mostly by the Itlemen, who were of Siberian and Mongolian origin. According to the best estimate, the precontact population of southern Kamchatka was about 25,000 to 30,000 people. Cossack pioneers killed many of these Itlemen directly and introduced diseases that killed many others, reducing the population to fewer than 5,000. Russian settlers immigrated to Kamchatka first for furs and later for fishing, mining, and military purposes. In 1995 the total population of Kamchatka was about 400,000, most of them Russian. Owing to hard economic times, many people had since returned to European Russia. By 2001, about 250,000 people lived in and around the biggest city in Kamchatka—Petropavlovsk; another 100,000 were scattered throughout the rest of the peninsula. Thus, while Kamchatka is about the same size and shape as Italy, it supports only $\frac{1}{165}$ as many people. Roads connect Petropavlovsk to outlying towns, but many villages have no roads. In addition, there are no roads connecting Kamchatka with anywhere else in the world. The nearest paved highway is in Irkustk, about 3,400 miles away.

In Montana, I live near the Selway-Bitterroot Wilderness, the largest wilderness in the lower forty-eight states. If I walk out my back door and head due west, I can travel 113 miles across forests and hills without crossing a road. That seems like a long distance, but in Kamchatka the wilderness stretches as far as New York is from San Francisco. The Trans-Siberian Railroad lies far to the south, so Kamchatka is accessible only by sea or air.

FRANZ AND I found a level, grassy platform between two grizzly trails. This beach, it was clear, was ruled by grizzlies, not people. We set up our tents, cooked dinner nervously, and went to sleep with wary alertness. But no excitement disrupted our slumber.

CONTINUING up the coast uneventfully, we landed through manageable surf on the evening of August 13. During the night, a large storm at sea generated steep surf, though the wind didn't reach us. We sat on the beach after breakfast, evaluating the situation.

"God, that breaker looks ugly. Whew, if we got caught by that one, it would crunch us for sure," I said.

"But look, after that there's a lull of three small waves. We could blast through them," Franz replied.

"You think so?"

"Yeah, it doesn't look too bad."

"Until you're out in it."

We dressed for sea, lashed everything securely, dragged both boats close to the water, and discussed our strategy. The first person to launch would have a partner to help push off the beach, but he would also be the guinea pig. The second person would have to launch alone, which was difficult. I turned away so Franz couldn't see me, picked up one small stone, and held out two closed fists, one with a stone and one without.

"Stone goes first."

Franz tapped my left hand and picked the stone.

He held his paddle and we watched the sea. Three big waves; two sets of small ones; four monster sets; one tiny break and three steep, ugly breaks: "NOW! GO! GO! GO!"

We pushed Franz's boat into the water until we were up to our armpits in foam, then Franz jumped aboard and paddled frantically. He rose over the first wave, the second, the third, and he was home free! No, he wasn't—a huge wave was roiling in, looming out of the deep green water. Franz dug his paddle, but his boat seemed stationary. The wave steepened, and suddenly Franz was sliding backward, almost vertical, racing helplessly toward the beach. The wave curled and his boat dropped sharply off its face. Franz spilled into the sea and the mast vibrated furiously, indicating that the stern had hit the sand with a thud. The boat righted itself and sloshed, broadside, in the surf. As I splashed into the water to help, I noticed a small black object floating in the white foam. It was Franz's rudder.

We wrestled the damaged boat back onto the beach and unpacked tools to replace the broken rudder with a spare one. The rumble of the surf faded into background noise and lost its urgency. Then the roar changed pitch and assumed mechanical overtones. When we looked up, a Russian military tank was roaring along the beach, with sand curling out from the treads like a wave. A man with a blue-and-white-striped sailor shirt was riding on the turret with an AK-47 assault rifle at his hip.

Franz put down his wrench and mumbled, "What next?"

The tank jerked to a halt, the armored hatch squeaked open, and a sweating, shirtless man in blue jeans popped out, followed by two raga-muffin teenagers and a white-bearded man in camouflage fatigues with a huge knife strapped around his waist. I half expected a hundred men to pour out like clowns from a circus car. The bearded man jumped down, walked over to us, and extended his hand with a broad smile.

"*My name is Alexander; I'm the commander.*"

We introduced ourselves and explained our journey and our present situation.

He surveyed the surf and remarked, "*Don't go anywhere.*"

Then he shouted a command, and the men scampered aboard the tank and dropped out of sight as if an enemy were about to open fire. The diesel roared to life and Alexander waved from the tank top like Yeltsin confronting parliament. Then he too dropped out of sight, and the beast clanked over a sand dune and disappeared.

They returned in an hour, and Alexander again approached us. He smiled and explained that there was no surf at a small cove a few miles up the beach. The men jumped down, and before we understood what was happening they had lifted our boats and loaded them on top of the tank.

"*You have ropes?*"

"*Da.*"

"*Good, we'll tie the boats down and go to the cove.*"

"*Harosho, ochen harosho* [good, very good]."

We secured the boats, and Franz and I rode on top of the tank while the driver revved the engine and whirred across the beach. After a few hundred yards, the tank lurched into an abrupt left turn and crunched through an alder thicket, shooting wood splinters and leaves to the side like a giant lawn mower. A startled grizzly bear flushed out of the brush and loped away. The tank turned again, like a robot, found a crude road, and headed inland toward a protected valley. Gnarled stone birches grew in abundance, reminding me that the entire world wasn't a harsh palette of stormy sea, rocky beach, and windswept tundra. The road curled up a steep hill, and the driver downshifted. Then the motor faltered, coughed, ran smoothly for an instant, and died.

The hatch squeaked open and Alexander's ragtag army jumped out like so many jack-in-the-boxes. Alexander pulled at his white beard, smiled, and pointed to my white beard. "*The tank is old, like you and me.*" We all climbed down and squatted in the dirt while Alexander and his shirtless mechanic conversed. I took two candy bars out of my pocket, cut them into equal shares, and passed them around. Alexander declined, pointing to his rotten teeth.

The mechanic said something I didn't understand; Alexander barked an order and the two teenagers ran down the tank track. Meanwhile, the mechanic opened a large armored hatch to gain access to the engine. If you don't speak a language well, you live in a mysterious present, only vaguely aware of past and future. If I asked the mechanic what was wrong, I probably wouldn't understand his answer. Yet I had been the default mechanic on an Alaskan fishing boat, and I knew diesel engines, so I guessed that the fuel pump had failed. If that were true, how were they going to fix it? Would the two young soldiers race out of the forest with a brand-new fuel pump in a neat blue and yellow box with black lettering on the side: "Fuel Pump—Tank—Russian Army—1943—part number AZ1436792"? We sat down to wait.

The boys returned with a plastic bucket and a rubber hose. The mechanic opened the fuel tank, slipped the tube down the hole, sucked on the tube until he had a mouthful of diesel, spat it out, and siphoned a few gallons into the bucket. Then he disconnected the metal fuel line and ordered one of the teenagers to stand over the engine with the bucket. He activated the siphon again and connected the hose directly to the fuel injectors. "Clever, very clever," I thought. Fuel pumps break, but you can always count on gravity.

The mechanic lowered himself into the belly of the beast and hit the starter button. A black puff of exhaust emerged and the engine sputtered to life. The open engine hatch and the human fuel pump had preempted our perch on the top of the tank, so Alexander motioned for me to sit in the gunner's seat with Franz crowded behind. A long time ago, someone had removed the cannon and welded shut the gunner's controls, but nevertheless I felt warlike, encased in armor and viewing the world through a periscope. It felt disconcertingly exhilarating to imagine myself being that dangerous.

We roared up the hill and down the other side to the protected cove, where gentle wavelets caressed the beach. The men unloaded our boats, waved good-bye, and drove to their small base on a nearby hill. Franz and I finished the rudder repair, cooked dinner, and went to sleep. The following morning Alexander walked into camp with a hot loaf of bread.

"*Hungry?*" he asked.

"*Da, we are always hungry.*"

"*Then you should stay home with your wife in a warm kitchen where there is lots of food and no surf.*"

I smiled, pulled out my knife, and cut myself a thick slice of bread.

"*How many years have you been sailing around in small boats like this?*"

"*Thirty.*"

In Russian, thirty and thirteen sound similar and my pronunciation is horrible, so he scratched two numbers, 30 and 13, in the sand. I pointed to 30.

He shook his head in friendly incredulousness, then grasped our hands, wished us good luck, and walked back toward his house on the hill where he was guarding Kamchatka with four men and a tank without a cannon or a fuel pump.

When he was out of earshot, Franz asked, "Would you remind me, Jon, what the cold war was all about, anyway?"

"I think it was about different concepts of ownership and payment."

We were tired and had been traveling together for a long time. Conversation was sparse, and political conversation was even sparser. We ate our bread in relaxed silence, then discussed the day's sailing strategy.

SIX days later, on August 21, we reached the entrance to Avacha Bay. Thousands of gulls, common murres, and pelagic cormorants nested on sea stacks that guarded the bay. Twin snow-covered volcanic peaks soared two miles above the coastal plain. These mountains were formed by the same tectonic subduction that gave birth to the Kuril Islands to the south and the Aleutians to the north. Mount Koryaksky is a perfect cone formed by successive layers of lava and ash that spewed out during repeated eruptions. On the other hand, its sister, Avachasky, has blown its summit to smithereens a few times. Each of these violent eruptions has left chaotic piles of rock and jumbled lava flows. The resultant asymmetrical mountain is now covered with snowfields and glistening glaciers. Avacha Bay is the best deepwater harbor on the east coast of Kamchatka. As a consequence, it was Vitus Bering's base for his historic exploration of Alaska. Today, the only significant cities on Kamchatka line the shores of Avacha Bay, and the Russian Pacific nuclear submarine fleet is based there. In a few weeks, fall gales would descend from the polar ice cap to turn the North Pacific into a maelstrom. Thus we decided to stop there and continue the following spring.

A killer whale swam off my starboard side, its curved dorsal fin knifing slowly through the water. After a few minutes, five more whales approached from the open sea. A seal bobbed to the surface a few hundred yards away, and the whales accelerated so rapidly that their noses rose out of the water, revealing their curved white chins. The pod split into two columns of three; the columns spread into two arcs and with military precision coalesced into a circle. Within seconds, the circle broke into six speeding whales charging toward a common center. The poor seal didn't have a chance. A small patch of blood colored the water, the whales sounded, and the blood dissipated into the great ocean.

I spilled the wind from my sail, wondering if the whales would return. My boat rocked with the waves, a seagull hovered, tucked its wings, dropped into the water, and flapped away with a small fish in its beak. But the sleek black-and-white beasts had disappeared.

Franz and I had seen many killer whales along the way, but only as dorsal fins sweeping through the water. I'd imagined the streamlined body and the curved white markings above the eyes that look like paste-on smiles against the shiny black skin. A few times in my life I'd seen orcas leap out of the water, but I'd never before witnessed a hunt. Orcas are on top of the marine food chain; they pursue smaller predators such as seals and sea lions, and they also feast on other species of whales much larger than they are. I had just witnessed six thirty-foot giants speeding through the water at twenty-five miles an hour in a synchronized attack. It was hardly a stretch, at that moment, to imagine Franz and me as tasty hors d'oeuvres.

Stone Age hunters of the North Pacific Rim knew that an orca could easily leap out of the water, crush a kayak, and spill its hapless human into the sea. Yet they also knew that orcas never attacked people. In trying to explain this paradox, our ancestors must have wondered, "Why am I surviving when survival is so improbable?" In response, they believed that their deities kept them alive.

According to the Ainu:

When we are fishing in the ocean, sometimes *repun-kamuy* [killer whales] come near our boat. When this happens we are supposed to give some of our lunch to them by throwing it in the ocean. It is said that the god of the ocean will eat it and give fishermen a good catch and a safe trip.

According to the Inuit:

A Cape Prince of Wales *anatquq* [shaman] had a boat. He and his crew went paddling out in it. So many killer whales came all around the boat that they couldn't move it . . . The *anatquq* tried to use his *anatquq* [shaman's powers], but the whales didn't go. Another man . . . thought, "This is the way they taught me long ago." He asked for some mittens. He put them on and got down inside the boat. He put his arms up in the air and started talking to himself. Then he sat down and the killer whales started to go. . . . People said that maybe he was praying. That is why the killer whales went away because he prayed instead of using *anatquq*.

To the Ainu, killer whales had the most powerful *kamuy* of any animal in the sea. But if a seafarer made the proper sacrifices and paid sufficient respect, the whales were allies, not enemies. Occasionally when killer whales hunted large prey such as gray whales, the hunted whale would swim up on the beach, become stranded, and provide a protein and fat bonanza for the Ainu. On the other side of the Pacific Rim, Alaskan Inuit recognized that killer whales were too powerful to confront even with a shaman's spell. Only prayers to the highest God ensured safety. From Japan to Alaska, aboriginal hunters pursued every other creature in their environment, but in all cultures, it was taboo to lift a harpoon against the killer whale.

After twenty-five years of expeditions in remote wildernesses, I'd come to appreciate the aboriginal animistic view of the world. When a storm swirls around you and dominates every sense, then the storm develops a personality and *kamuy*. Each wave within the storm has a unique shape and character, so it too has soul. The freshwater spring on Ekarma had a strong *kamuy*, and those moments under the green canopy by the precious water had become part of my personal wealth.

The killer whales visited us on the last day of our journey. It was a coincidence, not a miracle: I don't believe in miracles. Nevertheless, the powerful hunters, the churning water, and the sacrificial seal were my farewell kiss from the ocean, as if it were saying, "Good-bye, my friend. We've had a few bad times, but they're in the past. I meant no harm. Safe travels, and when you are far away, remember only our fond embraces. It's a long, uncertain passage from here to Alaska, but please come back. We're lifelong partners, you and I."

As Franz and I sailed into the protected bay, the swell subsided. A power plant belched black smoke, and dry docks resounded with the whir of cranes and the clank of metal against metal. Horns honked, fishing ships rumbled back and forth, and the hillsides were covered with rows of linear, uninspiring apartment buildings. We sailed past the industrial district and turned in when we saw an imposing statue of Lenin behind a large umbrella with the familiar red and white Coca-Cola logo. Curious bystanders helped pull our boats to shore, and a teenaged boy announced in faltering English that he would be our friend and interpreter. We ordered charcoal-broiled shashlik—grilled meat—from a beachfront vendor, wiped the drippings off our beards with the backs of our hands, and washed the meal down with ice-cold sodas. But I was already fidgety, impatient to return to sea.

Interlude

"I've been following [Kennewick Man's] tracks for my whole life, studying the things he left behind: campsites, dwellings, trash piles. I thought I knew who I was following, what he looked like. But then I finally caught up with him, and he turned around . . . and he wasn't who I expected to see."

James C. Chatters, *Ancient Encounters: Kennewick Man and the First Americans*

"The answer is never the answer. What's really interesting is the mystery. If you seek the mystery instead of the answer, you'll always be seeking. I've never seen anybody really find the answer—they think they have, so they stop thinking. But the job is to seek mystery . . ."

Ken Kesey

WE HAD sailed a paltry 1,000 miles of the 3,000-mile passage from Japan to Alaska. Yet standing on the shore beneath Lenin's fatherly gaze, the dangers of the Kurils behind us, I felt no sense of failure—only hope and gratitude. I had underestimated the scope, complexity, and rigors of a small-boat passage across the North Pacific Rim, and the ocean had spoken to us—but it hadn't destroyed us. I had fallen in love with this coastline, this ocean, this land, and the journey. After ordering another shashlik, I watched the sun set into the calm bay. It would be suicidal to continue north as winter approached, but I was determined to return the following year.

Even before reaching Petropavlovsk, Franz and I had talked about the continuing passage to Alaska, but he had already planned a river kayaking expedition in Peru the following year. Although I was disappointed, I wasn't going to let that roadblock interfere with my dream. As I sat on the beach, I thought about the lonely, surf-swept Arctic coast of northeast Siberia. Then I ran through a mental list of friends who might join me the following year: Chris, maybe; after that, no one.

Twenty years earlier, when I had decided to paddle a kayak around Cape Horn, all my friends smiled and replied something like, "Good idea, Jon. Send me a postcard from Puerto Williams." I impetuously pronounced that if an expedition is really worthwhile, no one will want to join you—and I set off alone. Then I made a mistake just shy of the Cape, became tangled in storm-driven kelp, shipwrecked, dislocated my shoulder, and endured that lonely walk back to a Chilean naval base. This misadventure had become a seminal episode in my life, but the lesson centered around a key judgment error that caused me to launch on a stormy day, not the arguable foolhardiness of attempting it alone. Over the following decades, that lesson stayed with me, and I continually sought to balance daring with caution, tenacity with common sense. The shifting blend brought me great joys and rewards, and I later returned and successfully completed my delayed passage around the Horn.

So, a partner would appear, or I would continue the expedition alone—it really didn't matter.

Franz and I had lunch with Martha and Yelena from Yelizovo Tour Service in Kamchatka. We told them all about the Kurils, and I asked about the bureaucratic hurdles for the continued passage north. They assured me that they could obtain the necessary permissions, but I would need another Russian guide. I objected, explaining that Jenya had been an expensive nuisance. They were intractable.

"Don't argue. The *pogranichniki* knows about you now. Without a guide you won't get your permissions, and without permission they'll shoot you out of the water."

The next day as I was lounging in their office, a tall, handsome, broad-shouldered blond man with a pressed sport coat and neatly trimmed beard walked in. He shook my hand, introduced himself as Misha, and spoke to Martha in rapid Russian. Martha explained that Misha was interested in joining me the following summer. I looked at him and smiled. He smiled back warmly, revealing a prominent gold tooth and disarming blue eyes. Weather had wrinkled his face, but he wasn't tan. I guessed that he had spent many years outside, but not recently.

"Do you speak English?"

"Yes."

"It will be a long, hard journey."

He looked at Martha quizzically and she translated into Russian. Then he responded in English.

"Yes."

"Do you know that Jenya left the expedition because he thought it was too hard?"

Martha translated.

"Yes."

"Are you sure you want to come?"

Martha translated a third time and Misha considered my question carefully.

"Maybe."

He smiled again and spoke slowly in English, "We talk more, I go now."

After he left, I asked Martha, "Has he ever been in a kayak or other small boat?"

"No."

"Has he ever been to sea in a boat of any size?"

"No, but he is a geologist and has spent fifteen field seasons in remote parts of Kamchatka."

I thought, "Oh, boy, here we go again. This is the same story she told me about Jenya." On the other hand, I was unlikely to find a competent Russian sea kayaker. Furthermore, Misha clearly wasn't another Jenya. Even though Misha seemed shy, he was confident and self-assured at the same time. I liked him immediately, but I wondered if I should base my expedition on this gut feeling. When the great British explorer Ernest Shackleton planned a multiyear expedition to Antarctica, he interviewed each prospective crew member for five minutes. If he had a positive first impression, he hired the man; if the impression was negative, he did not. Simple enough.

I'll never know exactly what personality traits Shackleton was looking for, but I suspect he wanted dreamers—men whose spirit would carry them through hardship and danger. I needed to know whether Misha was a romantic. I met him several times during the following week. He had received an undergraduate degree in hydrogeology from the prestigious mining institute in Saint Petersburg and had come to Kamchatka in 1980 to study groundwater. After perestroika, in 1988, the government imploded and Misha lost his job. During a short period of unemployment, he formed a company with several other hydrogeologists and privatized a parcel of land about fifty miles north of Petropavlovsk. This land contained three water reserves: a freshwater artesian well, a deep mineral-water well, and a hot spring. Misha's company built a modern factory to bottle and sell the artesian and mineral water. At the same time, they opened a tourist spa at the hot spring.

Misha had studied English at the university, and his conversation, rusty at first, improved dramatically every time we spoke. One afternoon he asked to see the WindRiders. We drove to the docks and entered the dilapidated, cavernous warehouse where the boats were stored. Although I had told Misha that the WindRiders were small, like a *baidarka*, he was visibly startled when he looked at them. He walked around one of the boats and lifted the stern to feel its weight. Then he took off his sport jacket, folded it carefully, handed it to me, and climbed into the cockpit, being careful not to scuff his shoes or smear dirt on his clean pants.

When he was seated, I asked him why he wanted to join me on this journey.

He remained thoughtful for a while, carefully choosing his words. "For fifteen years I work in wild nature. Now, five years I work in office. I make many papers. Only work. My health crashed. Now I need to see wild nature again."

We didn't talk for a few minutes, then he continued. "Maybe I will go with you. I will speak at my wife. I will speak at Martha after you return to America."

I FLEW home, and Chris met me at the airport. She was standing in the crowd, short and square shouldered; then she moved toward me with the easy grace of an athlete. When we had first met, she wore her blond hair in pigtails, but now that her hair was gray, she had cut it short to minimize cosmetic maintenance. We embraced, then held back to look at each other. Her angular Scandinavian face, with its slightly raised cheekbones and gray-hazel eyes, was so familiar. When we first met I would kiss the crow's-feet near her eyes to moisturize the skin and make the wrinkles go away. But twenty years of intense mountain sunlight had been stronger than my kisses. I held her again and kissed the weather-beaten skin near both eyes. Sometimes when we ski with strangers, young people don't seem enthusiastic about traveling in the backcountry with a fifty-year-old grandmother. But after a day in the mountains, Chris always earns people's respect through her stamina, judgment, grace on skis, and easygoing temperament.

We picked up my bags and stepped into the hot summer afternoon outside the airport. Two hours later we bounced up a steep hill to our driveway, with indented tire tracks and grass growing in the center. Ponderosa pine and Douglas fir closed in around us. A final turn brought us past the plywood shack that is my office, to our small brown house on the crest of a rise. I pulled past the firewood shed to a level platform and turned off the ignition.

Chris and I had chatted all the way home, but now there was a moment of silence. I needed to collect myself before returning to domestic life. But Chris's mind was elsewhere. "Are you going back next year?" she asked.

I still had both hands on the steering wheel. My surroundings felt so warm and comforting. Soon Chris and I would bustle around the kitchen together, cooking elk meat from the forest and lettuce and broccoli from our garden. Later we would climb the narrow stairs to our bed, in a tower, above the roof, surrounded by skylights that reveal the starlit sky. Tomorrow I would walk down to my office with a cup of mint tea and turn on the computer.

Was I going back next year?

"Yes. Do you want to come with me?"

Chris cut straight to technical details. "What kind of boat are you going to use?"

I laughed. "Does that mean you'll come?"

"It depends on the boat."

"OK. Let's go inside and get something to eat. Then I'll take a shower
and unpack. Then we can start planning for next year."

I HAD chosen the WindRiders because they were fast, yet Franz and I
had sailed only 1,000 miles in sixty-eight days, or 14.7 miles a day—2.3 miles
per day slower than I have averaged in a kayak. During one week of calm
weather, Franz and I had journeyed only 16 miles. Thus, in the unpredictable winds and steep seas of the Kurils, our high-speed, sporty sailing
trimarans were disappointingly slow.

On the positive side, the WindRiders were extraordinarily stable. Nights
at sea weren't comfortable, but we could doze without capsizing. I don't
think we could have survived the long passages in a single-hulled boat.
Looking ahead, however, I intended to follow the coast, and I wouldn't
need to sleep in a boat. The largest technical challenge for the upcoming
expedition would be landing and launching through the surf, and the Wind-
Riders were too heavy and awkward for that. They would surely invite
disaster.

The Bering Sea is turbulent. Warm water from Japan collides with cold
water from the Arctic Ocean to form steep waves, frequent storms, chaotic
currents, and drop-out-from-beneath-you surf. The kayak was invented
there. The aboriginal kayak was constructed of wooden ribs lashed together
with sinew or whale baleen and covered with sealskin. The oldest kayak
fragment is a 2,000-year-old piece of sealskin found in northwest Alaska.
The wear marks indicate that this ancient boat was similar to Inuit kayaks
built in the nineteenth century. A hundred miles away, on the Russian side
of the Bering Strait, archaeologists unearthed a model kayak from a grave,
also dated to about 2,000 years ago. No one knows when the first kayaks
were built, because thin wooden strips, sealskin, and sinew decompose easily. As a result, the oldest kayaks have long since rotted into the permafrost
peat. However, a double-bladed paddle and ivory cockpit fittings found on
the Aleutian Islands push kayak design to at least 4,000 years ago, and the
first kayaks may be even older.

Perhaps the greatest kayakers were the Aleuts, who colonized the Aleutian Islands 9,000 years ago, about the same time the Jomon sailed from
Japan. These extraordinarily strong people spent much of their lives in their

tiny and fragile crafts. The Aleut's strength has been scientifically proven. From a bone's density and shape—its rugosity—scientists can ascertain the strength of its attached muscles. According to William Laughlin, professor of anthropology at the University of Connecticut, an Aleut humerus—upper arm bone—exhibits the greatest rugosity ever recorded in a human arm. Captain James Cook, a careful navigator and accurate scientist, recorded that Aleut kayakers could sustain a paddle speed of 8 knots while carrying a load of fish; an Olympic paddler in a racing boat, by contrast, can sprint at 9 knots—only 1 knot faster, without cargo, and only for a short time. A Russian ethnologist reported that an Aleut messenger kayaked 120 nautical miles across open ocean in twenty-seven hours, averaging 4.4 knots. I can paddle for ten hours at 3 knots before reaching total exhaustion. Thus my range is about a quarter that of an Aleut.

Aboriginal people across the globe adapted boat design to their home oceans. It was no accident that Polynesians navigated the South Pacific in sailing catamarans while the Bering Sea people hunted from kayaks. Whereas a sailing craft is the most efficient vessel in the trade winds, a kayak is light and agile in surf and provides a low profile to the temperamental gales of a northern ocean.

A modern seventeen-foot expedition sea kayak weighs sixty-five pounds, light enough to lift with one arm yet seaworthy enough to cross an ocean. The secret lies in the unique intimacy between the paddler and the craft. You sit in a rowboat and stand on a yacht, but you stabilize a kayak with subtle motions of your pelvis and solar plexus. A kayak is like a long ski boot; it's a thin and tactile interface between your body and the medium you are sliding over. A yacht can bob on the waves without people aboard, but without its paddler a kayak is an unstable tube of plastic, fiberglass, or sealskin. Yacht racers talk enthusiastically about burying the leeward rail and sailing with "decks awash." In a kayak, every wave washes over the deck. If the seas are steep, waves will bury the boat altogether, and water may wash up to your armpits or even over your head. No alarm bells ring. Twist your hips to put the boat on edge, lean a paddle into the steep wall of water that threatens to engulf you, and the next moment you will be sitting on top of the wave like a child on a Ferris wheel, viewing the carnival below.

During Elizabethan times, when Europeans started exploring the Arctic, they repeatedly ignored aboriginal technology and attempted to overpower nature with heavy ships and steel tools. With uncanny regularity, brave and intelligent adventurers wandered into the ice with the wrong clothes, the wrong food, the wrong means of transportation, and the wrong attitude—and died. I would be foolish to ignore the aboriginal hunters of the Bering Sea and proceed with my modern, sporty WindRider. I needed a sea kayak.

THE previous year, Chris had been concerned about the weight of the WindRiders and the long crossings in the Kurils. But now that our passage would follow the coastline and use kayaks, she was eager to join the expedition. Fall slid into winter, and when the snow fell, Chris and I made our annual migration north to the mountains of British Columbia. In winter, our default activity is skiing. But when there was a good chance of an avalanche or when we couldn't find fresh powder, we continued our writing projects and worked together on expedition logistics. My two major sponsors, Gore-Tex and Polartec, generously extended their support for a second year. Prijon/Wildwasser donated three Kodiak sea kayaks. Lotus Designs supplied us with new anoraks and life jackets. Misha talked with his wife, she nodded a reluctant approval, and he agreed to accompany us. Martha and Lena obtained permissions.

During the ensuing months, new scientific discoveries confirmed Chatters's initial hypothesis that many of the earliest migrants to the Americas were Jomon or related East Asians. The Jomon lived on islands and were proven seafarers, and therefore it seemed reasonable that they had migrated by boat. But my passage through the Kurils had started me thinking, "Wow, that ocean is really gnarly. Maybe the whole maritime premise is wrong; maybe the Jomon walked along the coastline and crossed into Alaska by foot."

To date, unfortunately, archaeologists have found no Jomon villages between Japan and Alaska, but this lack of evidence doesn't tell us much. The sea level was lower during Kennewick Man's time than it is today. If the Jomon built camps or villages along the coastline, any remains would now be underwater. Thus the details of their migration may be buried in seafloor mud.

However, a powerful, albeit indirect, line of reasoning still supports the hypothesis that early migrants traveled by sea. About 18,000 years ago, ice age glaciers reached their southern extremity, terminating in an undulating line across the northern United States. This massive ice sheet comprised two separate glaciers. The Cordilleran Glacier covered the western mountains with a blanket of ice 4,000 feet (0.8 mile) thick. Today there is a huge valley between the Canadian Rockies and the Columbia Ranges, with undulating roads, marshes, and farmlands. But 18,000 years ago, this valley was filled to the top with ice, and meltwater flowed eastward, over the Continental Divide, toward the Atlantic Ocean. At the same time, the Laurentide Glacier inched westward from east-central Canada, moving *uphill* under incredible pressure from an ice bulge near Hudson Bay. During the long winters, heavy snowfall blanketed the glaciers and created a forbidding landscape of frigid, barren whiteness. Some of the snow melted during the summer, leaving gaping crevasses and wide, ice-choked rivers flowing across the surface of the ice. Most modern evidence indicates that the two glaciers were fused until about 11,500 years ago. This conclusion derives from analyses of sediment deposited by glaciers, and because paleontologists haven't found any animal bones dating from 21,000 to 11,500 years ago between the two huge ice sheets.

Yet anthropologists have found thirty-five villages or campsites in the Americas that are south of the glacier terminus and are more than 11,500 years old. The farthest south of these is Monte Verde, in southwestern Chile. If the glaciers were fused, then the hypothesis that Stone Age migrants walked across them to their southern terminus is impossible. These people may have been tough, but families couldn't have hiked 1,500 miles across a barren glacier with children and elders, with nothing to eat but the food they carried on their backs. At the same time, Pacific Ocean currents warmed the coastal route along Alaska and British Columbia. Geologist H. W. Josenhans estimates that the entire west coast of North America was ice free as early as 16,000 years ago and was vegetated and hospitable by 13,500 years ago. Fish and sea mammals would have been plentiful.

Scientists have found a 11,200-year-old skeleton in On Your Knees Cave on Prince of Wales Island in Southeast Alaska. Isotopic analysis of a bone indicates that this early settler ate fish and sea mammals almost exclusively. His diet and his very existence on an island assure us that he built boats, sailed along the coast, and hunted and fished on the open sea. Farther south, 11,000-year-old human bones have been found on Santa Rosa Island in Southern California. Today, Santa Rosa is thirty miles offshore from Santa Barbara, and even during the lowest sea level the island was fifteen miles from the mainland. Accordingly, the ancient inhabitants of Santa Rosa Island must have used boats.

Despite the growing wealth of anthropological data, no one yet knows exactly when the first humans migrated to the Americas, who they were, or where they came from. Scientists have found only a few camps or villages and can't trace the migration routes—at least not yet. But simple logic and limited data support the hypothesis that many of the first colonists to the New World sailed across a cold, tempestuous, foggy ocean, partially frozen in winter, crisscrossed by opposing currents, and buffeted by ferocious winds.

When I asked myself, yet again, why they made the journey, I recalled a conversation I had had many years before, while I was camped on the sea ice in the Canadian Arctic. At that time, most anthropologists supported the paradigm that the first migrants to the Americas walked across the Bering Land Bridge. Five of us were storm bound and dozing in a large canvas wall tent. One of my Inuit friends, Sam, broke the silence:

"You know, you white men are too crazy."

It seemed like a general statement of a cosmic condition, so I waited to see if he had any further explanation. After a moment, he continued. "White men say that the Inuit walked across from Siberia on the Bering Land Bridge. Isn't that right?"

I nodded. "Yeah, that's what they say."

"Well, do you guys think we're stupid?" Then he pointed his finger at me accusingly. "Do you think I'm stupid?"

He was agitated, and this conversation was turning personal. "No, I don't think you're stupid. What are you getting at, Sam?"

"Well, white men say that people lived in northeast Siberia for a long time. Do you think that we would sit on the shore, look across the straits, know that the hunting might be good over there, and then wait for ten thousand years until the ocean sank and the land bridge appeared? How stupid do you think we are? We'd build an umiak and paddle across. That's what we'd do. White men have crazy ideas sometimes."

Then he thought for a few minutes and repeated, "You white men are too crazy."

Judging from the emerging evidence, Sam had been right. His ancestors had built umiaks, kayaks, or dugout canoes and paddled across. But most important to me was the casual implication that the journey was "no big deal." Polar hunters accepted risk on the open sea as a part of life. Now, ten years after that conversation with Sam, I was determined to paddle the remaining 2,000 miles from Petropavlovsk to Alaska.

To Cape Rubicon

"We call them explorers, but I knew that look in their eyes. They were seekers and that is a different thing."

Alvah Simon, *North to the Night*

CHRIS AND I flew to Kamchatka on May 8, 2000, armed with fifteen permissions: entry visa, extended-stay visa, customs declaration for possession of extended-stay visa, visa extension of extended-stay visa, customs declaration for checked baggage, customs declaration for unaccompanied baggage (the kayaks), *pogranichniki* permission for Kamchatka, *pogranichniki* permission for Chukotka, FSB (internal police) permission, M-CH-S (rescue organization) of Kamchatka, M-CH-S of Chukotka, permission to enter Kronotsky Nature Preserve, permission to enter Beringia Nature Preserve, permission to camp near Petropavlovsk on our first night, and an amateur photography permit. Misha needed his own internal travel permissions plus a permit to own a shotgun (which he brought along for defense against bears and for hunting ducks and rabbits if we got hungry), authorization to travel with a shotgun, and a special, stamped permission (IZVSHCHENIE) to carry a shotgun in Kronotsky Nature Preserve. Martha and Lena spent 226 hours obtaining these permissions. They billed us at $5 per hour, for a total of $1,130, not counting substantial additional sums that disappeared rapidly into the black hole of Russian bureaucracy. Martha's file on our expedition was thicker than her reference book *501 Russian Verbs—Fully Conjugated in All Tenses and Alphabetically Arranged by Imperfective Infinitives*.

We took Misha to a secluded pond on a peaceful evening for a crash course in kayaking. He quickly learned how to sit in a kayak, paddle, and brace. After half an hour he paddled to shore and stood in front of Chris and me. "I am ready. We paddle to Alaska by our own hand." I didn't know what he was thinking, but I recalled an image from the previous year in the Kurils when my trimaran was breaking apart as phosphorescent-tipped waves loomed out of the night. Then I thought of Franz sliding backward in the surf and breaking his rudder. Misha was looking up at me, smiling and obviously happy. I didn't know whether I should share his enthusiasm or feel queasy and nervous over his irrational exuberance and fearlessness. I met his gaze—steady and confident.

Using simple sentences and monosyllabic words, I explained that the North Bering Sea is turbulent even during the summer months and we must race to reach Alaska before mid-September, when frequent gales would shriek across the ocean. We should expect to be scared and exhausted for the next few months.

Misha nodded. "I know this about the wild nature. I am strong."

It was too late to step back, find a new partner, or formulate a more prudent plan. This man was planning to paddle away from his wife, his two young daughters, and his job to join us on a dangerous venture over a capricious sea—with no kayaking skills and an unknown probability of success—all because he "loved the wild nature."

His enthusiasm and faith were contagious. I put my left hand on Chris's shoulder and reached out with my right to shake Misha's hand. Misha grasped my hand firmly and placed his free hand on Chris's other shoulder to complete the circle. Then I smiled. "OK, we will paddle to Alaska together."

Despite his apparent impulsiveness, Misha was a careful person, a trained scientist, a successful businessman. When I asked him where we could buy food along our route, he asked for a map and a pen. The first town north of Petropavlovsk was Ust' Kamchatsk, 350 miles away, though Misha marked the location of several lighthouses, meteorological stations, park wardens, and other small outposts along the route. People would invite us for dinner and perhaps give us a loaf of bread, but we wouldn't be able to buy food. I was amazed, once again, at the low population density of Russia's eastern coastline. We planned to pack food for three weeks, then restock at Ust' Kamchatsk. After our communication debacle during the previous summer, we carried a satellite phone. Misha packed a fishing pole for salmon. As a retired commercial fisherman, I'd never trusted a rod and reel as a serious food-gathering device, so I rigged two short gill nets.

Misha, Chris, and I launched into Petropavlovsk's oil-soaked harbor late in the afternoon of May 19. Nina, Misha's wife, cried, smearing the eyeliner that rimmed her lower eyelids. I took a few paddle strokes and turned my head to look back. Nina was waving; Misha's two bright-eyed blond daughters were clinging to their mother's waist; and all three shouted goodbye above the squeak of rusting cranes and the rumble of diesel engines. We cleared the industrial region of Petropavlovsk, paddled for a few hours, and made camp behind the last protected cape before the bay opened up to the open ocean.

Early the following morning, a dense fog hung across the ocean, suggesting, with a misty grin, an easy, uneventful trip and masking any nasty surprises that lay ahead.

When we reached the mouth of Avacha Bay and felt the ocean swell, Misha's steady paddling broke into a short, slapping motion. Chris and I had paddled for twenty years in all kinds of boats, in rivers and in the ocean, and the sea's motion spoke directly to muscle memory and long experience. Misha, on the other hand, had been in a kayak only a few hours and had never encountered turbulent water or even a gentle swell. He looked determined, though, and within a few minutes he began to balance the boat with his hips, in tune with the waves.

Three large sea stacks loomed out of the fog, simultaneously sinister and beckoning. An aged, decrepit dinghy was anchored near the rocks, and two lean, wrinkled men were jigging for cod.

"*Good morning. How's the fishing?*" Misha asked.

"*Fine. Where are you going?*"

"*Alaska.*"

"*Have a good trip.*"

They waved and laughed—a hearty, rolling laughter. Their guffaws led me to recall the maze of stupid mistakes I had spawned—and survived—over the past half century: In one vision, I was thirteen years old and rock climbing with Donny Cohen and Spiker Feen on mossy, wet, down-sloping shale with a worn cotton clothesline stolen from our neighbors' backyard. Years later, on an early morning in Providence, Rhode Island, I was stretched out over the tank of my motorcycle, throttle wide open, doing ninety miles an hour in a residential twenty-five-mile-per-hour zone, sparks flying as the muffler scraped the pavement. Then a protruding bolt on my bike caught a manhole cover, and the rear wheel rose off the ground and the bike was down, spinning wildly out of control. Thirteen years later, I was catapulting in the surf just north of Cape Horn, alone with my broken kayak. Next I was somersaulting down a mountainside in British Columbia in a roaring avalanche. And finally it dawned on me, as if it hadn't been obvious before, that my behavior hadn't matured with age. Right now I was setting out to paddle across the North Pacific Ocean with my wife, who, though brave, was on the small side for powering a boat through 2,000 miles of gale-roiled water, and with a friendly stranger who had never been in a kayak before. I had a sick feeling that the fishermen recognized my foolishness.

We turned north into the open sea. The fog lifted slightly until it hung a hundred feet above us, revealing a sand beach that rose to a flat plain. Dirty snowdrifts lurked in the shadows of the dunes, and yellowed grasses lay plastered to the earth between the snow patches. Like the grass, I felt constricted and bent by the cold, hoping for the warmth of spring. Abandoned military watchtowers stood at five-hundred-yard intervals, half shrouded in the mist. I didn't want to look at sinister reminders of Stalinist oppression and cold war paranoia; I wanted to marvel at the snow-capped volcanic peaks soaring above the coastal plain. But the ocean and the land were hidden behind the fog.

The fishermen's laughter lingered in my memory long after its sound had dissipated in the morning breeze. Yes, they were laughing at our obvious folly, yet they themselves were out here on this ocean in a leaky old rowboat. These men had survived dark decades of Soviet strangulation, half a century of bitterly cold Siberian winters, and the terrible economic depression of post-perestroika Russia. Maybe there was no rancor in their mirth, no petty criticism of our motives or sanity. Perhaps they accepted the simple fact that we were three people paddling toward Alaska, following some inexplicable dream, and their hearty guffaws were simply a little "tallyho" to speed us along our way.

As the sun brightened the morning sky, I tried to fathom the 2,000 miles of ocean that lay ahead, but the distance was too great. All I could see was a gray horizon and the empty beach with its abandoned cold war relics.

If the Jomon had left Japan simply to escape an enemy or find new hunting and fishing grounds, they would have achieved their goals by the time they reached Avacha Bay. Here, they were separated from past hostilities by the arduous passage across the Kurils. Avacha Bay is rich with food. If shelter and plenty were the limits of their imagination, why didn't they stop here? They already knew the ravages of travel; why did they set out again, this time into the Arctic?

One possibility is that the Jomon did stop here. Then, generations or centuries later, another group of adventurers set out to flee new enemies or escape a later famine. Thus the migration to the Americas could have been achieved in stages, incremental voyages, each one undertaken as a pragmatic response to an immediate need. I had started this adventure suspecting, instead, that the Jomon migration was, at least in part, a romantic quest. With the first 1,000 miles behind me and 2,000 miles ahead, I still wasn't sure whether and how this adventure might elucidate the personalities and motives of the sailors who paddled these waters between 20,000 and 9,500 years ago. I didn't know how the story would end, and I had no idea how or if I would find answers to my questions.

ON ALL previous kayak journeys, I'd paddled within the protective lee of islands or the Arctic ice pack. Even in the Kurils, Franz and I had spent most of our time in the Sea of Okhotsk, sheltered from the Pacific swells. But the Kamchatka coast is almost entirely exposed to the ocean. Surf pounded the beach with a shudder. We had 100 days and 2,000 miles to go.

I wondered how the Jomon managed surf in their heavy dugouts. They could have stayed at sea until they found a good natural harbor, but there are few protected inlets and coves along this coastline. Either the Jomon made long open-water passages or they tackled the surf. Either way, I admired their skill and courage.

I told myself that the doubts I was feeling were just first-day jitters. "The surf won't be a problem when we land," I repeated to myself. "We'll slide in on the backs of the waves, take one hit from a breaker, and accelerate smoothly onto the soft sand."

Late in the afternoon—tired, sore, and cramped—common sense demanded that we stop and camp. We grouped together to discuss our situation, and I volunteered to scout the landing. I turned toward shore, riding gentle waves. Thirty yards from the beach, however, the waves steepened abruptly. I back-paddled out to sea.

"It feels a little scary."

Chris and I had been lovers for twenty years and partners on seven major expeditions. We'd kayaked Arctic waters, climbed a previously unclimbed Himalayan peak, bicycled across the Gobi desert, and skied remote mountains in central Asia. I remembered the angle of her skis on a steep glaciated face; the dry, parched lips as we pushed our bicycles over a desert pass; and the broad smile as Inuit children gathered around the "kayak woman."

When we traveled together in the mountains, I carried more than my share of the weight, but now both of our boats were fully loaded. Chris was sixty pounds lighter than Misha or I, and she looked small in the long kayak. We had padded for eleven hours, and we all were tired. I wanted to offer warmth and support, but, now, two bad options presented themselves: We could crash-land through the surf, or we could continue along the seemingly infinite coast and try to find a better landing before dark.

"What do you think we should do?" I asked.

Misha shook his head. Chris thought for a moment and shrugged.

I looked at my watch. "It's six o'clock and we've got four hours of daylight left. We can go in here, or if we push hard and make thirty miles for the day, we'll reach the Nalichevo River. We'll be exhausted. But maybe we can paddle upriver and avoid the surf."

Misha smiled. "I am strong. I can paddle."

Chris looked at the surf, then back at me grimly. "This is only the first day of the expedition and my hands are already feeling numb, but I can go on."

I didn't say anything, but we continued northward. I remembered that during the previous winter Chris had developed a mild case of carpal tunnel syndrome, an inflammation of the medial nerve in her wrists. She was strong, physically and mentally, but a medical problem on the first day was worrying.

We paddled past the invisible landscape and ate dry bread for dinner. By 8:00 P.M. we reached a small cluster of shacks adjacent to a large river. Our boats rode gently on the swell.

Misha and Chris looked to me for a plan. "Let's inch a little closer and check out the river entrance." Chris nodded, but Misha didn't respond. His English was unpracticed, and I don't know how much he understood, but he heard the sound of collapsing surf, and that was enough. Chris and I paddled toward shore while Misha hung back, bobbing with the waves. His red boat lost color in the somber evening light, and as we paddled another fifty yards his boat disappeared periodically in the wave troughs, leaving an improbable head and shoulders riding an undulating sea.

The river looked calm and inviting, but as I left Chris and paddled closer I realized that the delta was turbulent. I peered over the backs of the steepening waves and tried to decipher a complex shear within the break zone. The breakers seemed to fold around a vortex. Were they twisting around rocks, or were they undercut by the river current? Could I find calm water near shore? What was that break to the right?

I back-paddled into deeper water and rejoined Chris. "I can't see what's going on, and this place makes me nervous. I think I'll take my chances with the beach surf south of the river mouth."

Chris nodded. "Sounds good," she said.

Chris and I paddled a hundred yards, and Misha paralleled our course farther out to sea. The surf was uniform for miles, so it didn't really matter where I landed. I lined up with one of the shacks and turned the boat toward shore.

"Guess I'll just do it."

Chris didn't say anything.

I paddled with long, steady strokes, talking to myself in the second person: "You're making too much fuss about this. You've surfed ocean waves before and thousands of river waves. Get on that puppy and ride her into the beach."

The waves steepened. Only a few yards from the beach, one wave passed beneath me, then a second. Then a wave curled into a break behind me, reaching steeply above my head. My kayak rose, and I expected the familiar surge of acceleration, but instead the bow dropped straight down and augured into the sand with an abrupt thud. The kayak teetered on its nose. I tried desperately to find purchase with my paddle, but the foaming break was too fast, and I lost control. With a sickening acceleration, the boat vaulted end over end and I landed on the beach—directly on my head. A sharp pain radiated from my neck and shot into my extremities. Instinctively I tried to set up for an Eskimo roll, a standard maneuver to right an overturned kayak, but you can't roll a kayak that isn't floating. Instead, I slid up the beach in the aerated swash, underneath the boat, grinding my face into the sand. When the wave reached its apex, I slid back down the beach, still under my boat, still riding on my cheek. Finally I was able to wiggle out of the cockpit, struggle to my feet, and drag my boat to safety. My head and face hurt, but I hadn't broken my neck. I was soaking wet, with sand embedded in my ears, nose, and belly button. But I had my paddle and all my gear. Welcome to Phase II, the North Pacific Ocean—birthplace of the kayak.

Misha paddled in without hesitation, and I marveled, "Was he foolish or brave?" A steep wave broke in front of his bow, but the swell behind it was relatively small. Misha glanced over his shoulder, then took a few rapid strokes. The foam cascaded over his head, and for a moment all I saw was a vague penumbra of red kayak beneath the white foam. A hat appeared, then a startled face, followed by an upright and stable boat. I raced into the water, grabbed his bow loop, and pulled him onto dry sand.

Chris missed her timing, as I had, and pitchpoled; she swam to shore. Her hair was plastered across her face, and a piece of seaweed hung off her ear. After we pulled her boat to safety, she reached toward me for a hug, and I held her warmly. Then someone in the shacks saw us, fired up an armored personnel carrier, and roared over the dunes to rescue us.

SOLDIERS without uniforms ushered us into their fort, which consisted of three wooden shacks shored up with driftwood logs and plastered with heavy tar paper. They piled coal into the *petchka* to dry our clothes and cook a hot meal. After dinner, Misha chatted with the men, but Chris and I were exhausted, so we crawled into cramped, sagging bunks and fell asleep.

In the morning we rumbled to the beach in the armored personnel carrier and surveyed the surf. The waves struck the shore obliquely, but the undertow ran straight back out to sea. If we floated down the beach with the undertow, the first wave would hit at a dangerous angle. I volunteered to help Chris and Misha launch, then follow by myself. We carried Chris's boat to the water's edge; she climbed in and pulled the sprayskirt tight.

"You OK, Chrissy?"

"OK," she replied nervously.

I held her bow into the waves. Chris's kayak floated on the foam, then rested back on the sand when the wave receded. We waited. Another wave broke and the foam washed up the beach, floating the kayak again. I dragged her a few feet closer to deep water. The foam slid seaward, tugging against the boat, but I fought to keep the bow aiming at the waves. Then the water receded again and her boat settled back onto the wet sand.

"I don't think I can hold your boat if we go out much farther. You ready?"

"Wait. The next two waves are big. Go on wave three . . . Wait . . . Wait . . . GO!"

I pulled the boat into the water, feeling the cold ocean press against my wet suit. Just before the next wave broke, Chris took a paddle stroke; I ducked under her upraised paddle blade and gave her stern a hefty push as she passed me. The momentum and her powerful paddling carried her over the breaking wave into deep water. Soon she was a small splash of color, appearing and disappearing in the swell.

Then it was Misha's turn. We tried the same technique but missed our timing, and a big wave caught him, capsized his boat, and spilled him into the sea.

I thought, "OK, this is the moment of truth. Will he react like Jenya? Is the expedition beginning its second day, or is it heading toward an ignoble ending?"

Misha swam to shore. We dragged his boat up the beach, rubbing shoulder against shoulder. When the boat was safe, we stood and stretched our backs.

Misha had a broad smile on his face. "It is Russian tradition to swim in every ocean that you sail in. Now we have all followed tradition. This is good. I love wild nature."

The sky, sea, and sand were dull gray. Behind us the armored vehicle, the distant shacks, and the soldiers were a mixture of gray, black, and dark green. Battered garbage from Petropavlovsk washed back and forth with the surf. Misha's orange parka and gold tooth were the only shiny objects in the whole sweep of land and sea.

I laughed. "It is a good Russian tradition. I, too, love wild nature."

We bailed out his boat, and Misha climbed in and launched successfully. Then it was my turn. Without help, I knew I couldn't keep my bow pointed into the waves and punch through the break. No way. I walked back and forth nervously. The commander walked across the wet sand.

"*Plocha* [bad]."

"*Da.*"

Then he pointed toward the river. A steep break crashed against the delta, but if I launched in the river, at least I would be floating and paddling when I hit the surf.

"*Da, reka* [river]."

The commander waved his arm, and four men carried my loaded boat to the river's edge. I settled into the cockpit, pulled the sprayskirt tight, and ferried into deep water. My soul relaxed to the familiar feel of river and boat. I eased into faster water and let the current pivot the kayak toward the sea.

Then I realized I had made a monstrous mistake. At the edge of the delta, the river current collided with the surf. In the Kurils, opposing currents had reared skyward to form standing waves, but here the two currents embraced and dove for the bottom, forming what river kayakers call a hole. A hole is roughly analogous to the bowl of a flushing toilet; all the water spirals downward. I looked at the rearing surf and the gaping hole and imagined myself back-surfing down the wave, catapulting, spilling out of my boat, attempting to swim in any direction, and drowning in the abyss. I had a quick memory of a previous incident where I had made one feckless stroke before a dangerous hole and come very close to dying. So this time I paddled for my life, digging deep, pulling hard, and concentrating on power and speed. The hole loomed closer, and I crossed into it. Then a breaking wave slammed into my chest, pummeling my body against the back deck with enough force to jar my sore neck. For a moment I was submerged in the foam with water rushing into my sinuses. Unable to see or paddle, fighting for air and clarity, I wondered, "Will I slip backward into the hole, or will my momentum carry me through?"

When my head rose above water, Misha and Chris were cheering.

I waved my paddle in salute and shouted, "To Alaska!"

WITH AN aching neck and stiff muscles, I joined my companions and headed north. The sea was calm, and a safe harbor lay an easy day's paddle away, but I knew that we would later face hundreds of miles of coastline with violent surf and no harbors. I whispered to myself, "Think one day ahead. No, just think of the present. Right now, you're safe."

The next few days slid past uneventfully as we followed the coast toward the high sea cliffs at Point Shipunsky. Time seemed to expand and contract—one hour tangible, the next fleeting and chimerical. Morning hours stretched into eternity, but afternoons sped by as if racing to reach Alaska before us. If time was playing with my brain, then my brain could play with time. We were paddling in an ocean four billion years old—more time than a human can fathom by experience or analogy. Only 150 million years ago, the towering cliffs along the shore weren't cliffs at all but layers of mud on the ocean floor. Slowly the mud compressed into soft shale. Then, as *Tyrannosaurus rex* terrorized fern-munching dinosaurs in Cretaceous swamps, powerful subterranean forces drove portions of the Pacific Ocean floor into Asia, smearing the shale onto the continent. At the same time, the intense heat and pressure of the collision cooked the shale into a metamorphic rock called argillite.

A horizontal band of white rock sliced through the pastel-pink argillite. Misha explained that the white rock was probably rich in quartz and had formed as magma or magma-heated groundwater intruded into the older argillite. After half a mile, we reached a place where tectonic forces had deformed the rock into gently arcing folds. Splotches of bright orange rock bordered the folds like colors on a Jackson Pollack painting.

Forty miles away, the 10,000-foot volcanic cone of Zhupanovskaya glistened with fresh, bright snow. Even farther in the distance, dimly visible in the slight haze, several other volcanoes floated above the coastal plain. Kamchatka is home to the densest concentration of volcanic peaks in the world, twenty-nine of which are still active. More had been active between 20,000 and 9,500 years ago when the Jomon seafarers followed this coast. Probably they saw steam rising from the lofty craters or red lava shooting into the night sky.

Gray-white bird droppings offset the pink, white, and orange rock. I guessed that the guano was a hundred years old. Patches of snow only a few months old completed the composition. Four billion years, 150 million years, 10,000 years, 100 years, and six months all merged in the metronomic beat of my paddle strokes.

We followed the cape as it veered southeast, pointing a finger across the Pacific. Cliffs disintegrated into small islands and sea stacks that reminded me of mud castles from my childhood. Fog descended across the sea, the wind went dead calm, and a gentle swell slurped against the rocks. When I paddled in close to ride the swell and its reflections, Arctic terns dive-bombed above my head, squawking like crabby dowagers. Seagulls fluttered off their nests like drifting snow, and murres dropped from the cliffs to gain airspeed, reminding me of falling rain. Amid all the commotion, a dozen stately cormorants rose on their pterodactyl-like wings.

WE CAMPED in a protected bay with no surf. Though it was the end of May, a nearby lake was frozen solid, the buds on the gnarled stone birches were only starting to swell, and snow formed a checkerboard pattern on the yellow tundra. Tracks in the snow revealed the distinct outlines of a grizzly's pads and claws; it must have passed through only hours before, after the sun had lost the strength to melt the fine detail in the tracks. Misha stooped and picked a small green shoot that looked like a wild onion. He explained that these plants, called *chirum-cha*, are rich in vitamin C and provided the early Cossack explorers with lifesaving respite from scurvy after a long, desperate winter. We picked a handful, tasted the garlic and onion flavor, and saved the rest for dinner.

If Stone Age travelers crossed the Kurils, continued this far north, and survived a Kamchatka winter, they must have welcomed the returning spring, eaten a few *chirum-cha*, and collected mussels and seagull eggs. Salmon were plentiful in the rivers, sea mammals thrived in the productive ocean, and game was abundant on the verdant steppe. Yet why, after surviving a single winter here, would they not have returned south, toward the temperate sun? Anthropologist Frederick West wrote:

> Richness of quarry could not alone account for hunters moving into such a region, nor could population pressure . . . It must be emphasized that the cold of northeast Siberia is totally unlike that of regions conventionally thought of as "northern." . . . It is not uncommon to find temperatures remaining in the range of −40°F to −50°F for protracted periods, with occasional descents to −75°F . . . Clearly Stone Age settlers and migrants had an extraordinarily high degree of adaptive sophistication together with a need not just to survive, but to succeed under the most arduous conditions ever faced by humans.

For some reason, the Arctic did not stop the relentless spread of humanity. In the 1980s, Russian archaeologist Yuri Mochanov investigated a Stone Age campsite on the Lena River in northeastern Siberia. This site, called Diring, lies at 61° north latitude, just south of the Arctic Circle. Even

during the warmest interglacial period, it was a harsh place, with hot summers and bitterly cold winters. Mochanov estimated that hominids lived in
Diring sometime between 3.2 and 1.8 million years ago, though more recent
research suggests that 1 million to 370,000 years ago is a more accurate
estimate. The Diring dwellers are assumed to be *Homo erectus* who lived
at least 250,000 years before our species, *Homo sapiens*, evolved. In 2001, a
Chinese team unearthed a 1.36 million-year-old *Homo erectus* site west of
Beijing. This site provides corroborating evidence that very ancient *erectus*
settled in regions dominated by cold, snowy winters.

Thus as soon as early hominids evolved the skeletal structure for efficient
walking, they marched out of their African homeland. Although many settled in the Middle East, a few restless adventurers moved past the warm paradise of the Mediterranean, crossed the fertile Asian steppe, and headed for
the coldest places on Earth. The wonderful enigma is that this exodus out of
Africa occurred before hominids developed sophisticated tools or language.
We can assume that they communicated through a series of grunts and cries,
and we know that they knapped crude hand axes, but these hominids were
primitive compared with the Cro-Magnon people, for example, who fashioned sophisticated tools and painted breathtaking art on cave walls.

One investigator commented that the Diring settlements in the Arctic
"imply a range of behaviors and adaptations that we have never given *Homo
erectus* credit for, from making mitts and boots, to controlling fire and having winter survival strategies." Another anthropologist noted that most
scientists believe that the Arctic must have slowed migration to the Western Hemisphere. However, in light of these new finds, he argued, "If people
were dealing with the cold that far north that long ago, then the Arctic
crossing or even a little bitty ice age . . . isn't going to stop them from getting to America."

After *erectus* colonized Asia, a new species, *Homo sapiens*, evolved in
Africa. Then, around 100,000 years ago, these modern humans followed
their earlier kin into Asia. *Homo sapiens* settled just south of the Arctic
Circle in western Siberia by 40,000 years ago, and north of the Arctic Circle by 27,000 years ago. They survived the frigid, dark winters and earned
their living by stabbing mammoths to death with pointed rocks tied to the
ends of long sticks.

As I ruminated about the past, I started a fire with dry grass. Misha unpacked the cooking pots, and Chris walked to a stream to collect water. The
warm blaze felt good against my cold fingers, and my mind drifted again.

From DNA studies, scientists estimate that there were only a few tens of thousands of *Homo sapiens* on Earth 40,000 years ago. There was ample room to settle in jungles and grasslands. The lush beaches of India and Southeast Asia were uncrowded. Anyone could fish off the coast of Greece without stepping on someone else's toes. So why would the Jomon and others move into Siberia?

British anthropologist Clive Gamble writes:

> Wildebeest could walk from the Serengeti to Stockholm. New York as well as Nairobi could have packs of hyenas. Chimpanzees have the brains and the omnivorous tastes to accomplish similar journeys . . . [These animals] are not limited by the environment but by themselves. At some point, however, some timewalkers [Stone Age wanderers] opened the desert door in Africa and moved north. The key they used was the evolution of behavior that co-opted the elements . . . and turned them into the trail of colonization.

Chimpanzees stayed in Africa eating nuts and fruit while mankind colonized every terrestrial ecosystem on the planet not covered by glaciers. And then—for better or for worse—we invented rocket ships and computers and learned how to play bridge and football. But Gamble's answer—"The key they used was the evolution of behavior . . ."—seems like a circular argument, as if he is saying, "Well, that's the way we behaved, so that's what happened."

My introduction to Kennewick Man echoed through my musings like a voice from a monk in a Tibetan monastery: "Paddle three thousand miles across the ocean wilderness, and when you come back, describe the sound of one hand clapping. Or, if you can't answer that one, tell me why people are the way they are. Tell me why *Homo erectus* migrated to Siberia or why Jomon families left their homes and sailed north, into the ice—into the unknown. And while you're at it, tell me why Jon Turk chooses to camp on these snow-covered beaches."

For the next three months I would sit in my kayak ashram repeating my silent mantra: "Paddle on the left, paddle on the right—one stroke a second, ten hours a day." Most of the summer would be infused with monotonous repetition. I'd have lots of time to think.

It was late May and I was sitting near a snowbank, warming my hands over a lively fire. Spoonbill sandpipers ran erratically along the beach, and semipalmated plovers stabbed for crustaceans in the moist sand. Out in the ocean, seals bobbed to the surface and eyed us curiously. Gulls hunted in the bay. A Steller's sea eagle lifted the feathers on its wing tips and circled slowly until it found a column of warm air rising over the beach. Then, riding the thermal, it glided inland. I added more wood to the fire and balanced the cooking pot over the blackened rocks.

THE following day we paddled toward the Zhupanova River. As we rounded the point into the estuary, we spied a seasonal fishing camp consisting of several shacks covered with tar paper and connected by wooden boardwalks. We landed a polite distance away and walked to the camp. Numerous skiffs lay upside down on the beach, and a fifty-foot fishing boat floated at anchor. A diesel generator thudded from an oily machine shed. The fishermen said they had arrived from Petropavlovsk a week earlier and planned to stay until mid-October. They offered us a *banyo*, then invited us to a dinner of crispy fried fish, tea, and bread.

The worn linoleum, lack of paint, and ubiquitous odor of grease and diesel reminded me of rough-and-tumble fishing camps in remote parts of Alaska. But in Alaska there were vegetables on the table and a bowl of fruit in the mess shack. I asked these men where they sold their fish, and they told me that Japanese buyers sailed into the bay with big freezer ships.

When I explained that I had been a commercial salmon fisherman, we talked about nets, fishing techniques, volume, and prices. Because their camp was several thousand miles closer to Japan than Alaska was, the Japanese paid fifty cents per pound more here than they paid for Alaskan fish.

I almost asked, "If you're getting good money for your fish, why don't you have fresh fruits and vegetables on the table?" But I preferred to listen and be patient. If I kept traveling all summer, the answers would come.

During dinner, the fishermen explained that the winter ice had broken up only two days before. A helicopter pilot reported dense pack ice a few miles north.

"*Sea ice?*" I asked, surprised. "*I didn't know that the ocean freezes this far south. Isn't the water along this coast too exposed and turbulent to freeze?*"

The men laughed and answered, "*This is Siberia, my friend.*"

Misha looked at me to be sure I understood.

The fishermen's mutt followed us back to camp. As we approached our tents, the dog charged off, barking and snapping, toward a grizzly bear prowling on a nearby hill. I had seen tracks in every camp since Franz and I first landed in Kamchatka the year before, but this was my first close encounter with a Russian bear. The grizzly moseyed down the hill, shoulder muscles rippling under baggy skin, seemingly oblivious to the small dog that darted in and out, snarling and nipping at its heels. Misha picked up his shotgun. He had one round of birdshot powered by a 16-gauge (relatively lightweight) powder charge. I was armed with an aerosol can of "bear-off" pepper spray, the size of a shaving cream can. I planned to wait until the bear—running at forty miles an hour—was ten feet away, then let loose with the aerosol spray. According to the manufacturer, it was absolutely guaranteed to divert a charging grizzly. Right!

In the Alaska backcountry I customarily carried a 12-gauge "streetsweeper," a powerful, short-barreled, pump-action riot gun with the ability to fire seven bear-stopping slugs in rapid succession. The mutt seemed to be our best defense right now.

The bear advanced until it was a hundred yards from our camp, settled on its haunches like a fat lady, and watched. The dog barked hysterically, darted close to the seated bruin, raced away, circled the bear, and made repeated mock charges. The bear feigned indifference. If he had been a person, the bear would have opened a newspaper and read the sports page. Twilight deepened into night, the cones in my retina lost their ability to discern color, and the dun-colored bear melded into the Kamchatka tundra. Perhaps we should have stood guard all night, but we were exhausted and needed sleep. Misha had spent fifteen field seasons in Kamchatka, and I asked him how we should respond to the bear.

"We may do sleep," he suggested.

I placed my headlamp and "bear-off" within easy reach, climbed into my sleeping bag, and closed my eyes. Chris pressed against me until we resembled two caterpillars snuggling inside their cocoons. I thought about the time twenty years ago when we had made love under the stars in the Utah desert, with sandstone spires casting moon shadows across the red earth. Then I remembered the accident five years before when we were climbing Mount Assiniboine in the Canadian Rockies. A handhold had pulled loose, and Chris had tumbled over backward, then somersaulted sickeningly down a steep snow slope toward a thousand-foot precipice. Her crampon dug in and she survivedbut with a torn anterior cruciate ligament in her knee. A few years later it was my turn for injury and near death, when I was swept off my skis by an avalanche in British Columbia. When I was in the hospital, with nine tubes draining fluids out of my body or pumping fluids in, Chris and I had held hands and vowed to be more careful.

Now, in this camp on the Kamchatka coast, I reached for the can of "bear-off" and wished for the comforting reassurance of my shotgun, with its worn wood and hefty but balanced swing weight. I tried to reason with myself: Every day when we went to sea, we faced the unseen potential of a fast-moving storm, wind against a lee shore, angry swell against sharp rocks. I told myself that this bear was no different from a storm that formed in the Pacific and moved toward us. I was here to enjoy and to be happy, not to live in fear. I tried to sleep, but I kept thinking that our flimsy nylon tent was no defense against a paw swipe that could crush a moose's skull.

The bear was still circling camp in the morning. It had chewed one of our dry bags and eaten a dozen candy bars, but it hadn't trashed our boats or destroyed essential gear. The dog had given up and gone home. Misha, Chris, and I clustered near the boats, and the bear walked down the hill steadily and purposefully. There were no trees to climb and nothing between the bruin and us but our inadequate weaponry. The bear closed in, unhurried—a hundred yards, fifty yards, twenty-five yards—with nose low and beady eyes staring straight at us.

At twenty-five yards, the bear seemed close enough to touch, its nose moist, its guard hairs silhouetted individually against the early morning light. It cocked its head like a puppy, curious and alert, then reared on its hind legs, hefting its tremendous bulk gracefully, like a dancer in baggy pajamas. Its forelegs hung limply over its chest, as a boxer holds his hands low before the opening bell. I noticed that the hair on its stomach was smoother and lighter than the hair on its legs. We all stood, frozen, dangerous predator facing dangerous predator. The bear's intense eyes stared out across its prominent nose, offset by small, almost cute ears.

A charging bear can cover twenty-five yards in about a second. Misha and I stood side by side. Chris stepped behind us.

Before the expedition, I had read a book about bear behavior. The author explained that when a bear approaches without charging, it is probing your strength and your intentions. If you make direct eye contact with the bear, you tell the grizzly, "I'm mean and aggressive and I challenge you." In response, the bear might attack. So, instead, you are supposed to look away nonchalantly and walk slowly sideways as if to say, "I know that you are there, Mr. Bear, but I'm the toughest thing on the block. I'm so tough that I can ignore you. You're a mosquito on my radar screen, so when you get tired of your silly antics, just go away."

Right! What did that author really know about bears? What did he know about Kamchatka bears? What did he know about this bear? At our previous camps on Kamchatka, we'd seen numerous fresh tracks, but not the creatures that made them. I assumed that these bears had known we were in the area and avoided us. This was an aggressive bear, clearly unafraid of people. It hadn't fled from the dog, and it had been hanging around our camp for ten hours. It had tasted our food. I wasn't sure how it was going to respond to the coy approach.

Neither was Misha. He lifted his gun, murmuring, "Maybe I shoot."

I had no moral objection, but I didn't trust his shotgun, and a wounded bear was a deadly bear. I gently pushed his barrel aside. "Wait."

As soon as I took my hand away, the barrel swung back as if on a spring. I aimed my aerosol can and looked straight at the bear, eyeball to eyeball.

Then I waved my arms and yelled, "Go away, bear!"

Chris piped up from behind in her female voice, "Go away, bear!" Misha waved his gun and yelled in Russian. The bear dropped onto all fours and sidled away as if saying, "I'm not scared of you guys but I was actually looking for food, and now if you'll stop that obnoxious racket I'll continue with my grazing."

The bear rolled a rock with its paw and licked at the exposed ants, staring intently at the snack and avoiding further eye contact. Then it slowly ambled across the tundra, nose to the ground, and disappeared over a low hill.

We breathed a collective sigh of relief and had a conference. If we paddled north, we would probably encounter pack ice; if we stayed, the bear might return. We loaded the boats and set out to sea.

AS WE paddled north, small chunks of ice bobbed in the swells. In the Canadian Arctic, ice moves in sheets, called pans, as large as a football field or even as big as a city. Near Greenland, massive glaciers break apart, or calve, to form glistening white icebergs taller than the mainmast of a nineteenth-century whaling ship. But this ice was composed of "bergy bits," chunks as small as a fist or as big as a pickup truck.

Monstrous, low-lying Canadian Arctic pans can crush a stout ship, but they pose little threat to a kayak. The pans rise only a foot or two off the water, so if they crunch together you can pull your kayak onto the ice, eat lunch, and walk casually toward your destination, dragging your boat as if it were a sled. The *Titanic* sank when it crashed into a towering Greenland berg, but a kayak is agile enough to snake around these glacial monsters. Paradoxically, the biggest danger for a kayak comes from dense concentrations of the smallest, least spectacular bergy bits. If the winds or currents compress such ice, you're stuck in a dense slush like a frozen daiquiri. You can't stand on it and you can't paddle through it, and your boat can be annihilated in seconds.

The ice became denser, the barometer dropped, cold rain fell, and the wind intensified. A storm was moving in, but the beach was a long, gently arcing coastal plain with steep surf and no protected landings. A rocky point, a good natural harbor, and a meteorological station lay a few miles north. If we reached the station, we would find a hot meal and a warm place to dry our clothes. So we did what thousands of sailors had done before us: we pushed on into obvious danger in the hope of finding shelter.

The rising wind ground the bergy bits against one another, creating crunching and tinkling sounds as an infinite number of crystals broke and dropped into the sea. As the tide ebbed, larger bergs were stranded on the beach, and the surf hurled bergy bits against the trapped ice. Landing now would be suicidal.

No one spoke of the danger, but we grimly increased our paddle speed as the ice thickened. At 4:00 P.M. we sighted the meteorological station as a speck in the distance. In another hour, the drab buildings stood out starkly on a high bluff. Smoke rose from stovepipes, and we could hear a diesel generator throbbing steadily against the wind.

But when we reached the point, I was struck by a sickening realization. We had expected an ice-free harbor; instead, the wind and currents had formed an eddy that had concentrated the ice. South of the point, rising surf was pounding into a consolidated wall of ice; north of the point, conditions were just as bad, and the coast stretched ahead another forty miles before the next harbor. The wind was increasing steadily, and waves were smashing the ice together, creating a roar that made the gale sound like a hurricane.

In the lee of the headland the water was calmer, but its surface was completely covered with bergy bits. I rammed into the consolidated mass, pushing the ice aside with my paddle, breaking a narrow channel for Misha and Chris. We inched slowly past rocky shoals toward a sandy beach. The surf was only moderate, yet car-sized bergs lifted and dropped with the swell, grinding against or falling over one another, and pounding against the beach. I paddled closer.

A steady, resolute female voice called out, "Jon, don't."

Misha added, "It is impossible. Impossible."

They were right. I back-paddled into deeper water, mashing my rudder against incoming bergs.

Misha pointed back toward the point. "Maybe there."

At first I thought he was nuts; all I could see was ice and rock. But then I realized that Misha, the neophyte, was thinking like a real kayaker. A kayak doesn't need a broad beach; all it needs is a tiny channel nestled between the bergs and the convoluted cliffs. The grinding ice generated a cacophony—dull bass rumbles mixed with the tintinnabulation of small crystals plopping into the sea.

A truck-sized berg floated toward the rocks and, like a billiard ball, bashed a smaller berg out of the way, leaving a two-foot-wide channel to shore. The larger berg ricocheted backward and impaled itself against a jagged rock. The next swell jostled the berg so it teetered like a boulder about to roll off a cliff. As soon as it broke loose, it would roll inward and close the channel. There was no time for discussion.

"I'm going in!"

I took a few strokes. A low ice pan between me and the shore seemed to rise and fall on the swell, but that was an illusion; the ice was beached, and I was riding on the wave. When my kayak settled into the trough, I stared at a three-foot ice cliff that blocked my passage to safety. But when a wave rose, its crest washed across the ice. If I could paddle across the crest at the perfect moment, I would reach safety. I paddled within a boat length of the ice, then back-paddled to remain stationary. If I landed at the wrong time, I would hit the pan, drift sideways, and probably capsize against the undercut ice. How much time did I need to accelerate the heavy boat? My kayak slid to the bottom of a swell while waves slapped against the glistening ice. I chose my moment and dug my paddle, hard and fast.

As I had planned, I closed the distance to shore just as the next swell lifted my kayak. I slid onto the ice, jumped out, pulled the kayak to safety, and raced back to the ice edge.

"NOW, NOW, NOW, CHRISSY! NOW!"

Chris raced into the slot, and her boat rose with the swell. I grabbed her bow and yanked her to safety.

A large berg floated off the shoal and drifted with the undertow. In seconds, it would float back in and close the channel.

"MISHA, MISHA, MISHA! PADDLE! PADDLE! PADDLE!"

A wave lifted Misha's boat and the berg at the same time. The berg rose, tilted, and struck Misha a glancing blow to the head. He missed a paddle stroke, and his kayak rotated into the undercut. I leaped into the waist-deep water, grabbed the kayak, and lifted it with all my strength. The big berg spun and closed the channel as I dragged Misha over the stationary ice to shore.

Misha sat in his cockpit with a scared look on his face. Then he broke into a broad grin.

"I am happy. I am so happy. I am so happy to be alive!"

A TWO-hundred-foot cliff loomed above us, and our small, rocky beach would be underwater at high tide. We lifted the boats onto a tall boulder above the tide line and surveyed the wet precipice. Rainwater dripped from Misha's hat, rolled down his nose and cheeks, collected on his chin, and fell to the earth. He looked up the cliff and pronounced, "Impossible."

Meanwhile, Chris was picking her way along the beach, scrambling over boulders. Her soft voice rose above the wind and the grinding ice.

"There's a gully over here. We can make it up."

We angled up a sloping plane of rock, kicked steps in the soft mud, and gained the next ledge. Grasping grass clumps as handholds, we ascended to the top of the cliff. The ramshackle cluster of tar-papered buildings looked dark and small in the evening light and the falling rain. Coal dust and rusting machinery lay half hidden under the flattened yellow grasses that gave no indication of spring growth. A rotund man with a white beard was dismantling a roofless shed. We stopped and silently watched him peel a board from the rotting structure and break it into firewood with a huge steel-handled ax that looked like a beheading tool for a medieval executioner. Then he tossed the pieces of wood into a wheelbarrow made of a leaky washtub bolted to two tiny solid rubber wheels, with bent and rusting pipe as handles.

The man looked up and saw us standing at the edge of the cliff in our bright orange and yellow parkas. He raced forward, grabbed my hand, and shook it with excessive enthusiasm while speaking to me in rapid Russian.

Misha laughed and translated, "Who are you? What are you? You look like you are the first amphibian rising out of the sea."

The man waited till Misha finished, then got so excited that his voice squeaked like that of a six year old. Because he was repeating himself, I understood his Russian the second time. "*Yes, amphibians rising out of the sea. Yes, you came from the bottom of the ocean. Who are you? Where did you come from?*"

Before Misha could answer, a tall, gaunt man stepped out of a house and walked toward us on a narrow, muddy path. He had sunken cheeks and thick glasses and wore tattered, baggy clothes held together with thread and string. Misha explained our expedition while the old man, Boris, kept squeaking, "*No, they are not Americans, they are amphibians. And one is a woman. Look, she is a woman.*" And then he shook my hand over and over again while repeating the Russian word for amphibian, in case I hadn't understood the joke. The gaunt man, named Andre, ushered us through an unheated veranda, filled with discarded machinery and old batteries, into his warm house.

We sat on rickety stools by a pine table under a single bare lightbulb hanging on a frayed wire. He piled coal into the *petchka*, boiled water, and bustled around to wash the week-old dirty dishes and remove greasy engine parts from the kitchen table. When the water was hot, he served tea with thick slices of stale bread, and rushed off. He returned a few minutes later with a gallon of fresh, clear vodka, still warm from the still.

Andre prepared the best food in his larder: canned peas, homemade pickles from last year's garden, *chirum-cha*, macaroni with canned meat, and strong black tea. And, of course, the vodka.

"*I am happy to welcome you.*"

He held his right hand over his heart, lifted his vodka glass with his left, and drained it.

I sensed that we were just starting with the toasts, so I took a small sip.

"*You are travelers, like the great Cossacks who settled this beautiful land. My land.*"

And we drank to that.

"*My grandparents were Cossack pioneers. We must drink to my ancestors, to the Cossacks.*"

We drank.

"*Now we must drink to my grandmother. She homesteaded on the Zhupanova*

River, where you camped last night. She is dead now, but she was a powerful woman."

For his grandmother, I was not allowed a polite sip. Andre ordered me to empty my glass. The vodka tasted smooth for home brew.

Andre pushed back his chair, adroitly jumped to his feet, and disappeared into his bedroom. He returned carrying a foot-long knife in a beautiful sealskin sheath. He held it in both hands and presented it to me, bowing slightly like a medieval page.

"My grandmother wants you to have this knife. I made it myself out of an old saw blade."

I accepted it with due solemnity, complimented his workmanship, and drank another toast.

"But," and he raised one finger in the air, *"it is not a gift; it is a promise. My grandmother always wanted to sail to Russian America, the place you call Alaska. You are traveling to Russian America, like my grandmother wanted to. You must make this journey for her. And when you arrive in Russian America, you must light a candle in a church, in her name. Her name is Evdocia. You must light a candle for Evdocia."* He stood unsteadily, held his hand over his heart, and ordered me, *"You must promise."*

I stood, held my hand over my heart, and promised.

We drank another healthy shot of vodka.

"But not a Catholic Church. You must promise this too."

I promised again. Then I tried to coax stories of Evdocia's life from Andre, but the vodka was winning and all he could do was toast Russian America, his grandmother, Cossacks, and travelers like us.

The Cossacks were analogous to American pioneers. In the seventeenth century, when the Puritans landed at Plymouth Rock, Cossacks were pushing thousands of miles across the frigid taiga, trapping fox, ermine, beaver, wolf, wolverine, and sable. According to one modern historian, "A few good fox pelts, alone, could buy 50 acres of land, a decent cabin, five horses, ten head of cattle, and twenty sheep."

Fox pelts were valuable, but sable was the currency for gifts and bribes within the Russian aristocracy. This small, arboreal weasel, twenty inches long and weighing four pounds, has a dense, silky undercoat with iridescent guard hairs that form the finest furs in the world. By the middle of the seventeenth century, the sable trade accounted for 10 percent of Russia's total gross national product. When the Russians were unwilling to send troops to support a crusade against the Turks, they donated 342,883 sable skins instead.

The Cossacks couldn't trap enough sables by themselves, so they extracted a fur tax, or *yasak*, from the aboriginal tribes. Typically, when Russian soldiers and settlers entered an aboriginal village, they imprisoned the elders in a squalid, hastily built stockade. The ransom, of course, was sable. If the local people refused or if they delivered poor-quality furs, the Russians killed the elders, burned the settlements, confiscated their reindeer, raped the women, and abducted the children.

This brutality was condoned because, in European eyes, the great hunter-gatherer nations of Siberia were barbarous savages. Even Krasheninnikov, the careful scientist, looked on the Kamchatka Koryaks with a curious disdain:

> They have extraordinary notions of Gods, of sins, and good actions. Their chief happiness consists in idleness and satisfying their natural lusts and appetites; these incline them towards singing, dancing, and relating love stories. Their greatest unhappiness or trouble is the want of these amusements; they shun this by all methods, even at the hazard of their lives, for they think it more eligible to die than to lead a life that is disagreeable to them . . . They have no notion of riches, fame, or honor; therefore covetousness, ambition, and pride are unknown among them.
>
> Although their manner of living be most nasty, and their actions be most stupid, they think themselves the happiest people in the world, and look upon the Russians who are settled among them with contempt.

The Koryak approach didn't sound so bad to me.

THE FOLLOWING morning we woke to howling wind and blowing snow. I sat up in my sleeping bag and wrote in my journal:

> We could survive the storm in a tent, but this house is fine. Not warm, because there's no fire in the *petchka*, not clean, charming, neat, or cobweb-free, but a solid concrete barrier against the gale.
>
> We need the rest. I try to concentrate on one muscle, tendon, or skin cell as it heals, then shout a hearty "hooray" as it becomes whole again.

Chris, too, was feeling the need for rest. Over the past week, the repetition and strain of paddling had aggravated her carpal tunnel syndrome to the point of constant pain. Even when she was sleeping, her hands would go numb and wake her with a tingly feeling. She tried taking anti-inflammatories, but they didn't work, and no other solutions presented themselves.

At midmorning we ventured outside. Snow filled the air and covered the landscape, masking the garbage and rusted machinery with a veneer of sparkling crystals. The wind had whipped the sea into whitecaps and multiple lines of surf. Bergy bits rode the waves, making it impossible to distinguish between spume and ice. Larger bergs accumulated on the beach and rolled in the swash with a deep-throated rumble. A kayaker would die out there within minutes. But the storm was also our friend, because it was breaking the bergs into splinters and washing them out to sea.

The ice had stopped us, but at the same time it opened a window of understanding. Between 10,000 and 18,000 years ago, the Pleistocene glaciers were receding and the Earth's temperature oscillated frequently and dramatically. For a few hundred years, the planet was abnormally warm and the Arctic seas were relatively balmy. Then the ice age cold returned with precipitous speed, and the northern seas froze solid. During those cold snaps, terrestrial game moved south, salmon streams froze solid, and sea mammals migrated to ice-free water. Even the heartiest travelers would die under such conditions. After the cold, the warm cycle repeated itself. If the Jomon migrants started their journey during a warm spell, they could have inched north incrementally, each generation moving a river valley or two farther along. But once they reached the southern edge of the Arctic, maybe at this very place or maybe a few hundred miles north, they would have needed to set caution aside and dash across the Arctic to reach Alaska, then turn south down the British Columbia coast. This mad dash wasn't the fingerprint of a practical, incremental migration. The Siberian Arctic, slowly emerging from the unimaginable cold of the ice age, was just too harsh and unpredictable. I was becoming more and more convinced that Kennewick Man or his ancestors moved quickly across unknown lands, driven by dreams infused, perhaps, with shamanism or even a touch of madness.

I walked back inside, picked up Andre's knife, and slipped it out of its sealskin sheath. Andre had carefully polished the old saw blade until it was shiny, but a few residual rust pits remained. This knife honored Evdocia's dream; now it represented my dream—and it was rapidly absorbing the weight of the Jomon dream as well. In this harshest of lands, I was finding a great concentration of dreams. I felt an odd responsibility to complete the old woman's interrupted journey.

We rested and waited while Andre finished his vodka and the storm blew itself out. On the morning of May 29, two days after our tempestuous landing, we launched into a calm, ice-free sea. During my passage through the Kurils, I had felt that Kennewick Man and his Jomon ancestors were helping guide my boat through incessant fogs. They had waited with me through the snowy winter and, when spring came, they paddled alongside our kayaks in their crude dugout. Now a new figure joined our entourage: Andre's grandmother. I saw Evdocia not as a grandmother darning socks by the fire but as a strong, young woman, statuesque, square shouldered, dressed in furs and canvas. She smiled politely at the Stone Age voyagers as she stepped into their dream canoe, picked up a paddle, and continued her interrupted voyage to Russian America.

We followed the coast into Kronotsky Zapavednick, the oldest nature preserve in the world. Alarmed by the prospect of a depleting sable population, Peter the Great set this land aside in 1705, centuries before most politicians thought about environmental issues. This noble concept was maintained through the czars, Stalin's era, the expansion of the Soviet Empire, and the economic turmoil that had followed the end of the cold war. We arrived here after paddling seventeen miles from the meteorological station to the Shumna River, where Andre had told us we would find a park warden's cabin that was generally uninhabited.

We landed through violent surf, and once again I pitchpoled and capsized, although Chris and Misha had clean runs to the beach. As we pulled our boats above the high tide line, a large orange helicopter landed, disturbing the peace with its high-pitched mechanical urgency. A man and a woman in brightly colored parkas stepped out, climbed gingerly down the bent ladder, and looked about warily, clutching their hats against the rotor wash. They appeared to be in their mid-fifties, and I guessed that they were American or European ecotourists. In another few moments a young woman appeared wearing a Russian imitation of an expensive parka. Finally a short, barrel-chested, white-haired man jumped to the ground, eschewing the steps. He was wearing plain clothes the color of the land, and his soft smile and weather-beaten face offset a phalanx of gold-capped front teeth. The man brushed past the others, approached us, and introduced himself as Vitali. Then he pointed to me but asked Misha, "*Why is he so wet?*"

Misha explained that I had *overkeeled* (capsized) in the surf. Vitali chuckled with a Santa Claus–worthy "Ho, Ho, Ho," then remarked, "*Tak* [so]*! Everyone overkeels now and then as they pass through life.*"

Vitali settled his tourists in the cleanest room of the warden's cabin and helped us install a wood-burning stove in a shedlike addition to the main house. Then the three of us, Vitali, the two tourists (from San Francisco), and a young female interpreter from Petropavlovsk convened for late afternoon tea. Vitali had been a low-level gangster in his younger years but had spent the past thirty years in the wilderness, studying grizzly bears. Although he had no university training, he had become an internationally recognized expert on grizzly behavior. I had learned about Vitali—indirectly—through a photograph he had taken. The foyer in Martha's house was dominated by his six-foot-high black-and-white photograph of an old grizzly walking through crusty spring snow, nose down and shoulders hunched, alert for grubs and roots. But the photograph wouldn't have been complete without the gnarled, weather-beaten birch with its leafless branches casting dark shadows. This wasn't a supple Robert Frost "swinging birches" tree but a twisted survivor of Kamchatka gales, and therefore a perfect foil for the bear. And now that I had met Vitali, I realized that the photograph was a spiritual self-portrait of the photographer, hardened and aged by this harsh land yet anticipating the return of another summer.

The following morning we woke to half a foot of new snow and a rising wind. Over breakfast, Misha told the story of our bear encounter at Zhupanova. Then I asked, "*How should we face a bear? Should we make eye contact or turn away? If we meet another bear, should we act aggressive or feign passive indifference?*"

Vitali responded, "*Every bear has its own personality and its own position in the hierarchy of bear society. Your response must factor in its age, sex, and social status. A strong dominant male in his prime is dedicated to maintaining his position on top of the pecking order. Don't challenge such a bear unless you're prepared to fight. On the other hand, a bear on the lower rungs of the social ladder is accustomed to backing down and will retreat if you confront it aggressively.*"

I explained that I couldn't categorize a bear's social status in an eye-blink. Vitali laughed with a playful twinkle. "*Learn fast before a bear eats you.*"

Vitali reached into a briefcase and pulled out a huge stack of black-and-white prints showing close-ups of happy, grumpy, and playful bears—eating, sitting, scratching, and rolling in the grass. He had taken all of these from twenty to thirty yards away with a 50 mm lens. I remarked that he must be a friend to the bears in this area. He put his hand on my shoulder. "*No. Bears have no friends. They are solitary creatures and come together only to mate. Bears are like me. They live alone.*"

Vitali explained that five years before there had been 25,000 bears on Kamchatka. But the average foreign bear hunter spends $12,000 in two weeks—a strong incentive for locals to guide tourists on bear hunts whether they have permits or not. As a result of hunting pressure, the population has been reduced to 10,000. I did the arithmetic out loud: 15,000 times $12,000 equals $180 million into an impoverished economy. "*Da,*" he said, nodding, "*I know. And the government pays me fifty dollars a month to monitor bear populations and to suggest sustainable harvest levels. But they listen to money, not to me.*"

Like a force of nature, Vitali seemed impervious to mortal harm. None of us could have guessed, sipping our tea, that in three short years he would crawl into a grizzly den to photograph a hibernating bear, and the waking bear would maul him to death.

E WAITED out the storm for two days, then went to sea again on June 1. We saw seven bears on June 3 and ten more the next day. Most of the time we were in the boats and the bears were rambling along the beach at low tide, munching seaweed and fishing in tide pools for starfish, crustaceans, or whatever they could find. I imagined that primitive people lived much like these bears. Anthropologists report that large calorie bonanzas from a successful seal or whale hunt were relatively rare, and people survived mostly by foraging.

Despite the fact that bears are generally shy and avoided our camps, I remembered a passage from Krasheninnikov: "The bears of Kamchatka are neither large nor fierce, and never fall upon people, unless they find them asleep; and then they seldom kill any one outright, but most commonly tear the scalp from the back of the head; and, when fiercer than ordinary, tear off some of the fleshy parts, but never eat the whole person."

Every book on safe camping practices recommends that you hoist your food into a tree or cache it far from camp at night, but "safe camping" practices didn't seem to apply here. We couldn't hang our food in trees because we were on the edge of the arctic tundra, and the trees were scarce in some places and nonexistent in others. Another alternative was to store our food in the boats, but if a bear destroyed a boat, one of us would have a long walk back to civilization.

After much discussion, we decided to leave our food in the kayaks and tie the boats directly to our tents. In theory, this nonconventional strategy protected us and our kayaks. If a nocturnal marauding bear molested the boats, it would surely jiggle the tents' guy lines. Alternatively, if the bear tried to attack us, perhaps it would be clumsy enough to stumble over the boats and also jiggle the guy lines. In either case, we would wake up and launch a counterattack with the inadequate shotgun and the untested "bear-off." The theory, though, was full of holes. Maybe a bear would step care-fully over the kayaks, then slash open our tent and eat us, or maybe it would just "tear off some of the fleshy parts."

Expeditions are about vulnerability, but they should also be about having fun. As a result, I've developed a defensive fatalism. I take all reasonable precautions, then try to relax. If I get crunched, so be it, but I'm not going to ruin a good time with constant fear.

Once we became accustomed to living with these great beasts, my jour-nal entries described bear signs and sightings as another component of the landscape. For example:

> It's June 4th and there is heavy snow down to the beach. We saw griz tracks of a mom and two cubs that were a few days old and fresher tracks of a large bear. A few grasses are greening near the ground on sunny hillsides, but the buds on the bushes and stunted trees aren't even swollen yet. I feel the harsh-ness of this place and this harshness has beauty. It's not necessarily the beauty of a picture, but the beauty of a feeling. And for whatever reason, people for all times have understood this feeling and have wandered into places like this.

We were depleting our food and the salmon were starting to move to-ward their spawning streams, so we set our nets whenever possible. I awoke at four in the morning of June 5, groggy, damp, and still hungry after an inadequate dinner the night before. My first thought was, "I hope we have fish in the net." I crawled out of the tent, looked over the ocean, and saw the net floats riding low in the water. We had our catch.

As I walked over the frozen summer snow, I noticed an unusual con-centration of seagulls soaring overhead. Then I realized that the beach was covered with a silvery carpet of sardines. Still half asleep, I marveled at the fish as if in a daydream. Some were still flapping in death throes, shining iri-descent rainbows in the first rays of daybreak. Others had thrashed until they were covered with sand, then collapsed into grimy, inert, cigar-shaped blobs. As I walked onto the beach, their bodies squished and oozed under my feet. As my mind cleared, I realized that the fish must have spawned during the night and washed onto the beach after laying their eggs. I thought, "Wow, what an upheaval of nature—the cycle of life—living, pro-creating, and dying. And now these fish are a protein bonanza for . . ." Then I woke up and finished the thought. "The cycle doesn't stop. In death there is life. Some animal is going to eat these fish. Seagulls, yes, and what else?"

I surveyed the landscape and saw two bears feeding along the beach.

"Think like Vitali would think!"

They were young bears, probably twins surviving their first year away from their mother. They were teenagers, so I decided to act like an adult and tell them what to do.

"Go away, bears!"

They interrupted their feeding and rose on their hind feet to catch my smell. As I sidled slowly toward the tent to grab my trusty can of "bear-off" the bears dropped back down onto all four feet.

"Chris, Misha! Wake up! Bears in camp!"

One bear retreated a few steps while the other gulped another mouthful of fish. Then they lumbered directly toward the tents. I called another warning, and Chris's head popped out through the door. I heard her high-pitched command, "Go away, bear!" Within moments Misha was standing in his underwear, waving his shotgun and yelling in Russian.

The bears ran away.

THE AINU believed that there were two circles of existence: the human world (*Ainu mosir*) and the spiritual world (*kamuy mosir*). Gods sent food and other gifts to the people; therefore, people must send gifts back to the gods. Grizzly bears, the most powerful terrestrial predator in the *Ainu mosir*, were welcomed as honored gods and were the preferred conduit for this gift exchange. Every spring, young Ainu hunters killed a female bear and kidnapped her cub. They raised the cub in captivity and loved it. When the bear was nearly full grown, elders began the *iyomante*, or bear-sending ceremony. After people offered prayers to the bear spirit, they led the bear around the village on a leash. Men danced around the bear and shot blunt ceremonial arrows at it. Then they strangled the bear between two logs. When the bear was dead, they skinned it and invited its spirit into a ceremonial house. There, an old woman told stories of heroic hunts and battles. Before the climax of the final episode, the woman abruptly ended her tale with a prayer to hasten the bear to the *kamuy mosir*, followed by an invitation asking the bear spirit to return next year to hear the ending. Thus the cycle of life would continue. The gods had sent this bear to the people, and the people had sent it back to the spirit world with the hope that it would return again.

The native Koryak and Itlemen of Kamchatka didn't have an equivalent ceremony, but they hunted bears for food. Krasheninnikov describes several ingenious snares, deadfalls, and traps. In addition, the bravest hunters met bears in hand-to-hand combat. A hunter held a short stiletto, pointed at both ends, in his right hand. He tied a three-foot leather thong to the stiletto and secured the thong around his wrist. He held a longer knife in his left hand. Thus armed, he charged a fifteen-hundred-pound, mature grizzly. As the man approached, the bear would rise on its hind legs and growl. Then, in Krasheninnikov's words, "The hunter, with great resolution and address, thrusts his hand into the bear's throat; placing there the stiletto, not only prevents the bear from shutting his mouth, but also gives him such exquisite pain that the bear can make no further resistance."

Once the bear was impaled, the hunter paraded it around by the leather thong and thus advertised his bravery to all his pals and potential girlfriends. Then the young man killed the bear with the knife in his left hand.

Krasheninnikov continued, saying, "The people look upon it as an affair of such honor to kill a bear in this manner, that whoever has this honor, is obliged to feast his neighbors; at which entertainment the bear's flesh is the principal dish; and as a trophy, the bones of the head and thighs are hung round about their huts."

Hunting grizzly bears in this manner is not a pragmatic way to procure food. It's a whole lot safer to pick minnows and kelp out of a tide pool, net salmon, or shoot caribou with a bow and arrow. No, killing a bear with a knife and a stiletto is clearly a display of courage—or foolhardiness. No other species besides ours hunts in a manner that exposes the hunter to maximum danger. No other species has deified and honored its most formidable adversaries. But then, no other species has colonized the globe.

I thought back to that day in the Kurils, a year before, when I had speculated that each person is a unique amalgam of three character traits: romantic, loco, and pragmatist. We think of hunting as a pragmatic activity—a means of putting food on the table. Yet the Ainu, Itlemen, and Koryak infused their bear hunting with romantic madness.

In the great sweep of humanity through time, from the Stone Age to the present, most people have behaved soberly, with a steady efficiency that brings reward more often than failure. Yet, in all times, there is abundant, even ubiquitous evidence of the romantic and the loco, and it seems clear to me that *Homo sapiens'* spectacular rise is based on this complex blend of diverse personality traits.

We pulled in our net and cooked a fresh fish for breakfast, constantly scanning the tundra in case the bears should return. Living among these wild and dangerous creatures, I felt a kinship with the aboriginal hunters of Kamchatka. Chris, Misha, and I weren't behaving any more pragmatically than they had. We could have been home earning money and growing vegetable gardens without worrying that a bear might eat us. But, then again, visions and seeking have thrived through two million years of evolution. Adventurers weren't some genetic experiment that failed, not a twig on the evolutionary bush that was destined to wither into oblivion. Although many adventurers died in the seeking, others led their people across the globe.

AMONG his belongings, Misha carried a torn, wrinkled plastic bag of herbs, which he called "my grasses." As near as I could understand, he had developed an ulcer over the past year and had visited an herbalist/healer. This woman had given him the herbs but had also told him that the root of his problem was intense pressure at work. She explained that her remedy would be effective only if he combined the herbs with deep mental relaxation. The previous winter, when Misha was contemplating joining us, his wife, Nina, had disapproved. But when his ulcer became more painful, he went to Nina one day and said simply, "I know that you don't want me to paddle to Alaska. But if I continue this life, if I only make papers every day, I will die young. If we are destined to share old age together—then I must paddle to Alaska."

Now Misha was with us, sharing this turbulent ocean and the peaceful meals around our campfires. One evening, as he was carefully brewing his grasses into tea, he told me that he probably didn't need the medicine anymore. "You have saved my life, Jon and Chris. This ocean has made me alive one more time."

"Then we are friends, forever," I replied.

We sat in silence, watching the flames lick the edges of the blackened teapot. Chris laughed and remarked, "Not everyone would find this journey—with surf, ice, grizzly bears, and storms—to be so relaxing. Some people would develop an ulcer out here, facing danger every day."

Misha thought about that and replied, "We are people who need the wild nature."

After a few more moments, he continued, "For me, for we, the wild nature is like a—I don't know the word in English. In Russian we say *narcotica.*"

"Yes," I replied. "We have the same word in English."

"So you know this word? Like a strong drug, you know? Much stronger than these grasses."

"Yes, I understand the word and what you are saying."

Misha continued. "Maybe sometimes it is not so good that we have this *narcotica* inside us. I leave Nina and the girls home alone all summer."

"I don't think that it is necessarily a matter of good or bad."

"Yes, Jon, this is true. Is it not sometimes very interesting? If I do not have the wild nature, my stomach cries out to me. My stomach eats himself. My stomach makes holes in himself, crying out for the wild nature."

Chris spoke softly, "Then why have most people built cities throughout history?"

Misha answered, "You speak that about most people. But those Jomon people, those people from Japan, they were not most people. Maybe their stomachs started to eat them and cry out that they must paddle to Alaska."

MISHA WAS a dreamer, but he was also the most careful man I have ever known. He was a tuned athlete who moved deliberately and made few mistakes. As the days passed, we honed our routine into an efficient sequence that minimized energy expenditure and risk.

One of the biggest technical problems was the steep, shore-break surf. After several violent pitchpoles, I developed a less painful landing technique: Instead of riding a wave nose first, I approached obliquely to the breakers. Just before a wave was about to crunch me, I spun the boat sideways, reached into the roiling mass with my paddle, and waited for the water to cascade over my head. Then, half buried in the foam and using my paddle as a stabilizing brace, I bounced onto the shore.

Launchings were more difficult. I always helped Misha and Chris by pushing their boats through the first line of breakers. Then, alone on the beach, I dragged my boat to the surf zone and made myself comfortable while the boat rested firmly on wet sand. Next, I wedged my paddle between my chin and my life jacket and scooted down the beach by pushing with my arms, until the boat floated on an incoming wave. At this point, the water was too shallow and aerated to use my paddle, so I continued pushing furiously with my hands. Usually, the outgoing wave raced back to sea ahead of me, leaving me stranded on the sand. I would sit there, vulnerable, watching the waves rear, break, and roll toward me. If I was lucky, the next wave would break close enough to float my kayak on six inches of water. Then I would grab my paddle and turn into the waves, hoping to blast through the breakers with a few frantic paddle strokes. Unfortunately, most of the time I floated out to sea on shallow foam, bouncing on the sand and desperately trying to keep the bow pointed into the break. The swash would wash me sideways and the next breaking wave would grab me like a football and hurl me back onto the beach, sometimes right side up, sometimes upside down, and sometimes half out of my boat. Then I would reorganize and try again. On average I reached deep water on the third try. By this time I was cold and wet. I would look around me at the sea and the sky, at my good friends bobbing gently in the waves, and exhale slowly to discharge the adrenaline and the fear. Then, the only way to stay warm was to start paddling—and not stop until dinnertime.

As we paddled slowly toward Cape Kronotsky, we noticed abundant waterfalls along the beaches. Every few hundred yards, a white cascade roared over colorful metamorphic rocks. Campsites were elusive, because cliffs bound the coastline and even the larger rivers dropped precipitously into the sea.

One afternoon I was thinking about our evening camp and wondering why there were so few river valleys and beaches along this stretch of coast. Then I realized that I had stumbled into a basic geology lesson. Given time, rivers and even small creeks erode rock and carve valleys, but this landscape was very young: tectonic forces were lifting the land faster than the rivers were cutting downward. As a result, the rivers remained perched above the sea.

Since leaving Japan I had been following the boundary between the Pacific Ocean Plate and the Eurasian Plate. Along this sinuous line, the floor of the Pacific Ocean is subducting into the hot bowels of the Earth, forming a trench six miles deep. If a person could magically walk along the seafloor south of Cape Kronotsky, he or she might climb the trench wall, a vertical rise greater than the height of Mount Everest. The descending ocean plate was churning the hot, soft subterranean rock to form the abundant volcanoes that dot the Kurils and the southern Kamchatka Peninsula.

Cape Kronotsky marks the place where the plate boundary veers eastward toward the Aleutians. We paddled calmly across the giant rift in the Earth, leaving the zone of active volcanoes behind us. Ahead lay the older rocks of continental Asia.

In addition to this geological change, we were entering the Bering Sea.

To the north, colliding currents and weather systems would form steep waves and sudden gales. I balanced my paddle gently in my hand, feeling its familiar contours; this was my motor and my ballast, the friend who would propel me into the Arctic.

When aboriginal voyagers reached Cape Kronotsky, they could have continued along the coast or headed east to follow the Aleutian Islands. The archaeological record is so scant that scientists can only guess at their route. I had assumed that these voyagers must have hugged the coast for several reasons: Even during the lowest sea level during the ice ages, the closest islands to the west lay invisible over the horizon. In addition, the Aleutian passage involves bigger waves, longer crossings, dangerous current shears, and more frequent storms. But after sailing and paddling close to 1,500 miles, I wasn't so sure. On the one hand, I had gained a profound respect for the violence and capriciousness of this ocean, which argued that the aboriginal mariners in their primitive boats followed the safer coastal route. On the other hand, I had gained an equal or even greater respect for the Stone Age travelers who had preceded us. If they could paddle a hollow log through the shear waves in the Kurils, if they could land and launch through violent surf in a boat that was as much as a hundred times heavier than my plastic kayak, then it seemed to me that they could do anything—including paddling into the open ocean to discover the Aleutian Islands.

Kayak historian Ken Brower wrote, "While the Eskimos liked to stay within sight of land, Aleuts kayaked over the horizon regularly, and on purpose. They went as far as the Kamchatka Peninsula, Japan, San Francisco and Baja California."

Dr. Alex Hrdlicka, a Smithsonian archaeologist, noted that Aleut and Inca mummies were buried with a feather thrust through the left earlobe. Such an oddly similar religious practice implies contact between the two widely disparate peoples. And if the Aleuts communicated with the Peruvians, how did they get there? By boat, I assume.

Thus all evidence indicates that the Jomon, the Aleuts, and other aboriginal inhabitants of this wild coastline were extremely competent mariners. Yet there is no compelling argument to outline the exact route of the first migrants to North America. We simply don't know how they got there. But I knew that Misha, Chris, and I would probably die if we set out across the open sea toward the Aleutians, so we continued northward, along the coast.

UST' Kamchatsk is the largest city in Kamchatka after Petropavlovsk and its suburbs. Ust' is located at the mouth of the Kamchatka River, the largest river on the peninsula and one of the richest salmon spawning rivers in the world. The Kamchatka River empties into the sea through a small slit in a ten-mile-long sandbar. At its mouth the river collides with ocean swell to create a dangerous break.

To avoid this break, we planned to camp ten miles southwest of Ust', drag our boats across the sandbar, and paddle inside the protected estuary. The wind was strong, and we landed through heavy surf. The following morning, as we portaged across the sand dunes to the estuary, a gentle headwind wafted out of the north, rustling the dune grasses. We slid our kayaks into a narrow slough, fifty yards wide, and paddled with the ease of Sunday picnickers on a bird-watching mission. A cuckoo called out and another answered. I had never heard these birds before, but they sounded for all the world like a Swiss clock, except that the call rose and fell in the vast tundra landscape rather than echoing in a small room. Two snow geese swam nervously away, then took flight amid a loud honking. Small wavelets slapped against our hulls, but we experienced no surf, no swell, and no fear of being blown out to sea.

The lines on Chris's weather-beaten face were relaxed for the first time on this expedition, and her eyes darted across the landscape. "Jon, I like this. I don't need the danger. I don't need the open ocean. It's hard to be hit by a big wave first thing in the morning and then stay soaked all day. My wrists hurt all the time and I'm sure that the carpal tunnel is aggravated by paddling into ocean swells and relentless headwinds. If there were a slough all the way to Alaska, I'd never look at the ocean again."

"There isn't a slough all the way to Alaska."

Chris ignored that comment and continued, "This place is truly a haven for ducks and geese. See how they're nesting and preparing for summer? And look along the shore at the salmon that have already come upriver, spawned, and died. The tundra is starting to green up and the creatures are all laying eggs and preparing for the next generation. We're surrounded by the circle of life."

Chris wasn't the only person to feel the safety and bounty of this place.

At Ushki, twenty miles upriver, archaeologists have uncovered twenty house foundations that form the largest late Paleolithic settlement in East Asia. Ushki people lived here 13,000 years ago, as the ice age glaciers were receding. Their elegantly pointed spearheads, knives, and scrapers resemble tools that were developed in central Asia, near the Gobi desert.

Ushki is the most prominent Stone Age site in Beringia and therefore critical to our understanding of migrations from Asia to North America. Originally, anthropologists speculated that the Clovis hunters of the American West were descendants of the Ushki. According to this hypothesis, migrants from Ushki walked slowly, over several generations, to Alaska, then veered south. However, this incremental migration hypothesis doesn't hold up, because the two cultures are contemporaneous: Ushki was settled 13,000 years ago, and the Clovis culture flourished in North America at about the same time. In a recent publication, anthropologist Ted Goebel, from the University of Nevada, speculates that the Ushki people migrated rapidly across the North Pacific Rim, or there is an older precursor village yet to be found.

Personally, I don't believe that people could have walked from Kamchatka to Oklahoma that rapidly, because the glaciers would have stopped them. Dr. Goebel doesn't speculate on any relationship between Jomon mariners and the Ushki people. The Jomon could have passed along this coast before the Ushki village was built or, alternatively, the settlers could have befriended the migrants—or fought with them.

The Ushki houses were built over shallow, circular excavations, with an entry passage and a stone-encircled hearth. The walls and roofs rotted away eons ago, so there is no picture of the completed houses. I wondered if they resembled eighteenth-century Itlemen dwellings, which were shaped like an hourglass, with a top cone perched upside down above a bottom cone. During the summer, people entered at ground level. They stored their salmon in the upper cone, where it would be safe from dogs and wild scavengers. In addition, sunlight from above and smoke from the cooking fires dried and preserved the fish. During the winter, when snow covered the ground-level entry and drifted to the rooftop, people walked over the snow to the roof, slid down the inverted cone, and entered their houses through the chimney. According to Krasheninnikov:

> They enter their huts by ladders commonly placed near the fire hearth, so that when they are heating their huts the steps of the ladder become so hot, and the smoke so thick, as almost to suffocate anyone who is not inured to bear it: but the natives find no difficulty in going in or out; and though they can only fix their toes on the steps of the ladder, they mount like squirrels.

Two hundred fifty years after Krasheninnikov visited Kamchatka, archaeologists uncovered a child's skeleton beneath one of the older Ushki houses. The skeleton was bound in a sitting position and laid to rest on a ritual mat made from the incisor teeth of lemmings. Red ochre dye was sprinkled around the grave.

Of all the abundant literature about the Ushki site, I find this "ritual mat made from the incisor teeth of lemmings" to be the most poignant and memorable image. A lemming is a rodent, four to seven inches long, so a lemming tooth has to be pretty small. How many teeth does it take to make a mat? How many incisors are there in a lemming? How would a Stone Age person with primitive tools drill holes in lemming teeth to sew them into a mat?

I can't answer any of these questions, but the picture is clear. Someone spent a lot of time, energy, and loving care to bury this child. Sometime, somewhere, and for some reason, people carefully collected lemming teeth, cleaned them, and wove a mat to carry their baby into the other world.

Almost every time I read about Stone Age life, I stumble onto some sentimental, time-wasting, or risky activity such as burying a child on a lemming-tooth mat, shoving a double-bladed stiletto into a grizzly bear's mouth and then leading it around by a leather thong, or paddling a dugout canoe from Japan to Alaska. The wonderful paradox is that inefficient endeavors aren't mere dead weight breaking the back of pragmatism; they are fundamental and essential components of humankind's success.

WE REACHED the Kamchatka River after lunch and ferried across the fast current. A huge pile of logs dominated a deteriorating wharf. These logs had been cut from the interior of Kamchatka, which has a more continental climate than the coast, with colder winters, warmer summers, and appreciably less wind. Trees are able to survive the cold winters and grow rapidly in the long, warm days of summer. As we paddled closer, we saw that the logs had been cut years ago and were rotting in the damp conditions. Rusting cranes cast oblique shadows across the docks. I estimated that the pile of logs was about three stories high and covered ten acres. Another almost equally large pile of sawn boards was rotting farther along the wharf, and beyond that we saw the steel skeleton of a huge building without roof, floor, or interior walls.

Before the 1980s, Soviet collectives shipped unprocessed logs to Japan. Then, in an effort to create more jobs, the government built a sawmill and was in the process of constructing a factory to manufacture doors and window frames. With the collapse of the Soviet Union, the managers lost their jobs, turned off the lights, and walked away. No one could write paychecks for the workers and no one could buy logs or lumber from agencies that didn't exist, so the entire timber industry collapsed overnight, leaving a huge mound of wealth to rot in an impoverished land.

We paddled toward a dock where a small crane was offloading fish from a barge. A sturdy, middle-aged man wearing a worn but expensive-looking leather jacket hailed: "*Who are you? What are you doing? Where are you coming from? Where are you going? We have food. We have a banyo. I want to meet you. My name is Victor.*"

Even before we could explain ourselves, he barked into a handheld radio and half a dozen rough-looking men appeared, hoisted our boats to shore, loaded them on a truck, and drove them to a small shack. As we followed on foot, Victor pointed out the shiny stainless steel sorting table where fresh sockeye, king, and silver salmon were being shunted into totes. A new Toyota forklift shuttled the loaded totes onto a waiting truck.

We stored our valuables in Victor's shack, changed into dry clothes, then jumped into his late-model pickup for a ride to the city's only hotel. After passing through the decaying industrial district, we reached an abandoned residential area. Most of the buildings had been demolished and were reduced to piles of rubble, jagged steel, torn wires, and broken plaster. The outside wall of one apartment complex had collapsed. A radiator hung in midair from a broken pipe, and a cracked toilet bowl listed precariously on a sagging floor.

Victor waved his hand out the truck window and lamented slowly in Russian so we could understand, "*You know Grozny? Da? In Chechnya? This is like Grozny in Chechnya. But worse. Worse than a city bombed by the Russian army.*"

He explained that before perestroika the population of Ust' Kamchatsk was 18,000 and the government had built new apartment buildings, a larger post office, and a modern municipal center. When the economy disintegrated, unemployment skyrocketed. People had no money to buy fuel, transportation networks collapsed, and the utilities shut down. Residents struggled without heat or electricity as winter temperatures plummeted to −40°F. The following summer, thousands of people left while the diehards scrambled to prepare for a second winter. They broke into abandoned apartment buildings and looted the household goods, wiring, and plumbing.

Then they dismantled walls with crowbars and pickaxes and salvaged interior lumber for firewood. By 1998 the city's population had dwindled by 75 percent, to less than five thousand.

Victor slammed on the brakes, and we slid through the dust in front of a four-story building with clapboard siding and no paint. A tiny sign on the corner announced in English and Russian, "Surf Hotel." We climbed a dusty, unlit stairway to the third floor and rapped on the concierge's window. She was sleeping on a couch and rose groggily. Misha explained that we needed two rooms.

"You want yours with a woman or without?" she asked Misha.

Misha blushed. *"No, thank you, without."*

Victor left us to settle in and returned later to show us his fishing operation. His employees set their nets near the mouth of the Kamchatka River, off-loaded the salmon at the dock, then trucked the fish to a modern flash-freezing plant. At the plant generators hummed, conveyor belts whirred, forklifts beeped, and the new freezers purred quietly. A Japanese buyer stood by, silently writing in a small notebook. I had read about the new Russian economy rising out of the ashes of the old Soviet system, but here I saw the contrast starkly, in the rotting logs and ruined buildings of the city compared with Victor's modern fish-processing operation.

Misha talked about his bottling plant near Petropavlovsk, and the two businessmen fell into easy conversation. After a while, Misha turned to Chris and me and exclaimed, "Gorbachev was Russia's biggest traitor. He sold Russia to the American CIA. Before Gorbachev, before perestroika, Russia was like this," and he pointed to Victor's freezers. "Then, overnight, it turned into that," and he waved his hand across a landscape of ruined apartment buildings and rotting logs and lumber. "The U.S. and Gorbachev did that to us. Now we must struggle to start again at the beginning."

I had always thought that Gorbachev was a hero and had never imagined that freedom was a CIA plot to destroy Russia from within, but I didn't argue.

Later that evening, Misha and Victor gave us a short course in modern Russian microeconomics. Misha explained that the government levied thirty-five separate taxes on his bottling plant totaling 80 percent of the gross. I shook my head. "No, that's impossible; they can't tax you on the gross." We had a long discussion about the difference between gross income and net profit. After all of us were convinced that we understood the definitions, Misha assured us that his taxes equaled 80 percent of the gross. Victor nodded in agreement.

"Then how do you operate?" I asked. "How do you pay your workers, buy equipment, meet your energy bills?"

There was a long silence. Then Misha started slowly, "The Western press talks about Russian mafia as if it is some group of evil men. But you don't learn the true story. I don't know exactly what mafia means. Yes, there are bad businessmen in Moscow. They kill people sometimes. Out here in Kamchatka there are not so many bad people. There are two choices in Kamchatka: no money or un-law. Everyone is un-law; every business is un-law. There is no other way." He shrugged. "Russian people have been through many hard times—under the czar, under Stalin, under perestroika. Russians have learned how to survive. There is always a way."

THERE are sixteen villages in the 1,650 miles between Ust' Kamchatsk and Providenya, our last town on the Russian coast. As a result, we expected to see people about once a week, which is either too often or not often enough, depending on your perspective. We bought food for a few weeks, trying to balance the desire to keep our boats light against the likelihood that the stores would be better in Ust' Kamchatsk than farther along the coast.

We paddled out of Ust' Kamchatsk on June 13 into a strong headwind. Every stroke was an effort, and every wave was a moving hill that pushed the kayaks southward toward Japan. I told myself, "Space out, forget what you're doing, and put in the hours. Don't even try to be inspired and don't think about your destination, because you can't fool yourself." By the third day, gusts shimmered across the water and I measured our speed by carefully monitoring diminutive landmarks on the cliffs. Yes, we were moving forward, but slowly, and my tendons ached. Chris was crying softly as she paddled, tears mixing with the salt spray.

"What's the matter, dear?" I asked, and she answered that her wrists hurt so badly that she could barely hold her paddle. I knew that we were expending too much energy for too little distance, so I turned to shore. When we reached the beach, the wind was not only lifting spume off the wave tops, it was blowing sand into our faces and rolling kelp along the beach like tumbleweed.

We found a protected beach, out of the prevailing winds, where alders grew head high, and pitched our tents. Then, because it seemed as though we might be here for a while, we went beachcombing for chairs. Chris found a yellow plastic crate with lettering in Japanese and English, "Sapporo Cider." A cold cider would have tasted good right then. Misha found a black plastic cylinder of mysterious origin, and I retrieved a thick block of white Styrofoam.

We sat beneath the alder canopy, built a smoky fire from damp driftwood, and brewed tea. Above us, a thin waterfall plunged over folded metamorphic rocks and carved a tunnel through a snowbank on the jumbled rocks below. Well-worn grizzly trails crossed the meadow at the edge of the alders. In the canopy, the leaves were beginning to burst out of their buds, but the bushes were bent and gnarled. I remarked that these alders had barely shed last year's snow before the snow fell again. As a result, they looked older than they really were. Misha answered that people in Kamchatka were like Kamchatka alders; human life expectancy on this coast is fifteen years less than it is in the large cities of western Russia.

That night a deep rumble seemed to rise out of the ground. I half woke and thought, "It's just a dream," but the noise compelled me to sit up. Outside the tent, gale-driven surf sounded like drumbeats beneath a wild orchestral overtone that might have started at the beginning of time. I fell back asleep but woke up early, and walked out to the bluff to watch the gale. Normally the surf formed one or two orderly lines, with discrete spaces between the breakers. Today the waves coalesced into a solid white band. I imagined paddling in the mayhem, buried by the foam, catapulting end over end, fighting for air, and struggling to reach the comfort of land. I shuddered at the thought and stomped on the rock bluff to assure myself that the earth was firm under my feet. Then I crawled back into the tent, slipped into my sleeping bag, and snuggled against Chris's warm body.

We settled in for a quiet domestic day. After breakfast I pulled out a small laminated map that surveyed the entire route from Petropavlovsk to Alaska. The scale of this map was too small for navigation, but it succinctly summarized where we had been and where we were going. Chris sat next to me as I crudely measured distances with a piece of dried grass. We'd been on the water twenty-nine days and had paddled nearly four hundred miles, one-fifth of the way to Alaska.

I looked up from the map. "Are you going to make it, Chrissy? Will your wrists hold up for another sixteen hundred miles?"

Chris was silent for a moment. "Usually I start off slowly on an expedition, and then I find my strength. But I haven't broken through the pain barrier. Maybe this is different. I don't know, Jon. I just don't know."

Chris and I had lived together so many years that we knew when words wouldn't change a situation. When there was nothing more to say, Chris stood up and walked into the bushes. After a short while, she returned with a walrus skull that she had found buried in the yellow grasses. Misha joined her and helped cut the tusks off with our tiny saw.

Over the past few weeks, Chris, Misha, and I had melded into a family. Maybe Chris's magic charm bound us together, or perhaps we were simply born soul mates. Chris and Misha seemed so engrossed with the walrus skull that I left them. After carving ergonomic curves into my Styrofoam, I moved it deep into the alders, out of the wind, and sat down to think.

Although I had set out on this journey to follow the Jomon migration from Japan to North America, as I paddled deeper into the wilderness I was hoping for more than a reenactment of a Stone Age journey. If I could understand *why* the Jomon migrated across the Arctic, I might also understand why the first Stone Age adventurer hollowed out a log and charged into the surf. Hunkered in an alder thicket, with a storm raging over the sea and grizzly tracks crisscrossing the tundra, I considered again the notion that a love of adventure helped transform bipedal primates into human beings.

THIRTY YEARS ago, when I was in college, I was taught that *Homo*'s recipe for success consisted of dexterous hands and a bigger brain. Yet the apelike hand, with counter-opposed thumb and forefinger, developed five million years before *Homo erectus* walked out of Africa. If our hands made us human, there was a huge time gap between cause and effect.

Nor can a big brain, by itself, explain our humanity. Hominid brain size tripled between 2 million years and about 100,000 years ago, yet tool design remained stagnant during a million years of the most rapid brain development.

A hand ax is a crude tool made by chipping an oval-shaped rock to a rough edge. *Homo erectus* held these tools in their palms and used them to chop, scrape, pound, and cut. Hand axes were useful for cleaning hides or cracking nuts, but they had none of the elegance of later Stone Age masterpieces such as the Clovis spear point or the Inuit harpoon. According to Rick Potts, director of Human Origins at the Smithsonian Institution:

> For more than one million years, the hand-axe was the dominant product of human technology . . . Distributed over Africa, Europe, and parts of Asia, the

hand-axe was the main stone design created and manufactured by hominids of the mid-Pleistocene. In our present world of rapid-fire technological advance, it is unthinkable that any single manufactured item could endure, much less remain dominant for so long . . . Today, we tamper with just about everything we create or lay our hands on. The hand-axe people just kept on making hand-axes.

Then, about 50,000 to 40,000 years ago, a massive renaissance called the Great Leap Forward occurred. New tool designs appeared rapidly, and almost simultaneously the *Homo sapiens* population soared. Many scientists argue that language was the required catalyst. Once people could communicate complex thoughts, they discussed concepts and ideas. Someone lashed a hand ax to a stick, another person suggested using a slimmer profile to make a spear point, and so on.

But we can't define our ancestors only by their tools. At the dawn of the Great Leap Forward, *Homo sapiens* painted on cave walls, carved figurines, made flutes, and buried their dead with tools and clothing for the afterlife. Thus rapid technological advances coincided with cultural, religious, and artistic explorations. If language was the catalyst, people were talking about more than hunting and food preparation. They held secret ceremonies deep in caves and painted pictures by the flickering light of campfires and torches. On cold winter nights, they played flutes around campfires. Art, music, and religion all consume resources without a direct, tangible return of food and shelter. Thus seemingly frivolous behavior was an integral component of the Great Leap Forward.

Language and culture are not unique to humans. Birds, monkeys, wolves, and bees communicate with one another. When chimpanzees hear a rival band moving into their territory, the males group together and hold one another's penises and grunt before battling the invaders. The gesture is a promise of togetherness in the face of danger; it is a cultural statement of tribal unity.

Stone Age people extended communication and cooperation far beyond that particular ritual. By working together, people quickly adapted and innovated. Bound by family ties, people made altruistic sacrifices to protect the tribe in time of danger or famine. Young hunters brought food to their elders; the elders contributed in turn by teaching their grandchildren and by knapping tools, building boats, and tanning hides. During famine, the elders remembered previous hard times and the secondary food sources that had sustained them. Perhaps they brokered peace treaties or settled disputes. The unity engendered by all these cultural activities bestowed Darwinian fitness on the tribe. Thus the lemming incisor mat was as critical to human development as the spearhead.

BUT WHERE does wanderlust fit into this picture?

In 2001, anthropologists found a 1.75-million-year-old hominid skull in the Republic of Georgia, near the Black Sea, pushing back yet further the time when our distant ancestors trekked out of Africa, adapting to dramatically changing environmental conditions along the way. But this ancient person had a tiny brain, huge canine teeth, and a thin, apelike brow. Surprisingly we started wandering before we were smart.

I believe that there was a reciprocal and symbiotic relationship between art, language, and technology on the one hand and wanderlust on the other. Clearly, extraordinary survival skills were needed for the migration into the Arctic and onward to the Western Hemisphere, but at the same time travelers accelerated the cultural and technological revolution.

It seems logical that once language tied individuals in a clan together, wanderers linked one clan to another. When someone in one valley developed a new tool, a sojourner carried that innovation to distant valleys— the first long-distance communication. Some adventurers died in lonely forests or on tempestuous seas, but cultural exchange strengthened the tribe sufficiently to outweigh the individual costs, and wanderlust thus bestowed an evolutionary advantage on the species.

Back in Ust' Kamchatsk, Victor had remarked that we were strange tourists, but Misha shook his head, saying, "*We're not tourists, we're puteshestveniks*." This commonly used Russian word has no direct English translation. A *puteshestvenik* is a wandering storyteller, one who carries the news, links cultures, and transfers technology. The word reaches back to times when men such as Krasheninnikov disappeared into Siberia for decades to bring news of Russia to the Koryak and report about the Koryak to the czarina. The incredible hospitality we had received at every nonmilitary outpost in the Kurils and Kamchatka was shown to us partly because the Russian people are naturally generous and partly because they have always fed, clothed, and protected their *puteshestveniks*. If we can extrapolate this hospitality back into the Stone Age, the gaunt and hungry wanderer was not a dangerous vagrant but an essential cornerstone of human culture.

FEELING CRAMPED and chilled, I stood and walked out of the alder thicket to survey the landscape. We were camped on the debris fan of an old landslide, and steep cliffs loomed above the gently sloping platform. To stretch my legs and get my blood flowing, I walked a few hundred yards to the south edge of the fan, then turned and walked to the north edge. I walked out to the beach, squinting to keep blowing sand out of my eyes. When the storm abated, we would continue northward, paddle stroke by paddle stroke. There were many adventures ahead of us, and lots of time to think.

THE wind died that afternoon, and even though the following morning dawned calm, the residual swells were still large. We loaded our boats and dragged them down to the beach. Misha planned to launch first, so he sat in the cockpit and pulled his sprayskirt tight. Each wave was much taller than a person sitting in a kayak, and the parallel breaks looked like impenetrable walls.

"Do you think you can make it out?" I asked nervously.

Misha muttered a phrase in Russian.

"What did you say?"

"Labor and Defend."

"What?"

Misha explained that the slogan was popular during the Soviet era. Athletes yelled "Labor and Defend" before a game. In grammar school, teachers warned their students that the Americans might launch a preemptive nuclear strike, but Russia would prevail if everyone "Labored and Defended." As we sat on the wet beach watching the surf, I told Misha that our teachers had warned us that the Russians might launch a preemptive nuclear strike against us. We were instructed to crawl under our desks and hold our hands over our heads when the sirens wailed and the sky filled with radioactive mushroom clouds. We both shook our heads sadly at the madness of it all.

I started pushing Misha toward the sea, but he asked me to stop. "Do you have a saying like 'Labor and Defend' that we can use before paddling into the breakers?"

I thought but could only come up with Crazy Horse's cry before the Battle of the Big Horn: "It is a good day to die!"

Neither Misha nor Chris liked that slogan. "Labor and Defend" won out.

That afternoon, summer burst onto the scene like a harried actress late for her on-stage cue. The sun was bright and warm, so we donned sunglasses and unzipped our parkas. We landed in a protected cove, spread out our wet clothes to dry, and stripped down to T-shirts. The low-lying tundra willows, barely a few inches high, were blanketed with rich green foliage. I checked my journal entry from our last camp; a scant ten hours and fifteen miles earlier the alder buds were barely starting to pop.

Two reindeer walked toward the beach, cocking their antlered heads as if wondering about these strangely colored mammals in their domain, then trotted off. These were the first reindeer we'd seen on this wild and sparsely inhabited coast. Sometimes a landscape is memorable not for what you see but for what you don't. In the Canadian Arctic in 1984, Chris and I had seen massive herds of caribou. One evening a herd moved slowly toward us, then ambled past our tent for six hours before the last stragglers disappeared over a low esker. I estimated their number at 10,000 or more. Other days we saw herds of several hundred to a thousand caribou, smaller groups of a dozen, or lone individuals walking along a shore. But we would see only two reindeer in almost four months in Kamchatka. When I asked Misha why there were no reindeer, he explained simply, "People shoot them all." Bereft of its largest herbivores, the wilderness was fractured and incomplete; in my memory, I see an undulating—but empty—expanse of grass, sedge, and willow.

The next day, June 20, we paddled across a calm sea. A dark mass, as large as a small island, rose and fell ahead of us in the gentle swell. As we approached, the mass resolved into discrete dots, and gradually I realized that the dots were black scoters, feeding peacefully. Sentries on the edge of the flock scanned the horizon with jerky head movements. When we were fifty yards away, the sentries took off, and the flock followed with a loud *whirr*. Seals bobbed to the surface and watched us with their whiskered, catlike faces. Delicate fork-tailed storm petrels swooped past on their swept-back wings, making sharp acrobatic turns while diving for fish. On shore, several Steller's sea eagles fed on the bloated carcass of a dead whale. Maybe the land had lost its reindeer, but the sea still teemed with life.

Then in the distance I saw a line of white on the sea, more reflective and elusive, more miragelike than a snowdrift on shore. I'd seen this before and knew what it was, but it couldn't be, not at 57° north latitude on the first day of summer in the open ocean. We were 600 miles south of the Arctic Circle. I've always associated sea ice with the midnight sun, but we were far south of that, still experiencing several hours of darkness every night. The white line had no right to be there on a peaceful day this far south, this late in the season. I thought, "I'm getting older and my eyes aren't as good as they used to be; maybe it's something else."

Chris and Misha paddled close, and Misha announced, "Maybe it is ice on the sea."

The three of us paddled side by side, stroke for stroke, and I felt the warmth of our friendship.

"Let's wait and see."

An hour later we were passing broken ice beached on the sand, and a few rogue bergy bits glistened as they bobbed on the gentle swell. We paddled north, and the ice became thicker.

Chris broke the silence. "What do you think, Jon?"

"The two best boats in the Arctic are the kayak and the nuclear-powered icebreaker. We're in kayaks."

"Don't be a smart-ass. Remember what happened at Zhupanova."

Misha asked what a smart-ass was; when Chris explained, he said nothing.

We stopped and analyzed the seascape. The Ozernaya River was only a few miles to the north. When I released my sprayskirt and sat on the cockpit rim to gain a better view, I saw a blue-brown channel a few hundred yards away, extending outward from the river mouth until it was choked off by sea ice. We reasoned that the colored channel marked a warm river current pushing a path through the otherwise dense pack.

I went first, ramming the bergy bits and larger bergs until they moved slowly out of our way, creating a narrow channel for Chris and Misha to follow. After about half an hour, we broke through to open water, surfed a gentle break at the delta, and entered a mirror-smooth estuary. Across the bay we saw a dilapidated cluster of shacks each sided with a curious mixture of gray tar paper and yellow, green, and pink plywood. Three boats were tied up along the beach, and smoke spiraled from the chimney of one of the shacks.

The caretaker, another Victor, guarded these buildings, which housed foreign bear hunters in spring and local fishermen during the summer. Victor was a strong, stocky man of medium height, in his mid-forties, with a neatly trimmed beard and bushy hair. He had spent six weeks here alone, then two weeks cooking for bear hunters, followed by another six weeks alone. Though taciturn and reserved, he was clearly glad for company. He made tea, sliced a loaf of bread, then dug into his pantry to find delicacies: canned peas, the last of his carrots, and a rare and valuable block of cheese.

Despite his generosity, Victor was bitter. The Soviet government had sent him to trade school to learn mechanics and truck driving. Under communism, life was easy. He went to work, came home, ate dinner with his wife, watched TV, and went to sleep. He had enough money for a yearly vacation to the Black Sea. But since perestroika he hadn't found a job, and his wife had left him. When I asked about basic freedoms, Victor said that he didn't care about basic freedoms. You can't eat freedom. So what if the communist TV was all lies? The capitalist TV was mostly lies too; what difference did it make? Even Misha spoke with bitterness about modern Russian capitalism. This theme was proving surprisingly ubiquitous. I wanted to diffuse another round of anger, so I smiled and said, "Labor and Defend." Misha smiled back and changed the subject.

Ice drifted in all afternoon, and by evening a dense pack churned against the rocky point north of Ozernaya. The following morning we climbed a bluff and scanned the coastline with binoculars.

If you toss ice cubes into a bathtub full of cold water, the cubes will disperse evenly throughout the tub. But ice doesn't behave this way in the open sea. The pack was jammed tightly against the coastline, then curved into a long seaward arc like Cape Cod. Just as Cape Cod was formed by current-driven sand, the barrier in front of us had formed as currents herded the ice.

A cold wind blew from the sea, and Chris lay down in the shelter of a small hillock. Misha trained his binoculars steadily at the distant ice as if to move it by sheer willpower. Soon I saw that Chris was eating something. I lay down. The earth felt warm and smelled of growth and decay. A few small cranberries remained from the previous autumn. I reached through the dried grass and inch-high woody bushes and picked a berry. It was freeze dried on the outside, with a pinhead-sized core that was succulent, juicy, and tart. I picked another. These berries were the first fresh fruit we had eaten since Ust', and I savored every morsel. Misha joined us on hands and knees, grazing along the hummocky ground.

Eventually I stood to stretch and scan the horizon. The beauty of the tundra is not like that of a calendar landscape with lofty peaks and tumbling glaciers. It's the feeling of infinite space. Those of us adapted to the reassuring confines of a folded or forested landscape must adjust to this expanse of sky lying low over a thin, featureless line of yellow-green earth. But once the feeling takes hold, you stop looking for images and let your spirit expand. In the tropics, the sun shines straight down, boring into the land and washing colors into a dull homogeneity. But in the Arctic, sunlight approaches obliquely, scattering in the atmosphere to accentuate the subtle yellows, browns, and greens and wash them into soft pastels. This lighting is like a gentle hand on your shoulder, reminding you to look for details even though the space around you seems empty. I reminded myself that in order to persevere through the three months ahead, I would need to look for soft accents in harsh images: the flowing, shaggy beauty of a grizzly bear's fur; the braided patterns of gray in a storm cloud; the curling symmetry of a breaking wave.

We passed a quiet afternoon in Victor's house. As the long twilight faded into a short, sub-Arctic night, I looked across the sea in the direction of home. Somewhere out there my father was still working as a chemist even though he had nominally retired years ago. My sister was engaged in medical statistics, my brother was making business deals, and my grandchildren were playing. A month of hard travel had rendered the outside world ethereal, like the twilight itself. All my life I had been darting in and out of the world I grew up in. I stayed in school long enough to earn my Ph.D., then worked as a carpenter, swinging a long, heavy framing hammer. I wrote academic textbooks, but retreated to the forest of Montana. Now I was paddling along this wild coast, immersed in the same powers that had ruled my Stone Age ancestors.

A month is a long time, or an eye-blink. It was long enough to adapt to this Arctic environment and stop craving the comforts of my opulent American life, and it was long enough to leave my body weary. I craved rest and relief from the monotony of paddling, and I knew, too, that a month was long enough to start my father worrying again. But on this quest to follow a Stone Age migration through a land ruled by millennial cycles of glacial cold and interglacial thaw, a month was an instant, a tiny speck in the eye of eternity.

We made pilgrimages to the bluff each morning and afternoon of the next three days, but the ice barrier remained packed against the shore. The storms around Zhupanova, the headwinds after Ust' Kamchatsk, and now this wait for the ice had reduced our average speed to 13.2 miles per day, and we were still 1,500 miles from Alaska. As often as I reminded myself that the journey was more important than the goal, I was determined to reach Alaska. We couldn't afford to wait.

On the third afternoon we scampered down the steep bluff to the beach. The tide had ebbed, leaving a dense pack of stranded ice chunks much larger than bergy bits—some as big as a suburban house. We jumped from berg to berg until we were on floating ice. Accustomed as we were to riding the swell on our haunches, the ice felt foreign underfoot. Standing on the ice together, we discussed our situation. Could we paddle around the ice, or would we have to wait until it broke up and floated away?

Expeditions are a game of risk, defined by probability and consequence. A high probability of mishap is acceptable if the consequences are low. If our passage around the ice were likely to cost us a good dousing and a hard day's work—but nothing more—we'd launch in a heartbeat. But if the consequence could well be death, then the probability of that calamity must be very low before we'd risk it. The coastline might be ice free around the point, fourteen miles ahead, but maybe not. If we paddled out there, the weather might remain calm or a storm might descend. If all of the "maybes" lined up in our favor, we'd be fine. But if even one of them went against us, we could be trapped on a stormy sea with nowhere to land, or we could be crushed in the ice. In either case, we would die.

As we walked back to Victor's cabin, I tried to think clearly. "The two best boats in the Arctic are the kayak and the nuclear-powered icebreaker," I had joked—and it was true. Yet we simply couldn't venture into the ice. There had to be a way, but I wasn't seeing it.

I walked in silence, watching my shoes make footprints in the sand as I thought. "A big ship was blessed with abundant horsepower, but a kayak was powerless and puny, so we had to be clever. I wasn't being clever enough."

Back in the cabin, I unfolded a map of the region. Victor poured tea, sliced another loaf of bread, and spread out butter and cheese.

"Jon, relax and eat," Chris urged.

I stared at the map, ignoring the tea and the food. "No, wait a minute. I've got an idea. We're kayakers; we can do something a nuclear-powered icebreaker can't do. We can drag our boats upriver to this low divide across the mountains. Look. From there it's less than a mile's portage to the next river that flows north. The entire route is only thirty miles as the crow flies, but this river empties into the ocean north of the peninsula—and I'll bet it will carry us north of the stranded ice. We can go around the ice by venturing inland."

Chris and Misha looked at me as if I were an alien.

THE following day Victor ferried us and our gear and boats up the Ozernaya River in his speedboat. At the confluence of a small, unnamed tributary, we slipped our kayaks into the water, and I paid him generously for his gas and time. He drifted seaward with the current, then started his motor and accelerated into the main channel. When the engine's drone faded, I felt the closeness of the land. Though vast and featureless, the tundra engenders a warm, secure feeling compared with the inscrutable harshness of the sea. Feeling hot, I stripped off my parka, until a swarm of Arctic mosquitoes enveloped me in a buzzing gray cloud.

Almost thirty years before, I had dragged a canoe across the Rat River Pass, a nineteenth-century trade route from the Canadian Northwest Territories to the rich gold mines and fur-trapping grounds in the Yukon. Now, with a white beard and graying hair, I was dragging and paddling my kayak across another mosquito-infested tundra in another far corner of the Earth. Apparently I was ineducable.

Where the river was more than knee deep, we paddled, but where it spread out into shallow riffles that gurgled over small stones, we got out and dragged our boats. We worked hard, but the river meandered so radically that we were heading in the wrong direction most of the time, and our straight-line speed toward the pass was a snail-like two miles per hour. The mosquitoes were thick and the frigid water numbed our feet, but at least we were safe in the placid river, moving generally north. As we passed numerous tributary streams, the main river became smaller and smaller until it was barely wider than our narrow kayaks.

After three days we reached the drainage divide, where the river opened into a tundra lake. It was bathed in evening light, and the reflections of snow-clad peaks shimmered in calm ripples. Two tundra swans swam side by side, rubbing necks in a fond embrace. For a time we stood by our boats in the cold water and listened to the silence. Then, almost reluctantly, we paddled across the deep, lapis-colored lake.

When we reached the other side, a broad smile crossed Misha's face. "I love the beautiful nature. For five years I work in office. I make many papers. Now we are in the most beautiful nature. Maybe only a few people have saw this lake. This swans is present to us from wild nature. I will remember this place forever."

We pitched our tents on a grassy plain adjacent to a stunted birch grove, and cooked dinner. Then Misha spread the map across his lap and announced, "I worried about tomorrow. Look. The river on the other side is very straight and steep. There will be big stones in the river. Water will crash over the stones. The water will move fast. It will turn white."

I didn't say anything.

"Don't you understand? Big stones—in the middle of the river—with water. The water will crash over the stones and turn white. Maybe you have never seen this before, but I am hydrogeologist. I know. Our boats will crash. We will crash. Everything will crash."

I explained that I had been a river kayaker for twenty years and had seen white water crashing over stones before. Having calculated the river's gradient and estimated its volume, I thought we could manage.

Misha wasn't convinced. "You may understand rivers, but you don't know anything about Kamchatka rivers. This is Russia," he said, concluding his final argument.

In truth, for three days I, too, had been worried about the rapids we'd meet on the way down. Our kayaks were elegantly designed for the sea, but they were lousy creek boats.

I turned to Misha and Chris. "Well, we're here. We can turn around, float back down the way we came, paddle back to Victor's, and wait for the ice to move out. Or we can head downstream, over the crashing water, back to the ocean, and manage somehow."

Chris and Misha were both born adventurers. I guessed that neither would want to turn back then, and neither did.

The next morning we dragged our kayaks over short stretches of tundra linked by bogs and kettle lakes until we found a tiny stream flowing north. The creek was so small that the boats barely floated, and we had to lift them to negotiate tight turns. When we reached the confluence with a larger stream, Misha was right—there were stones in the middle of the river, and white water was crashing around them. But I was right too: the stream was small, and its hydraulic energy was manageable. We tied ropes to the boats and lined them through the rapids without much problem. Logjams created the biggest frustration. Every twenty-five to fifty yards we had to stop and lift the heavy boats over tangled brush and deadfall. Mosquitoes swarmed around our heads and drew blood from exposed skin. Misha abandoned the river entirely and dragged his boat through the forest. At one point Chris sat down on a log in frustration and cried, until the mosquitoes jogged her back into action.

We were moving downstream, but progress was slow. We traveled about six miles that day and camped near the base of the mountains. The following day the river flattened out as it entered a broad delta, and on the third morning we paddled into a shallow, brackish estuary. The tide dropped and our boats sank into the mud, so we climbed out and sloshed through the ooze, dragging the kayaks. It was discouraging work. But looking out at the ocean, we could see that the main ice pack was clustered to the south. Our crazy plan had worked; we were north of the ice, with a clear path toward Alaska.

REACHING DEEPER water at last, we paddled across the bay toward a ramshackle collection of houses half sunken into the clay earth. One of the houses looked inhabited, so we paddled to shore. A worn path led us past bits of torn fishing net, rotting wooden skiffs, a wrecked three-wheeled motorcycle that looked incongruous in a land of no roads, and four skeletal snow machines that were slowly rusting into reddish-brown dust. The door to the house was held together by a collage of plywood scraps and white driftwood nailed together helter-skelter. The top hinge was made from the track of a snow machine, and the bottom hinge was cut from an orange plastic buoy. The weathered, toothless man who answered our knock looked as if he had just escaped from a gulag.

Uri blinked in the bright sunshine of the open doorway, looking at us quizzically. I sensed that his limp handshake wasn't an act of impoliteness but rather a ginger attempt to ascertain that I was both real and harmless. Remembering that he had forgotten his manners, he ushered us into his kitchen, where we sat on rickety stools around a stout table that supported a vise and a bench grinder while he fired up a smoky kerosene camp stove, boiled tea water, and heated a huge pot of borscht.

Misha told Uri of our travels, whereupon Uri started talking in a measured cadence. But his speech gradually accelerated until the words spilled out with the urgency of someone who hadn't talked with anyone for a long time.

Uri had moved there as a young newlywed in 1958, when the now-abandoned buildings had been a bustling town called Uka. He had been a seal hunter until seal hunting was banned, then he manned a meteorological station. When that was shut down, he took a job as caretaker for the fishing company that now owned the town. Unfortunately, the price of salmon caviar had been high last year, so the fishermen had overexploited the stock and decimated the resident salmon population. This year they hadn't bothered to return.

In 1971 Uri's wife and son had set out toward the town of Ossora to buy supplies. They motored their small skiff into the surf break, lost power, capsized, and drowned. Uri explained that he had lived alone since then.

When the soup was hot, he ladled out huge portions of borscht cooked with meat, beets, and cabbage. The meat tasted like mutton, but I didn't see any sheep nearby. Uri said it was "meat from town," as if there were two kinds of animals in this world: town animals and wild animals. I asked whether there were reindeer nearby; the surrounding tundra looked like prime pasture. Uri explained that reindeer had once thrived in the region, but during the cold war there had been a military base nearby, and soldiers had hunted all the game from helicopters. He hadn't seen a reindeer for years.

Misha shook his head sadly. "*No fish, no reindeer. That is the story of Russia. Too many bad czars, too many wars, too many years of communism, and now this. We have many resources, but we are poor.*"

Then suddenly Uri stopped talking as if he recognized, for the first time, that we were real people. "*And how did you get here? By baidarka? How did you get through the ice? Did you say, 'over the mountains'? I must go see your boats.*"

We stood up to walk outside with him, but he told us to sit and finish our dinner. Then he disappeared into the sunshine. Left alone, I asked Misha whether we should eat Uri's precious town meat. Misha reminded me that we were *puteshestveniks*, and Uri would be insulted if we didn't eat heartily.

Uri returned, shaking his head. "*Yes, baidarkas. They are so small. Alaska is still far away. My wife and son were killed in the surf in a much larger boat. A boat with a motor.*"

I wanted to explain that our kayaks were more seaworthy than an open skiff with a weary motor, but it wouldn't have been the right thing to say. Uri hadn't ventured onto the ocean for thirty years. He never left Uka during the summer; he drove to town once a year in winter, by snow machine, to pick up supplies. Uri was a villager; we were travelers.

IN HIS book on Stone Age migrations, Professor Alan Fix argued that most people stayed home unless a trigger such as famine or war initiated a migration. But he went on to say that his assumptions held for only 99 percent of a given population; the other 1 percent might go charging off into the wild for no good reason. An average band of hunter-gatherers numbered about thirty-five people. Thus, in any given generation, an average of one oddball in every three tribal units might be an adventurer and seeker. The Jomon had many tribal bands and lived in Japan for 10,000 years—four hundred generations. Looked at that way, the odds greatly favored a few people jumping in a boat and voyaging over the horizon.

I couldn't imagine living in Uka for forty-two years, and Uri couldn't imagine kayaking to Alaska. Just as Stone Age travelers had brought news of other lands, we brought Uri a little excitement and news of the outside world, and in return he fed us his precious town meat. The exchange was ancient and reciprocal.

Most people love their native land. The Yaghan of southern Chile believed that the cold, rainy, foggy, windswept bogs of Tierra del Fuego were the best home on Earth. The Hopi loved the desert, the Sioux sanctified the eroded gullies of the Black Hills, and the Seminoles gladly shared the Okefenokee with alligators. Most people are like Uri and stay close to home, but the Jomon and the Ainu after them were seafarers, and sooner or later seafarers make epic voyages.

The following morning we squirmed back into our cockpits while Uri wished us good luck with as many slogans as he could think of. "*May the seas be calm, the wind at your back, the fish plentiful . . .*"

Fog obscured the mouth of the estuary, and we navigated by the feel of the current and the first undulation of the ocean swell. Behind us we left the drone of delta mosquitoes. Ahead, surf beat against an offshore bar. If you adjust the volumes, mosquitoes sound similar to surf, soft and continuous. People sell audiotapes of "white sound" from rivers, jungle birds, surf, and wind, but I don't think anyone has tried selling a recording of mosquitoes. The melodious hum would be relaxing, but the connotations wouldn't work. No, I was happy to leave the embracing safety, the sticky mud, and the ubiquitous mosquitoes of the delta and feel my way blindly into the fog toward the pristine and, yes, violent sea.

W E REACHED Ossora on July 3 after a passage of 650 miles from Petropavlovsk. Prior to this expedition, my longest sea kayak passage had been 600 miles from Canada to Greenland. Now, instead of reaching the end of our journey, we were less than a third of the way. During the past week, Chris's wrists had hurt more and more, and she had been lagging behind, frequently wishing for an early camp. We both knew that in the months and miles ahead, her carpal tunnel would overpower her determination. There was no other solution, so she decided to quit. A cargo plane was leaving the next day with room for Chris and her kayak.

In her own words:

> For over a week north of Ust' Kamchatsk, the wind remained perpetually on our nose. We were in the kayaks for 10 or 12 hours every day, pushing hard to make miles. In the morning, after half an hour, each paddle stroke was an act of will because my hands and wrists were screaming. I forced myself to take ten good strokes between rests and then 15, then 20. Still I couldn't keep up with Jon and Misha. Finally in frustration and tears, I'd yell to Jon that I needed a quick rest and I would pop a few anti-inflammatories. Eventually

I swallowed pills each morning with breakfast, but I really needed to stop paddling and give my overworked hands a complete rest. Unfortunately, we didn't have time to rest and still make it to Alaska during the short summer season.

When we reached Ossora three weeks later, it hurt to tie my shoes or stuff my sleeping bag. My grip was so weak that I could barely hold my paddle by the end of the day, and the low point came when I couldn't even carry my sleeping bag from the boats to camp. Obviously, I couldn't continue. Ossora was the last village with an airport and a scheduled flight back to Petropavlovsk.

Retreat had been on my mind. I was vulnerable on this journey. Way back in March, when Jon and I were skiing in the backcountry of British Columbia, I had cartwheeled down a mountainside in a small avalanche. The tumbling fall wasn't fast enough to release my bindings, and I had ruptured the anterior cruciate ligament in my knee. My doctor told me I could go to Kamchatka, but he warned that my knee might be unstable. Jon and Misha had faithfully helped me in and out of the surf. I had moved cautiously and carefully. But now my wrists were stopping me, so after 650 miles and 43 days, I decided to head home.

Jon and Misha paddled out of Ossora Bay early on July 4, and I was on a plane headed to Petropavlovsk by three that afternoon. I dozed and woke up beneath a portrait of Lenin staring down from the forward cabin wall. The droning engine put me in a contemplative mood, and I thought back to the many adventures I've shared with Jon over our 20 years together. All of them have been physically demanding. My small stature misrepresents my strength. Although I'm only 5'3" and weigh 125 pounds, I'm very strong and have exceptional endurance. I usually just get stronger and stronger as we travel. This time I had hit the wall, and that frightened me. When we were paddling hard, I had often fantasized about returning to Montana, but I hated to leave Jon, Misha, and Kamchatka. I love the experience of being out in the wilderness for extended periods of time, while your mind and body adjust to the ancient pace of a landscape. Kamchatka was the wildest place I'd ever seen. Also, our group experience had bonded us strongly, and I feared that I might never see Misha again.

When I arrived in Petropavlosk, Yelena met me wearing a tank top and shorts. It was a hot summer in the city, and she handed me an ice cream cone as she grabbed my pack.

I fought back tears when Chris and I hugged on the beach. Then, in an action that was pure Chris, she attended to details in a moment of maximum emotion. She handed me an extra bottle of anti-inflammatories. "You may need these." Then she turned and walked toward the airport.

I wanted to go home with her, to hold her hand as we visited the ortho-pedic surgeon together, to support her if she needed an operation on her knee. Instead I tucked the pills in a dry bag that was lashed to my kayak. Chris and I had based our marriage on the premise that we wouldn't de-mand too much from each other. Right now we both knew that Chris had to go home and I wouldn't be happy if I abandoned the expedition to ac-company her.

I stared at the circle of disturbed sand where we had embraced and the small footprints that trailed away. At the far end of the footprints, Chris's figure was slowly receding.

Misha put his palm gently on my shoulder. "We must paddle to Alaska with our own hands," he said.

I smiled and he smiled back, flashing his shiny gold tooth. Misha wasn't returning to his wife and daughters. He had shown exceptional bravery, he was my friend, and we had come so far. We dragged our boats to the water's edge and slipped into the cockpits. The empty sea seemed emptier without Chris, and two fragile kayaks seemed so much more vulnerable than three. I grasped my paddle and said, "We must carry Evdocia's dream to Alaska."

Misha nodded. "We must go to the wild nature."

Then I pushed through the moist sand with my hands until the boat rocked comfortingly in the protected lagoon. A whiskered seal rose and eyed me curiously. I wiggled my hips to feel the balance, lifted my paddle, and swung north, with Misha beside me.

AGE was starting to creep up on us. Chris hadn't lost her indomitable will, but her wrists weren't as supple as they had been when we met. The same thing could happen to me. My left elbow tendon was hurting, so I straightened my arm and started every stroke by rotating my torso. Misha and I had 1,350 miles to go.

The wind was relatively light, the sun shone brightly, and the air was warm. We paddled across the lagoon and portaged over a narrow sandbar into the lazy swell of the open ocean. I started to sweat, so I shed my Gore-Tex shell and paddled in a Polartec sweatshirt. To combat the monotony, Misha slipped a list of English words in a plastic bag, propped it on the cockpit rim, and studied his vocabulary. I could have studied Russian, but I preferred to daydream and watch the ducks, gulls, and seals.

Pickings had been slim at the small village stores in Ossora, so lunch consisted of *sala* (salted pig fat), a small slice of cheese, and *colbasa* (hard, greasy sausage). I told myself to close my eyes, try not to visualize the insides of my arteries, and ignore all I'd learned about cholesterol. Present circumstances demanded that I forget about longevity and playing with great-grandchildren and concentrate on immediate needs. I gnawed off a big mouthful of raw fat and munched contentedly. Was this stuff any worse for my health than a fast-food burger and fries? I didn't know, but it surely packed high-octane go-power.

In the evening we pitched our tent on soft tundra moss overlooking the beach. For dinner we unpacked noodles and a small cube of chicken bouillon. I stared at the pathetically inadequate ingredients. We were paddling along the North Pacific coast, home of the largest salmon runs in the world, and it was foolish to eat poorly. Misha and I rigged our gill net with lines and weights, then I tied one end to my kayak, paddled a hundred yards out to sea, and anchored the net with a stone. Misha pulled the float line taut and secured it to a driftwood log on the beach. After I returned to shore, we built a fire. Within a few minutes, a flapping, silvery, five-pound salmon was tangled in the net.

We cleaned the fish, separated out the red caviar, and sliced the body into thick, juicy steaks. Then we rolled the steaks in flour and dropped them spattering and sizzling into the frying pan. I stood up and scanned the horizon for bears, but the tundra was empty. It was dangerous to cook fish in camp, but we would surely become weak and sick if we tried to paddle hard all summer on an inadequate diet. I thought back to Vitali again, remembering his white beard, warm smile, and sound advice.

"Your response to a bear must factor in its age, sex, and social status."

It seemed to me that a bear's behavior was linked to the health and integrity of the entire ecosystem. In times of abundance, bears suspend territorial battles and fish side by side in the same stream. I reasoned that if bears didn't fight with one another at such times, maybe they wouldn't want to mess with us. If Misha and I could look, act, and smell like "the baddest critters on the block"—maybe by nonchalantly cooking and eating our dinner in broad daylight—perhaps bears would deem it safer to catch their own fish than to steal ours.

My argument was full of holes, of course, but I knew we needed good food to sustain us. I scooped two steaming steaks into my bowl, poured the excess fat over my noodles, scanned the horizon again for danger, and sat cross-legged on a rock to eat. I wouldn't have minded being a little "badder" with my 12-gauge pump-action street-sweeper bear stopper by my side, but on the other hand it was exhilarating to be playing the pecking order game with fifteen-hundred-pound predators on an uninhabited coast of Siberia.

North Pacific salmon runs can be compared with other great animal migrations, such as the movement of bison over the North American plains or wildebeest across the African Serengeti. Yet salmon are unique in that they return to the exact same spot every year, on a nearly precise schedule. The Sioux lived in tepees so they could follow the bison, and the aboriginal Masai built temporary stick shelters that were abandoned when the rains dried up and the wildebeest wandered toward more abundant grass. In contrast, Pacific Rim people built permanent villages, secure in the assurance that their food would come to them. Stone Age inhabitants of the North Pacific Rim ate so much seafood that the chemical composition of their bones was nearly identical to that of dolphins.

The Jomon migration occurred more than 10,000 years ago, when the Earth was shedding the great weight of ice age glaciers. Before the ice ages, salmon lived in the North Pacific much as they do today. Adults swam upstream to their birthplace, then spawned and died. The following spring, the fry hatched, drifted down to the ocean, lived their adult life in salt water, then returned upstream to complete the cycle.

Although salmon are genetically programmed to return to the stream of their birth, the programming isn't perfect, and every year a few aberrants spawn in the wrong stream. In a stable climate these anomalous fish aren't significant, but when the ice age plunged our planet into a deep freeze, the northern streams froze solid, killing their resident salmon populations. Only the fish that spawned in warmer rivers to the south survived. Thus the oddballs became critical to the survival of the species.

As the late Harvard biologist Stephen Jay Gould argued: "The rules for survival change in extraordinary episodes, and the features that help species to prevail through catastrophic times are not the same as the sources of success in normal times."

The parallel with human populations seems obvious. For example, in the early twentieth century, my grandparents emigrated from Eastern Europe to America. Their migration was motivated by an adventurous urge to seek new vistas combined with a pragmatic desire to improve their economic status. Many of their friends and relatives stayed behind. Forty years later,

Hitler rose to power and murdered most of the Jews who had remained in Eastern Europe. Thus, arguably, I'm alive because my ancestors were willing to leave their homes and settle in a new land. My journey across the North Pacific wasn't an escape from oppression or warfare, but I believe that it was driven by a genetic propensity to wander that I inherited from my grandparents. I can only hope that my children and grandchildren will be free to follow their passions, too, whether those passions guide them home or over the horizon.

We finished our dinner and boiled water for tea. Misha and I had been traveling together long enough to develop routines, like those of an old married couple. Misha brewed strong tea for himself and very weak tea for me while I broke out a candy bar and carefully cut it in two. Misha took a small bite of his share and let the chocolate melt slowly in his mouth; I ate my half impatiently.

When I was finished, I stood and walked inland to stretch my legs and feel the sponginess of the soft earth. The tundra felt as vast and permanent as the sea, although 20,000 years ago—an eye-blink in geological time—this coastal plain was depressed under the weight of giant glaciers. The melting glaciers left behind a desolate landscape of naked bedrock. A few salmon swam up the northern rivers to spawn and die. In late summer, eagles and seagulls swooped down and grasped dying fish from their spawning pools. These birds lifted their meals a short distance, then settled on the ground to eat. As the fish became more abundant, the birds frequently abandoned uneaten morsels. These bits of fish accumulated in sheltered places, providing nutrients for mosses and later for the first grasses. Thus coastal soils all along the North Pacific Rim were formed partly from salmon.

Over time, other plants and animals migrated north behind the melting ice. Each species moved in its own way: Seeds blew on the wind, mink darted furtively from one stream to the next, and mammoths inched north behind the advancing soil. Sometime around 13,000 years ago, humans paddled or walked to Kamchatka to form settlements like those found at Ushki. And at about the same time, or not long after, the Jomon passed through here on their long journey to North America.

ON THE evening of July 5, Misha and I camped within sight of the next village, Il'pyrskiy. From the beach, I trained my binoculars on the smoke rising from the town generator. Tiny gray and black houses flanked the generator, and I visualized the interiors of the houses, with their bare lightbulbs, peeling paint, warm *petchka*s, and the rich aroma of baking bread. A trip to town would be a welcome break from the monotony of paddling, one stroke a second, sixty seconds a minute, ten to twelve hours a day, but Il'pyrskiy hugged the inner shore of a bay, a half-day's paddle out of our way. At some point, every adventurer struggles with the nature of his goals. Does a person climb Everest to reach the top or to experience the essence of the mountain? Were Misha and I paddling "along the Kamchatka coast" or "to Alaska"? We were woefully behind schedule, but then again the schedule and the destination were arbitrary constructs of our own minds. Other than our sponsors and family, few people in the world knew or cared about our existence, our goals, or our remote destination.

I looked up at Misha. "What do you think we should do?"

Misha pointed straight across the bay, away from Il'pyrskiy. "We must stay in wild nature." Then he held up his palms and stared into the cracked, salt-encrusted calluses. "We must paddle to Alaska by our own hands."

OK. We would skip the village and follow the mesmerizing trance of the horizon. This wasn't a tour of Kamchatka but a journey of unknown origins, inexplicable purpose, and uncertain consequence.

The next day we steered toward a prominent cliff on a peninsula fourteen miles across an open bay. During the five-hour crossing, we were vulnerable to a fast-moving storm that could blow us into the Pacific, but I didn't dwell on the possible cost; for most of the past two years, fear had been part of my daily routine. I checked the barometer and scanned the sky for signs of danger, then pressed my legs against the thigh braces to feel the connection between my body and my boat. A warm slice of bread, dry clothes, and friendly conversation in town would have been welcome, but Misha was right; we needed to remain in the wild nature. We would find comfort in our asceticism, our friendship, our ridiculously small boats, and our intimate communion with the sea.

I wondered whether the early Jomon migrants pushed on so relentlessly. Did they feel this love of the journey itself, or did they look longingly at slow-moving rivers and gentle coastal plains and ask, "What are we doing? Where are we going? Our boats are leaking. We need new nets. Two women are pregnant. The elders are tired. This is a good land; let's settle here."

I looked at my own journey. I was tired to my bones. Chris had left, and sometimes the passage to Alaska seemed nonsensical. Yet every day we woke at 4:00 A.M., paddled virtually nonstop for ten to twelve hours, then dragged our exhausted bodies onto the beach. Usually we fought boredom except when we were facing immediate danger. In the end, even if we succeeded, we would merely link two arbitrary dots on a globe, seemingly without purpose. Sometimes I wondered why we were continuing.

MY THOUGHTS kept circling as my paddle kept dipping, stroke after stroke. Again and again I conjured images of a Stone Age band of hunter-gatherers. If the group grew much larger than thirty-five people, they would deplete the local game and forage. If much smaller, there would be too few adults to share the tasks of defense, food gathering, and child rearing. The young men and women in the group would have had a limited choice of mates. Because mating of closely related family members is unhealthy, most young people would have chosen partners from neighboring bands. Thus Stone Age communities comprised a loose alliance of groups living close enough to one another to maintain a common language and cultural ties. Geneticists estimate that these alliances, or tribes, had to contain at least five hundred people for a healthy gene pool.

Imagine, for the sake of discussion, twenty bands of Jomon living on the north coast of Hokkaido. According to the most widely accepted model, a band that broke off and moved north into the Kurils must have stopped after a few days' travel—far enough to find fresh hunting and fishing but close enough to maintain contact with friends and relatives. After they established a colony, another group from Hokkaido might have leapfrogged them to settle on the next island farther north. This incremental migration could have proceeded over many generations. Consider an amoeba: one lobe protrudes outward to procure a toehold, then amorphous protoplasm from the center oozes beyond the first lobe, and so on, gradually carrying the organism along.

Thomas Dillehay, an anthropologist who specializes in the early settlement of the Americas, has argued for this model of slow, amoeboid migration, writing that the concept of rapid migration lacks appeal for three reasons:

> First, if we look at the earliest record of human migration in the Old World, we see very slow movement from region to region. Many areas were inhabited for hundreds of thousands of years after the first migration. . . .
> Second . . . if we have learned anything about more sophisticated cultures, it is that through time they tend to settle down rather than to become more nomadic . . .
> Third, as groups moved along the coast, they encountered hundreds of

hospitable deltas and river valleys that must have promised a rich life and a wide variety of lush environments . . .

Dillehay's argument is logical, yet human behavior isn't always logical. As my paddle dipped and rose, first one side, then the other, I kept thinking about the maverick 1 percent, the oddball 0.1 percent, or even the lunatic 0.01 percent. Often it's the crackpot, not the conservative, who breaks one mold and casts another.

Crackpots can make wonderful traveling companions. I'd been traveling with them since leaving Nemuro more than a year before in my physical journey and in my dream world. A few years ago, Kennewick Man had stepped out of a newspaper clipping to lure me across the Pacific, and now he had become a friend, sharing salmon steaks around a campfire, keeping watch for grizzly bears, and helping me through the surf. Now Evdocia had joined our group, silently bending her weight behind a rough, hand-carved paddle during the terrible monotony of peaceful days at sea.

There is no lack of scientific observations with which to counter Dillehay's incremental migration hypothesis. Igor Krupnik, a Russian anthropologist at the Smithsonian Institution, observed that 4,000 to 5,000 years ago, people of the Arctic Small Tool Tradition migrated quickly across North America:

> Archeologists agree that the similar profile and nearly identical age of aboriginal encampments throughout the Arctic from northeast Siberia, through Alaska, Canada, Greenland, and into Labrador offer proof of an extremely fast migration occurring along the Arctic coast of Siberia and North America.

Krupnik maintained too much analytic detachment to claim that this migration across 5,000 miles of the coldest environments on Earth was spectacular or marvelous. He merely stated that the migrants must have had a "reliable subsistence system" to complete their journey. But *why* did they choose to do it? Why didn't they migrate south? Or stay home?

According to Krupnik:

> . . . Among Arctic communities, migration was by no means always a consequence of famine, overpopulation, or any other crisis . . . The traditional residents of the Arctic were fully capable of purely human curiosity, wanderlust, or dreams of a "better life" to be found over the next pressure ridge.

Krupnik theorized that rapid migrations could be carried out only by robust, well-fed tribes who carried the reserves to travel—and keep traveling. Having studied the migrations of Paleosiberian people three-quarters of the way around the world—from the central Asian Arctic into north-east Siberia, across Beringia, and onward over the top of the Canadian Arc-tic into Greenland—Krupnik concluded that many of these migrations were much too fast to be explained solely by pragmatism. Rather, Paleo-lithic Arctic hunters must have been driven in no small part by romance, in-nate curiosity, and a sense of adventure. Krupnik quoted American geog-rapher Carl Sauer: "Folk who stuffed or starved, who took no heed of the tomorrow, could not have possessed the Earth or laid the foundations of human culture."

Pragmatism can explain a relocation to a nearby virgin seal-hunting bay from an established camp, but it can't readily explain why people would walk or paddle from Siberia to Labrador. Yet the Arctic Small Tool people zoomed across the circumpolar north 4,000 to 5,000 years ago. This proven exception to Dillehay's logic casts doubt on the universal merit of his hy-pothesis. By extension, it seems reasonable that Kennewick Man's Jomon ancestors could have made a similarly rapid passage across the North Pacific Rim sometime prior to 9,500 years ago.

If the Jomon moved incrementally, as Dillehay argued, then large num-bers of them must have lived along the Kuril and Kamchatka coasts for many generations. If this were true, why haven't archaeologists found re-mains of their villages or campsites? Perhaps ancient Jomon coastal vil-lages were flooded when sea level rose, and the record of their migration is now beneath the ocean. Yet in Hokkaido many Jomon moved upriver and built villages on higher ground, and they would reasonably have done the same had they maintained permanent settlements along the North Pacific Rim. An absence of interim settlements isn't proof of a rapid migration, but it's suggestive.

Climatological data also support the hypothesis that Jomon migrants charged ahead quickly. Scientists have studied paleoclimatic patterns by an-alyzing ice cores from the Greenland glaciers. These studies have shown that the Earth's temperature fluctuated dramatically, rapidly, and repeatedly during the ice sheet retreat from 18,000 years ago almost to the present. Century-long warm spells were punctuated by deep freezes, when the aver-age global temperature dropped by 20°F. (By comparison, the current global warming has raised Earth's average temperature about 1°F.) The Jomon migrants were tough, but they couldn't have survived the Arctic during a perpetual winter, when snow never left the earth, the salmon didn't return, and the sea froze solid for a hundred years. If they had moved piecemeal then, they would have died. Instead, they must have crossed the Arctic and traveled south along the Alaskan and British Columbian coast within a century-long period of favorable weather. According to James Chatters, the anthropologist who first analyzed Kennewick Man's bones:

> Immigration probably came in pulses rather than a continuous flow . . . Coastal Beringia was habitable for only short periods, between which it remained locked in permanent sea ice. It is easy to envision an Asian maritime culture expanding north into Kamchatka and out onto the Beringian coast, and exploring its way to America. When this first group was exterminated or forced to abandon the northernmost coast by the cooling climate, perhaps the peoples of Asia and America would have become separated, both culturally and biologically, until Beringia again became habitable and the process could be repeated.

Thus Chatters envisions relatively rapid migration pulses during episodic warm spells.

While assembling the WindRiders more than a year before, I had thought about the great distances, the stormy seas, and the fragility of Stone Age boats and wondered why people would cut all ties with their friends, families, potential mates, and allies. Why would they pass uninhabited lush valleys and rich salmon streams to paddle quickly and relentlessly toward the frigid Arctic? Warfare? Famine? No, to me that still didn't make sense. There was plenty of food in Kamchatka and few people to compete against. From the start of this journey, I had postulated that the original migrants might have been driven instead by romantic or spiritual motives or by a plain, old-fashioned love of adventure.

In 1988, Chris and I had kayaked from northern Canada to Greenland following the migration of Qitdlaq, an Inuit shaman. Qitdlaq was born around 1800 on the southeast coast of Baffin Island, in the Canadian Arctic. He became a powerful shaman, an *angakkuq*, who was obeyed and feared by his people. Sometime between 1830 and 1835, while hunting caribou, Qitdlaq crushed a companion's skull with a rock. None of the other hunters discussed the murder after they returned to camp, but another *angakkuq* saw it in a dream and ordered several sled dogs to attack Qitdlaq. Qitdlaq escaped and migrated north with a small group of loyal followers. Hounded by invisible *angakkuq*s, and restless at heart, Qitdlaq made frequent spirit journeys into uninhabited lands even farther north and returned to tell his people of abundant game and lush homesites. Finally the entire band set out for Greenland, guided by Qitdlaq's visions. Qitdlaq and his group covered 2,000 miles in ten years. This 200-mile-per-year average is considerably slower than the pace that Misha and I were maintaining but much faster than the migration speeds estimated by Dillehay.

Qitdlaq was a murderer and an outcast, but he was also a shaman, a charismatic leader, and a compulsive wanderer. He stopped for a few years after he had traveled far enough to escape his enemies. Food was plentiful in this interim camp. But then he saw a new land in a vision, and he packed up and moved with his band into the unknown. Pilgrims on a vision quest can travel much faster and farther than careful people searching for new hunting grounds. Perhaps the first Jomon migrants were more like Qitdlaq than the sober lot in Professor Dillehay's logic. Perhaps they followed a powerful chief; perhaps they followed a murderous madman. And sometimes, what is the difference?

MISHA AND I paddled to shore and camped on a thick carpet of moss. Each day's journey seemed an almost infinitesimal passage across the map, but gradually we were moving north. We were traveling into higher latitudes of longer summer sun about as rapidly as the season progressed and the days shortened. So far the two trends were neutralizing each other, and the number of daylight hours remained almost constant. Although at present we were enjoying long days and only a few hours of darkness, eventually season would defeat latitude, and night would overtake us. Arctic sedges had replaced the grasses that grew in southern Kamchatka, and the waist-high brush of the south had been replaced by willow "trees" that were half as tall as my middle finger. There were no streams at the tip of the peninsula where we were camped, so Misha left with the water bottles, saying, "I am hydrogeologist. I find water." I collected driftwood, and when Misha returned with water, we cooked dinner.

The Chinese Taoist philosopher Lao-Tzu taught that a person should be so content that he or she can view the smoke rising from a nearby village and never once feel compelled to walk down the road to visit the people who live there. Melville, though, had *Moby-Dick*'s narrator tell us that if you stay home too long, frustrations will build up until you wander around knocking people's hats off—or go to sea. Humanity isn't divided neatly into villagers on the one hand and wanderers on the other. Our species exhibits a broad and continuous distribution of personality types. Most Jomon stayed in their villages. Others sailed south to eat breadfruit and coconuts in Tahiti. A few paddled from Japan to North America.

I poured two cups of rice into the pot and added salmon steaks and wild onion to make a soup. Five yards away, an ermine poked its head from a small pile of rocks. Its back was brown but its stomach remained white, the color of winter. It inched into the daylight and stood on its hind legs, sniffing us, its muscles poised for action. I slowly reached for my camera, aimed, focused, and snapped the shutter. At the mechanical sound, the ermine disappeared so rapidly that I wondered if the film had caught it in the $^1/_{125}$th of a second of exposure time. I leaned back to absorb the sun. Dime-sized flowers reached out for light and heat, spreading their pollen, covering the tundra with splotches of purple, white, and yellow.

Misha and I hadn't talked for a while. I looked up and asked, "Misha, why do you think the Jomon paddled from Japan to Alaska?"

Misha thought for a while. "I don't know."

"OK, why are you paddling to Alaska?"

Misha didn't need to think about that. "I have spoke at you about this. Many times. Don't you remember? At home I am making too many papers. My health was crashed. I need to see wild nature."

"And now?" I asked.

His gold tooth shone as he smiled. "I am tired and sore, but I feel young and healthy."

W E SET out at 4:00 A.M. the following morning on a seventeen-mile crossing to the tip of the next peninsula. An offshore wind drove waves over our decks and pushed us steadily out to sea, so we adjusted course to compensate for the drift. When the distant hills ahead seemed to hide behind the rising sun, I steered instead toward low-angle rays that reflected off the wave tops and dispersed in long, undulating lines across the sea.

As the sun ascended, the fuzzy bluish outlines of the hills gradually sharpened into distinct ridges broken by gullies and small drainages. By early afternoon the hills appeared green and I could see a thin line of white sand between the sea and the tundra. The wind abated, and when we were close to land I saw a dense concentration of small, U-shaped black arches rising out of shoal water.

"What do you see there, Misha?"

"I don't know."

The curves were too smooth and graceful to be rock.

"Maybe they're mermaids sunbathing."

Misha didn't know what a mermaid was, so I explained.

As we drew gradually closer, the colors became more distinct. White-guano-covered rocks rose above floating dark green kelp. Between the kelp beds, the water was here light blue and there deep aquamarine, depending on its depth. The mysterious objects were jet black highlighted by a thin edge of sunlight. We slalomed around the shoals until one of the objects disappeared with a splash. Then, almost immediately, all of the arches wiggled and slithered into the sea. Sunlight reflected from water droplets that hung momentarily in the air. Then the droplets fell into expanding ripples, and gradually the ripples subsided, leaving no trace of the black curves. We stopped paddling and drifted. A few moments later, hundreds of whiskered seals bobbed to the surface, only their nose and eyes rising above the water. They all turned toward us, staring curiously.

They were seals, not mermaids, and had evidently slithered onto the rocks at low tide. When the rising tide flooded the rocks, the seals refused to quit sunbathing. Instead, they arched their backs, raising their heads and feet out of the water to absorb the precious summer sunlight. It seemed like an uncomfortable way to nap, but I'm not a seal.

We rounded the peninsula and camped on its eastern shore. The barometer dropped overnight, and the following morning lenticular clouds—dense and flat on the bottom and rounded on top, like flying saucers—crowned the cliffs. The effect was like gale-driven snow on a ridge-top cornice, or like grass bending in a summer breeze—a visible manifestation of wind. In fact, lenticular clouds are a harbinger of an impending storm. We decided to hug the coast toward the village of Vyvenka. A few miles out of town, we saw a forty-foot fishing boat moored alongside a large fish trap.

In Alaska, fishermen catch salmon in nets or on trolling lines, but the Russians use traps. To set a fish trap, the men first string a half mile of fine-mesh net from the shore straight out to sea. At the end of this net they rig a mazelike entrance into a large area enclosed by a second net. The linear net deflects salmon into the trap. After a few days, the fishermen pull the trap taut like a purse seine and collect the fish. This is no-nonsense commercial fishing, far removed from sport or the thrill of the chase.

One man on the back deck of the boat was preparing caviar while another peeled potatoes. They saw us and hollered greetings. We tied off our boats, balanced delicately on our tippy cockpit rims, and hoisted ourselves aboard. The captain climbed out of the narrow hatchway and ushered us into the crowded cabin, with its heavy smell of unwashed bodies and dead fish. A large table filled the aft portion of the cabin, and a double-decked sleeping platform was located forward. Six men sat around the table chatting while two dozed on reindeer hides spread across the bunk. The cook filled a wood-fired stove with driftwood to heat leftover fish stew and boil water for tea.

Misha explained our journey while I relaxed. When the food was hot, the captain ladled steaming stew into our bowls and put a loaf of fresh bread and a plate of red caviar on the table. All the men were Koryaks, with the high cheekbones and narrow eyes of aboriginal Siberians, though some had light-colored skin and one even had blue eyes inherited from intermarriage with nineteenth-century Cossacks or modern Russians.

I would have been content just to enjoy the warm food and my internal calm, but here was a chance to learn something of the folkways of these exotic fishermen. I slathered a thick layer of caviar over the fresh bread and wondered where to start.

During the previous winter, I had read about aboriginal salmon fishing across the Pacific Rim. In the book *First Fish, First People*, an Ainu elder described how her father placed the first salmon of the fall run on a ceremonial cutting board and passed it into the house through a special window reserved for the gods. The people then carried the first fish to a place of honor next to Fuchi, the chief goddess of the sacred hearth. Then,

> We took little piles of rice and malt for brewing sake, wrapped them up in paper, wrapped the paper in a bamboo leaf, and tied it all up nicely with shaved wood decorations. When the fish get to where the gods are, the little bundles become real bales of rice. So the fish gods make rice wine with it, and probably all the gods get together and drink it. And that was how we made sure that the salmon were happy and came back next year.

I took a bite of bread and caviar and washed it down with sugary hot tea. The captain had honored me by spooning the fish head into my bowl. I picked out the cheek meat, then ate the eyeballs.

"Misha, could you please ask these men how they honor the first salmon?"

Misha translated my question, but the men looked at me quizzically. I rephrased the question, but the fishermen and Misha were perplexed.

So I tried the third time, more simply, "*What do you do with the first salmon?*"

Everyone looked at me as if I were a bit daft.

"*We eat it.*"

I seemed never to acquire much information when I practiced journalism, so I shifted gears.

"*How's the fishing?*" I asked.

The captain shook his head. "*Not so good, but it's early yet.*"

One of the other men interjected, "*Last year was great; we caught two million pounds in this trap.*"

I whistled. "*Two million pounds—in this fish trap?*"

Misha told the men that I had been a commercial salmon fisherman in Alaska, and they looked at me with renewed interest.

The skipper paused as if weighing his thoughts. Then he asked how many fish we caught in Alaska and how much money we earned.

I looked around. Two million pounds is a tremendous catch, yet these men were obviously poor. I couldn't feign ignorance, and I didn't want to lie: "*Our boat employed a crew of four and caught 150,000 pounds in a good year. If fish wholesaled for $1.25 a pound, a crew member with a ten percent share could take home $18,750 in six weeks.*"

Everyone at the table stared straight at me, and the two men who were napping sat bolt upright in their bunks. The skipper found a pencil and made some calculations on the tablecloth.

"*Do you think that maybe the Japanese don't pay as much for Russian salmon?*"

I didn't want to make people feel bad, but I had to stick to the truth. "*Salmon are a commodity, traded internationally, like gold and oil. The Kamchatka salmon are high-quality fish. Japanese buyers will pay a high price for them.*"

The skipper wrote more numbers on the tablecloth. Finally he looked up. "*If the government and the mafia in Petropavlovsk only stole eighty percent of our earnings, we would all be rich. But now they steal ninety-five percent. We work for nothing.*"

We sat in silence, feeling the rocking of the boat and listening to the slurp of waves against the hull. The sea was rising, and the sailor in me snapped to. I stepped outside to an ominous gray sky and no wind. The combination of calm air and a rising sea meant that a storm was brewing at sea. If it were moving this way, we had to leave now or we would be trapped on this fishing boat.

W E PADDLED around the next point and toward a row of gray houses that stretched along the beach. Black smoke rose from a small electric generating station on the north end of town. Advance gusts of the storm wafted across the sea, painting the edges of the waves white. As we paddled closer, the tar-papered houses became more distinct. Between the houses, the ruins of concrete apartment buildings looked like fossilized skeletons of an extinct empire. But this wasn't ancient history. Soviet infrastructure and hegemony had collapsed only ten years before.

The rising wind roused the swell and drove a six-foot break almost vertically onto the beach. We paddled back and forth nervously, looking for the safest entry through the surf. I tightened the straps on my life vest and checked the lashings that secured the extra paddle and my sleeping bag to the deck. Then I inched closer, feeling the familiar, exhilarating steepening of each wave as it approached the shore. The kayak rose and accelerated and I turned it forty-five degrees to the wave.

Ka . . . woomph.

I leaned on my paddle as the water hit hard and buried me in foam. Then I rode the turbulence until the kayak bounced onto the beach, upright. Before I could jump out of the cockpit, two boys in ragged underpants and no shirts raced down the beach to grab the boat and hold it from sliding back out to sea.

"*Spaciba, spaciba,* thank you, thank you."

We dragged my boat above the waves, then turned to watch Misha's red kayak beyond the surf line. He made his initial move a little too soon, before the last of the big waves passed.

"Oh, shit!" I said above the sound of the surf

Misha's kayak rose, curled in the wave, and disappeared. Then I saw a splotch of red followed by a floating hat and a swimming body. The boys and I ran into the swash to grab his kayak, while Misha stood up, smiling, wet sand in his beard and his gold tooth glistening.

Misha talked with the boys, then they disappeared toward the houses. Within a few minutes, a tall man in army camouflage walked down to the beach. He was so muscular and broad chested that his legs looked skinny beneath his body. He walked with a bowlegged swagger, like a cowboy.

But he wasn't a horseman; he had developed his gait after a lifetime of riding snow machines and balancing on the decks of fishing boats. He introduced himself as Oleg, and we shook hands. Oleg pulled his moustache as he surveyed the storm, the brightly dressed but soaking-wet strangers, and the tiny plastic kayaks. He spoke to Misha, who instructed me to guard the boats, then the two men walked toward the houses.

A second man appeared on the beach. If Oleg looked like Jacob the farmer, this man looked like Esau the hunter. He was wiry, with a sharply angular face, pointed elfish ears, dark skin, and an impish smile that revealed four missing front teeth. A cigarette hung precariously off one canine tooth as if it were impaled there.

He stretched out his hand. "*Sergei*," he said.

"*Jon. Hello, how are you?*"

Sergei didn't bother with pleasantries but picked up my paddle and waved it in the air as if he were kayaking toward the horizon. Still waving the paddle, he walked down the beach until the waves slurped against his rubber boots. Then he turned, walked back toward me, and pantomimed that he wanted to sit in my boat. I nodded. He spun the kayak around to face the sea, slipped into the cockpit, and stared out at the angry surf.

Misha and Oleg returned. With a broad smile, and using a word I had taught him a few days before, Misha announced, "We have found our fairy godmother." Oleg motioned we should carry our kayaks toward a shed. After showing us where to secure our gear, he led us into a small house and built a welcoming fire in the *petchka*. We sat on rickety stools around a kitchen table. The tablecloth was white vinyl decorated with orange, purple, and red flowers that looked like a generic cross between tulips and roses. Knife marks sliced across the vinyl where someone hadn't bothered to use a cutting board. There was a mirror and a small sink in the far corner. A one-gallon bucket was nailed above the sink with a drop valve at its bottom. A few plates and cups perched in a dish drainer that was nailed to the wall.

Misha and I stripped out of our wet suits and baked by the *petchka* in our long underwear. When we were warm, we washed the salt off our hands and faces by tapping the drop valve and releasing water from the bucket; then we put on dry clothes. Soon a strongly built woman entered with a steaming teapot and a loaf of fresh bread. Her face was so round that her mouth seemed small and dwarfed. She set the food down and spoke in hesitant but grammatically correct English, "Hello, my name is Lydia. Welcome to our village. Welcome to our home." She grasped a piece of lint from my shirt and threw it in the fire, mumbling a short incantation in Koryak. Misha explained that she was banishing evil spirits that might be hiding in my clothing. We talked briefly about our journey, then Oleg, Sergei, and three other men trooped in and Lydia slipped away.

The men immediately started talking about hard times. During the Soviet era, two thousand people had lived in Vyvenka and the government had built concrete apartment buildings. A central heating plant pumped hot water through the apartments, and a generating station supplied electricity. The townspeople raised reindeer and caught salmon, and refrigerator ships transported the meat and fish south. Life wasn't luxurious, but it was comfortable and predictable.

Then, almost overnight, the Soviet infrastructure evaporated. The annual fuel tanker failed to arrive in 1996, so electric power became intermittent. In 1997 the electricity shut down for a year. The heating plant ran out of coal, and the Russian engineers flew south to find better jobs. For some reason they neglected to drain the system before they left, so the water froze and burst the pipes. The population of Vyvenka dropped to eight hundred. As winter closed in, the hearty Koryak pried the siding and windows off the frigid apartments, bashed in some of the concrete, and eviscerated the inner contents. They used the salvaged materials to build small homes that they could heat with driftwood. The market for reindeer meat evaporated. One day a Russian bureaucrat came to town and explained that all the fishing permits were now issued to large fishing companies in Petropavlovsk. The Koryak could no longer fish their own traps in their own village.

No one spoke for a moment, then Oleg, tight lipped and angry, added for emphasis, "*Now we work traps for the Russian companies, but they take all the profits.*"

Sergei added, "*There is a coal mine thirty miles from here, on Koryak land. The Russians use the coal in the town of Korpf, but for five years they wouldn't sell any to us.*"

Oleg continued, "*Geologists discovered a large platinum deposit upriver, and an American company opened a huge mine. They extracted $180 million dollars' worth of ore last year. But they don't hire many locals, and the money goes elsewhere.*"

I interrupted the conversation. If the storm slackened during the night, we would want to leave early in the morning. Was there a store in town where we could buy food?

"*Of course, we'll take you there.*"

We stepped outside. Wind was driving rain down the rutted street, past abandoned machinery and looted apartment buildings. Between the buildings, I caught glimpses of surf pounding against the beach. Oleg pointed toward a dilapidated concrete building, its green paint peeling, a few hundred yards away. I started to walk toward it, but he touched me lightly on the shoulder.

"Wait, Sergei will take you on his motorcycle."

At the end of World War II, the Russian army captured the BMW motorcycle factory in East Germany. They changed the name but maintained the factory. Thus the Ural motorcycle is a combination of generations-old German engineering and more modern Russian manufacture. The most popular model in Kamchatka has a sidecar for hauling passengers or freight. Sergei rolled his Ural from a shed, fumbled with the choke, kicked the starter several times, then pulled the wires off the spark plugs to blow on the contacts—more for good luck, I think, than any mechanical reason. Finally he kicked the starter again, and the engine coughed to life. As the honored American, I sat on a piece of plywood in the sidecar while Misha rode on a rusted metal bar behind Sergei's seat.

Sergei had a well-memorized, high-speed slalom course down the street. We snaked around three deep potholes, jumped onto the cracked sidewalk to avoid a huge mud puddle, skimmed past a telephone pole, dropped back on the street, and splashed to a stop in front of the grocery store.

Misha and I each had our own food fantasies. These dreams weren't unreasonable; I certainly didn't expect the abundance of a market in Petropavlovsk, much less the opulence of an American grocery store. Instead we both imagined stores like the one we had found in Ossora. I craved cheese and sausage; Misha hoped we could find garlic-flavored *sala*. We entered the store, stopped, and looked at each other silently. The room was dark and cavernous, with a hollow-sounding wood floor. The shelves were nearly empty.

A Koryak woman in a peasant kerchief stood forlornly by a dusty counter. When she saw us, she fingered her abacus expectantly.

"Cheese?" I asked.

"Nyet."

"Sausage?"

"Nyet."

"Bread?"

"Nyet."

"Sala?"

"Nyet."

We bought rice, sugar, flour, and hardtack crackers. Then she walked into the back room and returned holding a dusty twelve-ounce can of Dinty Moore beef stew. I had no idea where it might have come from or how long she had owned it, but I could see right away that she was a capitalist retailer who recognized the one rich customer of the decade.

Misha shook his head no, but she looked so dejected that I overruled. "*Da, harosho.*"

After we finished shopping, we told Sergei that we wanted to make a phone call to Martha, our contact in Petropavlovsk. When we were in Ossora, she had told us that an unseen problem was arising with our permissions and we should contact her at the next opportunity. Sergei explained that the Russian fishing company had a cell phone, so he revved up his machine and we raced to the boatyard.

Sergei and Misha went inside a small office while I waited in the maintenance shed. Two Koryak teenagers were engaged with early Iron Age technology, beating on an iron rod with a steel-handled sledgehammer and a dull hatchet. I had no idea what they were fabricating. Behind them, a Russian mechanic was tuning a new, polished Yamaha outboard motor.

WHEN THE Russian Cossacks first entered northern Kamchatka in 1697, they were repulsed by fierce Koryak warriors wearing bone-plated, seal-hide armor and walrus-skin helmets. Even after Russian reinforcements poured into the narrow neck of the peninsula, attacked isolated villages, and took hostages, the determined warriors kept fighting. But like the Apache and the Sioux in North America, the Koryak couldn't hold out forever. After sixty years of warfare—and their population had been reduced from 13,000 to 5,000—the surviving Koryak capitulated.

The Koryaks readjusted, then prospered under czarist rule. Lydia's grandfather, for one, had owned six thousand reindeer. Before the dark cloud of revolution hung over Russia in 1917, he traded reindeer meat with Yankee merchants from Alaska. For several years the Americans brought flour, tea, sugar, and noodles. Later the Koryak asked for Winchester rifles. As Lydia explained, "We wrapped some of those rifles in sealskin and seal fat and buried them. When hard times come, hidden rifles are worth more than food."

The victorious Red Army collectivized the old man's herd, and he died of despair a few months later. Meanwhile his brother hid in the mountains and continued trading with the Americans until the Red Army chased him down and shot him.

Once again the Koryaks were defeated, but not destroyed. After the old chiefs died out, the younger generation rebuilt and prospered. In the 1980s before perestroika, Oleg managed a collective that operated four fish traps. Sergei ran the reindeer collective that rebuilt the herds to 6,000. In town, generators hummed, bulldozers broke ground for new apartments, and refrigerated storehouses preserved meat and fish that were eventually loaded onto freezer ships.

Now the Koryaks were immersed in a third crisis that could be called the Road Warrior Age—half in and half out of the twenty-first century. When the electricity worked, the people got a distorted glimpse of the world through television. In summer Japanese ships moored offshore to buy fish and trade for supplies. Lydia had studied at the university in Petropavlovsk, and her daughter was a student now. Almost every male over the age of fourteen was an excellent mechanic. Yet Vyvenka was farther from a paved intercontinental highway than almost any place on Earth barring Antarctica and Greenland. In recent years communication had become undependable and fuel and spare parts had become scarce, leaving the Koryak with a curious combination of intermittent twenty-first-century technology and Stone Age skills.

MISHA REACHED Martha after an hour of frustrating dialing and recalcitrant operators. He learned that, for some reason, our permissions were out of order and we were instructed to report to a government agency in Anadyr. Well, Anadyr was seven hundred miles away, and we would worry about that problem later.

Sergei's motorcycle was out of gasoline, so he shook the dirt out of a tin can that was lying on the ground and begged a few ounces of fuel from the mechanic. When his tired machine sparked to life, he nudged it into gear and opened the throttle full bore for the half-mile ride back to the house. Lydia served us fried salmon with potatoes from her garden. Then the men left, and she sat down to talk.

She explained that she had learned English at the institute in Petropavlovsk because English is the language of the business world and might come in handy someday.

"Someday?" I asked.

She smiled. "Yes, maybe someday," and she waved her hand into the future. Then she explained, "Now each person must find his own way. Oleg manages the fishing fleet for the Russians. I teach school nine hours a day in an unheated classroom for $180 per month. Sergei refuses to work for a pittance on the fish traps, so he hunts and fishes for his food and makes a little money doing odd jobs and selling caviar."

She thought for a while. "The word *Koryak* is derived from *koyanga*, which means reindeer. We are 'the people of the deer.' When I was a little girl, you would look up on the hillside and see a forest of antlers swaying slowly across the tundra. After perestroika, the herders drank too much vodka. Some of the deer ran away. Wolves ate some. Poachers from the nearby villages of Tillichiki and Korpf killed some. The tax men came and took many. Now there are no deer in Vyvenka. We hunt seals in the spring, we fish in July, collect berries in August, and shoot hares in the winter."

She was having trouble finding words, and slipped into Russian. Misha translated. "*We know how to fish. We can raise reindeer, herd reindeer, and butcher reindeer. But we don't know how to raise money, buy a ship with a freezing unit, sail the coast, and market the meat in Petropavlovsk or Vladivostok. And we don't know how to bribe the right officials to get the fishing permits. So we are poor.*"

She paused before speaking again. "*Winters are long, especially when there is no electricity or television.*"

OR months I had slept in a flapping tent enveloped by the incessant sound of surf, so the eerie silence of a house was disconcerting. I woke at first light, dressed, and walked outside. Wind whistled through the narrow alley between the houses. We couldn't paddle that day, so I could have gone back to bed, but instead I leaned into the gale and walked toward the beach. A storm at sea seems to arise from the beginning of time, before the continents rose from the ocean depths.

Sergei appeared, ghostlike, by my side. His cigarette, fanned by the wind, glowed bright red. "*Maybe, no storm tomorrow.*"

"*Yes,*" I answered, "*maybe no storm tomorrow.*"

We walked back inside and started a fire in the *petchka*. After an hour, Lydia and Oleg brought bread and salmon caviar. They sat down, and Lydia explained that Moolynaut had conjured up this storm to hold Misha and me in town so we could visit.

I didn't know who Moolynaut was, but I smiled amiably all the same.

Lydia talked with Oleg in Russian for several minutes. When they were finished, Misha explained that we were planning to go upriver in Oleg's speedboat to visit Moolynaut.

After Lydia, Oleg, and Sergei left to prepare for the outing, Misha told me that Moolynaut was a ninety-six-year-old great-great-grandmother, the village's shaman and healer. I wasn't sure I understood everything I was hearing, but I sensed that it probably didn't matter. I'd been living in a vague limbo of partial comprehension throughout our voyage. More often than not, circumstances and situations revealed themselves if I was patient.

We packed tea, sugar, and bread and dressed warmly. Sergei wouldn't let us walk a few hundred yards down the street, but his motorcycle was out of gas again, so we waited for half an hour until he found a coffee-cupful of fuel. He poured most of it into the engine, splashed the remainder into the carburetor, and we took off, snaking around potholes, jumping onto the cracked sidewalk, and skimming past the telephone pole. A young boy, obviously accustomed to the routine, jumped out of the way as we dropped back on the street and skidded to a stop at the trail that led out of town.

We walked over a low hill, with Lydia pointing out every edible and medicinal plant along the way. Then we descended to the Vyvenka River, where Oleg was cleaning the spark plugs of his outboard motor. When the plugs were screwed back in place, we pushed the eighteen-foot speedboat to the water's edge. The still-raging storm patterned the estuary with whitecaps, so I zipped up my parka, preparing to be doused. Oleg and Lydia's dog, Wolfchuck, jumped to his accustomed perch on the bow deck, while Misha, Oleg, Lydia, Sergei, and I sat on wooden crates behind the windshield.

Oleg's outboard was the first get-up-and-go internal combustion engine I had seen since we had left Petropavlovsk. He revved the late-model Yamaha and the boat planed off, skipping and bouncing across the whitecaps. Wolfchuck tried to dig his claws into the aluminum deck to hang on, looking back occasionally as if to ask Oleg to slow down. We passed several dozen shacks along the riverbank. A net was strung from each of them, and Lydia explained that the net sites had been passed down through families. The government allowed each family to harvest five hundred pounds of fish a year, but with little food in the grocery store, and little money, people would starve on their allotment, so everyone cheated.

After half an hour, we motored around a bend in the river and into the lee of Man with Fast Shoes Hill. Lydia told me that, a long time ago, a hunter cut a new type of snowshoes from narrow, curved pieces of wood instead of the traditional webbed oval. Apparently this man could slide down the hill without walking, and every day in winter he would climb the hill just to slide down.

"I understand this man," I answered with a smile.

Oleg steered into a calm cove in front of a small shack. Without the wind, the summer sun felt warm. A man who looked about forty years old was in his boat, plucking fish out of the net, while on shore an old woman crouched on the ground, cleaning fish. We stopped briefly to talk with the man, who was Moolynaut's grandson, then motored to shore.

Moolynaut wore a dirty three-quarter-length blue coat, and her thin gray braids were bound in a crimson kerchief. She carried a long knife in a sheath that was angled across her abdomen, like a young warrior. She rose slowly, as if each creaky bone was reluctant to reorient itself. When she was half upright, her skeleton seemed to say "Enough!" She clutched her cane and hobbled toward us. Bent at the waist, she was a little over four feet two inches tall; even if she could have stood straight, she would have been less than five feet. She smiled, radiating warmth and friendship from her wrinkles. Then, after a few cursory pleasantries, she squatted back down on the ground and continued cleaning the almost iridescent red sockeye salmon with precise, steady strokes of her long knife.

Lydia ushered us into the shack and started a fire in a small sheet metal stove. Because Misha and I had been living outside all summer, I would have been more comfortable squatting on the grass outside, but I was the honored guest, so Lydia piled wood on the stove until the shack felt like a *banyo*. Moolynaut's summer dwelling was about twelve feet by fifteen feet, with two sleeping platforms covered with reindeer hides. One edge of a small table was nailed to the wall, and two rickety legs supported the other edge. There wasn't enough room for everyone to sit around the table for tea, so Sergei ripped the table out of the wall, moved it to the center of the room, and supported the legless end on an old crate and a few pieces of driftwood. Lydia directed me to sit as close to the red-hot stove as possible. Three men from a neighboring fish camp stopped by to visit.

Lydia explained that when Moolynaut was born, her mother dreamed that the young infant would be a shaman and healer. That was how she earned her name, which meant "woman who gives blood for the people." Moolynaut was healing people by the time she was a teenager, and afterward she learned spells to guard the reindeer herds from marauding wolves.

"Where does she get her power?" I asked.

"She was born with it." Then Lydia paused. "And she often eats the red mushroom."

"What?"

"The red mushroom. If you prepare it in a special way and eat it, the mushroom takes you to the other world and gives you special powers."

Lydia boiled water for tea, and Moolynaut hobbled into the shack. She reached across the table and ate three heaping spoonfuls of sugar from the community bowl, then sat on the sleeping platform. Lydia announced that I could ask questions now.

Caught off guard, I searched for something to ask. I wanted to say, "Tell me about all the transitions you have seen, from life under Czar Nicholas to the Bolshevik Revolution, to Stalin, and through perestroika, all viewed from this remoteness as if another planet, on a rich land now impoverished by a capricious government. Tell me about your power, where it came from, what it feels like inside, what you can do with it. And tell me, did you conjure up the storm to hold us here in Vyvenka?" But all that was too much, too soon, too presumptuous.

All across the north, the main topic of conversation was about animals, so instead I asked, "*Tell me a story about bears.*"

She smiled and clapped her hands in joy. Her wrinkled face opened into a huge smile, revealing teeth that were worn but largely intact. She broke off a piece of bread and ate it with a few more spoonfuls of sugar, then started talking in Koryak. Lydia, who was tired of speaking English, translated to Russian, and Misha translated to English.

"*Once when I was a little girl—a long time ago—I saw a bear. And I was very frightened. And the bear stood up and it was very big.*"

Moolynaut laughed until her whole body rocked. She clapped her hands again and rocked back and forth, smiling and chuckling. When she had composed herself, she continued.

"*And the bear ran away.*"

Then, satisfied that her story was finished, Moolynaut took one last spoonful of sugar and walked outside to clean more fish.

One of the fishermen realized that I had been hoping for more, so he asked, "*Would you like to know how we hunted bears in the old days?*" When I nodded, he continued. "*Several men would surround a bear, and the bear would stand to defend itself. The men in front of the bear would wave their spears in its face but stay out of range of its paws. Then other hunters would*

*dart in from behind and cut its Achilles' tendon. Once it was crippled, it was easy
to kill."*

"No," another man countered. "*The best way to kill a bear was to throw an
anorak* [parka] *at the bear when it was standing. The bear would reach out to
catch the anorak, and then, when its paws were occupied, a hunter could duck low
and thrust a spear into its heart."*

"Yeah, that worked," suggested a third. "*But it was much easier to catch them
while they were hibernating. First you must find a bear's den. Then one man
would take off all his clothes. You know in those days clothes were made of animal skins. Bears have a very good sense of smell so the hunter would have to remove his clothes so he wouldn't smell like a reindeer or a seal. The naked hunter
would crawl into the den while the bear was asleep and loop a rope around the
bear's neck. He had to be very careful not to wake the bear by touching its nose or
paws. Then the men who were outside would pull on the rope while the man in
the den would crawl behind the bear and push on its rump. Once they dragged the
bear into the open air, they would pounce on it with spears."*

"*Wow,*" I remarked. "*Those men must have been really strong and brave."*

"Not really," Sergei responded with his elfish smile. "*A bear is pretty small.
Before bears we hunted mammoths. Those men in the old days who hunted mammoths, they were the tough guys."*

Other men offered their opinions.

"*The warriors who fought the Russians were pretty tough."*

"*But not as tough as the runners."*

"*Who were the runners?"* I asked.

"*Sometimes, when a baby boy was born, his mother would see in a dream
that he was destined to be a runner. When a runner was ten years old, his father
would tie one end of a rope around his neck and the other end to a reindeer. Then
he would whip the reindeer into a run and the boy would have to run as fast as
the reindeer so he wouldn't be strangled. Once a runner was grown, he would
become a lookout. When the Russian Cossacks were coming, the lookout would
start a signal fire, but if it was too foggy he would carry the news by foot."*

"*Sometimes it wasn't the Cossacks, but the Koryak from Karaginsky Island."*

"*Yes, they were very bad men."*

"*They would come here to steal wives because they didn't have enough women
on Karaginsky Island."*

"*When the runner reached a river, he would use his spear as a pole vault and
jump across the river. A good runner could jump a hundred meters that way."*

"*How would they cross a really wide river?"* I asked. "*The Vyvenka River is
a lot more than a hundred meters across."*

"*Oh, to cross a wide river, the men would run very fast. Then they would spin their spears like a propeller and fly across.*"

All the men nodded in assent.

"*Let me ask you a question,*" I said. I explained our journey and the Jomon migration before us. "*Why do you think that those Jomon traveled so far under such hard conditions to find a new home? Why did they travel north toward the cold rather than south toward the tropics?*"

Everyone thought for a while, then one of the men spoke. "*I don't think that the migration was that big a deal. Those guys were tough. It would be no big deal to get in a boat and paddle to Alaska.*"

"*Yes, seals, bear, and salmon live all the way to Alaska. The people wouldn't have to learn new hunting techniques. It would be harder to migrate south, where they would have to learn how to live in a different land.*"

"*There are no salmon to the south. Who would want to move to a place where there are no salmon?*"

"*We all know how to catch salmon, but none of us knows how to climb a co-conut tree. Those guys who climb coconut trees are really tough.*"

Everyone laughed.

Sergei looked at me with a wry grin. "*Are you brave enough to take off your clothes and crawl into a bear's den? Of course not. Could you make a propeller out of a spear and fly across a river? Of course not. You and Misha—you're not very tough. And you're paddling to Alaska. If you could do it, tough guys could paddle to Alaska without making a big deal about it. Maybe these Jomon guys just went to Alaska because they were looking for a better life for themselves. People are always looking for a better life.*"

Lydia interrupted the conversation by serving lunch. She placed a huge king salmon head on my plate, along with mashed potatoes and wild onions. Everyone else had to make do with salmon steaks.

After lunch, we walked outside into the sunshine. Moolynaut stood, shouldered a load of fish, and slowly but confidently walked across a bouncy six-inch plank that spanned a gully. Once on the other side, she strung the fish on a drying rack.

Misha and I walked across to help her and to say good-bye. I desperately wanted to ask her, "Did you know that we were coming? Did you see it in a vision? Did you ask the spirits to bring the storm?" But the words wouldn't come.

She grasped me by the elbow, looked directly into my eyes, and spoke in Russian so Misha could translate: "*You must come back. You must come to visit the Holy Stone. It would be good for you. It would be good for our people.*"

AS WE motored downriver in Oleg's speedboat, I thought about my first meeting with a Siberian shaman. For most of our visit, Moolynaut had been more interested in cleaning fish than in talking to me. Was she teaching me a Zen lesson, showing by example that enlightenment derives from simple tasks rather than laborious conversation? Or was she simply an old lady cleaning fish? Or are they one and the same? Then I wondered why she had invited me to return to Vyvenka and visit the Holy Stone. Was the invitation a casual Koryak expression, like saying "see you later" rather than "good-bye"? Or was she really encouraging me to come back?

The wind was dropping and the gray clouds overhead were breaking apart, revealing small patches of blue. The boat skipped along smoothly, and Wolfchuck stood confidently on the front deck.

That evening as we were drinking tea, Oleg casually remarked, "*When you come to visit the Holy Stone, you understand that you will not be allowed to take pictures.*"

Sergei nodded. "*The last person who took pictures of the Holy Stone died three days later.*"

"*Drowned in the river,*" added Oleg.

In case I hadn't gotten the point, Sergei concluded, "*The people he was traveling with, they all died too—within a week. Evil spirits.*"

My first impulse was to exclaim, "Hey, wait a minute! Who says I'm coming back to Vyvenka?" I looked around the room; everyone was reacting as if I were destined to return. So I agreed to the camera ban.

Once the subject of evil spirits had been introduced, Lydia explained that the Koryak universe consists of five separate realms. We live in the middle, between two realms of goodness above and two realms of evil below. Sometimes spirits from the bottom level come to this world and inhabit a person. After a person dies, you are never sure whether the dead body is imbued with the person's spirit or with an invading evil spirit. You must carry the body onto the tundra and cremate it with tools and food for the afterlife. On the way home, you draw a sharp line in the dirt and say very loudly, "This is a river with lots of fish." Then, if the evil spirit were following you home, it would stop at the line so it could set its net and catch the fish. That way the evil spirit forgets to come to your house."

Lydia chuckled at the deception.

"Does this trick work all the time?" I asked.

Lydia didn't understand the question, so I tried again. "What happens if the evil spirit knows that the line is not a river? What happens if the evil spirit knows that you are trying to fool it?"

Misha translated and everyone talked rapidly in Russian.

Oleg replied, "*Yes, that happens sometimes. That is very bad.*"

Lydia became animated and spoke in English. "If the bad spirits cross the line, you must take ashes from your *petchka* and put them in the street. Then you make an X on your door with more ashes, and no one can go outside for several days. Then the spirit won't find you."

Misha translated into Russian and Sergei added, "*But if the spirit enters the house, it will take you too, and you will die.*"

Everyone nodded in somber agreement.

After a long silence, Oleg spoke. "*Once, the bad spirits tried to take me away. I was camping on the tundra, sleeping in my tent, and suddenly a soft furry animal sat on my chest, covering my mouth and nose and choking me. I knew that I was supposed to yell, 'Pai, pai,' which means 'Go away, devil,' but I couldn't yell because the furry thing was sitting on my chest and face. The thing felt heavier and heavier and was about to crush my chest. I couldn't breathe. Then a young man who was sleeping next to me woke up and started shaking me. The man shook me so hard that the furry thing slipped off my face and I quickly shouted, 'Pai! Pai!' And then the spirit disappeared.*"

Oleg waited for a few moments, then continued, "*I was fine, but the young man became sad the next day and every day he was sadder and sadder. He died ten days later.*"

I waited in respectful silence, then asked, "*Do you know why the spirits came for you?*"

"*No. There are bad shamans in the village. We call them cherny caldoons* [black witches]. *We all know these cherny caldoons. They are very dangerous. They send the devil spirits after you.*"

Lydia added, "Yes, the *cherny caldoons* are very smart. They are too smart to be fooled by lines in the dirt or ashes on your door. They are smart and dangerous. Sometimes they kill people. Sometimes they swim out to sea and tell the fish not to come back the next year. Then people starve."

"What would happen," I asked, "if there were a very, very *cherny caldoon?* What would happen if this *cherny caldoon* made the fish go away? The reindeer go away? The ducks and the seals go away? All the animals go away? Would people leave the village and find a new place to live?"

Misha translated and Oleg considered the question carefully. "*I don't know. If you tried to run away, the cherny caldoon might follow you. You would need to talk to a very powerful belee caldoon* [white witch]. *Maybe the belee caldoon would have a stronger spell and defeat the cherny caldoon. But maybe not. I suppose people might leave the village and travel far away. You would have to travel very far. Very, very far.*"

"Like to Alaska?"

Sergei leaned forward and asked quickly, "*Are you and Misha running from a cherny caldoon?*"

But Oleg changed the subject before I could answer. He explained that we had a long journey ahead and needed to discuss the weather and make plans for the morning.

THE STORM passed, and the following morning we blasted through the surf. We sat in our kayaks, feeling the closeness of the sea and our intense, six-week friendship. The opposite shore of the bay, twenty-eight miles away, appeared as a hazy blue line. A slight headwind brushed against my cheek and formed small ripples on the backs of the larger waves. The old dilemma faced us: We could paddle safely around the coastal perimeter of the bay, but the passage would take two days. If we headed straight east, we would be exposed to another dangerous crossing, but we'd be across in nine hours. Misha headed due east.

"Labor and Defend," he said.

"Yeah, Labor and Defend."

Despite the generosity of our hosts and the intriguing mystery of Moolynaut, I was happy to be back in my kayak, alone. I could stop talking, stop trying to understand Russian, stop being polite, and settle into the comforting monotony of paddling. In the space and void of the sea, my subconscious mind went to work, busily thinking but not immediately letting my conscious self in on the secret. But then, when Misha paddled close for a lunch break, I blurted out, "Misha, are we coming back to go to the Holy Stone?"

Misha looked over at me and smiled. "This is what I think about too."

"What's going on?" I asked. "You're a scientist. Do you believe that Moolynaut made a magic storm to bring us to Vyvenka? And if so, why?"

Misha pondered. "Yes, I am hydrogeologist. But this is Kamchatka. Sometimes science . . . How do you say it . . . Sometimes science does not talk to Kamchatka."

"Or maybe Kamchatka does not talk to science."

"Yes, maybe."

"Well, do you think that we should go to the Holy Stone?"

"First we must paddle to Alaska by our own hands. Then we will talk about this thing."

That evening I was so exhausted that I wrote only a few lines in my journal:

> We made the good (bad?) decision to cross the bay rather than take the safe route along the coastline. Scary headwind.
>
> Are we being smart or stupid? I don't know. Anyway, we keep pulling it off.

We didn't know it as we sat around the campfire that evening, but Misha and I were destined to return to Vyvenka not once but three more times— and Moolynaut would lead us through magical séances and mysterious passages. But that is a story for another time.

THE NEXT day we paddled south along the coast and neared Cape Govena at about three in the afternoon. We thought about camping in a tiny cove—more like a cleft in the rock—but the wind was light, the sea was calm, and the map showed some small coves around the point. Eager to make a few more miles, we pushed on.

Five killer whales glided past, parting the water with their tall, arched dorsal fins. Four adults swam in a diamond formation: one leader, two flanks, and one in the rear. A baby frolicked back and forth, lagging behind, then hurried to catch up. Cape Govena rose out of the sea—dark rock streaked with yellow and orange minerals formed under intense metamorphic heat from the bowels of the Earth. In front of us, the sea was divided by a line of seaweed, driftwood, and agitated foam. Though the ocean is vast beyond imagination, currents often collide along discrete borders, sometimes only a few feet wide. Current shears can be deadly, as Franz and I had learned the year before in the Kurils, so I stopped paddling to evaluate the situation. The Govena Peninsula formed a protective lee, and the sea was relatively calm behind us. But just ahead, beyond the line of detritus and foam, residual storm swells rolled in from the open ocean. Waves sheared off the calm water, forming a bubbly, agitated break. Misha didn't even slow down as he blasted through the shear and into the turbulent sea. I followed.

To our left, monster waves broke against a huge sea stack, sending a giant plume of spray into the sky. The adjectives—monster, huge, and giant—

are so imprecise as to be meaningless, but I had lost all sense of scale. Size and distance had warped my perception so that one instant these objects were no bigger than a pinhead, and then they filled the cosmos. My kayak rose on a wave, grandly gaining altitude, until the sea stack, the cliffs on the far shore, and even the thin strip of sandy beach stood out sharply. I was king of the mountain. Then I slid obliquely off the wave until towering walls of water surrounded me. The shore disappeared and Misha did as well, leaving me alone in a small yellow kayak on a limitless seascape.

Misha moved ahead with powerful strokes, seemingly unfazed by the commotion. Was this the same novice who, two months earlier, had paddled across a muddy pond with shaky hips and a hesitant stroke? After a mile we approached a small cove, but the swell broke violently against the rocks.

Misha stopped and I caught up to him. "This is too crazy," I yelled. "The nearest safe harbor is thirty-five miles around the point. It's four o'clock. We're tired. Let's go back to that cleft in the rocks before Cape Govena."

Misha smiled, and his gold tooth glistened. "I love the open sea."

I wanted to say, "Yeah, I love the open sea, too, but I also remember that day near Cape Horn when I catapulted down a breaking wave, spilled out of my boat, and dislocated my shoulder. I remember swimming for my life in a frigid sea, with a broken boat and a broken body. I remember walking for days along a windswept coast toward a Chilean naval base, and my eventual return to the United States—to orthopedic surgeons, needles, and a painful rehabilitation. I remember waiting seventeen years before I returned to Cape Horn to complete the journey."

What I said was, "Yeah, I love the open sea, too, but today I'm afraid of it."

We retreated past the sea stack, across the foamy white line, and into the lee of Cape Govena. Then we hauled our boats to shore. A forty-foot cone of avalanche debris had buried most of the beach. I looked toward the high mountain basin and imagined the churning, roiling wall of snow that had poured over the cliff during the winter. A waterfall cascaded onto the cone; to the right of that, storm surf had carved a small level platform out of the beach gravel, just large enough for one tent. But a grizzly bear trail crossed the platform. If we pitched our tent here, we would be breaking an obvious and fundamental adage:

DON'T PITCH YOUR TENT IN THE MIDDLE OF A GRIZZLY TRAIL!

But we had no other reasonable choice: It was late in the day, and this was the only safe landing spot for miles in either direction. We couldn't camp in the intertidal zone or on the cliff, so, after considerable discussion, we pitched our tent right smack-dab in the middle of the grizzly trail.

The following morning we studied fresh tracks. During the night, a large grizzly had descended from the high tundra, followed the well-worn trail, and stopped six feet from our tent. Scuff marks showed that the bear had shuffled back and forth before it walked around the tent and continued along the beach.

The next day, July 14, we paddled around Cape Govena again. The sky was an intense, primordial blue: pollution free. The storm waves had collapsed into gentle rollers that lifted our boats and cradled them in the troughs. Pillars of white spume rose as waves crashed into the sea stacks, but the break didn't evoke the urgency and terror of the previous afternoon.

Expedition time is measured in split seconds during a surf landing or by long hours in the slow passage of the afternoon sun or the rise and fall of the tides. Now we were molding our progress around a weekly cycle of storm, calm sea, and warm sun. Thinking back over the past two months, I remembered the cold, snowy spring and the sea ice. Now the tundra was blanketed with flowers and dominated by mosquitoes. Retreating deeper into memory, I thought about Franz and our adventures a year ago as we sailed from Nemuro and across the Kurils.

Surely the Jomon mariners traveled as we did, timing their movements to the rhythms of nature. As I paddled through the long afternoon thinking about the Jomon migration, I idly speculated on the unknowable: did some people return from the Americas to Asia to tell their friends and relatives about fertile lands and abundant game so far away?

I also wondered why the Jomon eventually died out in the Americas. Were they killed off by the more powerful Clovis hunters? Were the initial populations too small to be genetically sustainable? Or did the Jomon intermarry and assimilate with the later migrants? No one knows the answers to these questions. Perhaps no one ever will.

My reverie was interrupted when I looked down at my map. Several months before, sitting at my desk in Montana, I had drawn a red line on the chart. Now that red line corresponded with a nondescript and unnamed point off my port beam.

I called out to Misha, "We've come exactly 987 miles from Petropavlovsk. We are now halfway from Petropavlovsk to Alaska. We have 987 miles to go."

Misha looked at me, smiled, raised his fist, and cheered.

Yes, the journey was about living within nature's cycles. Soon the mosquitoes would lay their eggs and die, the tundra would turn from green to yellow, the nights would grow longer, and frost would rule the darkness. The ocean is unlike the mountains in that it has no summit and no downhill. We could expect just as many storms, mishaps, and hardships on the second half of the passage as on the first. But psychologically the half that lay ahead seemed shorter, the time and distance remaining more fathomable. Only 987 miles. Piece of cake.

EVERY day we paddled to exhaustion. Every evening I calculated our average speed, the remaining distance to Alaska, and our estimated arrival date. We were moving well, but we still hadn't made up for the time lost in June. "Time lost" is a funny idiom, more closely linked to the urban rat race than an ocean wilderness. What we were racing was the onset of another Arctic winter.

By the afternoon of July 18, we had paddled twenty miles since morning and were only three and a half days behind schedule. But then a rising headwind cut our speed by half, and the village of Apuka was still eight miles ahead. Suddenly my whole body revolted against our self-imposed itinerary, against another wet four-hour slog into interminable swells that relentlessly pushed us backward, sucked oxygen out of our muscle cells, and inflamed my overworked tendons.

"Hey, Misha! What do you think? Maybe we could camp here and paddle to town in the morning?"

WE LANDED on a rocky shore, changed into dry clothes, and scrambled up the hillside to look for a tent site, but the terrain was too steep. We should have changed back into our clammy, cold, wet paddling outfits and returned to sea, but a hot meal and a few hours of sleep sounded a lot more inviting, so we piled rocks into a crude tent platform between the high tide line and the hillside. That night the barometer dropped, the wind intensified, the tide rose, and the surf built. Waves beat against the shore, rolled inland, and struck our tent. The aluminum poles bent, the fabric shook, lines loosened, and water filtered through seams and zippers. Several times that night we had to wiggle out of our wet sleeping bags, clamber into the storm, and wallow in the rising surf to retie the lashings. By morning we were soaking wet, and the tide was still coming in.

I apologized to Misha for my lapse of resolve and stamina that had gotten us into this mess, and he smiled back warmly. I put my arm around his shoulder and thanked him for not being angry with me.

Four lines of breakers stretched along the coast, and curlicues of foam slithered like snakes between the breakers. Periodically the snakes seemed to bunch up, intertwine, and swim to the top of the next collapsing wave. We packed our bags in silence, loaded the boats, and sat on the rocks. The tide kept rising.

It was the classic sailor's nightmare: a storm, a lee shore, a rocky coast. We could either wait there and be battered against the rocks or try to paddle into deep water. Misha climbed into his cockpit and secured his sprayskirt. A rogue wave broke against his chest, and his kayak floated free before he was ready. The next wave rolled in and knocked him sideways, so I jumped into the water, grabbed his stern, pointed the boat straight, and pushed him seaward with all my strength.

Misha took a few powerful strokes and stopped to lower his rudder.

I shouted, "Forget the rudder! The next wave will hit you! PADDLE! PADDLE! PADDLE!"

But Misha ignored me. His rudder jammed, and he turned to fiddle with the line. Foam snakes coiled around his bow as if to squeeze the boat into a thin speck of crumpled plastic. Nothing could save him now—nothing but an elegant boat design and a few precisely timed paddle strokes. YES, the rudder dropped into place! He was paddling! His boat rose on the wave; he leaned forward, reached into the break, and propelled himself into the next herd of foam snakes. I stared at the colorful Lotus-flower logo on the back of his life jacket. A few moments later, he paddled into deep water.

Now it was my turn. I wedged my kayak between two rocks to stabilize it, slipped into the cockpit, tightened my sprayskirt, and stared into a seemingly impassable barrier of foam, rock, and wind. Then my perspective altered, as if I had changed lenses on a camera. With the wide-angle lens, all I saw was an infinite commotion, but when I snapped in the telephoto, I focused on that magical line that is the joy and salvation of every adventurer. With that clarity, I saw my boat hitting the breakers at 20 degrees off the perpendicular and flowing over the foam. In the same frame, I saw the timing, the precise position of my paddle, and the response of my hips.

A wave lifted my boat. I pushed clear of the rocks, dug my paddle into the aerated swash, found green water, and surged through the first wave with a few quick, powerful strokes. Then I took a deep breath—in case I rolled upside down and oxygen suddenly became a rare commodity. The foam snakes led me toward deep water.

The kayak rose into the dark, near-vertical liquid wall, and I stroked hard as the wave grinned its first white smile. My boat rose; I looked briefly into the sky and crested the wave, then dropped with a thud back into the foam snakes. There were two more breaking waves to go. Deep breaths. Think timing . . .

Misha cheered when I cleared the last line of surf.

"We have a saying in Russian," he told me. "The adventure is good if the final is good."

I thought for a moment, then responded, "In English we say, 'All's well that ends well.' "

Misha nodded. "Yes, how do you say that again?"

I repeated, then shouted, "Lunch in Apuka!" and pointed my paddle northward like a lance.

WE PADDLED around the point, rode wild surf into Apuka, and dragged our boats up the beach. A passing fisherman greeted us excitedly—the mayor of Vyvenka had telephoned ahead, and people were expecting us. The fisherman told us to wait, then rushed off to summon the mayor, Alexei, a short, round man, slightly balding, with a warm smile. He had already arranged for us to stay in the local schoolhouse. A man approached on a three-wheeled motorcycle that, like Sergei's, served as a pickup truck. He balanced Misha's boat on the sidecar, sped off to the school, then returned for mine.

The school was a long, one-story, wood-frame building sided with black tar paper. Inside, the students had painted tropical fish on the otherwise dreary, unlit hallway with its peeling paint and falling plaster. The classrooms were unheated, but the schoolteacher had built a fire in the kitchen stove, and we hung up our sopping gear. Then the mayor offered us a shower and led us to the electric generating station—the only source of running hot water in town. We entered a cavernous room that contained two large diesel motors, each about as tall as a person and twice as long. Both were still. One was missing the head, revealing the skeletal, oil-coated pistons. The second engine was slightly less denuded, but bolts were missing, wires and fuel lines dangled uselessly, and someone had removed one of the valve covers.

In an adjacent room, a third diesel rumbled, vibrating the building gently. The mayor shouted above the noise, explaining that the town couldn't buy replacement parts for the motors—the mechanic had cannibalized parts from the two older motors to keep this one running.

"*And when you can't find the part you need from the older motors?*" I asked. The mayor shrugged. "*Then we won't have any more electricity.*"

We walked past greasy spare parts and rusting drums of motor oil that were half hidden in the shadows. The room was about thirty feet high, with a gantry crane on the ceiling. Cables, chains, pulleys, and blocks hung from the crane and the steel catwalks that circled the room fifteen feet above our heads. It would have made a perfect setting for the final scene of a B-grade shoot-'em-up movie. In my imagination, I heard bullets ricocheting off dead machinery and watched the hero swing out of harm's way on clanking chains.

We climbed steel steps onto the catwalk and ahead to a small second-story room with a single showerhead. The water was warm enough not to be freezing but cold enough that we soaped up and rinsed off quickly before jumping back into our damp, smelly clothes. Then we walked to the mayor's office and sat on straight-backed wooden chairs in front of a plain wooden table. A green lamp cast a glow across the table. A faded red rotary telephone provided some forlorn assurance that we were in the twentieth century, or at least within spitting distance. The mayor sat at the head of the table, and a single white envelope—the only indication of commerce and politics—sat ominously in the center. After we exchanged pleasantries, he handed me the letter. It was from Martha in Petropavlovsk.

Martha asked how we were doing and wished us well. Then she explained that by the time we reached Apuka, we would be leaving Kamchatka and about to enter Chukotka, the oblast (equivalent to a state or province) on the extreme northeast edge of Siberia. Before we left Petropavlovsk, we had signed a contract promising to pay a travel agent named Sergei $500 for our permissions in Chukotka. Now Martha explained that complications had arisen. A few weeks ago, Sergei had sent a fax, apologizing obsequiously but at the same time explaining that the fee should have been $5,000. In addition, he had forgotten that we needed to pay M-CH-S, the official government rescue agency, which claimed that it must assume a heightened state of readiness to anticipate the probability of rescue. I was supposed to walk into the M-CH-S office in Anadyr with a huge stack of hundred-dollar bills. The officer at the front desk would then decide how many of the bills I should hand over to compensate the government for this heightened state of readiness.

I explained the content of the letter to Misha, and Misha translated for the mayor. We all sat in silence for a few moments.

The mayor shook his head. *"That is outrageous. Those fees are for tourists. You're not tourists, you are puteshestveniks. Puteshestveniks do not need to pay these fees. These men are robbers."*

I liked the ring of that title. Homer was a *puteshestvenik*, wandering from town to town, singing the Iliad and the Odyssey. Years later, when the Silk Road caravan drivers came to Macedonia from the east, young King Alexander welcomed them as *puteshestveniks*, not as tourists. Slave women washed their feet and brought them wine and olives. Then Alexander ushered the travelers into the royal chambers and listened to stories of India and other lands he wished to conquer.

JARED DIAMOND, Pulitzer Prize-winning author of *Guns, Germs, and Steel*, has written several articles on the importance of old people in Stone Age societies. He wrote, "For almost the whole of our evolutionary history, our repository of knowledge lay in the memories of people, not in books." Elsewhere he noted, "We cannot conceive of preliterate society's absolute dependence on old people as the equivalent of libraries." If old people were the databases of an individual clan, young *puteshestveniks* linked disparate clans and were Stone Age communication networks.

In Siberia, throughout the seventeenth, eighteenth, and nineteenth centuries, *puteshestveniks* were granted diplomatic immunity in times of warfare, because, as noncombatants, they could supply information to either side. Today, even though the Soviet Union sent the first man into space and built missiles and atomic weapons, the technological infrastructure in Siberia has collapsed. At present, there are no newspapers in Apuka. When the electric generator breaks down or runs out of fuel, often for weeks or months at a time, there is no television or radio. The red phone on the mayor's desk was connected to the nearby village of Pahachi and not to the outside world. Sometimes the mayor of Pahachi could patch a call to or from Apuka to Petropavlovsk, but often the connection failed. There wasn't a computer anywhere nearby. Misha and I carried the news. I knew the price of salmon on the international market. Misha talked about taxes and business affairs in Petropavlovsk. In addition, we provided entertainment, telling stories about our journey. We weren't tourists, but the bureaucrats in the big city of Anadyr wanted our money.

SEALS, sea lions, and sea otters were so ubiquitous that I stopped mentioning them in my journal. On July 22 we saw our first walrus, a tusked harbinger of the high Arctic ahead. Two days later we counted six more, and the following day we saw another hundred.

Misha was afraid of killer whales, but I was more afraid of walrus. Although killer whales are quite capable of crushing a kayak and eating its occupants, there is no historical record of them doing so. On the other hand, my Canadian Inuit friends had warned me repeatedly to beware of walrus. When Chris and I kayaked from Ellesmere Island to Greenland, an old hunter named Pijimini explained that rogue male walrus will lunge onto the deck of a kayak, tip it over, then suck out the kayaker's intestines with its powerful lips.

"The walrus doesn't eat the man," he explained. "It just likes the soft parts, the insides. The insides of a kayaker taste like clams, which is what walrus eat most of the time."

When I laughed and expressed disbelief, Pijimini was insulted.

"Inuit make jokes," he said. "But we never joke about dangers on the land or on the sea. Never!"

What a horrible way to die, splashing in a blood-red sea without your intestines! But we had no defenses against a ten-foot, two-thousand-pound aquatic bullet with a thick, rubbery hide and three-foot ivory tusks. When I expressed my fears, Misha assured me that Siberian walrus never attack kayaks.

I replied, "Siberian walrus don't attack kayaks because no one in Siberia paddles a kayak anymore. When these walrus see their first kayaks, maybe one will try an attack just to see what will happen."

Misha shook his head and answered, "No," without further explanation.

I wasn't convinced, but I stored my fear away in a mental antechamber where it could shut the door and socialize with a million other anxieties.

When a walrus rises from the depths, the top of its head appears first, followed by its whiskers, lips, and, finally, tusks. The beast looks about and spits a spray of water with its exhaled breath. Its diminutive nostrils are perched over the jowls and tusks like a pom-pom on a child's head. The huge jowls form an inverted V that reminds me of a painted scowl on a clown's face. At the same time, the walrus's sedate stare looks like that of a stern but friendly country burgher. Lewis Carroll understood this enigmatic appearance, making his walrus in *Through the Looking-Glass* both a sage and a joker:

> The time has come,
> The walrus said,
> To speak of many things:
> Of shoes and ships and sealing wax,
> Of cabbages and kings.

The Inuit in Canada believe that the walrus is more deadly than the polar bear, but whom do you meet in the afterlife, dancing jauntily on its back flipper on the bottom of the sea? The walrus, of course.

Walrus have several different swimming styles. Sometimes they hold their heads high and lunge with their necks as if they're reaching out with their tusks to pull themselves through the water. At other times the walrus holds its head down and plows through the water as if it were a giant mole shoving through a suburban lawn and leaving a bulge of dirt behind. When the walrus accelerates, its body rises above the surface, looking bloated and pink, like something dead and putrefying. The illusion of awkwardness dissipates as the beast lopes in graceful curves like a dolphin, ending each arc with a delicate flip of its tail, like a curtsy from a one-ton ballerina.

Before the introduction of rifles and explosive harpoon heads, Siberian Chukchi and Inuit generally hunted walrus that were sunbathing on shore. The trick was to crawl stealthily behind a sleeping giant, then stab it in the back of the neck, penetrating its brain or severing its spinal cord. Even though this approach was safer than hunting on the open sea, walrus often turned on their attackers with lightning speed and unbridled ferocity.

Hunting pressure didn't affect walrus populations significantly until Russian fur traders armed with firearms took a deadly toll on all the marine mammals of the North Pacific. In the eighteenth century, the Russian American Fur Trading Company harvested 1.2 million sea otters, 135,000 Steller's sea cows, 73,000 fur seals, and "tens of thousands" of walrus.

It was a dangerous business. In these foggy, storm-tossed Arctic waters, half of the ships launched by the Russian American Fur Trading Company sank. Again and again, skippers would move their clumsy square-rigged ships close to the coast, then a fogbank would close in and an on-shore wind blow up while most of the men were hunting from the longboats. The skeleton crew on board would desperately try to claw off-shore through shoals and sea stacks until the horrible sound of crunching wood on stone announced their fate.

The slaughter continued after the Russians sold Alaska to the Americans and Yankee seamen moved into the area. By the dawn of the twentieth century, Steller's sea cows were extinct, only a few isolated colonies of sea otters had survived, the fur seal population had been decimated from 3 million to 120,000, and the walrus population had crashed from 250,000 to 50,000.

In the twentieth century, the world community became alarmed at the destruction of North Pacific marine ecosystems. Numerous unilateral and international conservation efforts were enacted to preserve sea mammal populations; as a result, these species have rebounded. Today the North Pacific is threatened by overfishing, industrial pollution, and global warming, but as Misha and I inched north, we shared the sea with abundant walrus as well as seals, sea lions, and sea otters.

ON JULY 26, Misha and I launched our boats into what I called in my journal "another Bering Sea day." In the morning fog, mountains sometimes looked like clouds; at other times, clouds looked like mountains. A gray whale covered with barnacles rose and disappeared, resembling an ocean swell rather than an animal. The fog lifted and we crossed an open bay. From a distance the rock on the other side had appeared uniformly black, but as we approached we saw bands of red iron oxide crossing veins of pink granite. Orange lichen, green seaweed, white seagull guano, and light pink murre guano coated the rock. Murres stood shoulder to shoulder on the ledges, nervously shifting from foot to foot, while Northern fulmars hunted from the sky. Gargoyle-like boulders protruded from the cliffs at odd angles. In the ocean, thirty sea lions roared at us. One splashed into the water as we passed, but the others held their ground.

We had been at sea for more than two months, and life back home seemed unreal. I knew that in another two months I would jump back into that familiar world where I would read about danger in the news rather than witness it personally, and I would fill time with electronic stimuli. But for now my life was dominated by the tyrannical monotony of paddling—the same motion every day, all day, infused with an internal battle to overcome a deep, debilitating fatigue—punctuated by occasional intense adventures. To find joy, it was necessary to penetrate the monotony and tap the incredible richness of every slowly changing moment.

That evening we camped in a small bay. We had paddled twenty-eight miles and were bone tired, so we built a fire and cooked dinner quietly. As the water boiled for our evening tea, we heard a voice say "*Zdrastvoote.*" We were caught off-guard, completely unaware that another human was in the area.

A young Koryak man stood behind us. He was dressed in worn, dirty canvas pants and shirt, with deerskin boots and vest. Dark hair and a wispy moustache offset a shy smile.

"*Zdrastvoote,*" I answered. "*Sit down, have some tea.*"

The man explained that he was camped in the next valley with ten other reindeer herders and 2,500 reindeer. They had eaten all their flour, rice, tea, and sugar, so he had walked to the coast to look for passing ships. He explained that during storms, ships occasionally sought shelter in this small bay, and if he found one, he would trade reindeer meat for commodities.

Although we'd been paddling for more than two months, we had yet to see a ship anchored in a bay. It occurred to me that the herders must be pretty desperate to pin their hopes on a random encounter with a ship.

The young man explained that before perestroika, "special men" sailed ships into this bay every summer and traded clothes, tools, and commodities for meat. After perestroika, the "special men" stopped coming, and now the clan was out of food.

We answered that we didn't have enough extra food for ten people. The young man looked at our kayaks and nodded.

"*But please,*" Misha enjoined, "*have some tea with us before you go.*"

We added more water to the teapot, and I stood up to collect driftwood. A second man was walking across the tundra toward our camp. Even from a distance I could tell that he was older than our present guest, because he walked with a slight stoop. The old man wore a red wool sweater with deerskin vest, pants, and boots. He carried a spear in one hand and a rifle in the other.

"*Zdrastvoote. Come, have some tea.*"

The spear was made out of a piece of rusty metal bashed to a crude point and lashed to a driftwood pole. The point was deadly enough, to be sure, but it wasn't nearly as elegant as Stone Age obsidian points in museums. When the conversation lagged, I asked why he carried both a rifle and a spear.

He looked at me and grinned. "*No bullets for the rifle.*"

"*Then why do you carry the rifle at all?*"

He smiled again, "*Maybe you have some bullets and you will give me two or three.*"

Misha explained that we had a shotgun with shotgun shells. The old man tipped his head as if to say, "No harm trying."

I continued, "*Do you use the spear for hunting?*"

"*No, I use the spear to defend myself against bear attacks.*"

I whistled softly, half under my breath, wondering if he was better prepared with a rusty piece of metal tied to a stick than we were with the "bear-off" and the small-caliber shotgun.

The two Koryak men and Misha talked about the problems of shipping reindeer to market in the post-perestroika capitalism of modern Russia. We broke out two Snickers bars from our goody stash, cut them in half, and shared them four ways. When we were finished eating, the old man stood, grasped me by the elbow with his left hand, and held my right hand with his right. His smile revealed crooked brown teeth beneath his high cheekbones and Asian eyes. He spoke in Russian, and Misha didn't need to translate. "*You have a dangerous journey ahead of you. But you are puteshestveniks and you know about the danger. Good luck. Good luck. Be safe.*"

Then he shouldered his rifle, grasped his spear, and nodded for the young man to follow him home, across the tundra.

Little did we know that we would meet these men again, four years later, camped in a reindeer hide tent deep in the interior tundra.

A FEW days later we approached Cape Rubicon, an insignificant blip on the map guarded by shoals and sea stacks. Misha was excited about the historical connotations of the Cape, and kept reminding me that after we passed Rubicon, we, like Caesar, couldn't turn back. Gradually his enthusiasm became contagious, and I looked forward to our "crossing of the Rubicon."

A dense fog lurked a few hundred feet above us, leaving a strip of ocean and a narrow ribbon of sandy beaches, low tundra, and a hint of green hills. Then the fogbank coalesced into a low cloud and cold rain. We pulled our hoods over our heads and lost ourselves in solitary discomfort.

The wind intensified, and growing waves reflected off the rocks, creating a chaotic, uncomfortable sea. I felt sullen and dreary, but Misha grew animated. When we were abreast of the Cape, he raised his fist in the air and shouted, "Now we cannot go back. We will paddle to Alaska by our own hands." A drop of rainwater dripped off his hood onto his nose, paused for a second, then fell onto his lower lip. He licked it off with his tongue and resumed his broad smile.

I smiled back and waved my fist in the air, but my spirits couldn't rise to the occasion. The wind intensified, my body ached, and I wanted to camp. Steep cliffs dropped to the sea, and the nearest beach was three miles away.

I spoke softly to myself, "Three miles. No big deal. Two hours into this diabolical headwind." Then I paddled with syncopated, heavy strokes, driven from my torso, not my tired arms.

A storm was building, and the surf was formidable by the time we reached the beach. I was exhausted, but the routine was familiar, so, without fanfare, I paddled into the surf, dropped off a breaking wave, and leaned on my paddle, butting my head into the cascading foam. I was in the groove, past the point of return, like a ski jumper who has launched off the lip. But when I looked toward shore, I saw a large grizzly bear at the water's edge—immobile, feet far apart, long neck pointed straight toward me, with its nose sniffing to determine what I was and whether or not I was good to eat. It was too late to retreat, and my kayak was headed directly toward those treelike legs. I said a quiet "Oh shit!" as my adrenaline pumped, and then the bear turned on its heels and galloped over the sandbar. My kayak bounced on the sand and I jumped stiffly onto the beach. When I looked up, Misha was riding in on the next wave.

That night, storm gusts bent the flexible aluminum poles of our tent. I had learned to sleep in a high wind with one subconscious ear tuned to the storm outside. In the middle of the night, when the tent lurched violently, I knew even in my sleep that this was no wind-driven jolt. I was awake and alert immediately, and before I could think or act, Misha's body pressed against mine. We both screamed simultaneously, in English and in Russian, "GO AWAY, BEAR!" The sound of tearing nylon seemed deafening, and a claw entered our domain inches from my head. I fumbled for the "bear-off." The barrel of the shotgun brushed against my cheek as Misha swung his weapon in the dark. Suddenly the jerky motion subsided, and the tent resumed billowing with the storm.

We sat motionless, caught our breaths, then crawled outside and shined our headlamps into the empty blackness and the pouring rain. The bear could have ripped the tent to shreds in a single blow, but instead it had simply poked through the fabric with one claw, leaving a three-cornered rip only a few inches long on one side. We reasoned that the bear hadn't actually attacked but had simply probed this curious, funny-smelling, flapping object that had suddenly appeared in its domain. Reassured by this logic and driven by a bone-deep fatigue, we crawled back into the tent and slipped into our sleeping bags. Rain dripped through the hole, and I shifted toward Misha to stay out of the drips. His body was supple and reassuring, and I dozed fitfully.

A tent floor is made of waterproof material to keep moisture out, but if water is dripping through a hole in ceiling, the floor forms a basin that stores ever-deepening puddles. In the morning, our sleeping bags were soaked. We sat up, wiggled out of the deepest puddles, then sponged the tent floor with a pair of dirty underpants. Next we sewed up the hole, but to keep the water out, we really needed to dry the nylon and seal the seam with fabric cement.

I pumped up the stove to cook breakfast, but it wouldn't light. I went back outside, rummaged through my kayak to find the tool kit, and returned to disassemble the stove. After cleaning the oily jets and lubricating the pump, I tried again, but no luck. I took the stove apart a second time and tried to pull the generator wire out of the fuel line. I yanked, cajoled, and twisted. When that didn't work, Misha grasped the fuel line while I clamped a set of Vise-Grip pliers on the generator wire. We braced the soles of our feet against each other for maximum leverage and pulled with all our strength. Nada. The stove was irreparable.

I walked back into the rain and returned with two cold, stale energy bars from our emergency rations. It was nine in the morning. The storm had intensified, and we would need to wait through the wet, sullen, hungry day. I slipped into my sleeping bag and shivered until my body heat created a narrow zone of relative warmth and dryness. After dozing for a few hours, I woke and considered reading or writing in my journal. But when I moved even a few inches, I entered the wetter, colder corners of my sleeping bag. So I lay there, daydreaming and conducting an internal dialogue:

"These bear encounters are becoming too frequent, too close, and too spooky. How did you get yourself into this mess?" I asked myself accusingly.

"Well, that's a dumb question," I parried, stalling for time.

"Then give me a dumb answer."

I watched a raindrop run across the outside of the tent until it encountered the crude black stitching of my repair. The drop adhered to the thread, spread out, seeped through the seam, then re-formed and grew until it became heavy enough to plop onto the floor.

"OK, how did I get myself into this mess? Where should I start—a few hours ago, a day, a month?" As I half drifted toward sleep, I thought, "I've got all day, why don't I go back thirty years?"

ON A Sunday afternoon in April 1970, I was walking my dog through a high alpine meadow in the Colorado Rockies. The snow had just melted, and mist rose from the ground into the warm spring sunshine. My dog romped but then stopped abruptly and started digging furiously, sending clumps of grass into the air. He thrust his nose into the hole, barked excitedly, raced in quick circles, and dug again. At first I thought he was chasing rodents, but, no, he was simply smelling the warm, moist earth where bacteria, mites, and nematodes were emerging from their dormancy—their spore cases and eggs sacs—to munch and chew, turning vegetation into soil. Infected by his enthusiasm, I crawled on all fours and stuck my nose into one of his holes, breathed deeply, and absorbed the sweet odor of decay and renewal in the newly thawed earth. Then I lay on my back.

I knew then that I didn't want to return to work on Monday morning.

The next day I told my Ph.D. mentor that I wanted to quit. He recommended that I finish my thesis and then decide.

Here I was thirty years later. Misha was snoring, and I sat up to sponge out a puddle that was turning into a small stream and flowing toward my sleeping bag. Then I cuddled back into my warm spot, stared at the tent ceiling, and watched more drops roll, seep, re-form, and fall.

"So, how did I get into this mess?" I asked myself again. Images raced around my brain, charging toward conscious thought, elbowing others out of the way, then all coalescing in a gridlock at the synapses.

"Whoa, whoa, slow down!"

But there were too many images, so I reduced them to sound bites and let them through one at a time. I quit chemistry as soon as I earned my Ph.D. Followed by three wives, three children. Cutting ski trails with a chain saw in Colorado. Framing tract houses in Connecticut. Dabbling in horse logging and chicken farming in Maine. Fishing in Alaska. Winter in a one-room, dirt-floor cabin in Montana. Winter in a tepee in Wyoming. Junker cars. Writing, writing, writing. Eighteen major expeditions. Three reconstructive orthopedic surgeries. Three grandchildren, and counting.

Ultimately we're all driven by molecules deep inside. Genes assemble proteins; proteins burst into the brain and open locked synapses. Different people, different proteins, different synapses. Mine have driven me to smell newly thawed earth, to ski down steep mountains, to paddle my kayak in the open sea.

All my life, for better or worse, I've held true to one adage: listen to those proteins. When they open an alleyway that makes me feel good—whatever that means—I follow that path. That's why I was sleeping in this wet, cold puddle, wondering whether the storm would end before the grizzly returned. Because when I added up all the pluses and minuses, this was where I wanted to be.

And, I thought, it's where the Jomon wanted to be as well. When I think of them as people, not as subjects in a history book, it isn't at all strange to me that a few of them, following the call of their own proteins, paddled along this inimical coastline to another world.

I DOZED into sleep again, and when I woke up the tent was still.

In the classic movie about eastern Siberia, *Darzu the Hunter*, Darzu and the Russian survey party are hunkered down in a shelter waiting for a storm to end. Suddenly Darzu starts packing, saying, "It's time to go." The Russian officer asks him, "How do you know that the storm is ending?" Darzu looks back, incredulous that the officer is so unobservant. "The birds are singing, so the storm will soon be over."

For us, mosquitoes were the harbinger. When you heard mosquitoes buzzing under the rain fly, you knew that the wind had died and it was time to dry your soggy gear and head back to sea.

A Candle for Evdocia

"Our African exodus was the greatest of all human
journeys, a global endeavor that took our ancestors
over every conceivable obstacle thrown up by nature:
estuaries, deserts, mountain ranges, steppes and tundra, dense forests, fields of ice and snow, and sheer
distance . . . It is a testimony to human resilience and
resourcefulness that we overcame these hurdles in
a few dozen millennia, leaving only a handful of isolated ocean islands and the polar caps unconquered
until modern times."

Christopher Stringer and Robin McKie, *African Exodus: The
Origins of Modern Humanity*

IN THE morning we blasted through the surf and paddled north with long, steady strokes that stretched our cramped, cold muscles. Despite the day of rest, my left elbow tendon was inflamed, and I thought about Chris, gone for a month now. I pictured her angular face and short-cropped hair, and I longed for the familiarity we had shared for twenty years. But longing wouldn't bring her to me. I swallowed two anti-inflammatory pills and continued paddling. As Misha had said, we had passed the Rubicon, and there was no turning back.

A huge mass that looked like a rock shoal rose about ten yards away. The gray object was splotched with white, and a jagged scar cut across its surface. Barnacles grew between the spots and across the scar, forming a living collage. It was a gray whale, and when it rolled over, an eye bigger than a human head appeared a few feet from my boat.

Two months earlier I would have been startled and frightened, but distance, time, and pain seemed to have cleansed me of all but alertness, fatalism, and wonder.

I greeted the eye like a friend on the street, saying, "Hello, whale. How are you on this fine morning?"

The whale stared back at me as if trying to understand.

My kayak bobbed on a wave, slid sideways, and almost collided with the eye. The pupil expanded, and I stared into the dark opening as if it were a window into the whale's brain or a black hole opening on an alternative universe.

"Hello, whale. Finding enough to eat out here?"

It rolled over and evanesced slowly into the sea.

Soon we were seeing gray whales everywhere. It was hard to count them because one would appear, then vanish, before another popped up a few hundred yards away. Was that one or two? But even counting conservatively, we saw a few hundred whales that morning. Occasionally one surfaced, nose out of the water, as if standing on its tail to survey the terrestrial landscape that its ancestors had abandoned fifty million years ago. We paddled slalom through whale spouts. Water gurgled under our boats as whales swam beneath us. The powerful turbulence of their flukes rocked our kayaks, and I imagined a thirty-ton, forty-foot leviathan rising and lifting me into the air. Worse yet, what would happen if one of them accidentally—or maliciously—slapped one of us with its fluke?

I asked Misha whether we should paddle out to sea to avoid these close encounters, but he silently shook his head as if too stupefied to speak.

A whale swam into the breakers, its spout mixing with the frothing surf. Suddenly the creature lost its aura of power and invincibility. It seemed as if the next wave would wash it onto the sand, consigning it to a horrible death by starvation and desiccation. I wanted to grab its tail and drag it back into deep water, as you would pull a child by his shirt to prevent him from running across a busy street. A breaker surged over the whale's back. In my imagination, I felt the power of that wave as it accelerated my kayak toward the beach. Then I wondered, "Can a whale swim in reverse?" I knew that gray whales are bottom feeders and live in shallow water, but I had never imagined that they ventured within a body length of dry land. The leviathan must have bumped its chin on the bottom as its body undulated in the waves and bobbed in the foamy swath. Then it turned broadside and, with one powerful thrust, slipped back into deep water.

At midmorning we saw a grizzly bear tugging at the flesh of a juvenile gray whale that was dead on the beach. Another bear approached but backed off when the feeding bear charged. We paddled as close as we dared, riding the backs of the steepening breakers until I felt that one more stroke would drop us into the surf. The feeding bear watched us carefully and retreated a few steps, then reached back into the carcass with its powerful muzzle, leaned its massive weight backward, and shook its head vigorously to pull free a bloody mouthful of meat and blubber. Then, done feeding, it trotted over a dune. Once the dominant bear had left, the second bear settled in for its share of the bonanza.

Grays are the only members of the whale family that are exclusively benthic, or bottom, feeders. In the Bering Sea, one of their dietary staples is *Ampelisca macrocephela*, a quarter-inch-long crustacean similar to a sand flea. Each *Ampelisca* digs a tube into the bottom mud and waits in the tube to collect microscopic phytoplankton that die and sink from the surface. In a productive portion of the Bering Sea, 14,000 *Ampelisca* live in each square meter of mud. A whale rolls onto its side and sucks the mud, thereby ingesting whole metropolises of *Ampelisca*. With its baleen and half-ton tongue, it separates the protein-rich crustaceans from the mud and water. A single gray whale can eat one to two tons of crustaceans every day.

A pod of whales can't stay in one place for long without depleting its food supply. As a result, in late fall gray whales migrate from Siberia, across to Alaska, and down the west coast of North America to winter and calve along the sunny coast of Baja. Each spring they head north again, reaching Kamchatka by summer. The journey covers 7,000 miles each way—the longest mammalian migration on the planet.

Our whales disappeared by noon. Misha and I ate stale bread and leftover salmon, then continued northward. I scanned the horizon, but all I saw was a huge expanse of gray-green sea and a steel-gray sky. Locked between them, the land seemed a pencil-thin line of yellow beach offset by low-lying tundra. My hips rocked automatically with the easy roll of a gentle swell, and my mind wandered back to that vertiginous look into a gray whale's bottomless eye.

We all experience cross-species communication. A dog wags its tail and prances by the door to announce that it wants to go for a walk. A cat rubs against your leg when it would like to be scratched under the chin. Some communication had passed between the whale and me—the impression of intelligence in the depths of that pupil was unmistakable—but in this case the message was inscrutable.

I was tired and wanted to quit early, make camp, stretch out on the warm tundra, and take a long afternoon nap. But every hour and every mile carried us closer to Alaska, so I continued paddling, turning motion into a mantra, while I dropped into a suspended daydream. In that fuzzy dream space, whales represented the sea, the sea symbolized my journey, and my journey led to a reflection on the Jomon.

Acute observers of nature, Stone Age hunters would have known that gray whales were bottom feeders and lived in shallow water near the coast, never venturing far into the open ocean. These people must also have known that the gray whales off the Kamchatka Peninsula headed north in late fall and returned with their calves each summer—and that the whales needed ice-free water to survive. So, might not the Jomon therefore surmise that the coast to the north must at some point arc south again? If the migrating whales followed this coastline, they would curve across the Arctic and head south into ice-free waters. Stone Age mariners could thus have held a crude map of the North Pacific Rim in their heads, intuiting that if they followed the whales northward, they would eventually turn south toward warm water and unexplored lands. Could it be that the gray whale had become the totem spirit of a great shaman—and a compulsive wanderer? Maybe that shaman had looked into a whale's eye and read the message: "Follow me."

It was a musing born of space, silence, and boredom. Perhaps the image of a shaman following a gray whale is just a metaphor—nothing more. Nevertheless, between 20,000 and 9,500 years ago someone had the notion to paddle into the void—and a group of Jomon followed him.

Always when I try to make sense of this migration, I am inexorably drawn back two million years before the Jomon, to the dawn of humanity. By that time our hominid forebears were walking upright and starting to grow a large brain. Species of a new lineage, *Homo*, were beginning to thrive alongside their cousins, *Australopithecus*. For 97.5 percent of our present tenure on Earth, we hominids wouldn't so much as knap sophisticated stone tools, draw art on cave walls, bury our dead, or make music. And yet within a few hundred thousand years of learning how to walk upright, we walked out of our African homeland, crossed the desert, and migrated into Asia. Wandering, even before toolmaking or art, is a primordial hallmark of humanity.

How can we know what these first travelers were thinking or what drove them into the unknown? According to most anthropologists, *Homo* didn't even have language two million years ago. Our distant ancestors couldn't propose crossing a desert in the hope of finding a lush hunting ground on the other side. They just started wandering, driven by some internal spark that separates us from all other species on the planet.

Wanderlust is innate and ubiquitous; it has carried hominids to verdant oases and frigid tundras; it has occurred during times of warfare and famine as well as peace and opulence. As Misha and I experienced the terror and wonder of this North Pacific wilderness, I saw the call of the journey in that gray whale's eye.

THE Bering Sea is a shallow, oil-rich basin, and major petroleum deposits stretch from Siberia to Bristol Bay, Alaska. Approximately 1.75 billion barrels of oil and 5.4 trillion cubic feet of natural gas lie off the Chukotka coast. I was reminded again that this land has abundant resources: salmon, platinum, coal, and oil. The land is wealthy; only the people are poor.

The town of Meynypil'gyno lies at the confluence of two rivers. We feared that the river currents would collide against the ocean swell and create dangerous surf, so we landed twelve miles southwest of town and portaged into the protected river channel. An abandoned, rusting oil derrick cast geometric shadows across the softly undulating landscape.

Summer was progressing. The baby ducks were swimming strongly, though they were still clothed in yellow feathers and couldn't yet fly. Mothers herded their broods out of our way. The little ones peeped, and paddled so frantically that they practically rose out of the water.

The salmon run was at its apogee, and people were grouped along the shore, pulling nets, cleaning fish, and hanging the bright red meat to dry on large wooden racks. Some families lived in tar-paper shacks; others camped in circular tents called *yuranga*s, which are similar to Tibetan yurts and Mongolian *ger*s and are made of reindeer skins spread over a wooden frame. Typically, a *yuranga* is twenty feet in diameter, with a four-foot-high vertical wall and a domelike roof.

The river carried us to the village and we paddled to shore, where a fisherman offered us tea and salmon soup. We thanked him, stripped off our life jackets and sprayskirts, and warmed our hands over his driftwood fire. Before the soup was hot, the peaceful silence was rent by the roar of a revved-up diesel and the loud clanking of a steel-tracked armored personnel carrier (*visdichot*) that bore down on us at high speed. When the sinister machine lurched to a stop, six rough-looking men jumped down and surrounded us. I couldn't understand their exact words, but clearly they thought we were too important to eat fish soup with this lowly fisherman. Without asking our opinion, the men grabbed our heavily laden boats and hoisted them onto the roof of the *visdichot*.

Their leader, Vasilly, wore torn work clothes permanently stained by machine oil. He was a broad, big-boned man with a lot of muscle, a little extra fat, and an unkempt beard. He smiled warmly when he shook my hand, and I reflected that I didn't look that tidy either. Misha climbed on the roof with the boats and the men while Vasilly gestured that I should ride in the front seat. The cab was decorated with posters of bare-breasted women draped over the abundant chrome of customized Harley-Davidson motorcycles. Vasilly hit the starter button, and a dark cloud of exhaust belched out of the smokestack. My ears buzzed with the shriek and clank of tortured machinery. We made a hundred-yard dash to the first corner, cranked into an abrupt right turn, and came to a lurching stop in front of a large machine shed with several red hammer-and-sickle Soviet flags flying from the rooftop.

There were no automobiles in the outpost towns of northeastern Siberia.

If a vehicle wasn't powerful enough to churn through the mud, then it must be as light as a motorcycle so the driver could push it free when it got stuck. Vasilly owned a ten-ton *visdichot*, a six-wheel-drive army truck, and a bulldozer. Clearly, he was a man to be reckoned with.

He ushered us to his office, brushed aside greasy papers and motor parts, and laid out bread, salmon caviar, smoked salmon, and tea. I sliced a piece of bread and smeared it with a politely thin layer of caviar. Vasilly grabbed the bread out of my hands and heaped on five additional spoonfuls, until the tiny eggs rolled off the bread and spilled onto the desk.

"This is how we eat in Meynypil'gyno."

Before I finished my first bite, Vasilly aimed his long knife toward a smoked salmon on the desk and ordered, *"Eat!"*

Most people associate smoked salmon with New York lox served on a bagel with cream cheese. Wipe that image out of your mind. A Chukotka smoked salmon was a whole fish with skin, tail, fins, head, and pale white eyeballs in their death stare. The meat was dark, firm, smoky, and so rich that the oil dripped down our chins and oozed between our fingers. And instead of paying four dollars for a quarter pound of thin slices, we cut off monster chunks with our sheath knives, stuffed them in our mouths, and washed them down with deep gulps of that uniquely horrible, acidic Russian tea.

The phone rang. Vasilly nodded, then looked at us. *"The mayor wants to see you."*

"Oh, boy," I thought. "After all the money we gave Martha, we still don't have permission to enter Chukotka or paddle along the coast. Her letter said we owed another $5,000. We're in trouble, for sure."

We jumped into the *visdichot* and raced at full attack speed another hundred yards down the street. Vasilly dropped us off at city hall, and charged away as if he didn't want to be anywhere near the place. Misha and I climbed the rickety, unpainted wooden steps, opened the door, and entered a cavernous room that was softened by abundant philodendrons and geraniums, with tropical epiphytes drooping from the ceiling. In the center of the room, narrow steel tables were arranged in a T, with a woman sitting serenely at the head. She was dressed in a pressed blue pantsuit with bright purple frills offset by an immaculately clean white shirt. Her face was aged and beginning to wrinkle and her hair was completely white, but she was naturally beautiful. I guessed that she was about fifty. Bright red lipstick bordered a perfect, linear row of gold-capped teeth that dominated her smile. Her blue-gray eyes hid behind immense, goggle-like glasses.

She stood and we shook hands. Her palm was soft and delicate, so unlike Vasilly's. *"Welcome to Meynypil'gyno. My name is Anastasia. I am the mayor. I knew you were coming because they are broadcasting your passage on the radio. But the radio says so little. Please sit, tell me about your journey."*

I knew the story well enough to understand Misha's Russian, so I gazed around the room at the houseplants, indigenous to the Amazon rainforest, then nervously ran my finger along the fake wood grains in the steel table-top. When Misha was finished, I waited for the fateful question, "And where are your papers?"

But the question never came. We talked about the hardships of our journey and the hardships endured by the local residents. Anastasia explained that people had been hungry in Meynypil'gyno the winter before because the store had run out of food. Even now bread was rationed to three hundred grams per person per day. Then she shrugged and smiled. *"But we are Russians, and we always find a way."*

After an hour, she stood up. *"You travel and are not afraid. I live here and I'm not afraid. You overcome obstacles and so will we. We do these things because we are romantics."* We shook hands again, and Misha and I walked into the pastel Arctic twilight.

Vasilly returned with his *visdichot* and drove us seventy-five yards to the grocery store, but the store was closed, so we revved up the monster and roared another twenty-five yards to the storekeeper's house. Like Green Berets snatching a foreign diplomat from kidnappers, we encircled the merchant and whisked him into the armored vehicle. Vasilly hit the starter button, shoved the tired transmission into gear, did his best to do a tank wheelie in the middle of the potholed street, and clanked—pedal to the metal—toward the grocery emporium. Just when I thought we were going to smash through the exterior wall and drive right into the store, Vasilly slammed on the brakes and the beast skidded to a halt. I opened the door and stood on the track as if to wave to reporters and say, "Mission accomplished."

The store was dark and colorless, and its shelves were nearly bare. The owner took up station patiently behind the worn wooden counter with an abacus in his hand. I looked at an odd assortment of items too useless to buy: tubes of lipstick, a bottle of French cognac, and an elaborate and overpriced box of Swiss chocolate wrapped in an ornate red ribbon. Even though our stove was defunct, we cooked over campfires, so we bought rice, sugar, noodles, and more of that undrinkable Russian tea. Nimble fingers clicked the black and white beads of the abacus. *"Cooking oil?"* I asked.

The store owner hesitated as if deciding whether or not to part with his personal stash, then reached under the counter for a liter of oil. "*Bread?*" After another hesitation, he said, "*I can sell you two loaves.*" He went into the back to fetch the hidden bread, slid the hoarded loaves into our pile, and clicked the beads again.

"*Do you have anything else we might find good to eat?*"

The owner disappeared into the back room once more and returned with several glass jars of borscht. Normally I wouldn't carry glass jars on a kayak trip, but we had thrown normalcy aside a long time ago. Misha said, "*Schetiri*" (four), and I nodded in agreement.

After we left the store, Vasilly reassured us, "*Don't worry. I'll give you some real food—dried fish.*"

When we returned to Vasilly's, a bottle of vodka appeared. Soon Misha stopped translating, and I forgot even the small fragments of Russian I would normally understand. My mind wandered.

FRONTIERS ARE wonderful places. Where else can you work when you want, live by your wits, fire up your own private armored personnel carrier, and roar to a grocery store that may not have any food?

On the other hand, Meynypil'gyno was a hellhole characterized by few jobs and little food and choked by mud, dust, rain, fog, winter blizzards, and unimaginable isolation.

Who would want to live there?

Redneck motorheads like Vasilly. Romantic, frilly-dressed grandmothers like Anastasia. That's who.

Stephen J. Gould argued that variability within a species is fundamental to long-term evolutionary survival. Environments and ecosystems change constantly. If a species is too precisely adapted to a narrow niche, it runs the risk of extinction when the environment changes.

> Precise adaptation, with each part finely honed to perform a definite function in an optimal way, can only lead to blind alleys, dead ends, and extinction. In our world of radically and unpredictably changing environments, an evolutionary potential for creative responses requires that organisms possess an opposite set of attributes usually devalued in our culture: sloppiness, broad potential, quirkiness, unpredictability, and above all, massive redundancy. The key is flexibility, not admirable precision.

It's an essential and fundamental characteristic of humanity that some members of our species fly a Soviet flag and drive their armored personnel carrier around the old empire's margins, while others become shopkeepers in Saint Petersburg. And it was just as essential that most of the Jomon stay home and honor Fuchi, goddess of the hearth, while a few paddled north to discover a new world.

TWO days later we camped on a gravel bar near Cape Navarin. During the ice ages, when the sea level was lower than it is today, this was the beginning of the land bridge that led to North America. Perhaps Stone Age mammoth hunters had camped here along their walking route to Alaska. If the Jomon sailed to the Americas more than 9,500 years ago, Navarin would have been their most northerly point, because at that time the coastline veered southeast from there. North of us the sea was so shallow that if the Empire State Building rose from the seabed, visitors on the observation deck could watch the waves roll past twenty stories beneath them.

In Meynypil'gyno, Vasilly had warned us, "*Oh, you are paddling well. But wait till you get to Cape Navarin. There are big current shears at the Cape. There's a six-knot current setting against you. Watch out for standing vertical waves.*" Vasilly was a master of his turf, but apparently his neighborhood ended before Navarin. Beyond it lay the unknown—those blank white expanses on which ancient mapmakers wrote, "There be dragons." There are Vasillys wherever you go in this world.

In the morning, the sky was heavy and gray but the sea was flat. Ripples in the gentle swell blurred the reflections of our boats and bodies. We crossed the bay and approached the Cape. A sea stack rose incongruously from the water, bent erratically like a broken finger. Sea lions barked from a nearby shoal, while otters floated on their backs and eyed us curiously. The swell reflected from the rocks, but there were no shear waves and no adverse currents. Exhilarated by the unexpected ease of our passage, we paddled close to shore.

Farther out to sea, a large ship was motoring south. Joseph Conrad, my boyhood literary idol, claimed that deepwater sailors had the "right stuff," whereas coastal sailors were the wimps and wannabes who delivered the mail or carried the coal. When I was twelve, I resolved never to be a coastal sailor. Now I was in my mid-fifties, and as a Bristol Bay fisherman and a kayaker I'd seldom ventured more than five miles from the beach. No, I never became kin to Magellan, Drake, and Cook; instead, I reached back into history and joined the first mariners. I had been following their routes all my life, through the Arctic ice and now along the eastern edge of the eastern world. We shared the same passages until I felt that my Stone Age predecessors were riding in my boat or paddling alongside me. I understood the joy and terror of these seas; even more than that, I felt as if I were gaining an understanding of my ancestors who survived these harsh lands with a few stone tools and an indomitable will.

The waves broke first against an offshore shoal, while a residual swell broke against the beach. Misha and I paddled into the calm channel between the two lines of surf. This was the coastal ocean: intensely violent, the most biologically productive and geologically active region on Earth, where rocks, sea, and air collide. We stopped paddling to eat Vasilly's dried salmon. Pounding surf on both sides of our boats seemed abstractly chaotic compared with the calmness of our channel. Yes, this was where I loved to be—safe, but surrounded by turbulence.

I wiped the fish oil off my beard with my hand, but then my palms were too slippery to grasp my paddle. I smeared my hands against my once-new life jacket, then nodded to Misha, and we headed north. We still had 500 miles to go.

AFTER TWO more capes we reached a broad, protected bay. The clouds parted to reveal blue sky. Three killer whales were hunting salmon near the river mouth. As the whales surfaced and dove in graceful curves, their sleek black and white markings resembled the sunlight reflecting off the waves. Misha and I weren't observers of the seascape; we were part of it. We weren't simply watching the killer whales; we seemed to be swimming with them. And when we made camp, we would eat the same salmon they hunted. I felt as if the killer whales were there to remind us that our easy passage around Cape Navarin was a great gift, not a foregone conclusion.

On shore we saw a *visdichot* parked near a few shacks and smoke rising from a chimney, so we quit early and paddled to the beach. Frost had tilted the buildings, doorjambs were askew, and winter storms had ripped shingles from the roofs. A beautiful young Russian woman in shabby camp clothes asked us who we were and how we had gotten there. Then she pulled two stools from beneath a small, wood-plank table and set out plates and spoons. While feeding us dried fish, fish soup, fried fish balls, spaghetti with butter, bread, and bannock, she explained that the men were setting nets in the estuary. When we finished eating, she invited us to dinner in a few hours.

We wandered onto the beach to digest and to breathe the cool, fresh air. A young Chukchi girl, about ten years old, approached, carrying her baby brother in her arms. The Chukchi are the indigenous people of Chukotka, or northeast Siberia, and are related to the Koryak of Kamchatka. Once fierce and warlike, they were the last tribe in Siberia to succumb to Russian colonialism. The girl asked us to her *yuranga* for tea. I was tired and almost said no, but she won me with a delightful smile—a smile that only the fortunate few who are born happy can produce.

Misha and I nodded. "*Sure, we'd love to come to your yuranga.*" We walked a mile inland, past the beach and onto the soft tundra. The duff-colored skin tent was nestled among brown-green hills. Two reindeer sleds were parked outside, but there were no reindeer. The girl tugged at my parka to lead me inside.

Soft sunlight diffused through the smoke hole, and when my eyes adjusted I smiled to greet two young women and an elder. I walked a quarter turn clockwise around the central fire pit—as is customary throughout central and northeast Asia—and sat cross-legged on a reindeer skin. The soft odors of tanned hides, earth, drying fish, and wood smoke were immediately and luxuriously relaxing. One woman added driftwood to the smoldering fire, and smoke curled through the open hole in the roof. She hung a teapot over the flame while the young girl stood in the shadows and watched us intently. Two boys appeared and joined their sister.

The *yuranga* frame was built of weathered, whitened driftwood poles. I estimated that about a hundred reindeer skins had been needed to construct the covering. Some of the skins were old and rotting; the newer patches were more translucent.

Three hunters and a teenager ducked into the *yuranga* with a dozen ducks, a few geese, and a sack of salmon. We talked about our journey, our easy passage around Cape Navarin, and the dangers ahead. I asked whether they had reindeer to pull the sleds that were outside. The men shook their heads slowly. No, before perestroika they had herded two thousand reindeer, but then the government had placed such an exorbitant tax on living deer that they had killed their entire herd. Now the tax had been lifted (or perhaps there never had been a tax, only a deception by some corrupt official who pocketed the money), and they planned to start a new herd.

I asked one of the hunters if the family lived in this remote *yuranga* all winter, and this time he smiled. *"Yes."* Then he paused and explained, *"We don't have store food like cookies, butter, sugar, or tea, but we never starve out here. When the store runs out of food in the villages, then the village people starve."*

It was another example of Gould's argument that a diverse population has greater survival potential in a changing world than a homogeneous one. Today's eccentrics and mavericks may be tomorrow's survivors.

In the 1950s, when the Soviets built villages such as Vyvenka, Apuka, and Meynypil'gyno, the villages had electricity, fuel, warm houses, doctors, and schools. Life was good, birth rates rose, and infant mortality declined. Villagers had a short-lived adaptive advantage over people who remained in remote, primitive camps on the tundra. But then the infrastructure collapsed. Generators ran out of parts and fuel, heating systems broke down, pipes froze, and people shivered through long winters. The doctors flew back to western Russia. Stores ran out of food, and people starved. Birth rates dropped and infant mortality rose. Now the hunters who lived in *yuranga*s seemed better suited to survive.

Natural and sexual selection, the basic mechanisms of evolution, are simple and straightforward. A given character trait or physical attribute is favored if it helps an individual survive to reproductive age, find a mate, and produce children who in turn reproduce. Were individual survival the only determinant, a propensity for adventure might be a boon during catastrophic times and an impediment during prosperity. But survival is only one factor in the equation, and reproductive success might alter these outcomes.

In an evocative book *The Mating Mind: How Sexual Choice Shaped the Evolution of Human Nature*, Geoffrey Miller argued that sexual selection may favor the adventurous even in times of calm and plenty. Many animals have evolved inefficient body parts or behavioral patterns. A peacock's tail requires considerable energy to produce and carry around. At the same time, this gaudy, expensive appendage makes the peacock *more* visible and vulnerable to predators. According to Miller, evolution has selected for splendid tails only because peahens like them. This elaborate display is an advertisement that says, "Look, I am so robust that I can survive despite an absurdly inefficient tail. If you choose me as your mate, you will have robust babies." And the peahen swoons.

An inefficient attribute used as a sexual advertisement is called a "fitness indicator." Miller wrote:

Sexual ornaments and courtship behaviors must be costly in order to be fitness indicators. Their cost can take almost any form. They can increase risk from predators by making an animal more conspicuous with bright colors . . . They can burn up vast amounts of time and energy, like a bird song. They can demand a huge effort to obtain a small gift of meat, as in human tribal hunting . . . Male humans waste their time and energy getting graduate degrees, writing books, playing sports, fighting other men, painting pictures, playing jazz, and founding religious cults . . . What matters is the prodigious waste. The waste is what keeps the fitness indicators honest. The wastefulness of courtship is what makes it romantic. The wasteful dancing, the wasteful gift-giving, the wasteful conversation, the wasteful laughter, the wasteful foreplay, the wasteful adventures. From the viewpoint of "survival of the fittest," the waste looks mad and pointless and maladaptive . . . However, from the viewpoint of fitness indicator theory, this waste is the most efficient and reliable way to advertise someone's fitness.

Thus Miller argued that seemingly quixotic and foolhardy character traits are actually fitness indicators. If he's correct, Stone Age wanderers would have won a sexual advantage that offset their increased mortality. In turn, this sexual advantage would have maintained the adventurous spirit in the gene pool.

There is one final factor in the fitness equation. After mating, a person's genes survive only if his or her children mature and reproduce. Here, too, the adventurer may hold an edge under certain circumstances. Stone Age people lived in small family bands. Marriages within a band or even between closely spaced bands ran a high risk of inbreeding that would produce unhealthy offspring. Thus it was genetically advantageous to travel as far from home as possible to find a mate outside the immediate family or clan. And who traveled the farthest? The marginally insane dreamer who saw the map of a journey in a gray whale's eye and followed his vision to the ends of the Earth.

THE NEXT day a light tailwind pushed us northward. We paddled twenty-six miles in eight hours, made camp, set our net, and caught two salmon. We fried one in oil and boiled the other with borscht and noodles.

It seemed like a long time since I'd read the first newspaper article about Kennewick Man. All my life I've repudiated Fuchi, goddess of the hearth. This attitude has been costly. I never fit in with the social elite of my New England prep school. In college no fraternity would have me, and I ended up hanging out with rock and rollers and motorcycle thugs. Two wives left me. Potential employers have routinely shaken their heads, nervously averted their eyes from my hopeful gaze, and hired someone else. I've had the urge to shout back, "I mean no harm. I'm actually a nice guy. My only crime is that I listen to a few aberrant genes."

But the anger and the angst subsided a long time ago. I had come to understand that Stone Age migrants, Cossack *puteshestveniks*, itinerant jesters, and oddball adventurers like Misha and me had a place in history—and evolution—along with engineers, politicians, and farmers. And I was happy, camped on this windswept beach, leaning against a driftwood log, scanning the tundra for grizzly bears, and filling my belly with salmon. Misha and I lapsed into the warm silence of friendship.

IN THE morning we continued north toward Beringofski, the site of a large, active coal mine. Geologists estimate that there are 42 billion tons of coal in this region, enough to supply the entire U.S. coal consumption for four years.

About 100 million years ago, dinosaurs munched ferns in steamy, fetid swamps. Then the Eurasian continental plate drifted northward, inching slowly over the soft, hot asthenosphere deep within the Earth. Much later, the global climate cooled until glaciers buried this land under glistening ice. Recently the ice had melted, exposing broad, low-lying tundra that extended halfway around the world to Norway. And now, in Beringofski, cars drove on paved streets, and the clank of mining machinery rose above the sounds of wind and surf.

Misha and I paddled toward a steel breakwater that encircled a calm deepwater port.

"What do you think, Misha? We still don't have our permissions. There are soldiers and police here. Do you think we'll get in trouble?"

Misha shook his head. "It will be good. They know we come from wild nature. You worry too much."

A *pogranichniki* officer in his mid-fifties met us at the dock. Medals adorned his shirt and gold braid draped from his shoulders, but his wrinkled uniform reminded us that we were still on the frontier. He wrote our names and passport numbers in a shirt-pocket notebook, then we climbed into his military car and drove to the town hall.

The mayor was of medium build, jolly, and responsive. Though he walked with the briskness of someone with important business to attend to, he greeted me with a direct, friendly gaze. The mayor, his secretary, the *pogranichniki* officer, Misha, and I sat around a conference table. A clerk brought tea and chocolates. The chocolates were a treat, but they didn't fill my hungry stomach like bread and dried fish.

After exchanging pleasantries, the mayor placed both hands on the table. *"No visitors are allowed in this oblast without permission from the pogranichniki."* He looked at the officer for confirmation, and the officer nodded severely. *"And besides that, you need . . ."*—and he rattled off a long list of permissions that I'd never heard of. *"We know that you don't have any of these permissions. The officials in Anadyr were supposed to fax or mail the papers to Beringofski, but we never received them."*

He spoke to the secretary, and she raced out of the room. Then he picked up the phone. Misha stopped translating. I looked around the room and settled my gaze on the *pogranichniki* officer. A long ash grew on his cigarette, and there were no ashtrays at the table. He held the cigarette vertically to balance the ash while rummaging through his briefcase to find some ashtray-like device. Just as he found an empty matchbox, his hand jerked and the ash dropped onto the carpet. He looked up, but neither Misha nor the mayor had been watching. Then his eyes met mine and he smiled, winked, and held one finger to his lips. I nodded discreetly to let him know that his antics were safe with me, and he rubbed the ash into the carpet with his foot.

Suddenly his head jolted; the mayor was talking to him. *"We can't find their permissions. But the people in Anadyr had meant to send them. They forgot. Is it OK with you to let Jon and Misha proceed to Anadyr?"*

The *pogranichniki* officer smiled. *"Conyeshna* [of course], *that's fine with me."*

"OK, then," replied the mayor. *"Our business is finished."*

The mayor had another meeting to attend, but he summoned his deputy mayor to take us out to dinner. We went to a small cafe with loud music and no other patrons. A bored-looking waitress brought us a salad made of canned peas and corn mixed with fresh cucumbers, followed by a chopped cutlet served with an absurdly small portion of buttery mashed potatoes.

The deputy spent the whole dinner lauding the mayor's economic plan. "If we mine more coal, we'll make more money and create more jobs. Then people will buy more things, and we'll mine more coal to make the things that people are buying." It was the one-dimensional prodevelopment argument heard all over the world, at many levels from local to international.

The argument was more compelling in northeast Siberia, where people were poor and hungry, than in North America, where people drove their SUVs to the mall. But the argument neglected the law of unintended consequences—say, to salmon, whales, and walrus. I could have argued this, but to what purpose other than to risk offense with the patronizing smugness of the morally self-conscious well-to-do? The deputy mayor didn't want my opinions. The music was deafening, and one cracked speaker gurgled in its death throes. I wanted to be back in my kayak. I wasn't yet ready to jump back into the twenty-first century with all its promises and problems.

WE STAYED up late, drinking way too much vodka with the port commander. In the morning, Misha called the officials in Anadyr. He spoke, then listened, grim faced. After hanging up, he looked at me and said, "We must go now." I didn't ask any questions. I knew he would explain when we were alone.

North of Beringofski, the coastline arcs in a long series of sandbars, swamps, and estuaries, with no natural harbors. Luckily the wind was from the southwest, so we had an easy passage with minimal swell and surf. We paddled in silence, fighting hangovers and sleep deprivation. At lunch, Misha steered his boat close to mine.

"Do you know why the people in Anadyr didn't fax the permissions to Beringofski?" he asked.

"No, why?"

"They want us to come to town so they can charge us a lot of money for these permissions."

"How much?"

"I don't know. A lot."

"More than a thousand dollars?"

"Yes."

"What should we do?"

"I have been thinking about this. We must not go to Anadyr. We must paddle around the city and not stop."

I laughed with relief. "Misha, you're great. You left your job to join me. You had never been in a kayak before, and now we are almost to Alaska.

You've been my friend and my partner. You always have a plan. Thank you, thank you!"

Misha answered, "I have said this before. When I was in the city, my health crashed. Now I am strong again. Thank you, Jon. You have saved my life."

I smiled. "Labor and Defend. Let us paddle to Alaska by our own hands."

ON AUGUST 13 we reached Point Geka, at the entrance to Anadyr Bay. Misha unfolded our satellite phone and called Sergei, the agent in Anadyr who was responsible for handling our permissions. Misha explained that we would pay five hundred dollars for the *pogranichniki* permission and Sergei's commission. No more. No, this wasn't negotiable. No, we weren't coming to town. If Sergei wanted his money, he would have to find a skiff and motor out to us. We would be at Point Vasilya, at the north entrance of the bay, tomorrow. If he was upset about this, that was his problem.

"*That's right, if you want any money at all, meet us on the sandbar at Point Vasilya. No, our terms are nonnegotiable.*"

After the phone call, Misha walked out across the dunes. I suspected that he wanted to be alone, so I headed in the opposite direction. A hundred yards inland, I saw a small, circular depression in the tundra. I stepped inside, dug into the peat, and discovered that the rim was a foundation to an abandoned dwelling. Most northern people used the snow igloo when they were traveling or hunting on the sea ice. On land, they wintered in permanent igloos built of stone and tundra peat. This family home was ten feet in diameter, small enough to heat with a blubber lamp. Most likely the house had originally been roofed with a driftwood frame covered with skins and an insulating layer of snow. I imagined the original inhabitants huddled around a smoky lamp in this cramped, windowless space. During the short winter days, diffuse light would have filtered through the snow and skin roof, but December nights were cold, dark, and long.

Continuing my walk, I found six more foundations, all nestled behind a dune that provided shelter from frigid onshore winds. Seven family units with an average of four people per family added up to twenty-eight people, roughly the size of most hunter-gatherer clans throughout the world. Fifty yards beyond the last homesite was a much larger foundation, twenty-five to thirty feet in diameter. This must have been a community house for feasts, religious ceremonies, or political councils. Fifty walrus skulls were embedded in the outside rim, looking inward.

I sat cross-legged in the center and stared back at the empty eye sockets, overshadowed by the massive, jutting foreheads. Each skull must have told a story to those who lived here: a stealthy approach on foot and a quick spear thrust, or perhaps a daring chase from a skin boat. This was no accidental garbage heap. The village shaman knew that any hunter who sat within this ring would be filled with awe and exhilaration.

I imagined sitting in the sod and skin igloo while a winter gale flung fractured pack ice against the dune, feeling safe with my tribe, singing, beating on a deerskin drum, and staring into those blank eye sockets. The people who had built this cathedral hunted dangerous animals in a roiling sea using weapons of tooth and bone lashed to long sticks. They survived only because they respected the sea, the winter, the walrus, and the bears. From the walrus and the aboriginal hunters who pursued them, a ghostly mantra echoed in my brain: "Remember who's boss," it said. "Remember who's boss."

FROM ORAL accounts we know that Qitdlaq, the shaman who led his people from Baffin Island to Greenland, had evoked animal spirits to protect his tribe from danger. We can guess that the Jomon, too, were animists who drew strength from the walrus and their ghosts to endure hardship and isolation. Silently thanking the sea and its creatures for safe passage, and promising to respect them, I climbed to the dune and looked northeast, toward Alaska. Over the past two years I had sailed and paddled 2,700 miles, and now Misha and I had only a little more than 300 miles to go. But the crossing from Russia to Alaska weighed on my mind. Our exact route depended on permissions, and even the most favorable would require a long, open-water passage, beam-on to the strong current that flowed between the Arctic and Pacific oceans. It was already mid-August. The nights were growing longer. Any day now, cold, dense winter air would flow south from the North Pole and chase closely spaced gales across the Bering Sea. And we'd still be beckoned by the gray whale's eye while paddling with the walrus, sharing salmon with bears, and being guarded by a phalanx of killer whales. Yes, we were following Stone Age pilgrims who—like us—were addicted to the yaw and roll of a small boat on an endless ocean.

On the beach, our kayaks looked like insignificant red and yellow blobs—the merest flotsam of a big ship. Misha was walking toward camp with his familiar, lanky stride. For now, he was my tribe and I was his.

I turned again toward the circle of skulls. My Prijon Kodiak kayak, car-

bon-fiber paddle, Lotus Designs anorak, and Gore-Tex and Polartec clothing represented 9,500 or more years of technological advancement over
the gear used by Jomon sailors. But the ocean was primordial, and the significance of the skulls hadn't changed. Misha and I had to remain humble
and derive strength both from our partnership and ourselves. In 300 miles,
we would reach the far edge of Asia. Then we faced a long, exposed crossing to Alaska.

Through all these months, the crossing had been an abstract challenge
for the indeterminate future. But now I imagined this final passage: the
open sea; the current; the frailty of my battered, fifty-four-year-old body;
the sight of distant land, hazy in the salt air; the enveloping infinity of fog.
If Misha and I could stay calm and not make any big mistakes, we'd be OK.
No big mistakes. Remember who's boss.

THE next morning we paddled across the mouth of
Anadyr Bay toward the lighthouse at Point Vasilya. When we were close
to land, an offshore gale blew up with no warning. At the same time a
strong tidal current swept us east, into the open sea.

Every time you go to sea, you know that a combination of random, un-
fortunate events can turn the ocean against you. The hunters who sat in
the ring of walrus skulls knew this, and so did we. I remembered my
mantra: No big mistakes. Well, we hadn't made any. When we had broken
camp, the barometer had been steady and the sky was blue—but then luck
turned against us. This day we were only three miles from land, but if fate
were to pull a stunt like this on our long crossing, we'd surely die.

Powerless to paddle against both wind and tide, we drifted into deep water, arced around the current bulge, and only then battled toward shore. I
paddled at differing speeds to relieve the pressure on my elbow, but ultimately fear overpowered pain and pushed me into a hard, steady stroke.
I leaned into my paddle and stared at the waves as if to tell each one that it
could reduce my speed, it could splash cold salt water in my face, but it
wasn't going to kill me. After two hours of hard work, we ran through the
surf, pulled our boats above the high tide line, and walked inland to a small
cluster of buildings.

Mikhail, the lighthouse keeper, answered the door with surprise. "*Who are you? What are you doing? How did you get here? Didn't you know that the wind is gusting to forty-five miles an hour and the coast guard closed the port at Anadyr?*"

We explained our journey, and he invited us inside. After we changed into dry clothes, Misha asked if we could use Mikhail's radio to call Sergei. "*Of course, as soon as I finish fixing it.*"

During Soviet times, Mikhail had earned a Ph.D. in physics and was selected for special training in explosive nuclear devices—the very weaponry that was aimed at America. After perestroika, his salary as a nuclear researcher had fallen so far behind the rapidly rising rate of inflation that he could no longer afford rent and groceries. Finally he had taken a job as a lighthouse keeper, with room and board provided.

Mikhail served us tea and bread warm from the oven, then invited us into his shop, where he had been whittling a piece of driftwood with a sharp pocketknife. The radio at the lighthouse was another World War II vacuum tube monster—six feet high, twelve feet long, and three feet deep. The vacuum tubes generated considerable heat, and the cooling fan had broken. Mikhail was carving a new fan blade from driftwood. We waited for hours while he whittled, balanced, and whittled again. When he was finished, he bolted the new fan blade to the motor, and the assembly spun noiselessly. Then he fired up the radio so Misha could call Sergei.

Misha told Sergei where we were and agreed to call back when the storm abated. "*You know,*" Mikhail commented, "*those people in Anadyr are like fishermen. They see a fish like you and they cast their net. If you swim into it, they will take your money. But Misha is right. If you swim around the net, they won't chase you. They'll set their net for the next fish that swims by. They are not bad people. They just need to make a living. Like all of us. But you need to make a living, too. So don't give them your money.*"

The storm calmed after two days. Sergei told us that he would hitch a ride on a navy cutter and meet us at a protected landing near the lighthouse. At the appointed time, the fifty-foot ship nosed toward shore until its bow crunched into the sand. A sailor lowered a wooden ladder and a plump, boyish-looking man in bulky hip waders climbed awkwardly over the rail. He gingerly placed one foot on the ladder, tested his balance, and stepped down. Then he lowered the other foot to the next rung, tested his balance again, and moved lower. After an interminably long time, he splashed into the thigh-deep water and sloshed to the beach.

Misha squatted comfortably on his haunches. Sergei tried to squat, but the hip waders were so stiff that he couldn't bend his knees, so he remained standing. Misha motioned, "Please sit," as if offering the poor man a recliner. Sergei fiddled, tried to look dignified, then plopped down on his butt.

Misha waited for Sergei to speak, but Sergei didn't know what to say, so we listened to the wind, the distant surf, and the throb of the ship's diesel. The captain of the ship yelled through a bullhorn. "*Hurry up, I don't have all day.*"

Sergei blurted out, "*How did you come all this way in those tiny boats?*"

I responded in English, "It's about elegance, not power," and Misha translated. I don't know if Sergei understood. He cogitated for a while, shrugged, then read a list of fees that we were supposed to pay. When he was finished, Misha spoke deliberately, "*We're not paying those fees. We're not giving you any money. None at all.*"

Sergei stared, open mouthed.

Misha and I hadn't rehearsed this theater, but I immediately realized that Misha was playing the bad cop. I was apparently the good cop.

I waited while Sergei hesitated, then held up my hand. "Tell Sergei that I had originally agreed to pay him $500 for the permissions. I am a man of my word."

After Misha translated, I reached into my pocket, pulled out five crisp hundred-dollar bills, and laid them on the sand. Sergei's eyes brightened. Five hundred dollars is a lot of money in Chukotka. The wind lifted the bills and threatened to blow them into the ocean. Sergei grasped the notes and stuffed them in his pocket.

Misha waved his hand. "*That's all we're going to give you. Good-bye. You can go now.*"

Sergei moved his legs as if attempting to stand, but then he sat back and stared at me with a determined look on his face. Before he spoke, I reached into my pocket again, pulled out a sixth note, and held it toward him. "*Divide this up among all the other agencies. Make sure everyone gets something.*"

Sergei took the money and looked relieved. He handed me an official letter from the *pogranichniki*. I read enough to understand that we had permission to remain in Chukotka only until August 31. But we couldn't complete the journey by the end of the month. I had bought an expensive postponement of our problems, not a solution. I didn't know what to do, so I showed the paper to Misha. He read it, smiled at Sergei, extended his hand, and said, "*Good-bye. It was nice meeting you.*"

ON AUGUST 18 we paddled past large outcrops of now-familiar metamorphic rock. By noon the cliffs sloped toward a broad coastal plain. Huge flocks of common eiders fished in the estuaries; pairs of Pacific loons and a few Canada geese preferred the open waters outside the surf zone. Early in the afternoon, we approached a set of cliffs composed of granite speckled black and white.

This change in rock jolted me from my usual midafternoon daydreams. The basalt of the Kurils had cooled from molten magma blasted to the surface during volcanic eruptions. The sedimentary and metamorphic rock of Kamchatka had formed as tectonic forces crammed seafloor rocks and oceanic islands into Asia. But this granite was the basement of the continents. Geologically it made no sense, but spiritually it seemed fitting that the northeast edge of Asia, the world's largest continent, should be granite. Invisible beneath me, the rock extended under the North Bering Sea to Alaska. We were now paddling over the continental shelf that fuses Asia to North America. Geologically and emotionally, we were close to home.

The season, too, was changing. Ducklings had lost their baby feathers, and their new plumage was darker and thicker. They swam steadily and strongly, frequently beating their wings in preparation for that momentous day when they would fly. Each evening Misha and I picked two cups of ripe tundra berries, one for dessert and one to add zest to our otherwise tasteless breakfast mush. The sun hung lower in the sky, and by now the gloriously long Arctic days were punctuated by seven hours of true darkness. The mosquitoes that had plagued us for weeks now hid in the grass, held low by the near-freezing nighttime temperatures. I wanted to linger in this endgame, but instead we paddled to exhaustion every day. We simply had to reach Alaska before the onset of autumn gales.

On August 19 we reached the village of Uel'Kal, at 65°30' N, our farthest point north. We were less than a hundred miles south of the Arctic Circle, and from here we would follow the coastline east-southeast. We crossed through shearing tidal currents at Kresta Bay and spotted a small house on the eastern shore. A Russian marine biologist greeted us. She explained that, a few years before, 50,000 walrus had lived in the area, but during the past few years the population had dropped in half. She was certain that hunting pressure from local villages wasn't the problem and instead hypothesized that fluctuations in water temperature had reduced the local mollusk population, so the walrus had starved.

A motorboat arrived with two men from Uel'kal—both named Victor—and, incredibly, a Russian filmmaker, Afanassi, whom I had met in Seattle a few years earlier. The biologist retired to a private room and the five of us men went inside at sunset and cooked dinner by the flickering yellow light and deep shadow of a candle. The older Victor was a thirty-year-old Chukchi with a narrow face and high cheekbones; the younger was in his early twenties and his face looked boyish, due as much to his rounded Inuit cheeks as his youth. Afanassi, a Russian, was a jolly fellow with a bushy reddish-blond beard. We were five men from four cultures, bound by our passages across the North Bering Sea. The conversation focused on the immediate exigencies of our survival: storms, the oncoming winter, hunting, and the relative merits of rowboats and kayaks. Late in the evening, the older Victor pulled out a crumpled magazine article written by a prominent Russian anthropologist. The scientist claimed that before contact with Europeans, the northeast Siberians hunted walrus on the open sea. But Victor told us that the elders in Uel'kal believed that Stone Age people had mostly scavenged dead walrus and rarely hunted live ones.

"So, do you think the Russian scientist was wrong?" I asked.

The younger Victor answered, *"Those scientists don't know how vicious a walrus can be. Hunters speared walrus on land, but even that was dangerous."*

The older Victor added, *"Occasionally, young men would hunt a walrus in deep water to show how brave they were, so beautiful women would marry them."*

If that were true, walrus hunting on the open sea wasn't about food, hides, and ivory, it was about mating—another fitness indicator. Some young men died, but the winners married the most robust, fecund women.

Before we went to bed, the younger Victor told us that in two days we would pass another sandbar where walrus commonly haul out on the shore. He drew a line on the map. *"If walrus fill the entire beach from the tip of the bar to this small point, there will be 15,000 animals on the beach."*

The following morning we climbed an observation tower and scanned the beach with binoculars. Thirty-two male walrus were lying on their sides, stacked together like cordwood, their bodies touching. One of them rolled onto its stomach and wiggled its flippers under its body. Then ponderously, with its whole body rocking from side to side, it lifted one flipper into the air in an exaggerated mimelike movement. The flipper hung suspended, looking like a midget's leg capped by a huge clown shoe, while the walrus seemed to puzzle over what do to next. Then, *plop*, the foot fell to the sand, and the walrus' massive weight rotated over the flipper, with the adjacent skin crinkling into folds.

A second walrus ambled toward the water. The two walkers waved their tusks at each other, either to threaten hostilities or to say, "Hey, dude, let's go dig up some mollusks." Then the remaining thirty walrus rose in unison, waved their tusks, and waddled into the sea.

We returned to the house, waited for a favorable tide, and packed our bags. The older Victor asked, *"You guys have much food?"*

The store in Uel'kal had been bare, and the salmon run was winding down, so our supplies were low. Victor walked back into the house and returned with a bundle of dried walrus meat. *"This will keep you strong until you reach the next village, Enmelen."*

TWO DAYS later I woke early, crawled out of the tent, and saw two polar bears only fifty yards away. Curiously, my first thought wasn't fear or flight but exhilaration that we were now in the high Arctic, land of the white bear. The bears stood to watch me. They were juveniles, probably twins who had recently left their mother. Could I trust these teenagers to act rationally, or would they attack? Their huge paws hung listlessly against their chests—paws that can smash thick ice to snag a hidden seal; paws that can kill walrus; paws built to carry a two-thousand-pound animal over soft snow, and designed to stay unfrozen at -60°F. I walked slowly backward, intending to alert Misha and fetch my "bear-off." But when I moved, both bears jumped into the sea and swam away.

We ate breakfast and paddled into such a dense concentration of walrus that I felt as if I were witnessing an atavistic throwback to the pre-Columbian bison herds that once rumbled across the Great Plains. Paddling slowly and trying to think friendly walrus thoughts, we inched close to shore. They were there that day, all 15,000 of them, grunting like pigs, barking like dogs, waving their tusks, splashing into the water and then lumbering out, and surfacing all around our boats.

"Let's get out of here," I said. "I'm frightened."

Misha smiled. "Siberian walrus don't attack kayaks."

"Yeah. Well, you're more likely to be correct if we're twenty miles away."

Late that afternoon we approached Enmelen. A few miles from town we heard a deep-throated rumble from the north, and turned our kayaks to watch three giant trawlers without identity flags enter the bay. Through binoculars, I saw Far Eastern lettering: Chinese, Japanese, or Korean.

A typical Bering Sea trawler is three hundred feet long and pulls a net large enough to scoop up the Empire State Building. The net is designed to trap bottom feeders such as cod and pollock, but in the shallow water near Enmelen a trawl would also intercept salmon and other surface fish. In addition, trawling destroys seafloor habitats and kills untold numbers of mollusks, crabs, and other benthic species. A few days earlier, the Russian biologist had speculated that the decline in walrus population might be attributed to global temperature changes reducing the mollusk population, but I wondered how many mollusks these trawlers were killing. Was it enough to starve the walrus and cause the population decline? Then I wondered why foreign ships were operating so close to land, well within the 200-mile Russian territorial border. When I posed this question later to fishermen and government officials in Enmelen, everyone had the same answer: "*They are pirates.*"

My later investigations of the relationship between trawl fishing and walrus populations would turn up nothing specific, but I would learn that between the early 1980s and the late 1990s, when pollock fishing was at its apogee, Bering Sea fur seal populations declined from 1 million to 750,000, and the Steller sea lion population plunged from 250,000 to 80,000. At the same time, the sea otter population also crashed. Like walrus, sea otters eat mollusks.

The engine noise intensified, winches whirred, and chains clanked across metallic decks. I turned my kayak toward town, trying to block out the noise and remember other images. How many times in your life do you see 15,000 walrus?

SIX MONTHS earlier, in midwinter, the grocery store in Enmelen had run out of food and shut down. In spring, when reliable shipments could resume, the shopkeeper didn't have enough money to restock, so the store stayed closed. Misha and I walked to the back of the boarded-up building and knocked on the door. A plump, shy Inuit woman named Katrina invited us inside. Her husband, Anatoli, was sitting at the kitchen table drinking tea. Anatoli was thin, with a narrow face and high cheekbones offset by thick glasses that made him look more like a studious scholar than an Arctic hunter.

Katrina apologized that they couldn't sell us much food because they needed all the remaining supplies for their family. Then she disappeared behind a rickety door and returned with five pounds of noodles and a small bag of flour. "*I can sell you these noodles and I will bake you three loaves of bread.*

You can buy more food in Nunligran." I thanked her and counted a few bills, but Anatoli pushed my hand away.

"*The food is our gift, from one hunter to another.*"

Katrina looked disappointed, so I set the money on the table.

Anatoli slid the bills toward me and explained, "*These pieces of paper have value in the city where you can buy food. But out here, there is nothing to buy. If my family is starving this winter, this money will do me no good. Also, you are hunters and puteshestveniks. We don't take money from you.*"

The money stood between us, worn and crinkled, against a faded floral pattern on the plastic tablecloth.

"*It will help you some day,*" I rejoined, and pushed the money back across the table.

He hesitated, smiled, grasped the bills, and handed them to Katrina, who quickly stuffed them in her apron. Then Katrina served tea and disappeared. Anatoli explained that even though times were hard, people could avoid starvation if they hunted throughout the year. His eyes looked unnaturally magnified through the thick glasses as he continued, "*In winter, we hunt walrus and whales through narrow leads in moving ice. Sometimes the leads close up, blocking the way back to shore. We camp on the sea ice and it's not too bad if we've made a kill, because then we have meat. Last winter, we were trapped on an ice floe for two weeks before we could reach shore.*"

I imagined the forty-below temperatures, the frigid wind, the grinding ice, and the constant fear that a hurricane-force gale would blow them out to sea.

Anatoli continued simply, "*We were happy to reach shore, but we didn't land in the village, just on a lonely beach. Even though we weren't home, it was a lot safer than the ice floe.*" He waved his hand at Misha and me. "*You understand these things. You have paddled your kayaks from Japan.*"

"*And how long did it take to return to the village?*" I asked.

He shrugged. "*I don't remember, maybe a week. It didn't matter because we had lots of meat and we were on shore.*"

MISHA AND I were stormbound in Enmelen for two days. On the third morning, we paddled into a cold chop. The waves reflected off Cape Beringa into a confused sea, but the chop calmed as we continued along the rocky coast. Late in the afternoon we saw a small wooden whaleboat bobbing on the waves. It rose on a crest until silhouetted against the sky, then disappeared, seemingly sinking into the sea. An outboard motor started and the boat, carrying five dark figures, turned toward us. The hull was light

gray with worn green gunwales. Two men peered at the horizon with binoculars, two rested near their harpoons, and one managed the helm. I thought
that they would stop to chat, but they swung to within fifty yards, waved,
and headed toward the spout of a distant whale.

That was our entire encounter—two kayaks and a whaleboat passing
on a cloudy afternoon in late summer in the North Bering Sea. They
waved; we did too. I grabbed my camera and snapped the shutter, but the
boat was too far away for my wide-angle lens. When I edited the film two
months later, the whaleboat was tiny against a broad green ocean, and I
could barely see the five rounded, weather-beaten bodies wrapped in fur
and cloth anoraks. The photograph had no life or character to do justice to
what I'd seen, so I tossed it in the wastebasket. I'm left with the image of
an open whaleboat in that inimical sea.

When the boat settled into a trough, I had an irrational fear that the
waves would spill into the hull and drag it downward, but the boat always
reappeared, brave and saucy. As a small-boat sailor, I understood that the
whaleboat was seaworthy, yet it seemed so vulnerable. The waves loomed
higher than the hull, there was no deck to deflect a breaking sea, and the
tiny outboard could put up little fight against an Arctic gale. Moreover,
the animals those men were hunting were among the largest and most dangerous on the planet. Their harpoons were armed with pipe bombs that
were set to explode within the whale, but a harpooner can miss his mark,
and a wounded whale may turn on its attackers and smash their flimsy craft.
Moby-Dick was not just a metaphor.

Despite such dangers, the Inuit, Koryak, and Chukchi have thrived in
the Arctic for thousands of years—without motors, pipe-bomb harpoons,
and occasional shipments of noodles and flour. The Aleut paddled their
kayaks in the Aleutians, and the Jomon crossed this sea. And pre-Clovis
mammoth hunters walked over the land bridge.

What combination of hard-boiled conservatism, visionary adventur-
ousness, and outright impulsiveness kept people alive in a hunting society?
Any extreme wouldn't work: too conservative and they'd avoid hunting in
moving ice or hesitate at that crucial moment when they had to charge the
prey and thrust their spears; too brash and the uncalculated chances they
took would catch up with them, leaving at least some of their number
crushed, stomped, eaten, mauled, or drowned.

Every time a sperm meets an egg, all three behaviors—conservatism, ad-
venturousness, and impulsiveness—are jumbled into a new individual, each
miraculously unique. Over the two and a half million years of *hominid* evo-

lution—including 100,000 years for *Homo sapiens*—the global climate has varied dramatically from relative warmth to continental ice ages; plant and animal species have changed; warfare has devastated the land and peace has brought prosperity. Some people were hunters; others picked fruit, dug roots, and ate grubs and snails. Eventually most turned to agriculture. Somehow, in this swirling whirlpool of environment and personality, humanity has survived and prospered.

In the recent book *The Madness of Adam and Eve: How Schizophrenia Shaped Humanity*, author David Horrobin started with three observations: schizophrenia is substantially genetic; it is observed in all human populations; and acute schizophrenics are not likely to marry and bear healthy children. He then asked the obvious question, "Why has schizophrenia survived eons of natural selection?" His answer is that schizophrenia is not controlled by an on/off switch. An individual who is emotionally unable to function is unlikely to reproduce and pass his or her genes to the next generation, so that person's genes are lost forever. But individuals with a small amount of schizophrenia are often the most creative and successful members of society, and are therefore favored by evolution. As a result, schizophrenia is passed down from generation to generation despite the occasional dead ends that occur when a person inherits too much of a good thing.

I believe that the adventurous spirit is similar to schizophrenia. Mix in just the right amount, and a Stone Age hunter would have enough daring to spear a walrus during famine or win a bride. But, alas, the guy who crossed the line from brave to foolhardy might paddle out alone, do something foolish—and die. And how to know where that line lies? Young individuals die all the time trying to answer that question; even whole tribes die out for lack of that judgment. The critical balance—between what is daring and what is foolhardy—is written into the Jomons' story and ours.

O N AUGUST 29, after spending a night in Nunligran, Misha and I paddled into a snarling sky and a steep gray sea. Around noon I looked at my altimeter and was jolted to see that the apparent elevation had jumped from sea level to 850 feet in half an hour—the fastest and most dramatic drop in barometric pressure I had ever seen. Lenticular clouds gathered rapidly in the eastern sky, indicating that an intense gale was headed our way. We thought about landing immediately, but the low beach spread out into flat, unprotected tundra. The storm could last for days, and even a strong nylon tent can rip to shreds in an Arctic gale. We decided to paddle another mile to a sheltered lee behind low hills and granite outcrops.

Within minutes a strong gust hit us from the north, followed by an eerie calm. Then a second gust struck from the west, against my back. The kayak hull hissed as it accelerated, chasing its bow wake. Then calm again— followed by a south wind, and a third calm. The wind was spiraling counterclockwise around the low-pressure cell, and I felt as though we were being sucked into an abyss. Finally the wind pulsated from the east, lifting salt spray into a horizontally driven rain. During the bursts I held my paddle low so the blades wouldn't act as a sail and drive me backward or, worse yet, capsize me. I paddled as hard as I could between gusts and fixed my gaze on the rocky headland. We struggled for an hour and a half to gain one mile, and landed, wet and exhausted, near a narrow cleft in the granite. The cleft was only twenty feet long and ten feet wide, smaller than a living room in a suburban house, but it formed a serene shelter from the waterspouts that danced through a shimmering mist of rain and spray.

We pitched our tent and slept all afternoon. The next day I skirted the cliffs at low tide and emerged from our nook. As soon as I left the shelter, the wind hit so hard I almost lost my balance, but I leaned into the gusts and turned east to face the gale. The edges of my anorak flapped discordantly until they reached a resonant frequency and hummed in tune with the storm. The ocean was madness, with fingers of gray-green sea reaching upward to grasp the overpowering white. My eyes watered, swirls of cold air invaded my hood and penetrated my eardrums, and kelp rose off the sea, spiraling above my head.

Alaska lay only ninety miles to the southeast. Originally I had hoped to cross to Alaska via the Bering Strait, but both Russian and American customs officials had assured us that such a crossing was politically impossible. Instead, Misha and I had planned a longer and more dangerous passage to the Alaskan village of Gambell, on Saint Lawrence Island. Our route would follow the coast to Cape Chaplina, then turn almost due south for the thirty-eight-mile crossing to Gambell.

If we were motivated—and scared—we could probably maintain a three-knot paddling speed even in a steep, roiling sea. Thirty-eight miles at three knots meant nearly thirteen hours if the weather remained favorable. By the time we started the crossing, we'd have about fifteen hours of daylight. There wouldn't be much margin for error. I could overcome the exhaustion, the pain, and the fear, but I had no control over the weather. The day before we had been paddling half bored in a calm sea one moment, and half an hour later we were fighting desperately against a violent storm. A similarly unpredictable gale had struck us near Point Vasilya a few weeks before. We had survived both times because we were close to shore, but if a storm struck during our long crossing, it could kill us.

I searched for comforting optimism but instead remembered a haunting story from Nunligran. Every summer, Inuit and Chukchi people from Nunligran and neighboring villages motor across to Gambell to visit friends and relatives. In 1999 the crossing from Russia to Alaska was uneventful, but on the return trip fourteen boats were caught in a ferocious gale. Two twenty-five-foot whaleboats weathered the passage safely. The other boats were sixteen- or twenty-foot aluminum skiffs powered by fifty- or sixty-horsepower outboards. Six skiffs completed the passage safely, but three sank and three blew out to sea. Two people died, and a dozen were rescued.

I'd always thought that aboriginal mariners, who live in close communion with nature, have a sixth sense that alerts them to bad weather. Maybe that assumption was a fallacy. Fourteen boats had been caught unaware in a bad storm. Had their skippers been careless that day? Had they been drunk and partying? Or had the storm descended without warning?

I shuddered to imagine our fate in a similar situation. Even though I believe that a kayak is more seaworthy than an aluminum skiff, we didn't have a motor and were powerless to fight a strong crosswind or current. We couldn't predict the weather, and a storm could wash us out to sea, so we were playing Russian roulette. As an alternative, we could paddle to the port city of Providenya and fly home in an airplane. But after two years and 3,000 miles, that wasn't much of an option.

I turned out of the wind and headed back to our nook. Misha was brewing tea, and I wondered if he was thinking similar thoughts. I decided not to ask, because once you release your fears, they can become reason, and reason wasn't our friend right now.

THAT EVENING, the rising tide, a massive surf, and a storm surge lifted the ocean. Waves crashed against the sand and drove foam and seaweed up the beach. Misha and I discussed our situation and recalled that horrible night near Apuka when waves had battered our tent. But we didn't have many favorable options, so we tied our boats and tent to clefts in the solid granite and crawled into our sleeping bags. The tent was dry and comfortable, but it had no windows, and when I tried to look toward the sea, I saw only green nylon. I felt like a blind man whose sense of hearing was enhanced when his sight dissipated. When a wave rose, it produced a sucking sound, as if stealing power from the storm. Then it broke and the trapped air escaped with a roar, followed by a whistle. Finally the bubbly swash raced up the beach, rolling grains of sand like innumerable tiny billiard balls colliding on green felt. I unzipped the tent door and shined my headlamp into the darkness. Iridescent algae glowed only a few feet away, and the smell of the sea invaded my nostrils. I looked at my watch—an hour to high tide. Misha mumbled sleepily, "You worry too much, Jon." Embarrassed at my nervousness, I zipped the door and dozed—until I heard a more compelling *woomph*, a roarlike gurgle, and the buckling of aluminum and nylon as a wave struck our tent.

I woke with a start, thinking, "Maybe I'm not worrying enough."

Another wave broke and flung foam against our fragile shelter. I looked at my watch—it was five minutes to high tide. Half an hour later, the moon began loosening its gravitational grip, and the ocean slid back down the beach. We had escaped again, sobered but unscathed. We were living on a fine line, and I felt emotionally drained. Maybe I should hop on an airplane in Providenya, fly home, visit my children, and bounce my grandchildren on my knee. When I finally fell back asleep, I dreamed of walking through a carefully tended herb garden.

On the third day of the storm, August 31, I rummaged through my valuables to find the letter from Sergei in Anadyr. Our permission expired today. Misha watched me reading the letter.

"Jon, don't worry so much."

I didn't want to argue, and no one was going to walk down the lonely beach to hassle us, so I agreed. "Yes, you're right. I worry too much." Then I carefully folded the letter, wrapped it in plastic, and stowed it away.

To change the subject, we talked about America. I had extra frequent flier miles and invited Misha to spend a week in Montana. He had so many questions that we chatted and forgot our immediate troubles.

On September 1, Misha poked his head out of the tent and shouted, "It's a beautiful day!" That meant low, pregnant clouds, temperatures in the mid-forties, and a fifteen-mile-per-hour wind with occasional whitecaps, but no driving rain, no close-out surf, and no wind-driven spray. We launched and paddled eastward. Another storm held us down the following day. Then, finally, on September 3, we reached the mouth of Providenya Bay.

I N SEPTEMBER 1848, Thomas Moore, a British commander, sailed along this coast looking for signs of the lost Franklin Expedition, which had disappeared a few years before in the eastern Arctic. Moore hypothesized that Franklin had completed the fabled Northwest Passage, then had wrecked along this forbidding Siberian coast. The would-be rescue team encountered its own problems, however, when an onshore gale threatened to dash Moore's ship against the rocks. Running close-hauled and unable to claw offshore, the crew had almost given up hope when suddenly they peered into the mouth of a deepwater harbor. They concluded that God had saved them and named the bay Providence, now called Providenya. But from the moment we paddled into its calm waters, I sensed that this place would not be provident for us.

OUR *POGRANICHNIKI* permission had expired and our embarkation papers were in disarray, so I suggested to Misha that we avoid Providenya, just as we had passed around Anadyr.

"No one knows we are here right now," I argued. "Why don't we make camp, rest, and paddle to Alaska tomorrow?" I pointed south toward Saint Lawrence Island. "Look, it's just over there, across the horizon. We can almost see it. Our kayaks are so small that they'll look like two logs on Russian radar. We'll reach Alaska before anyone knows we've left."

Misha looked unconvinced, so I added, "We are in the wild nature. We must paddle to Alaska by our own hands. Labor and Defend."

Misha shook his head ruefully. "In Anadyr, small mafia men wanted our money; but in Providenya, the army, the coast guard, customs, immigrations, and *pogranichniki* are waiting for us. You don't paddle away from these men. You and I are friends, so we forget. We are crossing an old cold war border to visit our old enemy—America. If we cross to America without permission, they will never let us return to Russia again. That may not be so bad for you, but I have family in Petropavlovsk. It is my home."

So we turned into the protected bay and headed north, away from Alaska, toward the rusting cranes, idle docks, and fickle bureaucrats of Providenya.

After World War II, the Russians thought they could use large icebreakers to open a summer sea route across the Northeast Passage, from Europe, across the north coast of Siberia, to the Pacific. They enlarged Providenya to serve as an eastern terminal for the icebreakers, also making it a military base to defend against the hostile and aggressive Americans less than a hundred miles away. But the ice route never became economically practical, and the cold war ended, so the town collapsed.

Misha and I paddled between a sunken hulk and a docked harbor tug and pulled our boats ashore onto oil-soaked stones. Teenaged boys smoking cigarettes were leaning against a rusted, trackless *visdichot*. In town we found a woman who had once owned a small hotel. In the early 1990s, immediately after perestroika, five thousand tourists had visited the city every year—for a few years. But the bureaucratic obstacles became so labyrinthine that the flow of tourists trickled to six in 1999. The woman explained that I was the fourth foreigner to visit Providenya in 2000. Her hotel had closed, but she had friends who would sublet their apartment for a few days.

After we settled in, we set out to arrange permissions to paddle to Saint Lawrence Island, Alaska—the end of our journey.

Edward, the customs official, was a jolly, easygoing fellow with a dull job on the eastern edge of the eastern world. He opened a bottle of vodka and a jar of red caviar and sat back to chat. As far as he was concerned, our papers were in order and we were free to leave the country, in any direction and by any means—as long as we took our kayaks with us.

The *pogranichniki* commander was a young lieutenant who operated on the guiding principle that he would never ever do anything that could conceivably tarnish his resumé or blemish his career. He reasoned that if Misha and I died on the crossing to Gambell, the disaster might somehow reflect on his competence and judgment. Because he had nothing to gain by granting us permission and possibly something to lose, he shook his head "no." We were free to fly to Moscow, but because the planes leaving Providenya were small, we would have to leave our kayaks behind.

The police sergeant was a red-haired woman with shiny shoes, a starched white shirt, and two gold stars on her shoulder. She sat behind a spare wooden desk, frowning at our papers. She talked rapidly in Russian that Misha didn't bother to translate. Besides, I already knew our permission to remain in Chukotka had expired three days ago. She didn't care where we went or what we did, but we had to leave the city within twenty-four hours.

For two years our bureaucratic hassles had seemed relatively benign, and we occasionally even found theater in the pimply, uniformed, gun-toting guards. But when Misha and I stepped out of the police station, the long gray rows of nondescript apartments of Providenya, with their peeling paint, loomed inward like the barracks of a Soviet gulag. We walked aimlessly. Two army trucks and three jeeps careened through the potholed streets, splashing mud on us. We sat disconsolately on the concrete steps of an apartment building, and Misha stared into his callused palms. "We have come a long way. Many storms. We must paddle to Alaska by our own hands."

"We will paddle to Alaska by our own hands."

Misha smiled and put his hand on my shoulder. "Yes, Jon. We must."

THE FOLLOWING morning Misha tackled our political problems while I planned the crossing to Gambell. Through friends and business associates, Misha gained access to a friendly *pogranichniki* general in Petropavlovsk. The general called the red-haired woman with the shiny shoes, and when we returned to the police station she smiled warmly and handed us a one-week extension to our permissions.

But the young lieutenant was angry. We had gone over his head and now a general was involved, and that might end up blemishing his career. We had ratcheted our simple permission into a personal confrontation, and he wasn't going to budge. He explained that he took orders only from his immediate superior, and the general in Petropavlovsk presided over a different division.

Misha looked grim but not defeated. He had other friends; there were other generals. I gave him a large stack of rubles for long-distance phone calls, then concentrated on my own tasks. Our proposed crossing to Saint Lawrence Island was shorter than the long passages in the Kurils, but that was small consolation. Our kayaks were smaller than the WindRiders, it was late in the season, and gale frequency was increasing—and Franz and I had almost died in the Kurils.

I phoned Chris, who had been in contact with Professor Tom Weingartner, an oceanographer from the University of Alaska. She forwarded me a fax that read in part:

> The current is pretty swift between St Lawrence Island and Cape Chaplina . . . I wouldn't be surprised if the currents get up to 3 knots under southwesterly winds . . . The winds in the strait tend to blow stronger than what you will hear in a forecast because there is a channeling effect. I would encourage you to complete the crossing as early as possible because the weather worsens rapidly in September and it is not a place to be caught.

I left off reading to think about the howling gale of a few days before. Even if the weather were favorable, how would we cope with a three-knot crosscurrent when we could paddle only at three knots? Then I read the last two sentences: "Sounds like a fun trip. Good luck."

"Sure, thanks," I muttered to myself.

I telephoned the NOAA weather station in Anchorage and explained our proposed crossing. A meteorologist replied that from now until next July, fast-moving storms would dominate the North Bering Sea. Their exact movements were difficult to predict, but he was glad to help.

After four days, Misha found a general who overruled the lieutenant and sanctioned our crossing to Gambell—with one nonnegotiable caveat. Once the *pogranichniki* stamped our passports in Providenya, we couldn't land on Russian soil again. No stopping and no camping. Alexander, a policeman from Providenya, would follow us in an aluminum skiff to enforce this restriction. We had hoped to follow the coast for two days to Cape Chaplina, where the crossing was thirty-eight miles. However, this passage would entail two illegal camps. On the other hand, if we left directly from Providenya, as the lieutenant ordered, our crossing to Gambell would be sixty-six miles. Even if we could maintain a three-knot speed, the journey would take twenty-two hours.

I called the meteorologist in Anchorage again. He advised, "Leave at first light tomorrow morning. After that, expect a week of storms."

I asked if we could hope for twenty-two hours of favorable weather. He replied, "Don't count on it."

We had permission and a more-or-less favorable twelve-hour forecast, but our options were narrowing and our window of opportunity was slim. Misha wasn't deterred.

"Do you have another American $100 bill?" he asked.

I fished around in my pouch and handed him the note.

"I will talk to this man Alexander."

Even for a hundred dollars, Alexander couldn't defy the military. The C-note floated in the air between us. Alexander scratched his chin, then a broad smile crossed his face.

"Yes, the orders say that you can't camp on Russian soil after leaving Providenya. But we can load your kayaks in my skiff and motor south until we are thirty-eight miles from Gambell, the same distance as if you had left from Cape Chaplina. Then we put your kayaks in the water and you paddle the rest of the way."

I laughed. In Russia there is always a way. Even though we planned to use motorized support, we weren't despoiling our expedition by avoiding the crux crossing. It wasn't the most elegant ending, but it was the best we could hope for under the circumstances, and a whole lot better than an ignominious retreat by airplane.

Alexander reasoned that because he was now our escort, we should become drinking buddies. He was young—in his thirties—blond, strong, and good looking, of medium height and build. His father had been the town mechanic in Enmelen, and Alexander could nurse almost any motor to action with a pair of pliers, a screwdriver, wire, and a piece of driftwood, and he could keep it running for a decade after most men would have sung its requiem. At the same time, he sheepishly showed us that he had burned out three electric teapots in the week since his wife had flown to Anadyr to give birth to their first child. The teapots were stacked in a corner of his apartment, adjacent to a large hunk of whale meat that dripped its dark blood across the counter and onto the floor. Lace curtains and plastic flowers reminded me of his wife's domesticity, but if she remained in Anadyr for another week, the apartment would regress into a frontier bachelor pad.

Edward, the customs official, wasn't one to miss a good party. He walked in with three bottles of vodka, several jars of caviar, and two freshly baked loaves of bread. He filled our glasses, and we toasted Alexander's new baby, our journey, and Mother Russia.

I had two problems. First, I had stopped drinking twenty-five years before, and even though I still joined an occasional toast, I didn't like to get drunk. Second, Misha and I were about to embark on the longest, most dangerous kayak crossing of our lives. We hoped to reach Gambell during daylight hours, but if a current or wind pushed us off course, we might paddle all night in the treacherous, frigid waters of the North Bering Sea. It was madness to binge on vodka before we set off.

When I expressed my concerns to Misha, he rebuked, "This is Russia. Alexander will help us. The customs inspector must stamp our papers. If they want to drink vodka, we will drink."

I was annoyed at the drinking, annoyed at Alexander, and annoyed at Edward. But I may as well have been annoyed at the autumn storms or the inexorable current that flowed toward the North Pole. These men were helping me. They were my friends. And I was in Russia.

Alexander put a CD of heavy-metal rock into the boom box and turned the volume up until we had to shout to communicate. Edward refilled our glasses and proposed another toast. Bottoms up.

The alcohol rushed to my brain and my brain screamed back, "Stay strong, Jon. Start thinking strong, right now, despite this absurd party."

Alexander filled my glass a third time, but I knew to ignore it until someone demanded that I drink again. The three men were talking in Russian
and Misha had stopped translating, so I drifted into my own world.

I reviewed our situation. A thirty-eight-mile crossing at three knots
equals about thirteen hours of paddling, but what about the crosscurrent?
Gambell lies on a long, narrow peninsula jutting due north. If we drifted
only a few miles off course, we would miss our landfall and face a much
longer passage. It sounded like a tenth-grade word problem in trigonome-
try: "If Billy and Sally paddle at three knots in a three-knot crosscurrent,
will they reach Gambell before they run out of strength and die?" Let's see
now, the opposite over the hypotenuse, times the sine or cosine of something or other . . .

Even without the arithmetic, I knew we couldn't complete the crossing
during daylight, so we'd paddle into the night. But would we make it?

Alexander stood, gesticulating, raising his glass, and proposing another
toast. I knew I'd offend them if I didn't drink the damn vodka, so what the
hell . . .

I was trained as a scientist and believed in data and mathematics, so
why was I planning this crossing if the numbers didn't add up? More than
a year before, Franz and I had sat on a foggy beach and talked about living
close to that mysterious edge or dying by stepping over it. We had at first
decided to retreat, then changed our minds and continued northward. Now,
once again, I was very close to the edge.

Why was I ignoring the math?

I pulled the crumpled fax out of my pocket and reread it. "I wouldn't be
surprised if the currents get up to 3 knots under southwesterly winds." It
was only a possibility that the current would reach three knots, not a certainty. It was just a worst-case scenario.

The strongest ocean currents occur in narrow constrictions, as we had
experienced at the mouth of Anadyr Bay, or when there are large tidal differences, as we had encountered in the Kurils. But there were no narrow
constrictions or large tidal differences between Cape Chaplina and Gambell. Was this hypothetical three-knot current generated only during steady
winds or large storms? Was he giving me fatherly advice disguised as hard
data?

Ultimately, an adventurer bases life-and-death decisions on gut feelings: the feel of snow, rock, and the sea. I had been living in intimate contact with this ocean for two seasons. If a strong current ran along the coast,
why hadn't we encountered it close to shore? People had predicted strong

currents off Point Navarin, but we had paddled around the point in a flat sea. Suddenly I believed we would not encounter a three-knot current in the straits between Russia and Gambell. Was my belief a lethal example of foolish hubris? Was I willing to disagree with an oceanographer who had dedicated his entire career to studying this ocean—and to stake my life on a gut assumption?

I sat on my uncomfortable chair, with my vodka glass in front of me, staring at the plastic flowers and the bloody chunk of whale meat, and a voice from deep inside said, "You're going to paddle to Gambell, and you're going to make it."

W E WENT to bed at 2:00 A.M. and slept till 4:00. Struggling awake, I groggily programmed my GPS with the coordinates of Gambell, then added waypoints for several emergency landings in case we drifted off course. At first light we walked to the rusted steel container that served as Alexander's boat shed. I was hung over, bleary eyed, and grumpy. Misha and Alexander were sprightly and seemingly unfazed by the three bottles of vodka we'd consumed a few hours before. Misha and I packed enough water and snacks in our cockpits to stay alive for several days, then we stowed a few pounds of noodles and oatmeal in the rear compartments so we'd have something to eat if we landed on an uninhabited beach.

Edward walked to the dock, looking official in his neatly pressed uniform. He chatted briefly, wished us good luck, stamped our papers, and went back home to bed. The lieutenant drove up with four heavily armed soldiers to make sure we didn't pull any funny stuff at the last minute, and stamped our exit visas. I smiled and thanked him, but he turned away without looking at me.

We lashed the kayaks into Alexander's eighteen-foot aluminum skiff. He removed the spark plugs and cleaned the tips with his pocketknife, then screwed them back in. When he was satisfied with his engine repairs, he stashed six cans of gas under the thwarts, and nodded that we were ready.

The motor purred, and our wake fanned out symmetrically across the smooth waters of Providenya Bay. I shut my eyes and rested my chin against

my life jacket to doze and relax before our long paddle. An hour later I began to feel the ocean swell. The meteorologist had predicted wind from
the northwest, but instead the wind and swell were from the northeast,
moving exactly opposite to the predicted current. I let out a low whistle.
Would the wind neutralize the current, so we could paddle a straight
course? Why were we so lucky?

Alexander steered without compass, and I followed our course on my
GPS. At about 8:30, I told Alexander we were thirty-eight miles from
Gambell. By previous agreement, he was to drop us off at this random co-
ordinate on the open sea, but he grinned and kept the throttle wide open,
heading toward America. "Was he going to defect, leave his wife and newborn child, and take us all the way to Alaska?" I wondered. "Were we about
to be embroiled in a new political commotion?"

I hunkered down in the boat and waited. The current was undercutting
the swell, creating a steep, deepwater break. I didn't trust this open aluminum skiff with its uneasy roll in a beam sea. I wanted to be within the
waves, in my seaworthy kayak, with a sprayskirt pulled tightly over the
cockpit. The mileage on the GPS clicked down: 37.5 . . . 37.0 . . . When we
were 35 miles from Gambell, Alexander cut the engine and grinned. *"Here's
three extra miles for my friends."*

We unlashed the kayaks and dropped them into the sea, then climbed
over the gunwales and slipped into our cockpits. I wiggled my hips to feel
the swell, paddled into the lee of the skiff, and reached up to shake Alexander's hand. His grip was firm and his smile was friendly. The heavy skiff rose
above me on a wave, threatening to drop heavily on my deck. I pushed away
from the cold aluminum hull and stabilized the kayak with my paddle.
The motor started, the noise of the prop changed pitch as Alexander turned
into the wind, then the pitch changed again as he accelerated toward Russia. Misha paddled close.

"Labor and Defend."

"Da, Labor and Defend."

There was nothing else to say. We set a course at 128°, toward Gambell,
the small village perched on a narrow peninsula of Saint Lawrence Island.

After an hour of steady paddling, I checked the GPS. If the current were
driving us northeast or the wind were pushing us southwest, our GPS bearing would change. I scrolled through the display anxiously: position, speed,
course, distance to Gambell. I pressed a button—32 miles. Then I hit the
scroll again for bearing. That's what I wanted to know: bearing—128°.

I imagined the Arctic ice pack far to the north, groaning and crunching in an endless cacophony that had started when the Earth cooled in the early Paleocene epoch. To the south, warm waters pulsed from Japan, powered by a relentless drive to increase the Earth's entropy. And today these planetary winds, tides, currents, and waves were counterbalancing one another perfectly, so that our course and bearing were identical. We were paddling at 128° and moving at 128°. On my deathbed, I will thank the wild nature for this gift.

My arm ached, and I whispered hopefully to the anti-inflammatory drugs in my bloodstream, "Go for the elbow tendon! The left one!" But neither the drugs nor my prayers were effective. The sea was steep and laced with white. But these were trivial problems; our course and bearing were identical.

There was no immediate danger, just an abstract possibility of a rogue storm. We couldn't see land, so I watched the waves, thinking that by tomorrow I would be returning home to the green forests of continental Montana.

The waves seemed like individuals in a crowd. When you're walking in a crowd, the people around you are anonymous. Then you accidentally jostle against someone, and the mask of anonymity lifts ever so slightly. "He has warm eyes," "she wears ghastly perfume," "I wouldn't like to meet him in a dark alley," and so on. You say "excuse me" and drift apart. So it is with waves. The crowd was headed southwest with the steadfastness of weary commuters returning home from work. If I slipped into a daydream, the waves had faces but no individuality. But then a breaker would splash foam against my cheek, reminding me to watch the sea. The closest four waves were small and rounded, but the fifth was breaking with a thin white edge. Beyond that, a hundred yards away, another wave curled and collapsed into a broader band of white foam. It was a simple exercise of focusing on small nuances in shape and size. As the hours passed, the exercise became a game—a game with friends—because today the waves opposed the current and held us on course.

Misha's familiar red boat and brown hat rose on a crest, then sank out of sight. I remembered and marveled that he had never been in a kayak before the start of this journey.

By 11:00 A.M., I saw a thin, hazy line on the horizon—land.

Over the next few hours, the line metamorphosed into mirage-like images. First, the bluish edge became so distinct that I imagined the smell of exhaust fumes in the village and the shouts of children playing. Then the island seemed to be engulfed by waves, as if it were sinking into the sea. But optimism and pessimism were tempered by the steady digital readout of the GPS; we were moving at 2.8 miles per hour, like clockwork.

I concentrated on each wave and tried to maximize my power with each paddle stroke while minimizing the stress on my body. When waves curled and white foam hung above my head, I held the paddle blade flat and slid it across the water to maintain balance. Occasionally I scanned the sky, searching for some intimation of a storm. But innocuous gray clouds spread toward the horizon, and the sun drifted westward at a slow pace that mimicked our progress toward Gambell.

Every hour Misha and I stopped briefly, checked the GPS, nibbled a little food, chatted to break the lonely vastness of the sea, then picked up our paddles again. Gradually, ethereal outlines of land resolved into cliffs and hills. The sun dipped and the moon rose as the pastel day slid into a red twilight. The streetlights of Gambell twinkled like stars low on the horizon, their electric glow reminding me of the lighthouse above Svetia's kitchen when Franz and I were retreating from the horrible shear waves in the Kurils. When we were an hour from land, I thought again of home, with my dear Chris to welcome me. Then I thought about the Stone Age migrants before me who entered an unfamiliar and uninhabited land needing to find food and prepare for winter. For them, the adventure never ended.

NOW THAT my two-year expedition was virtually complete, the adventures and hardships blurred together into a soft-focus wash. So many times, reason had dictated that I turn back, but I had ignored these voices of sanity—and now Alaska was only an hour away. In my youth, I had assumed that romanticism is frilly faced and soft bellied, and logic and pragmatism must underlie strong deeds. But I didn't believe that anymore. Neither the Jomon nor I could have paddled to Alaska purely for material gain.

The long Arctic twilight began to fade inexorably into darkness, and the quiet of the open sea was punctuated by the ominous sound of surf. I had followed my internal voices for two years and 3,000 hardscrabble miles, and in that space and time I learned that great accomplishments can be driven by quixotic images and quiet but persistent dreams.

Lights darted back and forth as villagers drove their all-terrain vehicles to the beach. People were yelling. Misha asked what they were saying, and his question startled me, because he had always been the translator. I responded that they were cheering. I felt the familiar steepening of swells in shoal water and yelled back, waving my paddle toward the lights. No, it wasn't cheering; people were yelling instructions. I back-paddled furiously.

The words ululated through the surf and wind, all of them in English, a language that seemed foreign after all those months.

"Don't land here! Bad surf! Don't land here! Go east."

We paddled east for a mile to a small indent in the shoreline. Even there, the surf rumbled as it collapsed, reminding me of the break that had pitch-poled me near Petropavlovsk, 2,000 miles and almost four months before. I paddled closer and stared at one last wave out of a hundred billion before it. One last wave, and I would be safe. It rose and steepened; I stroked rapidly and ruddered the boat at an angle to the break.

Someone shouted urgently, "No, not like that!"

I ignored him. I was captain and master of this vessel. I knew this boat as no one else did. And in this moment, dropping into the foam, I was blissfully confident. The kayak fell, scooted sideways, and bounced on the sand. Eager hands grabbed the bow loop, the stern loop, and the sides. Suddenly, excited men lifted my kayak, with me in it, and ran triumphantly up the beach. People stood incongruously beneath me, reaching out to shake my hand as they shouted congratulations.

The men lowered me onto solid ground above the high tide line. My body was exhausted and tears welled up in my eyes. "Where's Misha?" I thought. "I have to give him a hug. I must laugh and cry with him." But before I could release my sprayskirt and stand, someone shoved a cell phone in my face. "Your wife is worried about you. You must call her. Right now!"

Still sitting in my kayak, I dialed the familiar number.

WE RESTED in Gambell for a day, then flew to Nome and booked a room in the Nome Nugget Hotel, on the main street. Mounted moose heads and gold pans advertised, "Welcome to the Frontier," but to us, this place was the pinnacle of civilization. We took showers, bounced on clean, firm beds like children, then went downstairs to pig out at the salad bar. During lunch, Misha reminded me that in June, when we were at Point Zhupanova, Andre had instructed us to light a candle in a church to carry his deceased great-grandmother's long-forgotten dream to Alaska.

In the recent excitement I had almost forgotten the dingy table, the candlelight, and the homemade vodka. Yes, I had held my hand to my heart and sworn to carry Evdocia's dream and spirit to Alaska. In Russia, you don't make such promises lightly.

After lunch, we crossed the street to the nearest church.

Our footsteps sounded hollow as we walked through the foyer toward a fluorescent light glowing from a small office.

The pastor looked up. "May I help you?"

Misha spoke first, in his heavy Russian accent, "We come to light a candle in your church."

"Excuse me?"

I explained our journey and continued, "Two generations ago, a Cossack woman homesteaded in Kamchatka. Her dream was to continue to Russian America—Alaska—but she never completed her journey. Because we were traveling in the old way, her grandson asked us to carry her dream to Alaska and light a candle in her honor."

The pastor looked at us in silence. I tried to imagine his thoughts. Even though Misha and I had showered, we were two big, rough-looking characters, with weathered faces and fish-oil-stained parkas.

Just in case the pastor didn't understand my English, Misha interjected, "We come from Russia. We paddle to Alaska with our own hands." He held up his palms, to show the pastor his calluses.

The pastor swiveled his office chair to face us. "Could you start at the beginning again?"

I repeated our story, then Misha repeated, "We paddle from Russia to Alaska with our own hands."

The pastor smiled. This was Nome, after all.

"What denomination was this woman?"

"I don't have the foggiest idea. Her grandson, Andre, said 'a church.'"

Misha corrected me. "He said, 'a church, but not a Catholic church.'"

The pastor looked at us carefully. "Well, why did you pick this church?"

"Coincidence. It's across the street from the hotel."

He thought again. Then he spoke slowly and softly. "Sure, we can light a candle for this woman. Sure."

The pastor didn't have any candles, so he sent us to the grocery store. When we returned, he was confident and relaxed. He invited us into the sanctuary and lit the candle. He asked Misha to offer a prayer, but Misha replied that he would rather pray silently. We bowed our heads. Then it was my turn, and I said a few words about Evdocia and the importance of following one's dreams.

The pastor started to speak. I could tell from the first sentence that he was revving up for an impromptu sermon, complete with a beginning, middle, and end. He understood our mission, but he was too clean and too earnest and I was too tired to listen. It wasn't a fatigue that could be assuaged by an afternoon nap. No, this exhaustion started deep in my bones, worked through the tendons, expanded into the abdomen and across the diaphragm, and rose into the brain. It was the kind of tired that made me want to sit in a rocking chair with a warm cup of chamomile tea and not get up for a month.

As the pastor's voice droned on, I looked into the candle and imagined all those waves—the friendly ones and the breaking giants. I saw Franz, Chris, and Misha blown by the wind and plastered with salt spray, and felt the smooth balance of the knife Andre had given me. Then I returned to the present, looked about the dimly lit sanctuary, watched Misha's serious face, and listened to the minister's somber reflections. It was funny—we were making quite a commotion over a woman we knew so little about. No one here had ever met Evdocia, and Andre had been too drunk to convey a picture of her personality or her life. Was she tall or short, slender or heavyset, gentle or strident? We just knew that she lived half of her dream, but not the other half.

No, I knew a lot more than that.

I knew that Evdocia was a powerful survivor as well as a dreamer. She walked, rode horses, or mushed a dog team across Arctic Siberia, then built a home in the wilderness and raised a family. She survived incredible isolation, deep snow, and the relentless gales of Kamchatka winters, and in spring she joyfully picked the first green shoots of *chirum-cha* that tasted of onion and garlic. Her face and hands must have been gnarled and weathered like the branches of a twisted stone birch. She wasn't a friend to the grizzly bears, because, as Vitali had assured me, bears have no friends, but she lived with the bruins and shared their salmon.

Then, for some reason, she failed to continue across the ocean to Alaska. If a person's dreams are expansive enough, eventually they will collide with the inexorable weight of time and old age. It's no shame to fail on the last dream.

Even though she fell short, she passed the vision down through the generations until it was entrusted to us. And Misha and I had carried Evdocia's dream to Alaska, just as we carried the genes of the first hominids who walked out of Africa and the Jomon sailors who paddled across the Pacific.

The pastor was still talking, but his words blurred into a background drone without definition or intensity. Right now all urgency was behind me, in that great ocean barrier that had stopped Evdocia. With the feel of the sea still vivid in my memory, I reached, once again, into the distant past and imagined stepping into a log canoe with fur-clad sailors.

I saw a stormy day. The travelers rounded a point and headed toward a small settlement nestled along the banks of a rich salmon stream. Village warriors raced to the shore, weapons in hand. Men and women in the canoe waved their paddles in a sign of peace. Once the villagers realized that the newcomers were *puteshestveniks*, not invaders, the young men put down their spears, and people bustled about to prepare a feast. Sitting in the glow of a warm campfire, the travelers offered a carefully knapped arrowhead as a gift. The arrowhead was not merely a weapon; it was an example of a new and innovative technology from a distant people. The exchange—food for technology—was ancient and reciprocal. Traveler, villager, romantic, pragmatist—each person contributed to humanity in his or her way.

Darkness descended, and a man from the village inched closer to a young woman from the canoes. She reached into a deerskin bag that was slung over her shoulder, removed a thin wooden flute, and began playing. The man slipped into the shadows, returned with a skin drum, and beat a rhythmic cadence in time with the flute. People began to dance.

Several days later, the man with the drum joined the travelers as they loaded their belongings and paddled out through the surf, still following their dream, their shaman, or the migratory route of the great whale.

Annotated Bibliography

Anthropology is such a fast-moving field that books cannot possibly keep pace with research developments. As a result, I've relied heavily on the following periodicals:

Nature, Science, Arctic Anthropology, Scientific American, Science News, Discover, Archaeology, Archaeology Odyssey, and *Discovering Archaeology.*

Anyone interested in digging deeper into the material presented in this book should start with four basic references, one about Kennewick Man written by his discoverer, and three about the settlement of the Americas, written by experts in the field:

Chatters, James C. *Ancient Encounters: Kennewick Man and the First Americans.* New York: Simon and Schuster, 2001.

Dillehay, Thomas. *The Settlement of the Americas.* New York: Basic Books, 2000.

Dixon, E. James. *Bones, Boats, and Bison: Archaeology and the First Colonization of Western North America.* Albuquerque: The University of New Mexico Press, 1999.

West, Frederick, ed. *American Beginnings: The Prehistory and Palaeoecology of Beringia.* Chicago: University of Chicago Press, 1996.

After I read about migrations to the Americas, I thought I'd broaden my perspective and learn about earlier human migrations out of Africa and human diasporas in general:

Luca, Luigi, and Francesco Cavalli-Sforza. *The Great Human Diasporas.* New York: Addison-Wesley, 1995.

Fix, Alan G. *Migration and Colonization in Human Microevolution.* Cambridge, England: Cambridge University Press, 1999.

Gamble, Clive. *Timewalkers: The Prehistory of Global Colonization.* Cambridge, Mass.: Harvard University Press, 1993.

In the next step, I read about migrations into the Arctic:

Krupnik, Igor. *Arctic Adaptations.* Hanover, N.H.: University Press of New England, 1993.

The Jomon were ancestors to the Ainu, who still live in modern Japan. Although no one can go back in time to study the folktales and religion of the Jomon, I gained insight by reading two books about the Ainu—one a memoir, and the other by a prominent anthropologist:

Fitzhugh, William W., and Chisato O. Dubreuil, eds. *Ainu, Spirit of a Northern People.* Seattle: Smithsonian Institution and University of Washington Press, 1999.

Shigeru, Kayano. *Our Land Was a Forest: An Ainu Memoir.* Boulder, Colo.:
Westview Press, 1994.

*The first-contact history of Kamchatka is elegantly chronicled by Russian explorer
Stephen Krasheninnikov. Thanks to the publishers of specialty books who maintain our
culture and history for little profit:*
Krasheninnikov, Stephen. *The History of Kamtschatka.* 1755. Translated and repub-
lished, Surrey, England: Richmond Publishing Company, 1973.

An excellent book chronicling the mentality and customs of hunter-gatherers is:
Brody, Hugh. *The Other Side of Eden: Hunters, Farmers, and the Shaping of the
World.* Toronto: Douglas & McIntyre, 2000.

My source for possible later migrations from Jomon settlements in Japan to Ecuador is:
Gilmore, Donald Y., and Linda S. McElroy, eds. *Across Before Columbus?
Evidence for Transoceanic Contact with the Americas prior to 1492.* Edgecomb,
Maine: The New England Antiquities Research Association, 1998.

*After sailing blind in the foggy Kurils, totally dependent on my satellite-activated GPS,
I read two books about Polynesian navigation, an old classic and a more modern sequel:*
Lewis, David. *The Voyaging Stars: Secrets of the Pacific Island Navigators.* New
York: W. W. Norton, 1978.
Thomas, Steve. *The Last Navigator.* Camden, Maine: International
Marine/McGraw-Hill, 1997.

*While I was reading about small-boat navigators in the ancient world, I dug up a fas-
cinating short book about the origin and development of the kayak:*
Zimmerly, David. *Qayaq: Kayaks of Alaska and Siberia.* Fairbanks: University of
Alaska Press, 1986.

My material on the history of Siberia was taken from:
Bobrick, Benson. *East of the Sun, The Epic Conquest and Tragic History of Siberia.*
New York: Poseidon Press, 1992.

*Two books (the first readable and the second technical) about the ecology of the North
Bering Sea are:*
Glavin, Terry. *The Last Great Sea.* Toronto: Greystone Books, 2000.
Jarvela, Laurie E. *The Navarin Basin Environment and Possible Consequences of
Planned Offshore Oil and Gas Development.* Washington, D.C.: U.S.
Department of Commerce, National Oceanic and Atmospheric
Administration, May 1994.

My factual material about gray whales was taken from:
Russell, Dick. *Eye of the Whale.* New York: Simon and Schuster, 2001.

The fitness indicator argument is derived from:
Miller, Geoffrey F. *The Mating Mind: How Sexual Choice Shaped the Evolution of Human Nature.* New York: Doubleday, 2000.

In A Candle for Evdocia, I make the parallel between wanderlust and schizophrenia. The evolutionary significance of schizophrenia is outlined in:
Horrobin, David. *The Madness of Adam and Eve: How Schizophrenia Shaped Humanity.* New York: Bantam Press, 2001.

Three books that supplied background, legend, narrative, and customs are:
Hall, Edwin S., Jr. *The Eskimo Storyteller, Folktales from Noatak, Alaska.* Fairbanks: University of Alaska Press, 1975.
Melville, Herman. *Moby-Dick.* 1851. New York: Signet, 1961.
Roche, Judith, and Meg McHutchison. *First Fish, First People: Salmon Tales of the North Pacific Rim.* Seattle: University of Washington Press, 1998.